Intellectual Precursors
of the Mexican Revolution
1900–1913

by James D. Cockcroft

UNIVERSITY OF TEXAS PRESS

AUSTIN AND LONDON

240926

International Standard Book Number 0-292-78379-5 (cloth);
0-292-73808-0 (paper)
Library of Congress Catalog Card Number 68-66318
Copyright © 1968, 1976 by James D. Cockcroft
Printed in the United States of America
First Paperback Printing, 1976

Intellectual Precursors of the Mexican Revolution

Latin American Monographs, No. 14

*Sponsored by the Institute of Latin American Studies
The University of Texas at Austin*

A los presos políticos

CONTENTS

ACKNOWLEDGMENTS

It is doubtful that this project ever would have been undertaken without the encouragement and advice of Professor Ronald Hilton, of Stanford University. For a careful reading of the manuscript, I am indebted to the following professors: Ronald Hilton and Bo Anderson, of Stanford; Otis A. Pease, of the University of Washington; Thomas F. McGann and Karl M. Schmitt, of the University of Texas at Austin.

In the many histories written about the Mexican Revolution, surprisingly little attention has been given to the roles of intellectuals and to certain basic sociological processes involved. I owe, therefore, a special debt of gratitude to Professor Anderson, who assisted me in my efforts to bring to light some of those roles and processes and who consulted with me on theoretical problems of the sociology of intellectuals and revolution.

My interpretation and research, for which I of course bear sole responsibility, have been greatly assisted by conversations with the following men: Professor Jesús Silva Herzog, of the Universidad Nacional Autónoma de México (UNAM); Professor Andre G. Frank, of Sir George Williams University, Montreal; the late Mexican historian Luis Chávez Orozco (1901–1966); and the late Antonio Díaz Soto y Gama (1880–1967), a Precursor of, and participant in, the Mexican Revolution. Also assisting in my research were Mexican geographer Ramón Alcorta Guerrero, whose personal library collection made possible my study of San Luis Potosí's social structure; Eugenio Martínez Núñez, whose material collected between 1912 and 1920, while living in close proximity to his friend Juan Sarabia, also a Precursor of the Mexican Revolution, aided in my study of San Luis Potosí's intellectuals; Ethel Duffy Turner and Nicolás T. Bernal, friends of Ricardo Flores Magón, another Precursor of the Mexican Revolution; and Luis González, who, in 1964, allowed me to use the index cards to a bibliography of newspaper articles on the Mexican Revolution, since published by the Colegio de México in two volumes as *Fuentes de la historia contemporánea de México periódicos y revistas* (Stanley R. Ross [compiler]).

I am also indebted to a score of Mexicans, Americans, and Europeans who provided invaluable suggestions in the course of this book's preparation, including the following persons: Arturo Arnáiz y Freg, Lyle C. Brown, Daniel Cosío Villegas, Agustín Cué Cánovas, Moisés Gonzáles Navarro, Martín Luis Guzmán, Friedrich Katz, Aurelio Manrique, Jr., Anita Meyer, Michael C. Meyer, Salvador Penilla López, Gustavo A. Pérez Trejo, Nereo Rodíguez Barragán, Ralph Roeder, Fernando Rosenzweig, Enrique Semo Caler, and James W. Wilkie.

The staffs of the libraries and archives listed in the Bibliography were extremely co-operative and helpful. I wish also to thank the staffs of the Institute of Latin American Studies (University of Texas at Austin) and the University of Texas Press for their assistance.

My research was done during a year and a half's residence in Mexico, made possible by an NDFL-related Fulbright-Hays Fellowship (1964–1966). A postdoctoral fellowship at the University of Texas, 1966–1967, facilitated the final writing.

J. D. C.

Antioch College
Yellow Springs, Ohio
July 26, 1967.

Preface to the Spanish Edition

Research into the social and economic structure of San Luis Potosí at the end of the nineteenth century, together with generally available data on Mexico as a whole, suggests that many traditional assumptions about Mexican history and problems of economic development must undergo revision. Agrarian feudalism did not exist in Mexico. While barbaric social relations between rich farmers and their labor force, the "peons," did characterize the Mexican countryside, these relations were not a product of "backwardness" or "traditionalism" in the usual sense. Rather, they reflected the uneven and combined development in Mexico of modern, capitalist forms of production with harsh and dictatorial social and political forms of control over the population. The vast majority of Mexicans in 1910 constituted what Porfirio Díaz's development minister and general director of agriculture both called a "rural proletariat"—landless peasants, working for "capitalist agriculture," in a system which combined wage labor and debt peonage and resembled feudalism in its barbarity but not in its fundamental arrangement of the means of production.

With the dawn of the twentieth century, the century of proletarian revolutions in the so-called backward or underdeveloped countries, Lenin and Trotsky began to detect the real nature of "underdevelopment" in rural areas and the importance of Karl Marx's original ideas

NOTE: Originally published in *Precursores intelectuales de la revolución mexicana* (Mexico City: Siglo XXI, 1971). © Siglo XXI Editores, S.A. Reprinted by permission.

on permanent (global, international) revolution. Lenin recognized, defined, and analyzed capitalist forms of production penetrating Russia's countryside. Trotsky went further. He insisted that Russia would be the scene of the first major proletarian revolution and that, because of the sharpness with which that general law of historic process, *unevenness*, revealed itself in backward countries, the Russian Revolution would *combine* stages of earlier human history, passing from industrial and preindustrial, bourgeois and prebourgeois forms of social organization to socialist ones in a very brief time, especially as other nations joined the international revolutionary process. Trotsky called this *the law of uneven and combined development*, by which he meant a drawing together of different stages of historical process, a combining of separate and disparate steps, "an amalgam of archaic with more contemporary forms," and he saw this law as especially applicable to those parts of the world less fully developed than Western Europe or *unevenly* developed in their adaptation of, and subjugation by, capitalist forms of production.

The first chapter of this book, written before I was familiar with Lenin's and Trotsky's ideas on Russia and the world proletarian revolution, presents the social and economic character of the Porfiriato for San Luis Potosí in almost exactly these terms. That other parts of Mexico experienced similar, if not identical, forms of uneven and combined capitalist development was acknowledged in 1910 by Díaz's cabinet ministers and has been documented since in such regional case studies as John Womack's *Zapata and the Mexican Revolution* (New York: Alfred A. Knopf, 1969; Mexico City: Siglo XXI, 1969).

While it is true that a domestic bourgeoisie did develop remarkable strength in Porfirian Mexico, it is also true that the power of this bourgeoisie rested on an increasing centralization of industry and finance—monopoly—and an almost total predominance of foreign capital. Mexico's most influential economic group was neither a rural aristocracy nor an urban bourgeoisie, members of which overlapped between city industry and country farm so thoroughly as to constitute an interlocking, ruling, domestic elite. Rather, the single most important economic group in Mexico was a *foreign* bourgeoisie. Ever more dependent upon foreign capital, Mexico's bourgeoisie developed *within itself* uneven, disunified, and conflicting segments, torn between the profits and advantages which accrued to them from their relationships of dependency, on the one hand, and their natural desires for independence (nationalism), on the other. When the Revolution of 1910 opened the floodgates of civil war, the Mexican bourgeoisie faced many "enemies": foreign capitalists (imperialists), foreign troops (Veracruz in 1914, the Pershing mission in 1916), aroused workers and peasants (proletariat), and, most obvious of all, the conservative, dictatorial, corrupt, and inflexible segments of the bourgeois class itself, exemplified by the Científicos, Díaz's *caballada*, and the most reactionary of the *hacendados*, industrialists, financiers, and merchants.

From the viewpoint of an enlightened Mexican bourgeois, 1910, 1913, and 1915 were years of crisis which called for flexibility, broad-mindedness, a number of unfulfillable promises, willingness to make some concessions, strong leadership in bourgeois hands to prevent "the rabble" from taking over, influence with key generals of the Mexican army—in brief, political opportunism. In bourgeois terms, what was needed was *civilian* rule, *civil law*, civil behavior, backed up with adequate military force—the orderly processes of bourgeois "democratic" politics, from which would flow all good things to all men in due time. Francisco I. Madero epitomized the naïveté, faith, and idealism of this bourgeois vision, as well as the bourgeois political leader's willingness to engage in unprincipled opportunism. Venustiano Carranza was more hardheaded than Madero, and more shrewdly opportunistic—a most fortunate circumstance for the Mexican bourgeoisie. Together, Madero and Carranza represented the enlightened elements of the Mexican bourgeois class in those years of strife.

The existence in 1910 of a capitalistic social structure, dominated by bourgeois elite families which were dependent in varying degrees upon foreign capital, makes it difficult to conclude, as many analysts have done, that the Mexican Revolution was in its essence a bourgeois (antifeudal) revolution. The dynamics of Mexico's uneven and combined development during the Porfiriato implied what, in effect, came to pass: an explosive confrontation between proletarians and capitalists. The Precursor Movement described in this book, especially after 1905, demanded, in fact, such a confrontation and helped to bring one about. It helped bring together workers and peasants to fight against the foreign capitalists and domestic bourgeoisie (*hacendados*, factory owners, railroad tycoons, mining magnates, bankers, merchants). These proletarian forces—miners, laborers, and peasants —won major battles against Díaz's *federales*, notably in Baja California, Chihuahua, and the extreme North and in Morelos, Puebla, and parts of the South. Bourgeois leaders like Madero and Carranza sought to stem this proletarian tide from the outset, and, because of the contradictions and disunities of class and geography operative in Mexico at the time, *they succeeded in significant part.*

As a result, the Mexican Revolution of 1910–1917 did little more than overthrow Porfirio Díaz and change part of the ideology of social change. The intense class conflict of that period has survived until this day; indeed, it has grown at a newly combined and uneven rate, as I will conclude in this preface. The only positive result of the Revolution of 1910–1917 was the 1917 Constitution, which expressed the change in ideology for Mexico's continued (but still capitalist) development.

The Constitution has rarely been honored in practice, however. Article 123 has been ignored or abused since the suppression of the 1959 railroad strike. Article 27 has had little effect since 1940, as suggested by the reality of 1975: *neolatifundismo* and over half the rural population landless. Even the bourgeoisie's frequent expressions of nationalism appear ritualistic and dishonest when viewed in the context of Mexico's increased economic dependence upon foreign capital and the growing control of the United States over Mexico's economy.

Radical changes in the class structure and in the power relationships between classes did not occur as a result of the Mexican Revolution, mainly because the worker-peasant thrust of the Revolution was blunted by Carranza's victory over Emiliano Zapata. Nominal unity between urban workers and the rural proletariat was shattered with the formulation of the pact between Obregón and the Casa del Obrero

Mundial in 1915. The consequences of that pact were not just the formation of "red battalions" of urban workers to fight against the workers and peasants in Pancho Villa's army. The consequences were more far-reaching. They involved a long-range misdevelopment of Mexico's organized labor movement, leading to the creation of a corrupt labor bureaucracy, resulting in only occasional gains for the working class, as in the 1930's, and making labor ever more dependent upon a government it did not—and could not—control. For almost four decades now, Mexican workers have had to live with constant or declining *real* wages and without the chance to develop their own class ideology and autonomy. The last sixty years of Mexican history are unintelligible without honest recognition of the immediate results of the Revolution in 1917: a defeated peasantry, a crippled and dependent labor movement, a wounded but victorious bourgeoisie, and, for a divided Mexican people, a paper triumph— the 1917 Constitution.

Surely these were not the causes for which millions of Mexican workers, peasants, and youth gave their lives and limbs in 1910–1917. The real goals of the Revolution were those proclaimed by the Precursors described in this book and their successors in Mexican history: Zapata, the petroleum workers who forced Cárdenas's hand in the 1930's, Vallejo, Jaramillo, Vázquez, Cabañas, and today's political prisoners who carry on the tradition initiated by the Precursors.

The anti-imperialist thrust of the Revolution in its "institutional" form has varied through the years, gaining strength when the workers mobilize, as during the crisis in the petroleum industry, 1936–1938, and losing strength when the domestic bourgeoisie feels less threatened from below and more amenable to profitable arrangements with foreign capitalists, as after World War II. The proletarian thrust of the Revolution has suffered similar ups and downs, undergoing defeat when workers and peasants divide against themselves (as in 1915), experiencing brief victories when they unite for common ends, as in the early years of the Cárdenas period. However, Cárdenas himself kept workers and peasants separated (CTM, CNC), and this has worked to the advantage of the domestic and foreign bourgeoisies ever since.

That Mexico's people remain conscious of their Revolutionary heritage and the gains they did win, at least on paper, in the 1917 Constitution, and the need to reassert themselves in an effort to revolutionize Mexican society and determine their own destinies, was manifested once more in 1968. Before the massacre of Tlatelolco, October 2, workers and peasants were rallying to the protest movement of the students. The internal dynamics of that movement, and of the independent labor union movement that ensued, have yet to be completely worked out.

Mexican readers of this book will recognize in the Río Blanco massacre of 1907 the same kind of power politics later manifested in the Plaza of Three Cultures. In the charges of "foreign influence" on the Precursor Movement (Ricardo Flores Magón was an Anarchist and therefore accused of disloyalty to Mexico), readers will recognize the recent allegations in Mexico that the 1968 student movement was somehow a product of foreign "subversion." A Mexican student involved in the demonstrations of 1968 was asked why he and his brothers and sisters carried the picture of Che Guevara, and the student answered:

. . . before anything else I want to make clear that ideologically we identify ourselves with the revolutionary thinking of José María Morelos and the brothers Flores Magón. For we consider that their struggles are not reduced to justice and freedom of their historical time but that they are of contemporary significance. With reference to the commandant Ernesto "El Che" Guevara, youth sees in him the prototype of the New Man who fought and gave his life, being consistent with his ideology. His humanism—to give himself unconditionally to the cause of the people—to the struggle against Yanquee Imperialism, the most pitiless brutal enemy keeping all the peoples in misery—all this identifies us profoundly with him.

In truth, historical struggles like those of the Precursors of the Mexican Revolution do have contemporary significance. Their spirit endures today.

James D. Cockcroft
Milwaukee, Wisconsin
October 2, 1969

Note to Chicano Readers of the Paperback Edition

This research was undertaken almost fifteen years ago with two particular readerships in mind: young Mexicans and young Chicanos. Mexicans did not have a Spanish edition until 1971, and an English-language paperback edition has taken almost a decade to appear. An author has little say in these matters—at least when inexperienced, as I was in the mid-1960's. Many Chicanos have discovered their own history—and that of Mexico—on their own. Their scholarship in the last decade has vastly enriched our understanding of Mexico and the United States. I hope that the research presented here will further in some small way the richer understanding Chicano scholarship has been providing us in recent years.

On many occasions in my writings, teaching, and public speaking, I have sought to bring to light the commonality of Chicano and Mexican working-class struggles (without denying the differences). For example, in my historical essay on Mexico (in *Latin America: The Struggle with Dependency and Beyond*, ed. Ronald H. Chilcote and Joel C. Edelstein [Cambridge, Mass.: Schenkman Publishing Company, 1974; distributed solely by Halsted Press—John Wiley & Sons, New York]), I wrote:

From 1846 to 1848, the Americans invaded Mexico ostensibly to force Mexico to pay off a multi-million dollar debt owed Americans who had lost properties during the War of Independence and subsequent Mexican civil wars, but in actuality to seize almost half of Mexico's territory as part of the United States' "manifest destiny," that is, imperialism. All Mexico got out of the Treaty of Guadalupe Hidalgo was fifteen million dollars to tank up its drained treasury, while the United States not only picked up some of the wealthiest territory of Mexico but also increased the wealth of U.S. railmen, farmers, and land tycoons by systematically violating treaty provisions guaranteeing the property and civil rights of those Mexicans remaining at their homesites in today's Southwestern United States.

In less than two generations after the War of 1848, almost twenty million acres were lost by Mexican-American citizens in the Southwest. This trend of swindle and thievery, with no fair judicial recourse, has continued to the present for the approximately fifteen million Mexican-Americans, or "Chicanos" as they now call themselves, residing in the Southwestern states covered by the Treaty of Guadalupe Hidalgo. For generations, Chicanos throughout the United States have been resisting the systematic subjugation that conquest, exploitation, and racism have been imposing upon them. Today, the Chicano movement in the United States has its own political party, its own youth militia, many outstanding leaders, a strong women's liberation section, and a growing consciousness of its roots in "la raza," or the race of Mexicans who have resisted subjugation since early times ("la raza" also refers to the human race, struggling to be free). Expressions of solidarity have become increasingly common between militant Chicano farm workers, welfare mothers, war veterans, and youth in the United States, and rebellious peasants, slum-dwellers, and students in Mexico. The strength of the Chicano movement is reflected in the savage repression it has evoked. Non-violent mass demonstrations have been broken up by gun-fire, resulting in the killing and wounding of scores of Chicanos, especially in Los Angeles. At least one confessed police agent has confirmed plots to assassinate Cesar Chavez, leader of the striking farm workers. In New Mexico, there has emerged a militant Chicano movement to reclaim the lands stolen from Chicanos after the Treaty of Guadalupe Hidalgo. The original leader of this land movement, Reies López Tijerina, won his own trial by defending himself without a lawyer in one case but was eventually sent to jail anyhow. Upon his release, López Tijerina had the sad and delicate duty of making public to his people at a Chicano and Puerto Rican conference, with prior permission from his wife, the nightmarish details of how police had repeatedly intimidated his wife and family while he was in jail, ending in their rape of his wife and her near-total nervous breakdown, as well as his own. Less publicized is the daily suffering of the Chicano people in general, who suffer such brutalities on a regular basis in their impoverished rural and urban "barrios." In a real and not rhetorical way, however, the

Chicanos are discovering their true history, their identity with "la raza," and they are forging a new unity among themselves and with other oppressed races and classes, especially among the poor in the United States.

For reasons of economic advantage and ethnic background, I have had the good fortune to be able to complete considerable research on Mexico, as well as on U.S. imperialism. Fortune, however, is as capricious as capitalist justice, especially when one dedicates one's life to the struggle against imperialism and for socialist revolution. Since completing my research in Mexico in 1966, I have been in the farm fields supporting striking farmworkers, in the barrios supporting the movements of Chicanos, Puerto Ricans, and others for national liberation, and, of course, among white workers and students pleading our common cause. Maintaining academic employment under such circumstances has been exceedingly difficult. I am threatened with being layed off from my fifth university job at this time, but I am more confident than ever that *venceremos*!

I, who have learned so much from the Chicanos, can only hope that my debt to them will be partially met with this research, which I have so longed to share with them. Slowly we are uncovering our buried history. In it, we find ourselves. Together, with those described in this book, we shout: "¡Viva la huelga! ¡Viva la Raza! ¡Viva la revolución!"

James D. Cockcroft
New Brunswick, New Jersey
May 1, 1976

INTELLECTUAL PRECURSORS OF THE
MEXICAN REVOLUTION, 1900–1913

Introduction

IN MEXICO, as in most developing countries experiencing rapid social change introduced by new economic forms ranging from Capitalism to Socialism, the word "intellectual" came to have a far broader connotation than it was to have in an established capitalist society like that of the United States. Historically, the noun "intellectual" might better be understood to mean an "educated" person, rather than a professional "educator"; a member of the intelligentsia, rather than of a select group of academics or authors. Mexican intellectuals, then, may be viewed as persons who possess, and continually make use of, an advanced education and relatively high standards of logic, criticism, and sustained ideological or technical conversation, acquired through either university instruction, professional training, or self-education (*autodidactos*). Among Mexico's intellectuals historically have been found professionals, university personnel, clergymen, high-level bureaucrats, artists, writers, philosophers, and some journalists.

Although intellectuals, like the working class, the peasantry, or the middle class, do form a recognizable social group, they are unique in the breadth of their social background. Intellectuals come from distinct classes, ranging from "low" to "high" in both economic resources and social status. Their education, rather than their economic or social status, unifies them into a group. Consequently, intellectuals can be more flexible than other groups in determining their loyalties to specific social or economic causes. This does not mean that social environment has only a minor effect on intellectuals. On the contrary, a study of intellectuals would be obviously incomplete if it did not take into account the influence of social background. In this context, a revolutionary intellectual, as distinguished from a revolutionary nonintellectual, may be examined in three particularly important respects: (1) in his shift, or occasional failure to shift, in personal identity, weak or strong, from one class to another; (2) the nature, cause, and timing of his shift, or failure to shift; and (3) the impact of his shift on the particular class with which he newly identifies, as well as the impact of the class and its values on the intellectual himself.[1]

In San Luis Potosí, so-called "cradle of the Revolution" (*cuna de la Revolución*), a small group of intellectuals began in 1900 to agitate for the goals of nineteenth-century Liberalism: democracy, anticlericalism, and free enterprise. These intellectuals addressed their appeal mainly to members of the upper and middle classes who felt resentment against the dictatorial policies of President Porfirio Díaz, whom they accused of betraying the very Liberalism he had championed upon taking power in 1877. The anti-Díaz movement that they helped launch has since become universally recognized as the Precursor Movement of the Mexican Revolution. The Precursor Movement is commonly defined as all political precedents of the Revolution of 1910–1917, including manifestoes, strikes, and armed uprisings, dating from the founding of San Luis Potosí's Club Liberal "Ponciano Arriaga" in 1900 to the outbreak of the Revolution in 1910.[2]

During the first three years of intensive agitation, intellectuals lead-

1 There is a considerable literature on the sociology of intellectuals, of which only a small fraction is cited in the Bibliography. Especially useful are the following: Karl Mannheim, *Ideology and Utopia*; Max Weber's essays in H. H. Gerth and C. Wright Mills (eds.), *From Max Weber*; and Roberto Michels, "Intellectuals," *Encyclopedia of the Social Sciences*, VII, 118–124.

2 There were other "Precursor" precedents prior to 1900, but only after 1900 did the precedents become *sustained*—a primary reason for naming and defining the Precursor Movement from that date.

ing the Precursor Movement broadened their appeal beyond traditional Liberalism to take in the demands of workers and peasants. By 1903, they were plotting for a violent revolution to overthrow Díaz and introduce profound social reforms. By August of 1910, more than two months prior to the call to arms issued by Francisco I. Madero, the press was referring to a peasant uprising in eastern San Luis Potosí as a "Precursor revolt."[3]

This book is a case study of intellectuals in the Mexican Revolution, with specific reference to four intellectuals from San Luis Potosí who played leadership roles in the Precursor Movement: engineer Camilo Arriaga, schoolteacher Librado Rivera, journalist and poet Juan Sarabia, and student and lawyer Antonio Díaz Soto y Gama. The lives and roles of two other prominent revolutionary intellectuals are also examined: Ricardo Flores Magón, Anarchist journalist who emerged as leader of the Precursor Movement's Partido Liberal Mexicano (PLM, 1905– 1911), and Francisco I. Madero, the Liberal landowner-businessman who led the Partido Nacional Antirreeleccionista (1910–1911), which triumphed after the overthrow of Díaz.

Although in agreement about the definition of the Precursor Movement, scholars remain in conflict about the definition of the Mexican Revolution. There is little doubt, however, that the 1917 Constitution represents the closest approximation to a Mexican consensus on the Revolution's goals. Therefore, for the purpose of this study, the term "Mexican Revolution" shall refer to those events which started on November 20, 1910, the date set by Madero for armed revolt, and culminated with the promulgation of the Constitution on February 5, 1917. Some authorities argue that the Revolution did not end in 1917, but continued until 1940 or goes on even today. This book cannot enter into that controversy more than indirectly. Its purpose is to present information concerning the nature of social forces generating the Revolution and affecting intellectuals' behavior during the earlier period. Insofar as the earlier period affected later developments, however, evidence presented here casts considerable doubt on the assertion that the Mexican Revolution was, or is, a "continuous" or "permanent" one.

[3] *El Estandarte*, August 7, 11, 12, 1910.

While by no means uniform in content or monolithic in effect, the 1917 Constitution did spell out radical change for Mexico in four important respects. First, in the realm of ideology, it established a new set of goals and ideals to guide the nation's life. Second, in the area of politics, it called for a new, less centralized, more democratic structure of national and local government. Third, in economics, it provided for a fairer distribution of the nation's wealth, severe limitation of foreign ownership, and agrarian and labor reform. Fourth, in social matters, it insisted upon the separation of Church and State, universal secular education, and respect for the equal rights of Indians, peasants, laborers, and all Mexicans.[4] Only the first change—that of ideology—has been fulfilled to any significant extent in the course of the Revolution and its aftermath. Dispute continues to rage on the questions of political democracy, economic nationalism, and social revolution.

Such dispute did not originate with events after 1917. Roots of the controversy go back to at least as early as the Precursor Movement. As intellectuals and political leaders formulated their ideologies for some kind of revolution or change in Mexico, what kind of social structure were they responding to or trying to alter? When the Revolution erupted and as it developed, was it bourgeois or proletarian? If bourgeois, then against what class or group were bourgeois revolutionaries fighting? If proletarian, then were workers and peasants pitted against the bourgeoisie?[5] If the bourgeoisie did withstand an assault from the lower classes, then was the bourgeoisie seeking its own revolutionary goals or merely preserving vested class interests?' Or, as many have argued, was the Mexican Revolution mainly an antifeudal revolution in which various bourgeois elements teamed with peasants and workers to throw out big landholders, modernize agriculture, and introduce a modern industrial system into a society bogged down in its "precapitalist" phase? These were questions which deeply concerned all revolu-

---

[4] *Constitución Política de los Estados Unidos Mexicanos* (official edition, 1917).

[5] The word "bourgeoisie" refers to that class primarily concerned with its own self-aggrandizement through profit-making in commerce, finance, and industry. In its purest form, the bourgeoisie constitutes the ruling class in a capitalist economy, as distinguished from a feudal economy, where a landholding aristocracy is the ruling class.

tionaries, especially—in terms of ideological conflict—Mexico's intellectuals.

While ideally a statistically designed research project, based on questionnaires or other modern social measurement techniques similar to those employed in the United States, might help to delineate the roles and conflicts among Mexico's intellectuals during the Precursor and early Revolutionary period, such an approach cannot be applied in this instance. There simply are not enough statistics of trustworthy caliber from that period. And the dead do not speak. However, there does exist sufficient data on the level of censuses, founding statutes of business concerns and political movements, newspapers, archival documents, personal letters, biographies, memoirs, and interviews with surviving revolutionaries or their relatives, to make possible a fairly clear overall picture of the relationship between intellectuals and the outbreak of the Revolution.

This is not to suggest that the relationship of intellectuals to the Revolution was strictly one-way, that is, that intellectuals to one degree or another stimulated the Revolution or provided its ideological basis without themselves altering their positions or attitudes as a result of revolutionary events. On the contrary, the two-way nature of the intellectuals' behavior—affecting the Revolution and being affected by the Revolution—must be considered if the intellectuals' role in the Revolution is to be fully understood.

By the word "ideology" is understood a coherent and publicly articulated set of ideas or opinions affecting one or more social groups. In Mexico during the "Porfiriato," as the regimen of Porfirio Díaz between 1877 and 1911 has commonly been termed, the ideologies of Social Darwinism, Liberalism, Socialism, and Anarchism all came to have an important impact on the nation's politics. The development of an ideology, however, cannot be understood solely in terms of its ideas or the impact of its ideas. Ideologies have to be examined in the larger social contexts in which they occur, flourish, or go neglected. Ideologies and their impact are, in this sense, intricately related to the emergence of important groups suffering specific grievances or having ambitions to be met. A political ideology, then, while by no means exclusively a rationalization for what a particular class wants to do anyway, may be construed as a charter of the ambitions and goals of a class acting in the political arena, alone or in coalition with other classes, or parts thereof.

In examining the roles of intellectuals in the preparation for, and development of, the Mexican Revolution, this book devotes considerable space to a study of the interrelationship between individuals, political ideologies, and class interests. To what extent, if at all, did individuals, groups, or classes articulate or respond to new ideologies upon encountering blocks to their ambitions or brooking other grievances? Was there much unrest among Mexico's different classes? If so, did there develop a willingness, however tentative, among discontented elements of one class to enter into political coalition with members of another class, in spite of ostensibly conflicting class interests, in order to change the political system of Mexico or otherwise achieve their goals?

Granted the genesis of the Precursor Movement in San Luis Potosí and its later division into principal branches led by Ricardo Flores Magón and Madero, the potential usefulness of a case study like this one, especially if supplemented in the future by other such case studies, becomes manifest. Five of the six intellectuals to be examined grew up either in San Luis Potosí or, in Madero's case, in a similar area of Mexico's mining North. Both the Precursor Movement and the Revolution were led, for the most part, by Northerners. In a detailed examination of the lives and roles of four prominent intellectuals from San Luis Potosí, along with those of Madero and Flores Magón, certain social, economic, and ideological forces affecting much of Mexico's intelligentsia may begin to emerge more clearly. While similarities between San Luis Potosí's social structure and that of the rest of Mexico can be observed, case studies of other important areas of the Mexican Revolution, such as Morelos, home state of peasant revolutionary leader Emiliano Zapata, will be required if scholars are to analyze in depth the complexities underlying most generalizations about Mexican society and the Revolution at the national level.

Similarly, further studies will be needed about other intellectuals who participated, or failed to participate, in the Mexican Revolution. Except for Díaz Soto y Gama, the six intellectuals examined in this book were most influential prior to 1913, not after. Therefore, post-1913 events are discussed solely to provide evidence on a tentative typology of intellectuals or to relate later developments to patterns and conditions already observed in the period between 1900 and 1913. Disputes involving the four "Potosinos" (as natives of San Luis Potosí are called) and Madero and Flores Magón were by no means necessarily unique. Indeed, divisions among these six intellectuals may have represented the kinds of disagreements affecting intellectuals in general during the Revolution. Finally, these six intellectuals and men like them either did or did not have a significant influence on the outbreak and development of the Revolution. Consideration of their careers will test the common assertion, succinctly put by Crane Brinton, "No ideas, no revolution."[6]

[6] Crane Briton, *The Anatomy of Revolution*, p. 52.

PART ONE

Intellectuals in the Social Milieu of the Porfiriato

CHAPTER ONE

Social and Economic Structure
in San Luis Potosí

C LIQUISH CONTROL of Mexico's economy and politics was a principal complaint of the Precursor Movement throughout the last decade of the Porfiriato. In San Luis Potosí, a handful of elite families,
often in co-operation with foreign businessmen, dominated economic,
political, and social life. A system of interlocking economic interests
between city, mine, and farm, tending toward increased industrialization, monopolization,[1] mechanization, profit-making, and participation
of foreign capital, resulted in significant changes throughout the state's

---

[1] The word "monopoly" may be defined as "unified or concerted discretionary control of the price at which purchasers in general can obtain a commodity or service and
of the supply which they can secure, or the control of price through supply, as distinct
from the lack of such control which marks the ideal situation of perfect competition"
(John Maurice Clark, "Monopoly," *Encyclopedia of the Social Sciences*, X, 623–
630). Pure monopoly, in either a buyers' or a sellers' market, is not frequent. The
principle of monopoly may be said to apply to many societies and may be extended
to any pervasive control of a given area, economic or otherwise—e.g., monopoly of
social status, or monopoly of political control.

social structure. Contrary to the claims of some authorities that "feudalism" and "stagnation" characterized the countryside, social change especially affected rural areas.

Economically, railroad-building and industrialization were the two most important innovative processes generating social change in Mexico during the Porfiriato. In its railroad development, San Luis Potosí was representative of the rest of the nation. Porfirio Díaz' rail-expansion program, which added fifteen thousand miles of right-of-way to the four hundred miles completed under Presidents Benito Juárez (1867–1872) and Sebastián Lerdo de Tejada (1872–1876), was financed primarily by foreign capital, mostly U.S., but also British and French.[2] San Luis Potosí's fantastic rail expansion between 1888 and 1902, which can be viewed graphically in Map 2, derived from the aims of foreigners in constructing railroads throughout Mexico: to extract and market mineral wealth, and to service populous industrializing areas where there existed abundant cheap labor (the state capital had nearly seventy thousand inhabitants by 1900).[3]

Railroads in San Luis Potosí ran from the state's silver, lead, and copper mines to the main north-south trunk line, to smelters, to factories, and to the port of Tampico on the Gulf of Mexico. Federal subsidies, state bonds, and concessions to prominent local businessmen and landholders like Juan B. Barragán, former San Luis Potosí governor (1869), financed the laying of the first track on the Tampico line in 1879. A year later, the U.S.-owned Mexican Central Railroad bought out all other interests and agreed to complete the railroad, which it did by 1890. Not long thereafter, Guggenheim mining interests extended this mining-transportation link by sea all the way from Tampico to Perth Amboy, New Jersey, where a new refinery completed integration of a nascent American mining dynasty from mine-mouth to the finished metal. A similar procedure of federal subsidies and business concessions was followed from 1881 to 1883 for construction of an east-west railroad connecting San Luis Potosí with Aguascalientes, site of a giant copper smelter built by the Guggenheims a decade later. President

---

[2] Raymond Vernon, *The Dilemma of Mexico's Development*, p. 39; Fernando Rosenzweig et al., *Historia moderna de México. El Porfiriato: la vida económica*, p. 1155.
[3] *Ibid.*; Dirección General de Estadística, *Censo*, 1900.

SAN LUIS POTOSI

Catorce
La Paz
Matehuala
Charcas
Guadalcázar
Ahualulco
Cd. del Maíz
San Luis Potosí
La Angostura
Ebano
Cárdenas
Rascón
Río Verde
Valles
Santa María del Río
Sierra Gorda
Tamazunchale

0   50   100
Scale   in   Miles

VMB

MAP 1

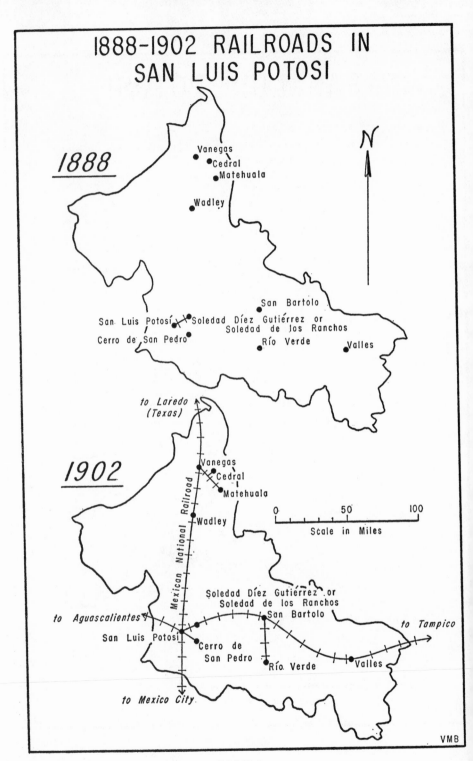

1888–1902 RAILROADS IN SAN LUIS POTOSI

1888

N

Vanegas
Cedral
Matehuala

Wadley

San Bartolo
San Luis Potosí
Soledad Díez Gutiérrez or
Soledad de los Ranchos
Cerro de San Pedro
Río Verde
Valles

1902

to Laredo
(Texas)

Vanegas
Cedral
Matehuala

Mexican National Railroad

Wadley

0   50   100
Scale in Miles

Soledad Díez Gutiérrez or
Soledad de los Ranchos
San Bartolo

to Aguascalientes
to Tampico
San Luis Potosí
Cerro de
San Pedro
Río Verde
Valles

to Mexico City

VMB

MAP 2

Díaz' rail policy after 1890 was strictly one of foreign concessions. U.S. business elements came to control the entire rail grid of San Luis Potosí and surrounding states. Of all foreign investments in Mexico during the Porfiriato, U.S. capital held majority control, and San Luis Potosí was hardly unrepresentative. Of total U.S. investments in Mexico, 83 per cent were in rails and mining—the two principal components of San Luis Potosí's economic infrastructure.[4]

Foreign economic investments were often encouraged and abetted by local businessmen of elite families, who welcomed new railroads to market their minerals and agricultural produce. In addition, a shrewd San Luis Potosí businessman who could wangle a railroad concession out of the Federal Government might sell it at a handsome profit to American investors. This was precisely what Governor Pedro Díez Gutiérrez did in 1888. The Governor, who accumulated an immense fortune while alternating the state governorship with his brother for two decades, sold his 5,500-peso-per-kilometer rail concession, which would have linked the northern mining complex of Matehuala with the agrarian hub of Río Verde, to the U.S.-owned Mexican National Railroad. Ignoring blueprints for running the line all the way to Río Verde, American engineers completed the shorter and cheaper link from Matehuala's mines to the north-south trunk line connecting Laredo (Texas) to Mexico City. President Díaz officially inaugurated the trunk line at ceremonies held in San Luis Potosí on November 1, 1888.[5]

Completion of such major railroads, together with the nationwide elimination of state and municipal import and marketing taxes in order to permit free interstate commerce, opened the gates to what most authorities agree was the period of fastest industrial growth during the

---

[4] Rosenzweig, pp. 493–544, 565 ff., 1066–1067, 1155; Primo Feliciano Velázquez, *Historia de San Luis Potosí,* IV, 72–73, 97–100; Harvey O'Connor, *The Guggenheims,* pp. 85–101; Juan B. Barragán, *Discurso pronunciado el 15 de septiembre de 1879 por el C. Lic. Juan B. Barragán, en la inauguración del primer tramo de Ferrocarril construido en el Estado* (pamphlet).

[5] Velázquez, IV, 72–73, 90–101, 162–163; Rosenzweig, Chaps. v, x; Isaac Grimaldo, *Gobernantes potosinos, 1590–1939;* Manuel Zepeda, *Opiniones de la prensa sobre las fiestas de inauguración del Ferrocarril Nacional Mexicano verificadas en la ciudad de San Luis Potosí los días 1°, 2, 3, y 4 de noviembre de 1888.* The Díez Gutiérrez fortune was estimated at three million pesos by Díaz braintruster Francisco Bulnes (*El verdadero Díaz y la Revolución,* pp. 165–167).

Porfiriato—1895 to 1901. As Mexican economist Fernando Rosen-zweig has observed: "The creation of new factories, a clear phenome-non since 1880, reached its apogee in this period, when foreign invest-ment turned to industrial activity."[6]

As in Mexico's railroad-building, so in its industrial development—foreigners dominated. Foreign capital brought in modern machinery for new medium and light industries. Concurrently, even though im-migrants constituted what might be called an "indigenous industrial class,"[7] foreign control of Mexico's new industries expanded and solid-ified during the last fifteen years of the Porfiriato. Financing of even "domestic" investments was often, at least indirectly, accomplished in significant part by non-Mexican capital. Examples of domestic financ-ing of foreign investment, also common, reflected a high degree of co-operation between Mexican and foreign businessmen.[8] In the last nine years of the Porfiriato, new investments by U.S., British, and French capitalists exceeded all their investments of the first twenty-three years of the Porfiriato. The most spectacular increase was in U.S. in-vestments, which more than quintupled between 1897 and 1911. As early as 1900, foreigners owned outright 172 of the 212 commercial establishments in the Federal District (Mexico City), and by 1911, foreign interests accounted for two-thirds of Mexico's total investment outside agriculture and the handicraft industries.[9]

Most influential of foreign industrial forces in the mining state of San Luis Potosí was the Guggenheim family's Sociedad Metalúrgica Mexicana, a subsidiary of American Smelting and Refining Company. By 1900, the Guggenheims already had established a thriving smelter at Monterrey, Nuevo León, and were casting about for new profitable mining ventures. Their engineers reported good opportunities through-out the North, including San Luis Potosí, which ranked seventh na-tionally in peso-value of mineral production (3,549,972) and second only to Zacatecas in number of men employed by the mining industry (10,767).[10] Guggenheim interests took over an incomplete and aban-

6 Rosenzweig, pp. 314, 326.

7 Vernon, pp. 44–45; cf. Rosenzweig, p. 453.

8 Velázquez, IV, 155–163; Vernon, pp. 44–45; Rosenzweig, pp. 1181–1184.

9 Rosenzweig, pp. 1125, 1162; Vernon, pp. 42–44.

10 *El Contemporáneo*, August 29, 1903; O'Connor, pp. 85–101.

doned rail link running east from San Luis Potosí toward Río Verde, in order to extract lead, silver, and gold from famed Cerro de San Pedro, original silver vein of the state and cause for the founding of the capital in the valley nearby in 1592. Then, on May 25, 1902, the Guggenheims' Sociedad Metalúrgica Mexicana bought the 42.3-kilometer railroad connecting Río Verde to San Bartolo on the San Luis Potosí–Tampico line, using "thousands of pesos given by large landholders . . . and fifty-cent contributions of many, many cooperating humble citizens."[11] Next, still in 1902, the Guggenheims established a multi-million-dollar smelting plant at Matehuala (lead, silver, and gold) and smaller smelters at San Luis Potosí and Wadley Railroad Station, about 40 kilometers southwest of Matehuala on the Mexican National Railroad (silver, antimony, bismuth, zinc, cobalt, and sulfur). By 1910, Guggenheim mining interests in all Mexico accounted for fifty million dollars' worth of common stock and an indeterminate amount of preferred stock. Throughout Mexico's North, the Guggenheims had "an almost complete monopoly on the metalurgical industry, upon which depended all progress in mining."[12]

In spite of a record of having collaborated with foreign capital, Mexico's bourgeoisie was not immune to the pressures of foreign competition and economic nationalism. While some Mexican businessmen profited from collaboration with foreigners, others suffered an economic squeeze. At the turn of the century, when the Liberal Clubs initiated by San Luis Potosí mining engineer Camilo Arriaga were beginning to manifest significant political opposition, there was much angry discussion about what Porfirio Díaz himself had criticized in 1876 as "selling the country to the nation next door."[13] Even the Cath-

---

[11] Velázquez, IV, 162–163; A. B. González, *Album Rioverdense, colección de escritos, datos históricos y estadísticos recogidos.* Histories by Velázquez, Manuel Muro, and Salvador Penilla López, listed in the Bibliography, agree that the name "Potosí" derives from the association in the Spaniards' minds between the silver found there in 1592 and the earlier gigantic silver strike made at Potosí, Bolivia, in 1544.

[12] Rosenzweig, pp. 283, 1092, 1184; Alfred Tischendorf, *Great Britain and Mexico in the Era of Porfirio Díaz*, pp. 72, 90.

[13] Díaz issued his Plan de Tuxtepec, January 15, 1876, to protest President Lerdo de Tejada's efforts at re-election and the sale of the national debt accumulated during the French intervention of 1862–1867 to the United States (text in Jesús Romero Flores, *Anales históricos de la Revolución Mexicana*, III, 212–215).

olic, Conservative San Luis Potosí newspaper *El Estandarte* was critical of "the Yankees' taking over of Mexico little by little."[14] By 1910,
foreigners owned one-seventh of Mexico's land surface.[15] Few scholars
would quibble with the assertion of the late Mexican economist Luis
Nicolau D'Olwer that antiforeign sentiment played a pivotal role in
the Mexican Revolution: ". . . all the acts for which Díaz is blamed,
and the consequent loss of prestige for his regime, are connected with
his policy of favoring foreign investments."[16]

Among San Luis Potosí's bourgeoisie, the end of the nineteenth
century was marked by political and economic uncertainty. Many elite
families were feeling the final effects of an economic slump (1892–
1895). Some, like the Barrenecheas and Coghlans, emerged with new
strength, and others, like the Arriagas, were still staggering from the
impact of the earlier crisis. These cases warrant examination because of
subsequent political developments and sociological implications concerning elite families and conflicts within Mexico's bourgeoisie. Camilo
Arriaga, a Liberal, was the man most responsible for initiating the Precursor Movement against Porfirio Díaz. Pedro Barrenechea, a Conservative influential in designating state governors, later lent financial aid
to Madero, the moderate Liberal elected President after the overthrow
of Díaz in 1911. Francisco M. Coghlan, by co-operating with U.S.
businessmen, parlayed mining profits into small and medium industry,
a not uncommon practice among heads of San Luis Potosí elite families.

The Arriaga family had founded its wealth on silver. It owned the
state's largest silver mines, incorporated as the Compañía Minera de la
Concepción. On January 16, 1893, the richest and largest mine at
Concepción caved in, thus undercutting the Arriagas' fortune. Three
months later, the sixty-six-year-old Casa de Moneda de San Luis Potosí,
major mint in the area, was closed down and its resources transferred
to Mexico City. Throughout this period—from 1892 to 1895—the
state of San Luis Potosí suffered a series of economic reversals: a severe
slump in the silver market, drought, famine, and typhus epidemics.

---

[14] *El Estandarte,* March 18, 1902.
[15] Rosenzweig, pp. 1106–1115; Vernon, p. 50; Frank Tannenbaum, *Mexico, the
Struggle for Peace and Bread,* pp. 140–141. Some estimates run as high as one-fifth.
[16] Rosenzweig, p. 183.

Consequently the economy became highly unstable. In the course of wild stock-market speculation, many mining shares traded hands. The Arriagas failed to recover fully from this economic infighting. The other major San Luis Potosí silver-mining concern at Santa Ana, directed by Coghlan and backed by U.S. capital, emerged strengthened.[17]

Before the end of the 1892–1895 slump, San Luis Potosí businessmen began clamoring for political changes at the Statehouse. In July of 1896, Barrenechea and other leading businessmen of San Luis Potosí went to Mexico City to confer with President Díaz. They urged the President to replace Governor Carlos Díez Gutiérrez with engineer Blas Escontría, who was appointed by Díaz after Díez Gutiérrez' death two years later. Escontría, the harried businessmen pleaded, was a partner in business enterprises of both Díez Gutiérrez and Barrenechea, among others. Therefore Escontría could be expected to encourage established economic interests. Since even Governor Díez Gutiérrez, a close friend of President Díaz, shared critical business interests with the Barrenecheas, such as the state's main brewery, there was no reason to suppose that the businessmen were interviewing the President because of economic rivalries with the Governor whom they wished replaced. Politically, however, Governor Díez Gutiérrez was vulnerable. He and his brother Pedro had ruled San Luis Potosí as governor for two decades. They had made mistakes, leading to a two-million-peso debt and "the ruin of San Luis Potosí." It was time for a change. A younger, more progressive and dynamic governor, someone like engineer Escontría, might break the economic logjam and assuage the public's discontent with decades of *caudillo*-style rule, argued the businessmen.[18]

[17] It was at this time that the Coghlan concern completed the installation of electricity and modern machinery provided by U.S. capital (Velázquez, IV, 103–104, 140–143); *El Estandarte*, 1892–1895, *passim*; Rosenzweig, pp. 230, 794; Compañía Minera de la Concepción, *Estatutos aprobados para el trabajo y laborío de la Mina de la Concepción ubicada en el Mineral de Catorce* (pamphlet) and *Contrato celebrado entre la Junta Directiva de la Compañía propietaria y explotadora de la Mina de la Concepción y Anexas, sitas en el Mineral de Catorce, Estado de San Luis Potosí, por una parte, y el Sr. Benigno Arriaga por sí o por la Compañía o Compañías que se organicen, para la compraventa de los metales de dichas minas* (pamphlet).

[18] Compañía Anónima Restauradora del Mineral de Ramos, *Estatutos de la Compañía Anónima Restauradora del Mineral de Ramos de San Luis Potosí, aprobados en junta celebrada el 7 diciembre de 1887* (pamphlet); Compañía Industrial "Cer-

Escontría was appointed governor in 1898. The major tactic he employed to confront the state's economic crisis was the same as that being used by President Díaz on a national level: incentives for investment by foreign capital. This was the time of the concerted Guggenheim economic invasion of the state. By 1910, the United States was receiving 77 per cent of Mexico's mineral exports, as compared to only 42 per cent at the start of the Porfiriato.[19]

There is every indication that San Luis Potosí businessmen, with obvious exceptions like Arriaga, at first welcomed this economic shot in the arm from U.S. capital. Although well-established mining concerns like those of the Barrenecheas did not relish U.S. efforts to buy them out, and smaller ones even protested publicly,[20] most businessmen, shaken by the 1895 crisis, felt they stood to gain by collaboration with their foreign counterparts. Since mineral production was lagging in San Luis Potosí when compared to that in other parts of the North, San Luis Potosí mining concerns welcomed expanded export facilities provided by new rail links to the North and the Gulf. Also the establishment of U.S.-financed lead and copper smelters and small steel

---

veceria de San Luis," S.A., *Estatutos de la Compañía Industrial "Cervecería de San Luis" Sociedad Anónima* (pamphlet); Compañía Anónima de Santa María de la Paz y Anexas, *Informes que a la Asamblea General Ordinaria de 31 de enero de 1901, rindieron los señores Presidente, Comisario y Director, acuerdos tomados y cuenta de produción y gastos del año de 1900* (pamphlet). In addition to such economic collaboration, the Díez Gutiérrez and Barrenechea families intermarried (Velázquez, IV, 175). San Luis Potosí's businessmen, received by President Díaz in the national palace's "Green Room," reinforced their argument with a letter signed by "various prominent residents of Matehuala" and having the support of the state's military zone commander, General Pedro A. González, and principal newspaper, *El Estandarte* (Velázquez, IV, 146–148). Although Velázquez does not specify Escontría as the businessmen's choice to replace Díez Gutiérrez, he confirms the nature of the complaints of the businessmen and implies that their wishes were met by Escontría's appointment as governor in 1898.

19 Rosenzweig, p. 241.

20 E.g., Manuel José Othón, *Apuntes que, para alegar de buena prueba ante el Señor Juez 3° de Letras del Partido de Mapimí, produce Don Jesús Revilla, patrocinado por el Lic. Manuel J. Othón, y representante jurídico de la Compañía Minera "Siderita" y Anexas, S.A. de S. Luis Potosí en el interdicto de despojo promovido contra la Compañía Minera y Fundidora "Descubridora"* (pamphlet).

plants in Matehuala and San Luis Potosí facilitated local expansion in the use of mineral products.[21]

Mexican businessmen, confronted with either economic slump or the need for more capital and machinery, had to work with whatever was available. Their needs happened to occur in an economically "under-developed" country at a time of rapid U.S. expansion around the world. It was only natural that they resorted to collaboration with U.S. investors, when the goals of both nations' upper bourgeoisies had so much in common: economic expansion, industrialization, and profit. However, this continued collaboration with foreigners by many of the bourgeoisie coincided with the first appeals to economic nationalism being expressed by the Precursor Movement in the early 1900's. Collaboration with foreign capital, however profitable for Mexican businessmen, served to increase further the degree of monopolization and foreign control of the nation's economy. At the time of the next major economic slump—1907–1911—Mexico's bourgeoisie would clamor for some kind of political change. By then, economic nationalism would be making more sense to them, since foreign control would have, in the meantime, increased noticeably; national economic progress would have slowed; and the Precursor Movement would have begun to influence national politics. These factors would affect revolutionary propensities among the bourgeoisie.

A characteristic of "underdeveloped" economies in general would seem to be an ambivalent feeling among bourgeoisie about the question of collaboration with foreign businessmen, as opposed to economic nationalism. Mexico's Revolution has often been described as a "nationalistic, bourgeois revolution," aimed at freeing the country from foreign domination. However, events in the 1917–1967 period would suggest that the historic ambivalence in Mexico's bourgeoisie has by no means been resolved in favor of economic nationalism. On the contrary,

[21] Rosenzweig, pp. 182, 224, 230, 241, 794, 1092; Fundición de Fierro de San Luis Potosí, *Estatutos de la Fundición de Fierro de San Luis Potosí, Sociedad Anónima incorporada bajo las leyes de la República Mexicana* (pamphlet). Although mining production rose impressively throughout the nation during the Porfiriato, San Luis Potosí failed to keep up with the national pace after 1895 (Jesús Silva Herzog, *El agrarismo mexicano y la reforma agraria*, p. 104).

in spite of occasional nationalistic outbursts like that of 1938 when the petroleum industry was nationalized, the Mexican bourgeoisie today —within the broader outlines of a "Mexicanization" policy allowing the Federal Government to require a company's capital to be 51 per cent owned by Mexicans—seems to be as willing as ever to collaborate with U.S. capital and less inclined than earlier in the century to support, or even tolerate, revolutionary calls for the nationalization of all industries or 100 per cent Mexican ownership.[22] The roots of these discussions on economic policy go back to at least as early as the events of 1900–1913, especially to the threat of an antibourgeois, revolutionary worker-peasant movement spawned by the Precursor Movement. In addition, the socio-economic realities influencing developments from 1900 to 1913 included precisely this ambivalence within Mexico's bourgeoisie about economic nationalism, as well as the inexorable problem of an "underdeveloped" country's economic dependence upon a "developed" one.

During the Porfiriato, collaboration by Mexican businessmen with foreign interests included bank loans when deemed necessary. Thus, for example, the Banco de San Luis Potosí provided Edward L. Doheny with fifty thousand pesos just when the U.S. oil magnate was about to give up petroleum exploration in the Huasteca[23] region around Ebano, early in 1904. Exploration continued, and in April of 1904, oil well "Fish No. 1" gushed black gold fifteen meters high and began a fifteen-hundred-barrel daily production. Thus began Mexico's oil boom —to the profit of foreigners, but with the assistance of nationals.[24]

22 Today there is considerable evidence that, because of increased bourgeois collaboration with foreigners and opposition to revolutionary movements or proposals for nationalization of industry, ambivalence among all bourgeoisies in Latin America has diminished to the point of insignificance. Mexico's at times "anti-U.S." foreign policy should not be misconstrued, as it concerns only the ticklish question of intervention in the internal affairs of other countries ("self-determination of peoples") or occasional border disputes, and not the Mexican Government's general guidelines of co-operation with foreign capital.

23 Thinly populated, well-watered, jagged eastern slopes and tropical lowlands of the extreme eastern part of San Luis Potosí; part of the larger geographical and cultural section of Mexico called "Huasteca" after the Huaxteco Indians, incorporating parts of Tamaulipas, Querétaro, Hidalgo, Tlaxcala, and Veracruz.

24 Velázquez, IV, 155–162; Tischendorf, pp. 125 ff.; Rosenzweig, pp. 1127–1129; Gabriel Antonio Menéndez, *Doheny el cruel,* pp. 288–293; Joaquín Meade, *La huas-*

The Mexican group responsible for abetting the oil boom in this case, the Banco de San Luis Potosí, had been established in 1897 by prominent San Luis Potosí businessmen, led by Ramón Alcázar and Gerardo and Eduardo Meade (a wealthy landholding family), who, with J. H. Bahnsen, had been granted a federal concession to issue paper money and bonds. The bank's capital was over a million pesos. It soon became the principal bank in the state, but collapsed during the Revolution.[25]

Families of landed wealth, as suggested by the case of the Meades and their Banco de San Luis Potosí, were quite conscious of new economic opportunities opening up with the inflow of U.S. capital and the completion of railroads and roads across the state. It was no coincidence that the first promotional organization of industrialists in San Luis Potosí was founded (May 27, 1905) as an "agricultural" and industrial center—the Centro Agrícola e Industrial Potosino. This organization was subsidized with more than fifteen thousand pesos by the state government, headed by landowner-industrialist Governor José María Espinosa y Cuevas. Its board of directors was composed of big landowners and cattlemen of the Espinosa y Cuevas, Hernández, and Barrenechea families, mining figures of the Cabrera and Barrenechea families, and industrialist Emeterio V. Lavín. Two of the state's biggest *latifundios* (large landholdings)—La Angostura and El Gogorrón, controlled by Espinosa y Cuevas, Hermanos, and miner-industrialist Felipe Muriedas, respectively—were well represented.

teca veracruzana, II, 135–145; E. L. Doheny, *A Brief Statement of the results accomplished by the Mexican Petroleum Company at Ebano, San Luis Potosí, México* (pamphlet). Besides Mexican bankers and large landowners, some medium-sized landholders sold property to foreign petroleum companies and came to form a provincial class of "new rich," according to Gregorio López y Fuentes, *Huasteca,* pp. 37–52, 89.

[25] Banco de San Luis Potosí, S.A., *Banco de San Luis Potosí, S. A. Concesiones, estatutos y extractos de la ley general de 19 de marzo de 1897 de Instituciones de Crédito* (pamphlet). Federico J. Meade's Haciendas Anexas was one of the biggest estates in the state, sprawling over 104,000 hectares and including part of the state of Tamaulipas (A. Fremont, *Obras de irrigación en las Haciendas Anexas y abastecimiento de la Presa de Guadalupe, San Luis Potosí* [pamphlet]). At the time of Federico Meade's death in 1909, his wealth was estimated at more than three million dollars, according to the Methodist monthly *La Ofrenda Escolar,* September, 1909, p. 134.

The new agrarian-industrial Centro welcomed such U.S. investment in local industry as the Guggenheim foundries; the Fundición de Fierro de San Luis Potosí, founded in 1904 to produce screws, nuts, and bolts; and the F. L. Schaefer Shoe Company, established in 1903–1904, and sold a year later to Coghlan y Compañía. Coghlan's company also controlled shares in the Fundición de Fierro de San Luis Potosí. The massive overlap between mining, landed, and industrial wealth, both domestic and foreign—a principal complaint of the Precursor Movement—was manifested by the Muriedas and Coghlan cases.[26]

Diagram 1 presents a graphic picture of the overlap between elite families in San Luis Potosí in mining, agriculture, industry, commerce, and politics. Because of the lack of adequate or complete statistical studies on estate sizes, ownership, and investment of agricultural capital in nonagricultural commercial activity, Diagram 1 is no more than a representation of what presently available evidence indicates about San Luis Potosí's social structure during the Porfiriato. It is based largely on founding statutes and annual reports published by mining, industrial, commercial, and agricultural firms in San Luis Potosí, supplemented by newspaper accounts of the time, memories of surviving citizens of the state, and the writings of contemporaries and historians. On the basis of evidence from these diversified sources, the elite families listed in Diagram 1 are not only representative; they are also the most often-cited examples of large landholders and big miners in San Luis Potosí. The Barragán, Espinosa y Cuevas, Hernández, Meade, and Muriedas families seem to have controlled the state's largest *latifundios*. As Governor Rafael Nieto pointed out in 1921, the Espinosa y Cuevas' Hacienda La Angostura alone accounted for more than one-tenth of the land area of the so-called "Central" portion of the state of San Luis Potosí, while six haciendas made up more than a quarter of the land in the "West" and seven haciendas more than a fifth of the "East."[27]

26 Velázquez, IV, 194–197; Centro Agrícola e Industrial Potosino, *Primer Concurso de Ganadería, septiembre de 1906* (pamphlet); Fundición de Fierro de San Luis Potosí, *Estatutos de la Fundición* (pamphlet). Engineers hired by Muriedas were responsible for developing the state's system of artesian wells (1906–1910), culminating with the inauguration of a hydroelectric plant in 1910. Muriedas was considered a major industrialist because of his mining interests and shipping concerns.

27 Rafael Nieto, *Exposición de los motivos que el Ejecutivo del Edo. tuvo para*

DIAGRAM 1
ELITE FAMILIES[1] IN SAN LUIS POTOSÍ

Mining	Governors	Land (Including Urban)
ARRIAGA	Barragán (1869)	Arriaga
BARRENECHEA	DIEZ GUTIERREZ (1876–1898)	BARRAGAN
CABRERA	Escontría (1898–1904)	Barrenechea
COGHLAN	Espinosa y Cuevas (1905–1911)	Díez Gutiérrez
Díez Gutiérrez	Hernández (1874–1876)	ESPINOSA Y CUEVAS
ESCONTRIA		HERNANDEZ
Espinosa		Ipiña
HERNANDEZ		MEADE
IPIÑA	Centro Agrícola e Industrial	MURIEDAS
MURIEDAS	Barrenechea	
OTHON	Cabrera	Small and Medium Industry
OBERON	Espinosa y Cuevas	
VIRAMONTES	Hernández	Barragán
ZAMANILLO	Lavín	Barrenechea
		BUENO
		Cabrera
		Coghlan
		Díez Gutiérrez
		Espinosa y Cuevas
		Hernández
Transportation and Construction	Banking	LAVIN
		Muriedas
Cabrera	Alcázar	Soberón
LAVIN	Bahnsen	Viramontes
Muriedas	Meade	Zamanillo

[1] Names printed in solid capitals indicate, insofar as it is possible to ascertain, the original source : sources of a family's wealth during the Porfiriato; names in capital and lower case indicate to what other major economic enterprises an elite family spread its interests.

This system of interlocking control by elite families in the state's economic, political, and social life alienated much of the middle class and even elements of the upper class, as in the case of Camilo Arriaga. Monolithic social control by families of the upper class blocked the advance of people from classes immediately below. Finally, elite families contributed to, and profited from, basic social changes during the

---

pedir al H. Congreso, la expedición de la Ley Agraria (pamphlet); Velázquez, IV, 175–177; Section II-E of the Bibliography, "Pamphlets."

Porfiriato which seriously affected expectations of the vast majority of the state's population, then living in the countryside.

To appreciate social change in Mexico's countryside, it is useful to understand how large landholders acquired and developed their wealth and how they farmed. Nearly all industrialists-farmers brought together in the Centro Agrícola e Industrial Potosino had developed during the Díaz regime, or earlier, a tremendous reservoir of landed wealth through inheritance, questionable legal practices (juggling of land titles, etc.), or energetic land-grabbing under the protection of Articles 26 and 27 of the 1857 Constitution and the 1883 and 1894 "vacant-land" (*baldío*) laws.

The Liberal authors of the 1857 Constitution, devotees of economic liberalism and free enterprise, had called for dividing all corporately held property, which meant both Church lands and the Indians' traditional communally held *ejidos*. Articles 26 and 27 thus provided ideal conditions for the development of private property in Mexico, a prime goal of Liberals. Recent statistical research at the Colegio de México suggests that an inordinately large number of Liberals benefited from the Reform Laws of 1857. Most of the Church and Indian lands apparently were bought up by merchants and professionals, including bureaucrats of the Liberal government; some large landholders and land speculators also benefited. Peasants, unable to compete to begin with, were further impoverished by the 5 per cent *alcabala*, or import and marketing tax. The 1857 Constitution thus intensified, rather than mitigated, land hunger among the peasantry.[28]

With unusual foresight, Ponciano Arriaga, great-uncle of the initiator of the Precursor Movement (Camilo Arriaga), warned of the dangerous consequences of the 1857 Constitution's failure to handle the land problem adequately. Although believing the right of private property to be inviolable, Arriaga nevertheless told the constitutional delegates that they had failed to define property rights precisely enough to avoid the advent of "monopolistic capitalism." Arriaga, who chaired the committee that edited Article 27 of the Constitution, proposed his

---

[28] Jan Bazant, "La desamortización de los bienes corporativos en 1856," *Historia Mexicana*, XVI, No. 2 (October–December, 1966), 193–212.

own solution: elimination of *latifundios*, provision of land for all peasants, and a tax system favoring the poor. These proposals were rejected unanimously by the constitutional delegates, who by their votes showed where their own economic interests lay.[29]

The *baldío* laws of 1883 and 1894 only increased the pace of land monopolization for what Ponciano Arriaga had called "the exclusive use of the capitalists." Under this ingenious legislation, all restrictions on land sales were removed. Land-survey companies were contracted by the government to locate and measure *baldíos*, receiving one-third of all lands surveyed as compensation.

The results of such opportunities for land speculation were statistically expressed by the 1910 census. Of rural family heads in Mexico, 96.6 per cent held no land at all. There were only 411,096 landholding farmers and 840 *hacendados* (large landowners). Of Mexico's total population, 80 per cent depended upon agricultural wages—a sizable agrarian labor force in a country undergoing incipient industrialization. In San Luis Potosí, the percentages were almost identical.[30]

In its pattern of ever-expanding *latifundios* and more and more landless peasants and rural wage earners, Mexican agriculture was not, as often has been supposed, "feudal." Rather, it was capitalist.

"Feudalism" may be defined as that socio-economic system characterized by a closed economy unconcerned with the accumulation of capital and its progressive reinvestment for profit. The vassal owns his plot of land (fief) and in exchange provides the lord certain services, often military. The feudal community is a self-contained, self-sustaining one founded primarily on relationships between lords and vassals rather than on kinship or an open, money-based economy or the presence of a strong State. Often, the lord's seigniory, or manor, is farmed by tenant farmers. Feudalism was prevalent during the Middle Ages in Europe, when "the absence of an easy flow of sales and purchases such as exists in present day societies prevented the formation of agricultural

[29] Ponciano Arriaga, *Voto particular del C. Ponciano Arriaga sobre el derecho de propiedad* (pamphlet).
[30] Census of 1910, cited in various works, e.g., Silva Herzog, pp. 122–123; Nieto.

or industrial salaried classes and of any body of functionaries remuner-
ated periodically in money."[31]

"Capitalism," on the other hand, may be defined as that socio-
economic system in which all or most of the means of production and
distribution (lands, factories, railroads, etc.) are privately owned and
operated for profit, the accumulation of capital, and the progressive
reinvestment of capital, with a corresponding development of wage
labor, salaried classes, and regularly paid functionaries, all of whom
interrelate within a relatively open, competitive market economy. Tendencies toward the formation of giant corporations and monopolistic
control of sales and purchases are common to most capitalistic societies.
The ruling class in a capitalistic society, as distinguished from that in
a feudal society, is not simply a landholding aristocracy, but rather a
bourgeoisie.

As Rosenzweig has observed, Mexican agriculture during the Porfiriato was "a new *latifundista* agriculture, oriented toward the market
. . . and employment of wage labor."[32] Production of commercial
commodities like cotton and sugar doubled in less than forty years
under Díaz.[33] In San Luis Potosí, commercial-minded *latifundistas* like
the Espinosa y Cuevas brothers took advantage of the recently completed rail network to develop a small-scale tomato export business via
Tampico, as well as trade in cattle, hides, henequen (seventh state in
henequen production in 1907), cotton, oranges (third in 1907),

[31] Marc Bloch, "European Feudalism," *Encyclopedia of the Social Sciences*, VI,
203–210.

Recent scholarship suggests that traditional views of feudalism's closed economy
may have to undergo some revision to allow for cases of market commerce that did
occur (Sidney R. Packard, *The Process of Historical Revision: New Viewpoints in
Medieval European History*).

[32] Rosenzweig, p. 315; Fernando Rosenzweig, "El desarrollo económico de México
de 1877 a 1911," *El Trimestre Económico*, XXXII, No. 127 (July–September,
1965), 427. The most important work being done on this particular theme of "capitalism—not feudalism" in Latin America is probably that of Andre G. Frank
(*Capitalism and Underdevelopment in Latin America*), who alerted me to this concept during my research when I was already drawing such conclusions on the basis
of available evidence, which I apply here only to the Porfiriato.

[33] Vernon, p. 43.

limes, lemons, custard-apples, plums, and peanuts. For the internal market, the state's largest farmers profitably produced basic food commodities like maize and beans, under the protective cover of a 100 per cent import tariff on competitive foodstuffs undergoing price declines on the world market.[34]

A glance at Diagram 1 suggests how commercial-minded San Luis Potosí elite-family *hacendados* were. All five families listed whose wealth was founded on land were also active in industry or banking. Moreover, three of them held shares in mining companies, and two of them were represented on the board of directors of the Centro Agrícola e Industrial Potosino.

One of the Precursors' chief complaints, especially after the formation of the Partido Liberal Mexicano (PLM) in 1905, was directed against Mexican capitalism. This capitalism had a real base in the countryside. It is significant that high officials in the Díaz government wrote socio-economic analyses in precisely the same terms as those used by the PLM and in confirmation of the picture given here, especially with reference to capitalist instead of feudal agriculture. For example, in early 1911, Díaz' Development Minister Olegario Molina described Mexican agriculture as "capitalist exploitation." Lauro Viadas, General Director of Agriculture and a chief collaborator of the Development Minister, contributed a statistical study confirming Molina's conclusions. Viadas described land hunger, a steady rise in prices on consumer goods and in rural and urban land values, "concentration of all kinds of production in the hands of a few," the rising cost of food staples, low cost of labor, and consequent "reduced production costs

---

[34] San Luis Potosí also accounted for half of the nation's production of prickly pears (used as a vegetable or main dish, as well as in honeys and drinks), and much of the nation's *lechuguilla* fiber, extracted from a cactus-like plant for use in handbags, sacks, and coarse rope; both items were produced commercially on haciendas (Rosenzweig, *Historia moderna*, p. 57;; Eugenio Martínez Núñez, *Juan Sarabia, apóstol y mártir de la Revolución Mexicana*, I, 32). There were two railroad stations within the borders of the Espinosa y Cuevas' Hacienda La Angostura (Silva Herzog, p. 124). On crop production, including exports, see Rosenzweig, *Historia moderna*, pp. 46–49, 57–58, 74, 123–124; Eduardo Chávez, *Estación Agrícola Experimental de Río Verde, San Luis Potosí* (pamphlet). On internal food market, Rosenzweig, *Historia moderna*, p. 47; Tannenbaum, pp. 140–146; Henry Bamford Parkes, *A History of Mexico*, p. 306.

and increased profits" as "capitalist agriculture . . . lacking a noncapital-
ist farmer element."[35]

The major structural change in Mexico's countryside under this
system of capitalist agriculture was not the entrenchment of alleged
feudal patterns but rather the considerable expansion of a rural working
class, as the Development Minister asserted and the 1910 census confirmed. Viadas expressed a corollary to the Minister's analysis when
he wrote that, except for "capitalist" farmers, the Mexican countryside
no longer contained "the farmer element, furnished with the indispensable resources necessary for family farming." The only remedy to the
sharpening conflicts between rural "proletarians" and "capitalist" farmers, according to both the Development Minister and the Director of
Agriculture, was to convert "as great a number as possible of the proletarians into property holders."[36]

Concurrent with this structural change in Mexico's countryside was
the introduction of modern machinery and transportation. This was the
case not only in San Luis Potosí and other mining states but also in
more traditional farming areas, such as Morelos, native state of Emiliano Zapata. There the railroad, which reached Tepoztlán in 1897,
opened up new commercial possibilities, and mechanization was introduced on large modernized farms. Trade flourished, the charcoal-mak-
ing industry was launched, wire fences and steel plows were introduced,
and even a cultural renaissance occurred. Private-property holders like
the Zapata family lost their lands, as did the communal-land holders
(*ejidatarios*), to big commercial farmers, interested in expanding the
sugar industry in Morelos by developing large plantations with cheap
labor and by constructing sugar mills on the plantations themselves.
These mills were connected by railroad with urban industries (e.g.,
rum distilleries). Thus at the turn of the century sugar mills sprang up
in the rural communities of Tepoztlán, Tlalneplantla, Cuautenco, and
Jonacatepec (scene of Zapata's first major battle in the Revolution).
Except for the Federal District, Morelos was by 1911 the most com-

---

[35] Silva Herzog, pp. 161–163; text in Jesús Silva Herzog (ed.), *Colección de
folletos para la historia de la Revolución Mexicana: la cuestión de la tierra*, I, 112 ff.
[36] *Ibid.*

mercialized state south of Coahuila and west of Veracruz in all Mexico (based on per capita retail sales).[37]

Because of structural changes introduced by this increased pace of capitalist agricultural development in Mexico's countryside during the Porfiriato, a relatively static situation became highly dynamic. Many peasants experienced economic frustration and downward mobility— from small property holder or *ejidatario* to rural proletarian. For a few, however, there was social progress to foreman, miller, mechanic, or administrator. For economically deprived subsistence farmers and landless peons, employment on large plantations may have offered some slight—at best seasonal—economic relief.

Most peasants felt a strong sense of resentment about the changes being introduced into their lives. In an economy of rising prices on basic staples, the landowners' offer to the peasants of low wages in exchange for their labor on land that often originally had been theirs seemed unfair, or exploitive. Sociologically, an increasingly unbalanced structure, characterized by unfair exchange, was developing in Mexico's countryside. Earlier examples of unbalanced rural structures in Mexican history, in spite of ostensibly "stable" or "balanced" conditions, had resulted in violent peasant or Indian revolts, as in the case of the so-called "caste war" of 1847 in Yucatán. Behind the façade of the *Paz porfiriana*, there existed in the countryside a state of considerable social imbalance, worker resentment, and potential violence.[38]

Thus, the process of social change taking place during the Porfiriato went beyond the new industries springing up in the cities and, by means of railroads and new farming techniques, reached into the remote confines of Mexico's supposedly "feudal" countryside. Agriculture became an eminently capitalistic enterprise, as land was bought and sold on an open land market and peasants were further incorporated

[37] Rosenzweig, "El desarrollo," *El Trimestre Económico*, 415–417; Moisés González Navarro, *Historia moderna de Mexico. El Porfiriato: la vida social*, pp. 144, 211; Oscar Lewis, *Life in a Mexican Village; Tepoztlán Restudied*, pp. xxv, 433–437; Gral. Gildardo Magaña, *Emiliano Zapata y el agrarismo en México*, Vol. I; Alberto Morales Jiménez, *Hombres de la Revolución Mexicana*, p. 210.

[38] Nelson Reed, *The Caste War of Yucatan;* Andrés Molina Enríquez, *Los grandes problemas nacionales.*

into the wage labor system. The existence of this capitalistic social structure, dominated by bourgeois elite families, makes it difficult to conclude, as many writers have done, that the Mexican Revolution was in its essence a bourgeois (antifeudal) revolution. In the sense of economic nationalism, or protest against undemocratic politics, or anticlericalism, or dissatisfaction with economic slow-down, the Revolution to some degree did command at least tentative bourgeois backing. The structure of Mexico's society, however, implied an eventual confrontation between proletarians and capitalists. It therefore should come as no surprise that the main political force of the Precursor Movement —the PLM—as well as major political movements that emerged during the Revolution, brought together workers and peasants to fight against the bourgeoisie. For these participants, this was an anticapitalistic revolution.

CHAPTER TWO

Nascent Political Coalitions

SOCIAL CHANGE during the Porfiriato affected, and ultimately frustrated, the expectations of peasants, small property holders, artisans, urban workers, miners, small businessmen, and, during the economic decline of 1907–1911, people from all classes, including large-scale industrialists and *hacendados*. Consequently, protests and unrest among different classes became more common as the Porfiriato drew to a close. When articulate dissenters began to form tentative coalitions uniting otherwise conflicting class interests politically against the Díaz regime, significant change was bound to occur.

Among the upper class, publicly expressed dissent first came from big landholders, the group usually considered most privileged under Díaz. Not all landowners were able to survive the 1908 credit crisis which, in San Luis Potosí as in most of Mexico, was accompanied by a drought and food shortages. In addition to their financial difficulties, *hacendados* no longer could draw upon so large a rural labor force as they had been able to in the past. Mining had drained off needed field hands from the haciendas by offering better wages. So had newer, modernized cotton plantations and textile and other factories, which sprang up in the North after the coming of the railroad.

In 1907 there was a panic on Wall Street, a depression in the world henequen market, and a sharp decrease in export prices of cotton and industrial minerals. These developments put a severe strain on Mexico's economy. Accustomed to using land as collateral, *hacendados* had come to depend heavily on mortgages and credits which they had used to speculate, to invest in urban lands, to place in industrial or commercial enterprises, or simply to live off (inflation reducing their real debt in the long run). Finance Minister José Yves Limantour's modernized banking system had, until the 1907 crisis, continued the tradition of renewing old loans to the landholders as a matter of course. However, as Raymond Vernon states: "With the shortage of funds in 1907, the margin of safety of the banks was suddenly imperiled. Banks were forced to curtail credit sharply; and despite efforts by the government to bail out the banks, the swollen debt of the haciendas was squeezed back."[1]

Limantour endeavored to rescue the nation's foundering banks by calling in mortgages and prohibiting long-term credits to the already-insolvent *hacendados,* at a time when market conditions made long-term credits more in demand than ever. These new credit restrictions evoked a storm of protest from *hacendados.* According to Francisco Bulnes, a leading adviser of Porfirio Díaz but no friend of Limantour's, "The planters wanted to take vengeance on the Científicos because, with the promulgation of the banking laws of 1908, their virtual robbing of the banks ceased."[2]

The "Científicos," of whom Bulnes was one, were Díaz' braintrust of Positivists and Social Darwinists who emphasized doing everything in politics and economics according to the rules of "science," rather than to the rules of "metaphysics" or "religion." *El Estandarte,* repre-

---

[1] Raymond Vernon, *The Dilemma of Mexico's Development,* p. 55.

[2] Francisco Bulnes, *The Whole Truth about Mexico—President Wilson's Responsibility,* p. 146. In defense of Limantour's policy, see Joaquín D. Casasús, *Las reformas a la ley de instituciones de crédito y las instituciones de crédito en México en 1908,* originally published in 1908 in Mexico City's Catholic daily *El Tiempo,* and Francisco Barrera Lavalle, *Estudios sobre el origen desenvolvimiento y legislación de las instituciones de crédito en México.*

senting the point of view of landed elite families in San Luis Potosí, printed the landowners' attacks against Limantour and the Científicos on its front page.

Most articulate and bitter of Limantour's critics during this period was landowner Toribio Esquivel Obregón, later a leading political supporter of Francisco I. Madero.[3] According to Esquivel Obregón, panic did not exist among the public but at the banks, which had lost confidence in "that [in] which the public has most confidence, that which merits the most credit, namely, the land." Consequently, he argued, curtailment of long-term credits to landholders had undercut the very foundation of Mexican banking. "Alarm" was spreading through all sectors of business, and the banks themselves would soon be "bankrupt." Moreover, Esquivel Obregón said, the banks did not in fact lack funds to back credits, since between 1906 and 1908 bank deposits had increased, not declined.[4]

Other landowners echoed Esquivel Obregón's protest, and, by 1911, laws were being proposed in the national Congress to assure long-term credits for *hacendados*.[5] A supporter of Esquivel Obregón's position was Mexican-American industrialist-farmer Oscar J. Braniff, a multimillionaire and an adviser to President Díaz.[6] In 1911, Braniff and Esquivel Obregón served as diplomatic bridges between the Díaz regime and Madero during negotiations of the Ciudad Juárez peace treaties, which replaced Díaz with an interim President until Madero's election five months later. Esquivel Obregón had been an active Anti-reelectionist (pro-Madero), and at one point a possible Presidential candidate for the Anti-reelectionists; but as revolutionary events de-

---

[3] *El Estandarte*, May 12, July 14, 16, 17, 1908. These articles by Esquivel Obregón were originally published in *El Tiempo*, and have since been collected by Luis Chávez Orozco and published in *La crisis agrícola de México en 1908, en su aspecto crediticio*. Bulnes later provided the most all-encompassing attack on Limantour in *El verdadero Díaz y la Revolución*, pp. 240 ff.

[4] Esquivel Obregón, *in* Chávez Orozco, pp. 14, 23–24, 32.

[5] Chávez Orozco, pp. 41–42 (Cámara de Diputados, *Diario de los Debates*, December 1, 1911, and October 16, 1912).

[6] Oscar J. Braniff, *Observaciones sobre el fomento agrícola considerado como base para la ampliación del crédito agrícola en México* (1910), reprinted in Jesús Silva Herzog, *Colección de folletos para la historia de la Revolución Mexicana: la cuestión de la tierra*, I, 21–74; Bulnes, *El verdadero*, pp. 141, 168, and *passim*.

veloped in late 1910 and early 1911, he had assumed an increasingly conservative position. Later he became Minister of Finance under President Victoriano Huerta (1913–1914), the general who led the *coup d'état* against President Madero.[7]

Such political zigzags by leading spokesmen of Mexico's bourgeoisie were, in part, a manifestation of the conflicts they felt between the demands of economic nationalism and the need for politico-economic stability. Esquivel Obregón represented a general feeling among many *hacendados* who were "damned if they did and damned if they didn't" oppose Díaz. With Díaz, they were cursed with the credit crisis; without him, they faced the prospect of armed peasants and a national revolution. Many landowners joined the Madero movement and became its conservative wing, while others did not emerge as publicly recognized political powers until the reactionary Huerta regime. Younger, idealistic members of their class—like Madero himself, or San Luis Potosí's Juan F. Barragán—became revolutionaries, usually against their parents' most emphatic caveats. Young Barragán, scion of a Mexican President and of one of the largest landholding families in all of San Luis Potosí, first served Díaz but later, in 1911, worked closely with Gustavo Madero, Francisco's brother and political manager. In 1913, Barragán led peasants from his father's Hacienda del Carrizal in an armed revolt against Huerta—an instance of a political coalition between landholders and peasants. Later, Barragán became Venustiano Carranza's Chief of Staff and, according to some, his most intimate confidant[8] (Carranza's faction was to emerge triumphant with-

---

[7] Manuel González Ramírez, *La revolución social de México: las ideas—la violencia*, pp. 173–174; Charles C. Cumberland, *Mexican Revolution: Genesis under Madero*, pp. 140–151; Stanley R. Ross, *Francisco I. Madero, Apostle of Mexican Democracy*, pp. 159–168; José Yves Limantour, *Apuntes sobre mi vida pública*, pp. 224–226, 272–296; Toribio Esquivel Obregón, *Democracia y personalismo—Relatos y comentarios sobre política actual*, pp. 78–83.

[8] Luis F. Bustamante, *Quién es el Crol. Juan B. Barragán* and *Perfiles y bocetos revolucionarios*; Vicente Blasco Ibáñez, *Mexico in Revolution*, p. 103. Matilde Cabrera Ipiña de Corci (*Cuatro grandes dinastías mexicanas en los descendientes de los hermanos Fernández de Lima y Barragán*) traces Barragán's lineage back to not only Spanish nobility but also to the original rulers of the Toltecas, Chichimecas, Huaxtecos, and Aztecs (via Doña Isabel de Moctezuma). The Barragáns intermarried with other leading San Luis Potosí families, such as that of Governor Carlos Díez Gutiérrez. The author of the book, Cabrera Ipiña, was herself related to the Barragáns

in the Revolution in 1916). Madero must be considered of a middle generation of these *hacendados*—not younger—as he was thirty-seven years of age when in 1910 he launched his revolutionary protest, the Plan de San Luis Potosí.

This Plan, in its call for significant political change, may be compared to the French nobles' calling of the Estates General in 1789. Both calls came from discontented members of economically and socially elite families, who protested government centralization, the taking away of their political power in parliaments and provincial assemblies, and economic infringement upon their "rights" through taxation (France) or the withdrawal of accustomed credits (Mexico) because of the Government's increased concern about the chronic shortage of money. Like the French nobles, Mexican *hacendados* and farmers-industrialists solicited the support of the middle class and elements of the peasantry (Article 3 of the Plan de San Luis Potosí pledged the return of despoiled lands "to their original owners"). Dissenters from the upper class were thus becoming amenable to political coalitions with other classes, in spite of ostensible conflicts of interest, because of their feeling of strong resentment under the "old regime."[9]

Not only *hacendados* but also a number of new bourgeois entrepreneurs, industrialists, and merchants felt checked in their advance by the economic slump of 1907, by the new restrictions on bank credits, and by the increased strength of rich, monopolizing foreigners. As Rosen-

---

through the families of Octaviano B. Cabrera, president of the Centro Agrícola e Industrial Potosino, and José Encarnación Ipiña, another large landholder and miner with his roots in the Spanish nobility. See also Joaquín Meade, *Semblanza de D. José Encarnación Ipiña.* For an indication of Barragán power in September, 1910, in Ciudad del Maíz, gateway to the Huasteca and agrarian center of San Luis Potosí's northeast, see Ciudad del Maíz (Ayuntamiento de) y Junta Local del Centenario, *Corona patriótica a la memoria de los héroes de la Independencia Nacional en el Primer Centenario de su gloriosa iniciación* (pamphlet), which lists at least six influential Barragáns, including Jacobo as president of the Ayuntamiento de Ciudad del Maíz (city council), and Juan F. and Florencio as aldermen (*regidores*). Although later a Maderista, as of January 22, 1911 (*El Estandarte*), Juan F. Barragán was running the Ciudad del Maíz government, loyal to Díaz, as acting Presidente Municipal.

[9] Georges Lefebvre, *The Coming of the French Revolution,* pp. 7–34; Crane Brinton, *The Anatomy of Revolution,* pp. 28–41. Madero devoted only one paragraph of Article 3 of his Plan de San Luis Potosí to agrarian reform.

zweig has observed: "In the difficult years at the beginning of the twentieth century, along toward 1906–1907, the large companies with foreign capital withstood the crisis profitably, while many of the small Mexican factories closed their doors."[10]

Among resentful industrialists in San Luis Potosí were some elite-family businessmen who commanded considerable resources of their own. It is perhaps significant that some of these businessmen and even reputable Conservatives helped gain the release of Madero from the San Luis Potosí penitentiary on July 22, 1910. After his release and until his escape into U.S. exile ten weeks later, Madero was confined to the city of San Luis Potosí. He moved into an apartment of land-owner-banker Federico Meade's Palacio Monumental. Madero, who had been running for President as the Anti-reelectionist candidate, had been arrested in early June during a campaign swing through San Luis Potosí, Coahuila, and Nuevo León, on charges ranging from "aiding a fugitive" to "fomenting a rebellion" but really because his campaign had been drawing large crowds and represented a political threat to Díaz. (Elections were held that summer, but there were many irregularities; Díaz was officially declared winner on October 4.) Key figures in persuading the Díaz government to order Madero's release on bond were the Bishop of San Luis Potosí, Ignacio Montes de Oca y Obregón, and the state's leading nonforeign industrialist, Pedro Barrenechea. Montes de Oca y Obregón had been for a long time, as we shall see, a leading apologist for the Díaz regime and a notorious baiter of Liberals; in fact, his proclamations helped provoke the launching of the Precursor Movement in 1900.[11]

Barrenechea posted Madero's ten-thousand-peso bond. A year later, he would run for governor *against* the candidate favored by Madero. Nevertheless, Barrenechea represented a growing malaise among Mexi-

10 Fernando Rosenzweig et al., *Historia moderna de México. El Porfiriato: la vida económica,* pp. 322–323.

11 *El Estandarte,* July 23, 1910, which noted that Madero's release was delayed while officials considered disqualifying Barrenechea as bondsman because of his having properties scattered beyond San Luis Potosí into other states and Mexico City; Barrenechea's lawyers succeeded in thwarting that legalistic delaying tactic. Cf. Jesús Silva Herzog, *Breve historia de la Revolución Mexicana,* I, 125; Primo Feliciano Velázquez, *Historia de San Luis Potosí,* p. 218; and Ross, pp. 105–109.

co's independent, expansion-minded businessmen. He had, while co-operating with foreign capital, developed considerable independent wealth, and he stood a chance of multiplying it many times if freed from the competition and expanding control of foreign monopolies. This probability was suggested by his founding in 1914 an oil company controlled entirely by San Luis Potosí businessmen, not long after the establishment of a no-concession and stamp-tax policy on foreign petroleum concerns by the Madero government.[12] Even the Díaz regime had recognized growing antiforeign sentiment among the upper bourgeoisie when in 1908 it had arranged for Mexican purchase of majority interests in the nation's railroads—although Esquivel Obregón, among others, alleged that the entire deal was fraudulent. Government control of the railroads was "nominal," Esquivel Obregón claimed, and "Yankee businesses were behind the deal."[13]

There were good reasons why most of Mexico's bourgeoisie, with the exception of a few well-placed monopolists, or buyers, sellers, and agents connected with foreign companies, suffered what Crane Brinton has felicitously characterized as "economic cramps"[14] during the last decade of the Porfiriato and were therefore willing to consider tentative political coalitions uniting different classes in opposition against Díaz. Nineteenth-century advantages for industrialists and merchants, offered by low wages, a depreciating peso, growing urban demand, and support of foreign capital, were beginning to dissipate. Money wages in pesos rose, although because of inflation and other factors real wages declined from 42 to 36 centavos a day.[15] The value of the peso was pegged to the gold standard in 1905, thus ending the heyday of Mexican silver and leading to the constriction of credit. Prices of primary agricultural goods like sugar (for the large brewing industry) and cotton (for textile manufacturers) rose sharply, as did the cost of imported capital goods. Finally, internal consumption dropped off with

---

[12] Compañía Petrolífera "La Carolina," S.A., *Compañía Petrolífera Mexicana "La Carolina,"* S.A. (pamphlet); Silva Herzog, *Breve historia*, I, 230–231; Ross, p. 143.

[13] Esquivel Obregón, "Las consecuencias de nuestra política ferrocarrilera, *El Estandarte*, June 16, 1908; Rosenzweig, *Historia moderna*, pp. 612–633; Bulnes, *El verdadero*, pp. 241–250; Henry Bamford Parkes, *History of Mexico*, p. 301.

[14] Brinton, p. 36.

[15] Rosenzweig, *Historia moderna*, p. 339.

the failure of the peasantry to enter the market and with the cutback in workers' real wages. The rate of growth in national industrial production between 1900 and 1910 dropped considerably when compared to the 1890–1900 period. Cotton and sugar fell under the control of monopolies, largely foreign, as mining had done earlier. After 1907, profits dropped, plants shut down, and monopolization increased apace; and, except for sugar, internal consumption decreased sharply. For a shrewd bourgeois Mexican with a grain of nationalism and an eye for profit, some kind of political and economic change to increase his voice in government, challenge foreign monopolies, and open up an internal market by bringing the peasantry into the consumer economy seemed desirable by 1911.[16]

Unrest among Mexico's small middle class, especially among professionals, was also on the increase. In San Luis Potosí, the middle class consisted of managers and administrators in large commercial operations, as well as smaller shopkeepers, merchants, and vendors, or the traditional petty bourgeoisie. It included lawyers, doctors, engineers, teachers, journalists, and other professionals.[17] At the bottom of the middle class were well-paid skilled laborers, such as plant foremen, chief engineers, master mechanics, and their immediate assistants in rails, mining, textiles, breweries, shoe factories, etc., and a few successful artisans who survived the competitive wave of mechanization and benefited from improved marketing channels. Finally, the middle class included the middle and lower bureaucracy—that segment not sharing the benefits enjoyed by the Científico-dominated top of the govern-

---

[16] For documentation with primary sources, see Rosenzweig, *Historia moderna*, pp. 314–339. Later, of course, such powerful industrialists as Barrenechea coalesced with other elite families and *hacendados* in both business and agriculture to attempt to maintain the Madero phase of the Revolution within respectable bourgeois bounds. Even though the French nobles and the Mexican elites may have opened the doors to revolution by means of their protests, socially they stood as much to lose as even the most progressive and enlightened businessman or *hacendado* might stand to gain.

[17] Silva Herzog (*Breve historia*, I, 40–41) correctly suggests that an occasional lawyer or doctor, with a large, socially eminent clientele, belonged to the elite families controlling the state's economic and social life. For example, Dr. Antonio F. Alonso's name appeared frequently on the high-society pages of *El Estandarte;* in 1912, Dr. Alonso was elected to the nation's 26th Congress. See *El País*, July 18, 1912; *El Estandarte*, 1900–1912, *passim*; Joaquín Meade, *Hemerografía potosina, historia del periodismo en San Luis Potosí, 1828–1956*, p. 78.

mental and administrative structure. As Francisco Bulnes wrote at the time of the Revolution: ". . . the hatred of the lower bureaucracies for the higher had assumed unheard of proportions. The lower bureaucracy was not socialistic, but it wanted a new order of things."[18]

These middle-class sectors, with some significant exceptions like schoolteachers, had expanded during the industrial and commercial growth of the Porfiriato, when there was a certain degree of social progress from the lower classes to the middle, from country to city, from farm to factory, and from labor to commerce.[19] Retail trade in San Luis Potosí increased 7.29 per cent annually from 1896 to 1908, making the state "one of the most commercialized in the Republic."[20] For the middle class, there was not in this period a corresponding rise in living standards and social status. Food prices doubled, rents and taxes became insufferable, and middle-class elements were denied entry into elite social clubs or bureaucratic cliques.[21] People in the middle class were further angered by a revenue system which they considered to tax unfairly and to favor the rich at the expense of "the little man." Manuel González Ramírez has shown that serious localized uprisings against President Díaz in Chihuahua in 1889, 1893, 1895, and 1896 all occurred as essentially middle-class protests against unfair and excessive taxation.[22]

From July, 1908, to January, 1909, food stalls in San Luis Potosí's main marketplaces closed down as small merchants and vendors, as well as butchers, protested "double taxation" in municipal, state, federal, and private space-rents and taxes. At the same time, consumers were objecting to price hikes on basic commodities. A drought crippled the state's food and water supply, leading *El Estandarte* to call 1909

[18] Bulnes, *The Whole Truth,* p. 142.

[19] Normal-school enrollments in Mexico dropped from 3,689 in 1900 to 2,552 in 1907, while educational needs were rising proportionately to population growth and increased urbanization (Moisés González Navarro, *Historia moderna de México. El Porfiriato: la vida social,* pp. 30–39, 667).

[20] Rosenzweig, *Historia moderna,* p. 747, and "El desarrollo," *El Trimestre Económico,* pp. 415–417.

[21] Vernon, pp. 53–54, 204; González Ramírez, pp. 17–21, 41–42; Silva Herzog, *El agrarismo mexicano y la reforma agraria,* pp. 127–129, and *Breve historia,* I, 34–35; Parkes, p. 308.

[22] González Ramírez, pp. 17–21, 41–42.

"the year of calamities." In the fall of 1909, a frost killed many crops, costing the nation fourteen million pesos and San Luis Potosí one million pesos. From 1908 to 1911, the state's retail trade declined more than a million pesos. During the 1907–1911 period, the nation as a whole suffered a general economic slump which left no class untouched.[23]

So far as many, but not all, of Mexico's economically pinched intellectuals from the middle class were concerned, the next social revolution in Mexico would be started by "middle-class intellectuals" and the "intellectual proletariat," as schoolteacher-engineer Félix F. Palavicini asserted in 1905. Palavicini, who in 1915 was to become Carranza's Secretary of Public Instruction, believed that Mexico's intellectuals had been the main dynamic force throughout the Republic's history, from the War of Independence to the more recent "intellectual development and economic tranquillity of the Republic." Therefore, he warned, "the middle-class intellectual," when confronted by "hunger at the gates," reduced salaries, lack of clothing, "indecent" housing, and the high cost of bread and "inferior" meat, would become a revolutionary: ". . . the intellectual proletariat will undertake its own defense." Palavicini provided many examples of how "middle-class poverty" was developing in Mexico, as inflation raced ahead of consumption capacity.[24]

Further tension was created in the middle class by frustrations suffered with respect to social status. On the one hand, individuals making some degree of economic progress were denied the higher status they felt they deserved, in part bcause of the high cost of status and its associated symbols: imported clothing and food, French education, Paris residences, European vacations, and city and country houses. In addition, members of the upper class were concerned with preserving socially aristocratic customs, not with broadening social boundaries to include people from classes "beneath" them. True, money could still, as in colonial times, buy status—and this the most successful of new industrialists and merchants did, thereby joining the ranks of the upper

23 *El Estandarte,* July 10, August 5, 21, 1908; May 30, October 19, 1909; and *passim.* Rosenzweig, *Historia moderna,* p. 747 and Chaps. 3, 4, 6, 7.
24 Félix F. Palavicini, *Mi vida revolucionaria,* pp. 16–17.

bourgeoisie. Most of the middle class, however, were unable to command the economic resources necessary to display the kind of high status prevalent during the Porfiriato.

On the other hand, traditionally respected, honored, and to an extent politically powerful professionals, especially lawyers, often experienced social frustration and a decline in status, unless they held high government positions or had family connections with the ruling political powers. It is perhaps significant that José Vasconcelos, Antonio Díaz Soto y Gama, and Luis Cabrera, three of the Mexican Revolution's most famous lawyer-intellectual participants from the middle class, all experienced this sense of status demotion personally. The best positions Vasconcelos and Díaz Soto y Gama could obtain, prior to the Revolution, were clerical posts from 1909 to 1910 in a U.S. law firm serving various business corporations. Cabrera, meanwhile, finding the path to political power blocked by the cliquish Científicos and unwilling to become a nameless adjunct to a corporation, turned to journalism and wrote a series of articles during 1909–1910 under an assumed name, accusing the Científicos of corruption, thievery, and political skulduggery.[25]

Regardless of Palavicini's prophecy, these discontented intellectuals from the middle class could not create a revolution by themselves. Only in coalition with leaders from other classes could they bring about the overthrow of Díaz. The combination of nationalist, expansion-minded businessmen, disgruntled *hacendados,* economically and socially blocked elements of the middle class, and occasional peasant groups that formed behind Madero in 1909–1910 represented the kind of political coalition needed to change the system against which they all held grievances. The social background of the seven men elected to the executive board of Madero's Centro Antirreeleccionista in May, 1909, to oppose Díaz' re-election, is suggestive of the range of class interests that could be brought together in such a coalition. Four of the board members were petty-bourgeois intellectuals from low-status groups:

[25] José Vasconcelos, *Ulises criollo* in *Obras completas,* I, 582, 692; Luis Cabrera (Lic. Blas Urrea), *Obras políticas,* pp. 3–142, *passim.* Cf. Richard Hofstadter's description of the "status revolution" in the United States at the turn of the century, on the eve of the "Progressive era," when businessmen succeeded lawyers as leaders of social and political development (*The Age of Reform: From Bryan to F. D. R.,* pp. 155–163).

Palavicini, lawyer-philosopher Vasconcelos, and journalists Filomeno Mata and Paulino Martínez. The other three members were intellectuals from the upper class: Madero, Esquivel Obregón, and lawyer Emilio Vázquez Gómez (brother of Dr. Francisco Vázquez Gómez— the personal physician of Limantour and Díaz and Vice Presidential candidate of Madero in 1910).[26]

By 1910, however, another coalition of classes was opposing Díaz as forcibly as Madero's coalition, and with greater violence: the Partido Liberal Mexicano, major political force of the Precursor Movement. The PLM coalition involved workers, peasants, small merchants, and a generally lower- and lower-middle-class composition. Like the Madero movement, it had an intellectual leadership and a strong, if clandestine, press. Political coalitions embracing restless proletarians were recognized by progovernment and antigovernment forces alike as either threats to a progressive-bourgeois mode of economic development or means to a change of the old regime for some kind of new one, be it proletarian or progressive-bourgeois in nature.

Grievances among the lower classes made middle-class complaints look mild by comparison. Most disastrous for peasants and workers during the Porfiriato was the growing gap between wages and the cost of basic staples. Between 1876 and 1910, maize prices increased 108 per cent, bean prices 163 per cent, and chile prices 147 per cent; since wages increased only 60 per cent during the same period, real income for the masses declined an estimated 57 per cent.[27] Díaz braintruster Francisco Bulnes, who earlier had propounded "scientific proof" of the superiority of foreigners, conceded that by 1910 "poverty had driven the majority of the Mexican people to the edge of the grave."[28]

Compounding this disaster for the masses was their own competition among themselves for jobs. In San Luis Potosí, for example, huge numbers of workers moved in and out of the state in desperate quest for employment. Rural laborers flocked north into the United States as

---

26 Cumberland, pp. 62–63; Limantour, p. 212; Francisco Vázquez Gómez, *Memorias políticas* (1909–1913).

27 González Ramírez, pp. 20–21; Silva Herzog, *Breve historia*, I, 34–35, and *El agrarismo*, pp. 127–129.

28 Bulnes, *El verdadero*, cited in Silva Herzog, *El agrarismo*, p. 128; González Navarro, pp. 151, 157.

braceros, making San Luis Potosí the fifth state in order of out-migration in 1900. On the other hand, workers from other states flooded into San Luis Potosí, converting the state capital from Mexico's eleventh most populous city in 1860 to its fifth in 1900. By 1908, *El Estandarte* reported, San Luis Potosí's main avenues were "choked with the unemployed."[29]

Contributing to the job crisis was the introduction of modern labor-saving machinery in Mexico's factories and on its farms. Machines displaced many workers. For example, the textile industry, which from 1877 to 1888 had doubled its labor force, now streamlined production, laid off sixteen thousand workers (or 26 per cent) between 1895 and 1910, and forced the shutdown of uncompetitive artisan shops and small factories. Production per textile factory increased 55 per cent, but "a good part of the artisans became unemployed in the face of the advancing forces of the new industrialism."[30]

These displaced and disgruntled artisans provided an impetus for labor organization among urban workers. As early as 1864, artisans had founded the Círculo de Obreros, the first of a series of "sociedades mutualistas" aiming through co-operative pooling of workers' resources to provide medical care and social assistance to injured or laid-off workers. Mutualist societies prevailed as a form of fairly innocuous labor organization into the twentieth century, when labor unions underwent vigorous expansion for the purposes of striking and engaging in direct confrontation against capitalists. The influence of European Socialism on artisans and labor organizers was evident as early as the period 1870–1875, with the founding of such proletarian newspapers as *Clases Productores, La Revolución, El Socialista, La Comuna, La Huelga,* and *El Obrero Internacional.* Mexico's first full-fledged labor unions began to appear after 1880. By 1900, two of the nation's three principal labor groups were run by Europe-oriented Anarchists.[31]

[29] Moisés T. de la Peña, *El pueblo y su tierra: mito y realidad de la reforma agraria en México,* pp. 111, 115, 126, 146; *El Estandarte,* June 3, 1908.

[30] Rosenzweig, *Historia moderna,* pp. 322–323, 402.

[31] González Navarro, pp. 355–371; Roberto de la Cerda Silva, *El movimiento obrero en México,* p. 57; Antonio Escobedo Acevedo, "Periódicos socialistas de México, 1871–1880," *El Libro y el Pueblo,* XIII, No. 1 (January–February, 1935), 3–14; Alberto Bremauntz, *Panorama social de las revoluciones de México,* pp. 143–149. The

Although strikes were forbidden during the Porfiriato, more than 250 occurred. Of these, 25 in 1907 alone were classified as "major." Strikes took place especially in those industries most affected by new types of machinery and by foreign investment, such as textiles, rails, mines, and tobacco. No document was so revealing of workers' demands—nor so influential upon Article 123 of the 1917 Constitution, labor's "bill of rights"—as the 1906 Program of the PLM. The consensus among scholars is that no strikes were so devastating as those led by the PLM or its sympathizers from 1906 to 1908.[32]

In San Luis Potosí, labor unrest began at the mines and later spread to railroads and textiles. Miners struck in 1884 at Charcas and Matehuala and in 1886 at Catorce. In January of 1901, Matehualan miners reportedly "paralyzed" the mines for a month in a strike against high maize prices and poor work conditions. In a new incident on August 1, 1903, workers at the Guggenheims' Compañía Metalúrgica were fired upon by company police, and federal troops were called in. No miners were killed, but fifty-five were arrested, and their comrades decided to go on strike. The Ingenio de Morales was primarily affected, as nearly a thousand workers joined the walkout. After 1903, mining unrest was kept down by armed force until early 1911.

-----

best collection of primary sources can be found in works by Luis Chávez Orozco, listed in Section II–F, "Books," of the Bibliography. Cf. Manuel Díaz Ramírez, *Apuntes históricos del movimiento obrero y campesino de México, 1844–1880*, and Linda Mascona Davidoff, "Orígenes del socialismo en México, 1867–1876" (unpublished thesis). On San Luis Potosí mutualism, consult Section II–E, "Pamphlets," of the Bibliography; *El Estandarte*, April 19, 1904; Manuel González Ramírez (ed.), *Fuentes para historia de la Revolución Mexicana*, IV, 621, 635. The concept of "mutualism" was given its fullest theoretical formulation in the mid-nineteenth century by the French revolutionary Pierre-Joseph Proudhon (1809–1865). Proudhon, whose dictum "What is property? Property is theft" influenced the thinking of the Precursors of the Mexican Revolution, envisaged the world of the future "as a great federation of communes and workers' co-operatives, based economically on a pattern of individuals and small groups possessing (not owning) their means of production, and bound by contracts of exchange and mutual credit which will assure to each individual the product of his own labor" (George Woodcock, *Anarchism: A History of Libertarian Ideas and Movements*, p. 20).

32 González Navarro, p. 298; Miguel Velasco Valdés, *La prerrevolución y el hombre de la calle*, pp. 150–163.

During the fighting against Díaz' Army that erupted in 1911, Ma-tehualan miners and peasants joined forces to help win San Luis Potosí for the Revolution. They were assisted by peasants and miners from Guanajuato and peasant forces from eastern San Luis Potosí led by student-lawyer Pedro Antonio de los Santos. From 1911 to 1913, under the rule of President Madero, miners at Matehuala, La Paz, Catorce, and elsewhere boldly held an almost uninterrupted series of strikes. Troops were often sent in by the "Revolutionary" government, and more than a few miners were shot down.[33]

Among San Luis Potosí's railroad workers, the story was pretty much the same. During the last decade of the Porfiriato, an exceptionally strong workers' movement developed among railroad employees. Because of its importance nationally, this movement's strikes and influence are not discussed in this chapter but rather in connection with the Precursor Movement overall, especially the PLM strikes of 1906–1908, to which Chapter Six is devoted.

Nationwide textile and railroad strikes from 1906 to 1908 failed in San Luis Potosí, as elsewhere. Nevertheless, the defeated strikers contributed to revolutionary successes during 1910–1911. According to newspaper accounts, rail workers participated in the 1910 dynamiting of major rail lines in San Luis Potosí and the 1911 fighting against federal troops that helped bring victory to Madero. Under the relatively more democratic rule of Madero, rail workers again struck. New suppressions occurred, but there remained no doubt that Mexican workers, influenced by social change and strong politico-ideological leadership (PLM, Anarchists, Socialists), were insisting on fairer treatment.

Similar pressures of revolt from below were developing in Mexico's countryside, where peasants were suffering new hardships under the impact of capitalist agriculture. Social relationships on the farm were changing from relatively co-operative communal organization (*ejido*) to owner-foreman-worker-peon hierarchies. This is not to say that there did not exist hierarchical patterns of social organization in the country-

[33] González Navarro, p. 313; Velázquez, IV, 163; *El Estandarte*, 1900–1912, e.g., February 7, May 16, 1901; November 1–21, 1911; January 21, 1912; *El Contemporáneo*, January 20, 27, 1901.

side and within *ejidos* prior to the changes implemented during the Porfiriato. Rather, the degree and nature of hierarchical organization underwent change, resulting in a more formalized and permanent division of labor and greater distances separating groups. As the peasants assumed more regularized working schedules and routines, superimposed from above for the profit of others instead of from within for their own *ejido,* they became at least dimly aware of new conditions, new exploitation, and new demands. For many peasants, traditional normative systems were giving way, either to new values or to new conflicts between the ends desired and their abilities to achieve them. The means available to them for accomplishing their ends were becoming ever more limited and harsh.

Two kinds of appeal were to be made to landless peasants and rural proletarians during the Revolution. The first was simply to return lands to the peasantry. This appeal took different forms, ranging from the cautious and unfulfilled promises of upper-class leaders like Madero to the militant demands of peasant revolutionaries like Zapata. Falling between those two extremes was revolutionary leader Alvaro Obregón, who often spoke out for peasants and workers within a broad political coalition led by *hacendado* Venustiano Carranza. Both Zapata and Obregón came from families with small landholdings and a generally petty-bourgeois outlook. Zapata's status was on the decline, having had his lands taken away from him during the Porfiriato and having been forced to serve in the Army. Obregón, on the other hand, was on the way up. He had advanced from the rank of employee on a Sonoran chickpea hacienda to that of owner of a small piece of former government land. If sociologists are correct in their view that severe social dislocation—whether involving rapid upward (if blocked) mobility or rapid downward mobility—has often produced heightened social-psychological tensions, then it should come as no surprise that revolutionary leadership was produced, as in the case of Zapata and Obregón, by individuals moving in opposite directions on the social continuum. Zapata was clearly more radical and charismatic in his handling of the agrarian problem than was Obregón, perhaps because he was more disillusioned than Obregón. Moreover, Zapata did not share Obregón's esteem for capitalist agriculture. Obregón had made an auspicious start toward large-scale commercial farming in Sonora through his cultivation of chickpeas for the growing export market.[34]

The second kind of appeal made to the peasantry was that of the PLM, which demanded that rural proletarians "seize all the means of production," which meant both land and machines. These two appeals ⊢—to return farm land to the peasants, on the one hand, or to seize all means of production, on the other—were distinct in social derivation. By comparison with the Zapata movement, the PLM derived more from industrial workers, small merchants, and petty-bourgeois intellectuals than from peasant workers, *ejidatarios,* and small property holders. Nevertheless, the two appeals ultimately had much in common so far as the peasantry was concerned, judging both from the later Zapata-PLM alliance and from the tendency for peasants to grab lands and mills spontaneously during the Revolution.

It would be a mistake to assume, however, that prior to the appearance of persuasive leaders like Zapata, or in the absence of broad political coalitions like that involving Obregón and Carranza, Mexico's peasantry accepted without protest the radical changes imposed upon it during the Porfiriato. On the contrary, the 1876–1900 period was characterized by frequent localized peasant revolts, to which San Luis Potosí was hardly immune. The record of these intermittent revolts indicates that peasants felt strong enough resentment against new conditions being imposed upon them to rebel at almost any time. Indeed, a tradition of localized peasant revolt established over the decades helped prepare the ground for the nationwide Revolution of 1910–1917.[35]

Peasant revolts occurred in San Luis Potosí in 1849, 1856, 1879, 1882, 1905, and 1910.[36] From 1879 to 1883, Indian peasants of the

---

[34] Gral. Gildardo Magaña, *Emiliano Zapata y el agrarismo en México,* I, *passim;* Alberto Morales Jiménez, *Hombres de la Revolución Mexicana,* pp. 183–191, 207–218; Antonio Díaz Soto y Gama, *La revolución agraria del sur y Emiliano Zapata, su caudillo;* Djed Bórquez (pseud. of Juan de Dios Bojórquez), *Forjadores de la Revolución Mexicana,* pp. 26–35, 45–53; John W. F. Dulles, *Yesterday in Mexico,* pp. 4, 24, 26; Alvaro Obregón, *Ocho mil kilómetros en campaña.*

[35] Consult Bremauntz, Chávez Orozco, González Navarro, González Ramírez, Silva Herzog.

[36] On 1849, consult the pamphlet by Eleuterio Quiroz and that by O. L. A. in

Huasteca, numbering more than three thousand armed men, kept central and eastern San Luis Potosí in a state of constant unrest. Described as "anarchists" and "communists" by Governor Pedro Díez Gutiérrez, these Indians used the slogan "Land to the tiller!" They attacked sprawling haciendas of the Barragán family, as well as the Hacienda La Pendenci of the Governor's own family. Troops led by General Bernardo Reyes finally crushed the revolt, at great cost of life. Although little was reported about these Huasteca revolts after 1883, it was no coincidence that when the Revolution broke out in 1910–1911, *El Estandarte* reported rebel successes in precisely those places where peasant disturbances had occurred earlier: Río Verde, the Sierra Gorda, Tamazunchale, Ahualulco, Santa María del Río, and Ciudad del Maíz.[37]

As in the case of San Luis Potosí's striking rail workers, so too with the state's peasantry: the PLM provided ideological impetus and revolutionary leadership. Peasants in the Ciudad del Maíz area, stirred by PLM propaganda that caused American Ambassador David E. Thompson to warn the Department of State in 1906 of possible anti-American riots there, rose up against American owners of the Hacienda Minas Viejas in 1905. Peasant unrest spread to Guadalcázar and Potreritos to the west. The peasants claimed that their lands had been "stolen" from them by Americans and other *hacendados* of the region. On August 12, 1905, the leader of the Minas Viejas revolt, PLM member Vicente Cedillo, issued the "Agrarian Proclamation of Social Order," which clearly reflected the influence of PLM ideas in its call for land redistri-

---

Section II–E of the Bibliography. At that time, one large landholder complained of *ejidatarios'* "first experiment of communism" on Mexican soil (see the book by Francisca de Paula Pérez Gálvez, Section II–F of the Bibliography, and the pamphlet by Pedro Quintana, Section II–E). On 1856, when Indians on the Veracruz border of San Luis Potosí declared an Anarchist-type revolt calling for "death to private property" and communal sharing of land, wives, and services, consult *Rebelión y plan de los indios huaxtecos de Tantoyuca, 1856* (Bibliography, Section II–E, "Pamphlets"), pp. 15–22.

37 *Ibid.*; Nereo Rodríguez Barragán, *El canónigo Mauricio Zavala, apóstol del agrarismo en el Valle del Maíz*, pp. 3–24; pamphlets in Section II–E of the Bibliography by Ahualulco (Ayuntamiento de), Juan Othón, Santa María del Río (San Luis Potosí), and Santa María del Río (Vecinos de); *El Estandarte*, November, 1910–May, 1911.

bution and other measures of agrarian reform. The Minas Viejas revolt failed, but by August of 1910, peasants in San Luis Potosí's Huasteca were once more engaged in armed rebellion against oppressive district leaders and landowners.[38]

This upswell of revolt from among the lower classes spread to other parts of the state. From 1906 to 1909, a series of fires swept through San Luis Potosí haciendas, destroying sugar and other crops. Affected haciendas were often American-owned, and the fires were "caused" by anti-American sentiment, according to *El Estandarte*. South of the city of San Luis Potosí, field workers in the Villa de Arriaga valley began mass out-migration in 1909, when crops failed and the government tried to tax tenant farmers for their small subsistence plots. *El Estandarte* reported "the working people" to be "in an impossible situation." These peasants made willing recruits for schoolteacher Cándido Navarro's rag-tag workers' army when it swept through from Guanajuato on its way to San Luis Potosí in May of 1911. North of the state capital, in Soledad de los Ranchos (Díez Gutiérrez), peasants began arming themselves in mid-1910. They later joined Matehualan revolutionaries sweeping south toward the capital. Many of these peasants pledged their loyalty to the Madero movement because of the Plan de San Luis Potosí's promise to return despoiled lands to original owners. As the tempo of railroad bombings, hacienda fires, and peasant revolts quickened during 1910, the San Luis Potosí penitentiary filled to overflowing. According to official count, there were more than seven hundred prisoners by November 24, 1910, just four days after the date set by Madero for his followers to rebel.[39]

In brief, by 1910 there were abundant signs that peasants and workers were ready to take up arms, declare strikes, or engage in acts of

---

[38] Ambassador David E. Thompson to U.S. Secretary of State, September 8, 1906, in U.S. Department of State Archives, Numerical File, 1906–1910, file number 100 (hereafter referred to as State, followed by file number); Rodríguez Barragán, p. 15; the pamphlet Potreritos (dueños y vecinos de), *Manifestación que los dueños y vecinos de Potreritos, sito en Guadalcázar, San Luis Potosí, hacen a sus amigos y a las personas amantes de la justicia; El Contemporáneo,* March 5, 1905; *El Estandarte,* August 7, 11, 12, September 2, 1910.

[39] *El Estandarte,* April 6, May 30, September 12, 14, October 27, 1909; November 1, 25, 1910; and *passim.*

sabotage, as they had done in the past, either alone or in coalition with other classes. Many of them already had fallen in with the PLM revolutionary movement. Peasants were attracted by Article 3 of Madero's Plan de San Luis Potosí (the Plan contained no reference to labor). Noteworthy was the willingness of upper-class elements with huge landed estates, men like Madero, Carranza, and Barragán, to enter into coalition with the peasantry, in spite of their ostensibly conflicting economic interests, in order to overthrow Díaz and obtain new means to achieve their goals.

In view of increasing tensions among all classes, 1908 was an inopportune time for Porfirio Díaz to offer to retire at the end of his term (1910) and to encourage independent, democratic political movements, as he did in his famous interview with American journalist James Creelman.[40] Nor was it opportune to begin asking for investigations of the agrarian problem, investigations which produced publicly circulated agrarian-reform ideas within the Díaz administration itself.[41] The aging dictator obviously was not familiar with De Tocqueville's dictum that "it oftener happens that when a people which has put up with an oppressive rule over a long period without protest suddenly finds the government relaxing its pressure, it takes up arms against it."[42]

Yet for the past few years Díaz' closest advisers had been warning him of the revolutionary consequences of increasing resentment among the populace. In part, the resentment itself and the expanding impact of PLM propaganda had probably led Díaz to experiment with new political ideas at the end of his regime. A number of factors made some kind of forthcoming social upheaval evident even to Díaz' advisers: the groundswell of revolt from below; adequate national revolutionary leadership in the PLM and Anti-reelectionist movements; Díaz' declin-

[40] James Creelman, "Interview with Porfirio Díaz," *Pearson's Magazine*, XIX, No. 3 (March, 1908), 241–277.

[41] Silva Herzog, *Colección de folletos*, I, II, and *El agrarismo*, Chap. 5. Bulnes claimed that Díaz' forty-five-million-dollar irrigation allotments from 1908 to 1910 were proof of the regime's "serious, well planned, definitely decided and energetically launched" program to tackle the agrarian problem (*The Whole Truth*, p. 98).

[42] Alexis de Tocqueville, *The Old Régime and the French Revolution*, p. 176.

ing physical condition; [43] the prolonged gravity of the 1907 economic crisis; and the increasing dissent of elite-family, bourgeois, middle-class, intellectual, and proletarian elements, many of them willing to unify into tentative political coalitions in order to overthrow Díaz.

In 1906, Porfirio Díaz' friend Rafael de Zayas Enríquez carried out the President's request for an investigation of "the socialist movement," that is, the PLM. Zayas Enríquez confirmed the picture given here and clairvoyantly warned the President, in August of 1906:

Make no mistake about it: the present movement is not isolated, nor is it confined to the working class. On the contrary, it is very widespread, and in it are participating, directly or indirectly, individuals from all social classes: from the wealthy, in a small proportion; from the bourgeoisie, in a larger proportion; from the lower classes, in a growing quantity, urged along by the other two.

. . . .

The small [PLM] movements that have been taking place until now in Cananea, Aguascalientes, Chihuahua and even in this very capital, in the name of the working-class question, precursors of those that are being prepared in other major centers of the country, are no more than dress rehearsals in force, expansion, and strength, to find out how much support they can count on and to calculate just how far they can go.

. . . .

The accumulated experience of history teaches us that, when no one looks after the people, the people take care of themselves; and when the people take care of themselves, it is no river that runs along in its riverbed, but a deluge that inundates.[44]

---

[43] According to Limantour (p. 257), Díaz suffered from "cerebral fatigue, lapses of memory, and frequent drowsiness."

[44] Rafael de Zayas Enríquez, *Porfirio Díaz, la evolución de su vida*, pp. 216–234.

CHAPTER THREE

The Revolutionary Intellectuals:
Social Background

MOST OF Mexico's revolutionary intellectuals came from outside the ranks of what scholars have characterized, in varying language, as Porfirio Díaz' "Científico Establishment." The Científicos were a select group of intellectuals, professionals, and businessmen who shared the Positivist and Social Darwinist philosophy expressed in the works of Auguste Comte and Herbert Spencer, and who succeeded in influencing Mexico's educational institutions and overall national policies accordingly. Their emergence as a dominant intellectual force in the late nineteenth century coincided with the increased rate of industrialization in Mexico; by fair means and foul, many Científicos became notoriously rich. In part a result, in part a cause, of national trends toward monopolistic, elite-family capitalism, the Científico movement would hardly have been viable in the absence of rapid business expansion; nor would such expansion have occurred as peaceably as it did under Díaz without the presence of the Científicos for policy guidance.[1] As Leopoldo Zea has noted, Social Darwinism's emphasis on "survival of the fittest" and measured evolutionary progress, in lieu of violent revolutionary change, provided Mexico's bourgeoisie the kind of ideology it needed to develop and believe in its own class consciousness, at a time when the nation was exhausted from fifty years of civil war and responsive to new incentives for economic growth.[2]

In 1892, the distinguished Liberal Justo Sierra joined Rosendo Pineda, Miguel S. Macedo, Joaquín D. Casasús, Porfirio Díaz' father-in-law Manuel Romero Rubio, and the President's new Minister of Finance, José Yves Limantour, among others, in founding the Unión Liberal, later known as the Partido Científico, which proclaimed as a policy guideline the Positivist slogan "Order and Progress." During the next two decades, the Científicos developed a monopoly of political, economic, and administrative power that caused considerable resentment among those intellectuals outside "the Establishment."

The "independents," as the "out" intellectuals fashioned themselves, found it increasingly difficult to advance within the system. As the biographies and memoirs of revolutionary intellectuals like lawyer-philosopher Vasconcelos, engineer Palavicini, lawyers Cabrera and Díaz Soto y Gama, and lawyer-journalist Federico González Garza indicate, the "outs" found it difficult to gain promotions or acquire jobs in desired locations at satisfactory pay. They had to work long hours, and often at more than one job, to make ends meet. Although the number of positions available in the lower bureaucracy increased under Díaz, chances for advancement from clerical and understudy positions to higher levels in law, business, journalism, government, or other areas were slim in the highly stratified social, economic, and political system of the Porfiriato.

At times, the independents found themselves behaving in typical

---

[1] In addition, of course, Social Darwinism throughout the world enjoyed its heyday during this period, especially in the United States and Europe, the two major locales of Mexico's intellectual heritage. The Científicos' new emphasis on foreign investment in Mexico derived in part from their admiration for economic and intellectual developments then sweeping the capitals of the West.

[2] Leopoldo Zea, *El positivismo en México*, pp. 79, 173, and *passim*.

Latin American patterns of petty competition among themselves for jobs in the lower echelons of government (*empleomanía*). At other times, they withdrew into themselves to write or think out their ideas about changing the system that "oppressed" them. With increasing frequency, they sought new forums by means of which they might express their dissent. Some took up journalism, which often catapulted them into public speaking and opposition politics. In 1909, a significant number of independent Mexican intellectuals, including Vasconcelos, Isidro Fabela, and literary giant Alfonso Reyes, the son of General Bernardo Reyes, together with occasional foreigners like Pedro Henríquez Ureña of Santo Domingo, founded a scholarly discussion club known as the Ateneo de la Juventud. The Ateneo, which met regularly in Mexico City, consisted of students, writers, artists, professionals, and teachers committed to free intellectual inquiry and a search for new intellectual concepts to replace the "scientism" and "dogmatism" of Positivism.[3]

Typical of these intellectuals' alienation was not only Palavicini's claim that an "intellectual proletariat" would inevitably lead Mexico's next social revolution (an essentially intellectual argument), but also the moral and political protest of men like González Garza, who in 1909 linked specific dissents of intellectuals with the more general theme of "oppression of the people by a dictatorial State."[4] Politically, the independents at first aligned themselves with the insurrectionary PLM or with the more moderate Madero movement. Some of them, like poet Reyes, avoided the political arena altogether. As opportunity for public political protest expanded after the overthrow of Díaz in 1911, many intellectuals became leaders and advisers of divergent political movements. Schoolteacher Otilio Montaño, for example, helped Emiliano Zapata write the revolutionary Plan de Ayala (November 25 or 28, 1911). Lawyer and one-time schoolteacher Cabrera became princi-

---

[3] José Vasconcelos, *Ulises criollo* in *Obras completas*; Félix F. Palavicini, *Mi vida revolucionaria*; Luis Cabrera, *Obras políticas*; Federico González Garza, *La Revolución Mexicana. Mi contribución político-literaria;* Díaz Soto y Gama, interviews; Moisés González Navarro, *Historia moderna de México. El Porfiriato: la vida social,* pp. 383–528; Samuel Ramos, *Historia de la filosofía en México,* pp. 127–149; Zea, pp. 34–35; and Ateneo de la Juventud, *Conferencias del Ateneo de la Juventud.*

[4] González Garza, pp. 21–23.

pal adviser to "First Chief" Venustiano Carranza (1913–1919). Cabrera was the main author of Carranza's labor and agrarian decrees of December 12, 1914, and January 6, 1915.[5] Author Martín Luis Guzmán served as a secretary in the war camp of Pancho Villa.[6] More than a dozen "intellectuals of high or medium stature" led the formation and propaganda campaign of the industrial workers' Casa del Obrero Mundial, 1912–1916. In the early years of the Revolution, idealistic agronomy students from Mexico City's Escuela Nacional de Agricultura y Veterinaria treked to Morelos and the surrounding area controlled by Zapata to effect immediate agrarian reform.[7]

The foregoing is not to suggest that debate and reformist tendencies were limited to "out" intellectuals. On the contrary, a vigorous minority of Científicos engaged in frequent self-criticism, while searching for new ways to confront the growing protests and demands of groups unfavored by rapid social change introduced during the dictatorship of Porfirio Díaz. For example, as early as 1904, Francisco Bulnes, even while nominating Díaz for a sixth re-election, stunned complacent convention delegates by warning them in unusually inflammatory language that Mexico's people were fed up with personalist rule and wanted an end to re-electionism, the introduction of free political parties, and "the open clash of ideas, interests, and emotions."[8] This, of course, was the political line espoused by Madero in 1910, six years later.

Initially, the effect of such self-criticism inside the Científico movement was little more than nominal. No actual liberalization in politics occurred. However, during 1907–1908, a number of published protests

[5] Gral. Gildardo Magaña, *Emiliano Zapata y el agrarismo en México*, II, 111–139; Alberto Bremauntz, *Panorama social de las revoluciónes de México*, pp. 184–189, and Alberto Bremauntz, *La batalla ideológica en México*, pp. 173–174; Jesús Silva Herzog, *Breve historia de la Revolución Mexicana*, II, 160–174; and Henry Bamford Parkes, *A History of Mexico*, p. 352.

[6] Martín Luis Guzmán, interview, December 11, 1964, and Martín Luis Guzmán, *El águila y la serpiente*.

[7] Silva Herzog, *Breve historia*, I, 225–226, quoted here; Antonio Díaz Soto y Gama, *La revolución agraria del sur y Emiliano Zapata, su caudillo*, pp. 214–222; Djed Bórquez, *Crónica del constituyente*, pp. 34–35.

[8] Quoted in José López–Portillo y Rojas, *Elevación y caída de Porfirio Díaz*, pp. 249–253.

by Científicos or their sympathizers against social and political conditions under Díaz suggested the presence of more than an isolated and powerless dissenting group within the Administration. Díaz' 1908 "Creelman interview" may have been, in part, an effort to counteract, in as innocuous a manner as possible, these signs of opposition from within his Administration. Some men who were later to become prominent revolutionaries were still at this time important officials lending service to the Díaz regime, with varying degrees of loyalty and conviction. They included, for example, Porfirista Senator and Governor Venustiano Carranza.[9]

During 1909–1910, many intellectuals who previously had identified with either the Científicos or the Díaz regime, or both, consciously hedged their bets on Mexico's political future. To an extent, at least at first, Madero himself represented this tendency among high-status intellectuals to waver between alliance with Díaz and outright opposition. Less than a month prior to Díaz' final resignation, in fact, Madero was reported as demanding only the Vice President's removal from office.[10] Such behavior derived in part from the feeling of ambivalence on questions of nationalism and political change then plaguing the Mexican bourgeoisie in general.

Intellectuals of the Upper Class

The pressures operating upon Madero and other intellectuals of his class were distinct from those affecting petty-bourgeois intellectuals like Ricardo Flores Magón. Similarly, in the cases of Camilo Arriaga, Antonio Díaz Soto y Gama, Juan Sarabia, and Librado Rivera, various social and personal forces were involved. An examination of the lives of these men, supplemented by a comparison of their revolutionary propensities to those of other intellectuals of their economic class, so-

[9] Manuel M. Alegre, *¡Aun es tiempo!* (pamphlet); Esteban Maqueo Castellanos, *Algunos problemas nacionales;* Querido Moheno, *¿Hacia dónde vamos?;* Francisco de P. Sentíes, *La organización política de México;* Esteban Maqueo Castellanos, interview, *El Demócrata,* September 11–12, 1924; Alberto Morales Jiménez, *Hombres de la Revolución Mexicana,* p. 243; Charles C. Cumberland, *Mexican Revolution: Genesis under Madero,* pp. 44–54; Stanley R. Ross, *Francisco I. Madero: Apostle of Mexican Democracy,* pp. 46–52.

[10] Ross, pp. 159–169; Cumberland, pp. 146–151.

cial rank, educational experience, or geographical region, may bring into focus the outline of a tentative sociological typology of revolutionary intellectuals which, while necessarily incomplete, should prove useful in further delineating the complex relationship between intellectuals and the Mexican Revolution.

Francisco I. Madero

Francisco I. Madero (1873–1913) came from Mexico's small, wealthy, upper stratum of elite families, and as such was, from the start of his adult life, a high-status intellectual "removed, virtually isolated, from the majority of the Mexican people and their problems."[11] The Madero family, which by 1910 accounted for one of the ten largest fortunes in Mexico, fit perfectly the pattern of monopolistic, elite-family control of regional society, economics, and politics observed in San Luis Potosí. In fact, Francisco I. Madero's mining interests spread from his native state of Coahuila into San Luis Potosí. Francisco's grandfather, Evaristo Madero, founded the first bank in Mexico's extreme North, the Bank of Nuevo León in Monterrey, center of Mexico's nascent iron and steel industry. Evaristo helped extend the family's interests from cotton and guayule haciendas into cattle and hides, textile factories, wine distilleries, copper mines and refineries, iron and steel mills, and banking, from Coahuila in the North to as far south as Mérida (Yucatán).

As in the cases of other elite families, the Maderos cultivated political power and influence. From 1880 to 1884, Evaristo Madero was governor of Coahuila. The family maintained a long and close friendship with Finance Minister Limantour. As late as 1909, Francisco I. Madero wrote letters to Porfirio Díaz reporting on irrigation projects and addressing the President as "friend." Madero compared Díaz to Pedro II, the enlightened emperor who ruled Brazil for fifty years and then abdicated without a struggle in 1889.[12]

[11] Ross, p. 5.

[12] Madero to Díaz, February 2, 1909, in Francisco I. Madero, *Archivo de Francisco I. Madero: Epistolario (1900–1909)*, pp. 316–317; Ross, pp. 3, 12; Cumberland, pp. 30, 36; Manuel Tinoco, *Informe sobre los minerales de Guadalcázar, Sta. María del Tecomite y Rincón de Petros, del Estado de San Luis Potosí* (pamphlet).

Like the rest of his family, Francisco I. Madero was a firm believer in free enterprise, easy credit, and the modernization of agriculture. From an early age, he sought an education that would prepare him for life in big business, having found two years of Jesuit primary education depressingly "somber and irrational" (in spite of a transient religious conversion). Madero was educated at the School of Advanced Commercial Studies in Paris. There he learned modern techniques of manufacture, market analysis, and cost-price determinations. In 1892–1893, he went to the University of California, Berkeley, where he studied new agricultural technology. On his father's estates he introduced modern machinery and a high-yield American cotton, while also building new guayule factories. According to Stanley R. Ross, "Madero merits recognition as a leading pioneer in the development of the Laguna region which became one of the most productive areas of Mexico." By 1902, Madero had parlayed his profits into a personal fortune of more than a quarter of a million dollars.[13]

Thus, unlike his elite-family colleague and friend Camilo Arriaga of San Luis Potosí, who suffered economic decline during this 1895–1902 period, Madero was expanding his family's wealth. This explains in part why Madero, by his own admission, was politically ignorant at a time when Arriaga was launching the Precursor Movement. Only upon hearing of the bloody massacre of Liberal Club members in Monterrey by troops of General Bernardo Reyes on April 2, 1903, was Madero shocked out of his complacency into incipient political consciousness. Nevertheless, he did not commit himself to serious and sustained political opposition until 1909—after his family's wealth had been threatened by the 1906–1908 credit and trade crisis. In 1908, Madero credited the financial wizardry of his uncle, Ernesto, with literally saving the family from bankruptcy. As he wrote his grandfather, ". . . the principal article we export [cotton] was the item hardest hit by the American crisis." Throughout 1908 and on into 1909, the Madero family was negotiating for a sizable loan, a factor which caused Madero

---

13 Madero, pp. 2–7, 172–173, *passim*; Ross, pp. 6–12; Cumberland, pp. 30–36. The Laguna region is a basin area two hundred miles west of Monterrey on the border of Coahuila and Durango, which in modern times became the source of half of Mexico's cotton crop and much of its wheat.

to delay publication of his book *La sucesión presidencial en 1910* "until the settlement of my father's credits." By November 20, 1910, the date set by Madero for a nationwide revolution against Díaz, the family wealth was threatened with confiscation; family debts to various Mexican banks were said to total eight million pesos. In brief, there were more than ideological causes for Madero's considering the potential utility of political change in Mexico. For Madero, as for many of the class from which he came, there was private economic reason to be concerned during 1909–1910.[14]

Ideologically, Madero drew his inspiration from the idealistic philosophy of Allán Kardec, whose journal *Revue Spirite* he avidly read. In fact, Madero attributed his political transformation to the influence of spiritism. His tendency to consult a planchette before making important political decisions has since become part of Madero folklore. Throughout 1906–1908, Madero maintained a copious correspondence on spiritism and, as a Coahuilan delegate, attended national Spiritist Congresses in Mexico City. He told the Spiritist Congress of 1908 that he anticipated "the liberation of humanity by means of school and science." In the science of medicine, Madero believed fervently in homeopathy. Politically, he added to his idealism an unshakable belief in democracy and free-enterprising industrial progress.[15]

In sum, Madero was a high-status intellectual from an elite family of Mexico's North who, in general, remained aloof from the problems of Mexico's masses. Economically and personally, he was on good terms with the Díaz regime. Culturally of the *gente decente* (aristocracy or upper class), Madero was French-educated. Ideologically, he was a spiritist, a free enterpriser, and a democrat. Politically, he was at first complacent, but, after the 1906–1908 economic crisis, he was willing

[14] Madero to Evaristo Madero, September 19, 1908, to Mercedes G. de Madero, December 22, 1908, and to Francisco Madero, December 26, 1908, in Madero, pp. 233, 271, 276; Francisco I. Madero, *La sucesión presidencial en 1910*, pp. 8–10; Ross, pp. 12, 51–57; Cumberland, pp. 36, 56–57; U.S. Senate, *Investigation of Mexican Affairs* (1920), I, 735, cited in Cumberland, p. 125. As Part Two of the present volume indicates in more detail, Madero flirted with active opposition to the Díaz regime prior to 1909. However, there is little evidence to suggest that Madero's politics were the cause of his family's economic woes, which stemmed largely from the nationwide 1906–1908 recession.

[15] Madero's letters in Madero, *Archivo;* Cumberland, pp. 33–36; Ross, pp. 8, 9, 19.

to enter into coalition with leaders from other classes in order to change Mexico's political system. Sociologically, he represented a growing dissent among Mexican intellectuals as expressed in small part by a handful of younger- and middle-generation sons of elite families. Unlike most of Mexico's revolutionary intellectuals, Madero was not an "out" intellectual. Rather, until 1909 at least, he was, like lawyer-*hacendado* Carranza and others of his class, decidedly an "in" intellectual.

Camilo Arriaga

San Luis Potosí mining engineer Camilo Arriaga (1862–1945) was, like Madero, a high-status intellectual from an elite family of Mexico's North. Unlike Madero, however, Arriaga was only briefly an "in" intellectual. From an early date, Arriaga cast his lot with both the "out" intellectuals and, to a significant extent, Mexico's middle and lower classes. Arriaga's family suffered major economic reversals during the decade when Madero and the rest of the upper class were, in general, progressing economically (1892–1902). Arriaga came to represent an altogether more radical tendency among Mexico's dissenting intellectuals than that exemplified by Madero. Yet, subject as he was to the conflicts plaguing most of Mexico's bourgeoisie, Arriaga never was to resolve the ideological and political tensions which accompanied his partial shift in interest from one class to another.

The Arriaga family had founded its wealth on mining, principally silver. Arriaga mines extended into other northern states and as far south as Morelos. The family's economic interests also included a number of rural and urban landed properties, some of which it farmed or rented, and others of which it developed commercially, as in the case of San Luis Potosí's Hotel Jardín.

Like other elite families, the Arriagas cultivated political power. Camilo's father, Benigno, was the nephew of Ponciano Arriaga, two-time congressman, aide to Benito Juárez, and reform-minded delegate to the 1857 Constitutional Convention. Benigno had accompanied Ponciano and President Juárez north from San Luis Potosí in 1863–1864, when Liberals were fleeing the French Army. During the 1876 revolt of General Porfirio Díaz against the re-election efforts of Lerdo de

Tejada, Benigno and other Liberals threw their support to Díaz. Díaz showed his gratitude by rewarding the Arriaga family with government posts and personal attention. In 1888, with Camilo's father already a national senator, President Díaz had San Luis Potosí Governor Carlos Díez Gutiérrez name Camilo a deputy (*diputado*) in the state legislature. In 1890, when his father died, Camilo, then only twenty-eight years old, was promoted by Díaz to deputy in the national Congress, a post which he held until 1898. As late as 1908, after a decade of political opposition by Camilo, the dictator was still willing to assist Arriaga financially and to maintain the family friendship.[16]

Able to read at the age of three, Camilo Arriaga was encouraged by the family in his intellectual endeavors. In 1875, he entered the Escuela Nacional Preparatoria in Mexico City, then under the direction of Gabino Barreda, the "maestro" of the Mexican Positivists. In spite of the heady atmosphere of the Positivist converts, Camilo began to read the works of Proudhon, Marx, Engels, Bakunin, and other European Socialists and Anarchists. Later, before his 1900 Liberal declaration of revolt, Arriaga went to France, where he procured his subsequently famous library of European radical books and pamphlets.[17] In 1880, he entered Mexico City's Escuela Nacional de Ingenieros. He became the first in the Arriaga family line to obtain a degree in mining engineering. In 1884, he began his field work at his father's mines in Pachuca (Hidalgo) and Guanajuato. His engineering degree in hand, Camilo went to work at the family mines in Morelos in 1887. He had defended his graduate thesis against a committee headed by Francisco Bulnes. Bulnes opposed Camilo's defense of bi-metalism, which, by

[16] Manuel Ramírez Arriaga, "Camilo Arriaga," *Repertorio de la Revolución*, No. 4 (May 1, 1960), pp. 7–28. The main source for Arriaga's biography has been Santiago R. de la Vega, who wrote nothing extensive on Arriaga except "Los precursores de la Revolución" (*El Universal*, November 20, 1932, magazine section), upon which Ramírez Arriaga draws heavily in addition to interviews with De la Vega (now deceased). Other biographers draw on Ramírez Arriaga. Therefore, all biographical data in this section can be confirmed in Ramírez Arriaga. Subsequent footnotes will refer to sources expanding or going beyond points raised by Ramírez Arriaga.

[17] Rosendo Salazar, "Camilo Arriaga trajo de Francia el socialismo," *El Nacional*, November 25, 1959; Morales Jiménez, p. 37, and Alberto Morales Jiménez, "Camilo Arriaga, una vida ejemplar," *El Nacional*, June 28, 1945.

that time, had contributed significantly to the development of the Arriaga family's silver-mining interests.[18]

The Arriaga family tradition of participating actively in politics at critical times, as well as Camilo's ideological formation, influenced by his upbringing in an atmosphere of militant Liberalism and his readings in Socialism and Anarchism, contributed to the willingness and independence with which he made the transition from silent collaborator of the Díaz regime to its active, militant opponent in 1900. His dissent, in actuality not sudden or unanticipated, also related to his family's unstable financial situation.

Camilo's first notable political protest occurred in part for economic reasons, during the regime of President Manuel González (1880–1884), an Army man who had assisted Díaz in overthrowing Lerdo de Tejada in 1876. Díaz had chosen González to replace him as President in order to live up to the 1876 revolt's slogan of "Effective Suffrage" and "No Re-election." During a slump in the silver market, President González proposed that small coins up to one peso be converted from silver content to nickel. This angered many Mexicans, who had a sentimental attachment to their shiny silver pieces. Arriaga, whose family mining interests were largely in silver, led student demonstrations against the conversion proposal. Popular unrest grew, and González reluctantly shelved his project. Nationalists were further angered by President González' abrogation of the old Spanish law giving the State subsoil rights, a step which in effect sold away much of Mexico's mineral wealth to foreigners.[19]

---

[18] The adoption of bi-metalism was established in Mexico in 1867, with 16.5 ounces of silver equal to 1 ounce of gold. The demand for silver at first shot up, to the immediate advantage of the Arriagas. However, with the introduction of more efficient mining methods and the discovery of new mines, a surplus of silver developed on the world market, in part the cause of the severe slump in the price of silver from 1892 to 1895. By 1905, 39 ounces of silver equaled 1 ounce of gold. This decline in the value of silver, upon which the Mexican peso was founded, contributed not only to the Arriagas' economic crisis but also to the drop in real wages of workers and peasants during the Porfiriato (Jesús Silva Herzog, *El agrarismo mexicano y la reforma agraria*, pp. 129–130).

[19] Ramírez Arriaga, 12; Anonymous, "Don Camilo Arriaga, ilustre precursor de la Revolución," *El Popular*, June 27, 1945. I am indebted to Mexican economist-historian Silva Herzog for his consultations with me on the subject.

For the next decade, Arriaga remained politically unobtrusive. However, his financial situation grew worse with the 1892–1895 crisis. When the flouting of anticlerical provisions of the Reform Laws by state governors came to his attention in 1898, Arriaga rose in Congress to deliver an excoriation of the Church and its political collaborators. A minority of deputies, including Bulnes, joined Arriaga in his Liberal protest. All of them, except Bulnes, were dismissed from Congress by Díaz that same year. For Bulnes, this incident was a prelude to his 1904 incantation for political democracy at the Díaz political convention. For Arriaga, it was the turning point of his career. Using the capital he had left from the 1892–1895 crisis, Arriaga poured his money and effort into forming a political opposition movement against Díaz. By 1906, his funds almost exhausted, Arriaga would be consoled by his friend Madero in his futile "fights against the usurers . . . those slaves of their own moneybags."[20]

Arriaga left Mexico City in 1899 to return to San Luis Potosí, where he soon became a friend of politically dissenting Liberal youths like Juan Sarabia, Antonio Díaz Soto y Gama, Benjamín Millán, Humberto Macías Valadés, Rosalío Bustamante, and a score of others who lent numerical weight and vocal support to his crusade for Liberalism, launched publicly a year later. This new generation of young idealists met with Arriaga regularly in his home behind the Arriagas' Hotel Jardín, "to read and comment upon works by the most advanced revolutionary authors of the time."[21] Arriaga's identification with his own class had already become weakened by his economic decline, ideological formation, and political setbacks. Now he was beginning to take seriously the problems of other classes and their potential political effects.

Although Arriaga's leadership of the Precursor Movement became increasingly radical, spokesmen for his class at first failed to realize the full implications of his opposition. San Luis Potosí's moderate weekly *El Contemporáneo* initially praised Arriaga and the Liberals for their anticlericalism, but by 1902 the newspaper condemned them as "seditious imbeciles." Even the Conservative *El Estandarte* absolved Arriaga

[20] Madero to Arriaga, March 4, 1906, in Madero, *Archivo*, pp. 149–150.
[21] Eugenio Martínez Núñez, *La revolución en el estado de San Luis Potosí (1900–1917)*, p. 9; Díaz Soto y Gama, interview, March 19, 1965.

from responsibility for the militant anticlericalism of the movement, spearheaded by "Masons and Protestants." By mid-1901, however, *El Estandarte* was branding Arriaga and his followers as "revolutionaries," "Jacobins," "false saviors," and potential "tyrants."[22] Elite families of San Luis Potosí and the North in general were shocked when Ricardo Flores Magón, an Anarchist whose name has since been mistakenly applied to the Precursor Movement overall (*magonismo*), described Camilo Arriaga as "the soul of the current political movement."[23] Later, some elite families would be more willing to support political opposition movements, if only tacitly, as in the case of Pedro Barrenechea, who would help bail Madero out of jail in 1910 and later try to keep the Revolution within respectable, bourgeois bounds. In the early years of the Precursor Movement, however, elite families produced only occasional figures like Camilo Arriaga.

One of those few figures was poet and Anarchist Práxedis G. Guerrero (1882–1910), with whom Arriaga bears some comparison. Guerrero came from a rich, landholding family of Guanajuato and represented a younger generation of elite-family offspring than that of Arriaga and Madero. Guerrero, like Arriaga, began his revolt early. Unlike Arriaga, however, Guerrero committed himself to Anarchism and forsook all his family and wealth for a life of poverty, poetry, revolutionary combat, and martyrdom.

Arriaga, then, among revolutionary figures of his class, fell politically and ideologically somewhere between Guerrero to the Left and Madero and Carranza to the Right. Like Carranza and Madero, Arriaga guarded the family fortune, attempting to devote it rationally to a revolutionary cause. So too, his Liberalism ultimately emerged stronger than the radical ideas which he helped to disseminate. Likewise, he was willing to lead revolts, peaceful at first (1900–1903), violent later (1911, Tacubaya). However, unlike Carranza and Madero, Arriaga began his anti-Díaz revolt early; fomented and remained with the Precursor Movement when others of his class were hardly aware of its existence; shifted his identification significantly toward the lower classes;

22 *El Contemporáneo*, September 20, 1900; February 7, 1901; February 6, 23, 1902; *El Estandarte*, February 7, 12, March 1, 19, June 18, August 2, 1901.

23 *Regeneración*, February 23, 1901.

and never was as moderate in his politics—or as successful—as Madero and Carranza.[24]

As an intellectual, Arriaga was more representative of dissent by professionals than of dissent by elite-family elements. In addition to rebellious lawyers like Federico González Garza, Antonio Díaz Soto y Gama, and Luis Cabrera, there were many engineers and doctors active in the Revolution. During the 1910–1913 period, engineers proposed carefully researched agrarian-reform measures. One of them, engineer Pastor Rouaix, Carranza's Secretary of Agriculture and Development, joined "Jacobins" at the Querétaro Constitutional Convention in radicalizing Carranza's innocuous agrarian-reform proposals into Article 27 of the 1917 Constitution.[25] When Arriaga began the Precursor Movement in 1900, a large number of doctors, teachers, and other professionals signed his anticlerical manifesto. Those from the upper class, however, like Dr. Antonio F. Alonso, tended to withdraw from the movement when they realized its increasingly radical nature. Some prominent professionals, like Dr. Rafael Cepeda of Coahuila, who moved to San Luis Potosí at the turn of the century, were politically awakened by the Precursor Movement and ultimately joined the violent revolution against Díaz. Cepeda helped Madero to escape from San Luis Potosí in early October, 1910, and to complete his Plan de San Luis Potosí from U.S. exile in early November. Cepeda later became governor of San Luis Potosí (1911–1913).[26]

In terms of revolutionary intellectual types, what this picture suggests is that businessmen and professionals from the upper class occa-

---

[24] Eugenio Martínez Núñez, *La vida heroica de Práxedis G. Guerrero (apuntes históricos del movimiento social mexicano desde 1900 hasta 1910)*; Morales Jiménez, pp. 241–250.

[25] Bórquez, *Crónica del constituyente*, pp. 232, 583–639.

[26] Rafael Cepeda, *De mis memorias—Apuntes anecdóticos de la revolución* (pamphlet); Isaac Grimaldo, *Rasgos biográficos del Dr. Rafael Cepeda;* Reynaldo Pérez Gallardo, *Apuntes para la historia. ¿Dónde surgió la primera chispa de la Revolución?;* Luis F. Bustamante, *La defensa de "El Ebano." Los libertarios*, pp. 227–248, and Luis F. Bustamante, *Perfiles y bocetos revolucionarios*, p. 17; *El Estandarte*, October 11, 1910; Cumberland, p. 121. For Cepeda's first money contribution to the PLM, November, 1905, consult Archivo de la Secretaría de Relaciones Exteriores, colocación number L–E–918 (hereafter referred to as Relaciones, followed by colocación number).

sionally, as in the cases of Arriaga and Madero, contributed to critical revolutionary developments (1900–1903, 1910–1911). In widely varying degrees, these high-status intellectuals, by seeking political coalition with leaders of other classes, reflected the tensions of the class from which they came. Similarly, to the extent that they shifted their interests from one class to another, these intellectuals altered their revolutionary ideologies from Liberalism toward violent Anarchism. As widely divergent as their ideologies were, Madero, Arriaga, and Guerrero shared with the archpriest of Anarchism, Prince Peter Kropotkin of Russia, a propensity for unusual idealism, often capable of theoretical cultivation only among the highest, most leisure-abetted strata of society. In the case of Arriaga, a high-status intellectual served as "the Mexican Revolution's precursor par excellence," by introducing discontented elements from other classes to the revolutionary works of Socialism and Anarchism. As Santiago R. de la Vega later recalled: "He introduced us to Karl Marx and 'the gentle Prince' Kropotkin. . . . Thanks to Camilo, or 'Camilito' as we called him, the entire Stock collection from Paris formed part of our luggage in prison."[27]

Intellectuals of the Middle and Lower Classes

It was precisely among restless intellectuals from the middle and lower classes that Arriaga's recommended readings had their profound-

[27] De la Vega. Prince Peter Alexeivich Kropotkin (1842–1921) of Russia was considered to be the main theoretician of communistic Anarchism, even as Michael Bakunin (1814–1876) was viewed as Anarchism's main proponent of collectivist Anarchism. Bakunin "replaced Proudhon's insistence on individual possession by the idea of possession by voluntary institutions, with the right to the enjoyment of his individual product or its equivalent still assured to the individual worker" (George Woodcock, *Anarchism: A History of Libertarian Ideas and Movements*, p. 20). Kropotkin went beyond Bakunin by attacking the wage system in all its forms and by calling for a literal communism "that would allow everyone to take, according to his wishes, from the common storehouses, on the basis of the slogan: 'From each according to his means, to each according to his needs'" (*ibid.*, p. 21). Kropotkin edited *Le Révolté* (Geneva, 1879–1885; Paris, 1885–1894), the movement's principal organ devoted to theory. The "Librairie Stock" was a prominent publishing house and library in Paris which, through its "Bibliothèque anarchiste," distributed the works of Europe's leading Anarchists, and through its "Bibliothèque cosmopolite" assembled the works of noteworthy authors (Tolstoi, Ibsen, Hugo, Kipling and others). It was there that Arriaga obtained much of his collection of revolutionary works.

est impact. Díaz Soto y Gama, Juan Sarabia, Rivera, and Ricardo Flores Magón, like most of the revolutionary intellectuals known to historians of the 1910–1917 period, came from petty-bourgeois or even semi-proletarian environments. Unlike Madero and Arriaga, they were low-status intellectuals who, by force of circumstances, were close to the Mexican people and their problems. All four of them, influenced by Arriaga's library, became revolutionaries of the Left. Two of them were from the city, two from the country. In general terms, they were representative of revolutionary tendencies among low-status, "out" intellectuals during the final decade of the Porfiriato.

Antonio Díaz Soto y Gama

Antonio Díaz Soto y Gama (1880–1967) was one of sixteen children born to Liberal provincial lawyer Conrado Díaz Soto and Catholic housewife Concepción Gama in San Luis Potosí. The family resided in a modestly middle-class home which, because of Concepción's prolific childbearing and the unprofitable honesty of Conrado, became poorer as the years passed. Conrado Díaz Soto was nicknamed "Don Honrado" for having used court injunctions to expose the fraudulent bookkeeping of a foreign banking concern. This caused a local scandal which earned the Díaz Soto family the unrelenting antagonism of San Luis Potosí's "business elite."[28] Antonio was brought up in an anti-Díaz atmosphere; confronting him each day as he returned from school was a large photograph of Sebastián Lerdo de Tejada, displayed prominently in the family's parlor. His father frequently lectured him in Liberal dictums and aphorisms. Antonio's law thesis, finished in 1900 when he was twenty years old, emphasized municipal democracy as the foundation of true Liberalism.

Antonio was affected, however, by more than the ideas of nineteenth-century Liberalism. The works of the French Revolution in Arriaga's library also inspired him, as did such Anarchist and Socialist works as: Kropotkin's *La conquista del pan, Memorias de un revolucionario, La ética, el estado y la revolución,* and *El apoyo mutuo, como factor de*

---

[28] Antonio Díaz Soto y Gama, interview, March 25, 1965. This interview and those of January 23, March 19, 1965, and January 15, 1966, are the most satisfactory sources of biographical data provided here.

progreso entre los animales y los hombres; Jacques Élisée Réclus' *Evolución, revolución y el ideal anarquista;* and various books by Bakunin, Carlos Malato, Proudhon, and Marx. During the last decade of the Porfiriato, these works became readily available in San Luis Potosí and other Mexican cities at roughly twenty-five centavos a copy, owing to the publishing and distributing efforts of a Spanish publishing house, Editorial Maucci. In the late nineteenth century, Maucci, a wealthy idealist with Anarchist leanings, set up a printing press in Mexico. Díaz Soto y Gama did not meet Maucci until 1910, when the two men became good friends. Antonio's interest in Anarchism, as he has subsequently stated, was the primary cause of his friendship with Ricardo Flores Magón, begun in 1900–1901 when, as president of San Luis Potosí's Student Liberal Committee, he invited Ricardo to attend the First Liberal Congress of February, 1901.[29]

Díaz Soto y Gama viewed the 1901 convention of Liberal Clubs at the First Liberal Congress as an excellent façade behind which he and other young radicals could develop their Anarchist and Socialist ideas. As he later recalled, perhaps with some exaggeration, "All of us were Anarchists through and through."[30] Antonio contributed to the Liberal façade by reading to the 1901 convention delegates his law thesis, in which he made such moderate assertions as the following: "There is a

29 *Ibid.;* Silva Herzog, interview, December 9, 1965; Florencio Barrera Fuentes, *Historia de la Revolución Mexicana: la etapa precursora,* p. 43; Ethel Duffy Turner, *Ricardo Flores Magón y el Partido Liberal Mexicano,* p. 22; *Regeneración,* January 31, 1901. Réclus (1830–1905), noted French geographer, author of the nineteen-volume *Nouvelle géographie universelle* (Paris: 1875–1894), and veteran of the Paris Commune (1871), worked out the theory of Anarchist communism with Kropotkin while Kropotkin was editing *Le Révolté* in Geneva, 1879–1885. He wrote *L'Evolution, la révolution, et l'idéal anarchiste* in 1898. Malato (1857—?) was the son of an Italian father but was born and educated in France. From 1897 on, Malato headed the Paris Anarchist movement. He wrote among other works, *Prison fin de siècle, Révolution chrétienne et Révolution sociale, De la Commune á l'Anarchie,* and *Philosophie de l' Anarchie.* Later, in the 1900's, Malato opposed Syndicalist tendencies in the Anarchist movement.

30 Díaz Soto y Gama, interviews; Duffy Turner, p. 22. Díaz Soto y Gama used the words "Anarchist," "Socialist," and "Communist" interchangeably in those days, as evidenced by his letter of November 3, 1903, to Ricardo Flores Magón, in Relaciones, L–E–918, and Eugenio Martínez Núñez, *Juan Sarabia, apóstol y mártir de la Revolución Mexicana,* I, 192–199.

time and place for everything, even democracy; Robespierre and Saint-Just were ridiculous in their untimely extremism. . . . violent revolution must be avoided, but reform is necessary." However, other parts of Díaz Soto y Gama's law thesis brought the delegates to their feet, with applause from the radicals and bewildered murmurs among the moderates: "The Constitution is a myth. . . . the national conscience has been corrupted, public opinion is sick of Caesarism." Among those to whom Díaz Soto y Gama dedicated his thesis was Camilo Arriaga, to whom he owed so much intellectually.[31]

Díaz Soto y Gama's first political involvement was as an idealistic student from an increasingly impoverished middle-class family, anxious to right the wrongs that he saw all about him in the industrially expanding city of San Luis Potosí. His father's failure to advance economically for having been "too honest," the sight of beggars on the city streets, and the stories of workers' hardships related to him by Juan Sarabia, as well as the literature he was reading in those days, contributed to the impressionable young law student's willingness to identify with the lower class and express his political revolt publicly. On July 18, 1899, the anniversary of Juárez' death, Díaz Soto y Gama joined Ismael Quiróz and Emiliano Z. López, two fellow students at San Luis Potosí's Instituto Científico y Literario del Estado (today's state university), in leading a street demonstration which reached a climax in front of the San Luis Potosí Military Zone Headquarters with unison cries of "Death to Porfirio Díaz! Death to Porfirio Díaz!" Unknown to the student demonstrators, the commandant of the military zone, General Julio Cervantes, was an old Juarista and therefore was reluctant to take repressive measures. Porfirio Díaz, less hesitant, had General Cervantes immediately replaced as head of the San Luis Potosí Military Zone.[32]

Later, in January, 1901, Díaz Soto y Gama was jailed a week for having circulated a broadside critical of the actions of San Luis Potosí's judiciary. Defending himself against charges of libel, Díaz Soto y Gama claimed he had criticized officials in their public capacities and not their private lives, an attack which fell within the purview of freedom of the press.[33] Seven months later Díaz Soto y Gama was to return to jail because of his attacks on an official higher up: President Díaz.

Not without reason has Díaz Soto y Gama, master of revolutionary rhetoric and a veritable terror in parliamentary debate, been called the Danton of the Mexican Revolution, the figure from the French Revolution whom he most admired. Like Georges Jacques Danton, Díaz Soto y Gama had received a good education but encountered difficulty in obtaining employment. He had to work, to support his family, a fact which kept him out of the revolutionary struggle in large part from 1904 to 1910. However, in spite of his education, he found himself cut off from social or economic advancement. With Danton, he might have said: "I could not buy any office, as I had no money. . . . Then the Revolution took place. I and all those like me hastened to join it, because the former regime had given us a good education without affording us an opening for our abilities."[34]

Student protests were frequent during the Porfiriato. For example, in 1892 more than sixty students of Mexico City's Escuela Nacional Preparatoria were arrested for publicly protesting Díaz' re-election. Eighteen years prior to Madero's movement of the same name, the "Centro Antirreeleccionista" of these students, among whom was Ricardo Flores Magón, helped to put out the newspaper *El Demócrata*. By the end of 1893, the student movement was suppressed. It did not rekindle until the 1899–1901 San Luis Potosí demonstrations and manifestoes. That movement in turn was suppressed, but student unrest erupted anew during the 1908–1911 period, as even a casual reading of the national press confirms. At that time in San Luis Potosí, a small but vocal group of Maderista students appeared, including law student Pedro Antonio de los Santos, poet Jesús Silva Herzog, and future Governor of San Luis Potosí (1923–1925) Aurelio Manrique, Jr.[35]

If Antonio Díaz Soto y Gama was representative of the rebelliousness of Mexican students, he was equally representative of the signifi-

33 Martínez Núñez, *Juan Sarabia*, I, 21; *El Contemporáneo*, January 27, 1901.

34 Gaetano Salvemini, *The French Revolution, 1788–1792*, p. 303; Díaz Soto y Gama, interviews; Robert E. Quirk, *The Mexican Revolution, 1914–1915: The Convention of Aguascalientes*, p. 153.

35 Duffy Turner, p. 18; Barrera Fuentes, pp. 27–28; Silva Herzog, interview, December 5, 1964; Aurelio Manrique, Jr., interview, March 2, 1965.

cant role played in the Revolution by persons trained in law. Not all Mexicans with the title of "lawyer"—*licenciado*—were practicing lawyers. Many, like Díaz Soto y Gama and González Garza, failed to achieve much more than the university law degree, a relatively early and easy step in the career process. Nevertheless, their legal training made them familiar with the intricacies of the law and skilled in debate methods. The word "lawyer" is, therefore, used here to mean *licenciado*, a concept far broader than its English equivalent. Both Madero and Carranza attracted a large number of younger lawyers to their movements, men who had felt cut off by the Científicos.

A reading of either the 1914 Aguascalientes Convention or the 1916–1917 Querétaro Constitutional Congress debates, to say nothing of the Congressional record of the 26th Congress (1912–1913), confirms the predominant role played by lawyers during the Revolution (some of whom were also effective in the counterrevolutionary camp, of course). Díaz Soto y Gama himself typified the debating power of the younger, more radical lawyers when he threw the 1914 Aguascalientes Convention into wild confusion by crumpling the Mexican flag in his fist and asserting that it symbolized "the lie of history" since "our independence was no independence for the native race, but for the creoles alone," a sensational challenge that brought leveled pistols before his chest.[36]

In their capacities as intellectuals, lawyers have earned considerable fame in histories of the Mexican Revolution, especially with respect to their contributions to the ideology of agrarian reform. Luis Cabrera's December 3, 1912, address to Congress calling for the restitution of communal lands to the peasants and Carranza's January 6, 1915, agrarian-reform decree have often been heralded as the major precursors of Article 27 of the 1917 Constitution—as, within Carranza's "Constitutionalist" branch of the Revolution, they were. Prior to 1912, persons trained in the law were influential in drafting a score of agrarian-reform ideas ranging from the 1906 PLM Program and Article 3 of Madero's Plan de San Luis Potosí to assorted Porfirista proposals. The two major intellectual contributions most often cited among these ear-

[36] Quirk, pp. 109–111.

lier proposals were both by lawyers: Wistano Luis Orozco's 1895 volume exposing the ruthless land-grabbing taking place under the *baldío* legislation of 1883 and 1894, and Andrés Molina Enríquez' 1909 criticism of the *latifundio* system.[37] Molina Enríquez drew heavily on Orozco,[38] and later scholars have drawn heavily on Molina Enríquez.[39]

Yet close examination of the works of the two men reveals that both were typical nineteenth-century Liberals preoccupied with fulfilling the ideals of Article 27 of the 1857 Constitution, which called for the breaking up of *ejidos* and the development of private property. In 1911, as revolutionary events began to polarize Mexico's intellectuals, Orozco emerged as a fighting free-enterpriser, insisting that private property is sacrosanct. Molina Enríquez, on the other hand, went to jail for his revolutionary proclamations, which included recognition that violence was necessary for land distribution to occur but still expressed the hope that after the Revolution free enterprise would predominate.[40]

Although as intellectual precursors of the Mexican Revolution Orozco and Molina Enríquez did not develop the kind of anti-Díaz, Socialist- and Anarchist-oriented ideas and political activism of lawyers like Díaz Soto y Gama or the sponsors of the 1906 and 1908 PLM revolts, still their 1895 and 1909 books, written with high praise for Díaz, did serve to alert a number of moderates and Conservatives to an impending crisis and the need for reform. Molina Enríquez' greatest influence

---

[37] Jesús Silva Herzog, *El agrarismo*, pp. 104–208, 233–237, 246–256, and *Colección de folletos para la historia de la Revolución Mexicana: la cuestión de la tierra,* I, II; Wistano Luis Orozco, *Legislación y jurisprudencia sobre terrenos baldíos;* Andrés Molina Enríquez, *Los grandes problemas nacionales.* Agrarian histories in the Bibliography duplicate much of Silva Herzog and one another.

[38] Molina Enríquez, pp. 84 ff., and Andrés Molina Enríquez, *Filosofía de mis ideas sobre reformas agrarias,* in Silva Herzog, *Colección de folletos,* I, 250.

[39] E.g., Cumberland (Chap. 1), who accepts Molina Enríquez' at-times racist ethnological analysis of classes, in which mestizos are seen to be the future hope of Mexico, and creoles, or white Mexicans "uncontaminated" by Indian blood, are viewed as Mexico's domineering upper class.

[40] Orozco and Molina Enríquez issued pamphlets contesting one another (Silva Herzog, *Colección de folletos,* I, 193–264). In August, 1911, Molina Enríquez proclaimed his Plan de Texcoco in an abortive revolt (Manuel González Ramírez [ed.], *Fuentes para la historia de la Revolución Mexicana,* I, 71–72).

was felt during consultations among the "Jacobins" of the 1916–1917 Querétaro Constitutional Convention, when he helped reformulate Carranza's modest agrarian proposals into the solid content of Article 27 of the 1917 Constitution.[41]

If Díaz Soto y Gama felt himself impelled to revolution by the social injustices he observed in San Luis Potosí, Orozco preferred to carry his protests to the courts of law. There he exposed the despoilation of lands of the Moctezuma Indians in fertile regions of San Luis Potosí's Huasteca by such monopolistic, land-grabbing *hacendados* as the Barragáns and Espinosa y Cuevas.[42] Thus, San Luis Potosí was the breeding ground of Precursor protests that ran the gamut from violent revolution to peaceful, legalistic protest.

Juan Sarabia

By comparison with Díaz Soto y Gama, journalist-poet Juan Sarabia (1882–1920) suffered even greater frustrations than those one might expect in the life of a petty-bourgeois intellectual. Unlike Díaz Soto y Gama, Juan Sarabia failed to finish his formal education and was therefore obliged to work with his hands—a traditional mark of low culture and proletarian necessity in Mexico and the rest of Latin America.

Juan's father was a humble musician, conductor of a military band in San Luis Potosí. Although Juan completed primary school with excellent grades, he rebelled against "the exaggerated scholasticism" of the Instituto Científico y Literario del Estado.[43] When school authorities protested Juan's attitude, his father yanked him from the classroom and put him to work in a cobbler's shop. This work lasted only a few months, for Juan's father, called to Mexico City on business, decided to take his son with him. In the nation's capital, Juan learned the rudiments of printing at night school. After five months, in June, 1895, Juan's instruction was cut short by his father's sudden death.

---

[41] Bórquez, *Crónica del constituyente*, p. 232.

[42] In 1905, when San Luis Potosí landowners brought some slanderous charges against him, Orozco was sentenced to jail. See Orozco's works in Sections II-E and II-F of the Bibliography.

[43] Martínez Núñez, *Juan Sarabia* I, 4. This work is the best source for biographical data on Sarabia and is used in this section unless otherwise stated.

Forced to return to San Luis Potosí to support his mother and sister, Juan, only fourteen years old, at first worked at a local library. Finding the pay there inadequate, he went to work in the dark moist pits of Guanajuato's El Cabezón mine. The hardships he suffered in the pits, as well as the sufferings of children, adults, and old folk that he witnessed among the miners, so sickened him that he returned home after only six months on the job. His mother then found him a temporary position as an apprentice in the San Luis Potosí–Zacatecas telegraph office. Eventually, Juan was laid off as under age. However, he was not too young to work for ten months, until May, 1898, at the Fundición de Morales foundry,[44] where he weighed freight cars from ten to twelve hours a day. The work was debilitating, and Juan, although unhappy at leaving friends like Antonio Díaz Soto y Gama with whom he discussed politics and read poetry under the city's street lamps, was persuaded by his mother to take employment as a printer in Mexico City. The new job lasted three months, because the employer died and the plant was closed down. When Juan returned to San Luis Potosí, he fell ill with pneumonia and then smallpox. His unemployment left his family impoverished. Still convalescent, he obtained a temporary job in the state tax department.

These job experiences in his formative years affected Juan's later career. Most importantly, he became embittered against employers and the upper class and sensitized to the sufferings of the working class, into whose ranks economic circumstances had temporarily forced him. His knowledge of printing served him well as journalist and manifesto-writer. Even his apprenticeship in the telegraph office was not wasted, for during his incommunicado jail days at Mexico City's Belén Prison, in 1903, Juan tapped telegraphic signals to Ricardo Flores Magón in the cell on his right and to Enrique Flores Magón on his left, thus maintaining ideological and tactical unity before the authorities.[45]

During those same formative years, Juan Sarabia educated himself at home, after work. He wrote poetry. He became enchanted with the

---

[44] Three kilometers west of the state capital and not to be confused with the foundry at Matehuala.

[45] Enrique Flores Magón, "La vida de los Flores Magón," *Todo*, May 1, 1934; Alfonso Cravioto, "Algunos recuerdos de Belén," *El Nacional*, March 22, 1933.

works of Verne, Hugo, Tolstoi, Zola, Gorki, and Kropotkin.[46] When fourteen years old, Juan wrote this verse about his situation:

> Como fantasma aterrador y frío
> Contemplo allá muy lejos mi pasado,
> Y envuelto en el turbión de lo ignorado
> Siento llegar mi porvenir sombrío.
>
> Si miro hacia adelante, hallo el vacío,
> Y si en mi alma despierto lo olvidado,
> Me encuentro como siempre desdichado
> Y siento el corazón lleno de hastío.[47]

Besides this kind of melancholy, disillusioned verse, Sarabia wrote comic love poems and, when only fifteen, a series of satiric verses—his mature style as a poet—in the weekly sheet *El Bromista*,[48] which he printed as his first effort to ridicule the exaggerated poses and stances of conservative San Luis Potosí society. The variety of his verse suggested already a "dual character" in Juan, which his colleagues later described as a moodiness shifting unexpectedly from boisterous joy and wit to quiet, withdrawn solemnity. It was the quality of wit and carefreeness, however, which most distinguished Juan Sarabia in contrast to Madero, Arriaga, Díaz Soto y Gama, Rivera, and Ricardo Flores Magón.

In 1899, at the age of seventeen, Juan received economic assistance from Camilo Arriaga.[49] He quit his government job and began publish-

---

[46] Víctor A. Monjaras, "Los precursores de la Revolución: Juan Sarabia," *Todo,* October 31, 1933.

[47] Martínez Núñez, *Juan Sarabia,* I, 9. A loose translation of the poem, with no attempt at rhyme or meter, would be the following:

> Like a chilled and horrible apparition
> My past I contemplate yonder,
> And enveloped in the rush of the unknown
> I feel upon me my somber future.
>
> If I look forward, I meet with the void,
> And if in my soul I revive the forgotten,
> I find myself as always miserable
> And I feel the heart full of loathing.

[48] Not listed in the Bibliography because there is no collection of it to be found.

[49] According to Rafael Ramos Pedrueza ("Semblanzas revolucionarias: Juan Sarabia," *El Popular,* December 22, 1942), Sarabia received forty pesos a month at the state tax department, while Arriaga gave him sixty pesos a month to publish the opposition newspapers.

ing *El Demócrata,* which attacked clericalism in the Díaz government, servility among government employees, and injustices perpetrated by the state judiciary. This cost him some friendships he had formed with elite families, including that of his sweetheart, for whom he had written love poetry for years. When *El Demócrata* closed down in 1900, Sarabia began printing *El Porvenir* along the same lines. By 1901, Juan Sarabia, still in his teens, was secretary of San Luis Potosí's Club Liberal "Ponciano Arriaga." In addition to *El Porvenir,* he edited the club's newspaper, *Renacimiento,* tending to radicalize its program beyond anticlericalism, although not with the kind of militant Anarchism already envisioned by Rivera and Ricardo Flores Magón.

As a poet, Juan Sarabia was not particularly representative of a growing literary revolt against Porfirio Díaz. San Luis Potosí poet laureate Manuel José Othón was more typical—concerned more with art for art's sake than with politics. However, some poets, including San Luis Potosí's José María Facha, briefly joined the Liberal Club movement against Díaz. San Luis Potosí's Dolores Jiménez y Muro became a Socialist agitator and later a prominent Zapatista. Many poets became affiliated with the Ateneo de la Juventud during 1909–1910.[50]

As a journalist, Sarabia was more representative. The distribution of Mexican newspapers increased rapidly during the Porfiriato, from one per 53,858 people in 1884, to one per 9,337 people in 1907.[51] Although most journalists followed the Díaz line, a vigorous minority were in the vanguard of the Precursor Movement, in spite of violent suppression of their papers and ample rewards for conformity.

Regional investigation, in San Luis Potosí at least, suggests just how important journalists were at the local level in the outbreak and development of the Mexican Revolution. In San Luis Potosí, Luis F. Bustamante served as *El Estandarte*'s main correspondent traveling with the revolutionary armies in early 1911. Bustamante wrote flattering accounts of the Revolution's leaders, and later joined the Constitutionalist cause, where he covered the Obregón-Villa battles and propagandized

---

50 *El Contemporáneo,* September 20, 1900; Teodoro Hernández, "Precursores de la Revolución," *El Popular,* July 12, 1943; Ateneo de la Juventud.
51 González Navarro, p. 681.

for Socialism and Anarchism.[52] The support of journalist Dionisio L. Hernández of Matehuala for the Liberal Club movement resulted in his receiving a sentence of more than a year in prison (1902–1903).[53] San Luis Potosí's Humberto Macías Valadés signed Arriaga's 1900 manifesto, joined the Club Liberal "Ponciano Arriaga," helped found Mexico City's *El Hijo del Ahuizote,* was imprisoned, and later returned to San Luis Potosí, where, in 1906, he vainly plotted for the scheduled PLM revolt. In 1911, he emerged as a vocal Maderista.[54] Another San Luis Potosí journalist, Ramón M. Santoscoy, suffered innumerable jailings. Santoscoy wrote the satiric biweekly *La Esfinge;* backed Madero and later Carranza; and joined Dr. Rafael Cepeda in plotting the escape of Madero from San Luis Potosí in October of 1910.[55] In addition, Juan Sarabia's cousin, journalist Manuel Sarabia, participated in the PLM revolts of 1906 and 1908, and Camilo Arriaga's cousin, Rafael Vélez Arriaga, owned the press on which were printed the San Luis Potosí opposition newspapers *El Demófilo, Renacimiento,* and *El Porvenir* in the early 1900's. Both men were jailed from time to time.[56] Finally, San Luis Potosí contributed another rebellious journalist in the person of Paulino de la Luz Mendoza, editor of *La Opinión Pública,* who was held in jail from 1909 to 1911.[57]

San Luis Potosí's most famous contribution to the cause of revolutionary journalism, however, was Filomeno Mata (1842–1911), founder of Mexico City's daily *Diario del Hogar* (1881). For thirty years, in spite of more than thirty arrests, Mata maintained a relentless attack against the Díaz regime. It can be argued that Mata's independent journalism constituted the most significant sustained protest prior to the Precursor Movement itself. When illness forced him to resign as

[52] Luis F. Bustamante's works are listed in Section II-F of the Bibliography.

[53] Barrera Fuentes, pp. 117–118; Club Liberal "Ponciano Arriaga" manifesto of February 23, 1903.

[54] Humberto Macías Valadés, interview, *El Demócrata,* August 28, 1924; Martínez Núñez' unpublished "Humberto Macías Valadés"; Barrera Fuentes, p. 145.

[55] Bustamante, *La defensa de "El Ebano,"* pp. 244–248.

[56] Barrera Fuentes, pp. 101, 117; Joaquín Meade, *Hemerografía potosina, historia del periodismo en San Luis Potosí, 1828–1956,* p. 76; Martínez Núñez' unpublished "Manuel Sarabia."

[57] Paulino de la Luz Mendoza, *Queja* and *Los burgueses potosinos y su censor.*

editor in 1911, he handed the editorship of *Diario del Hogar* over to Juan Sarabia. Earlier, in 1902, Mata's contemporary, Daniel Cabrera, an uncle of Luis Cabrera, had made a similar move by inviting Ricardo Flores Magón to edit *El Hijo del Ahuizote*. Clearly, the older, relatively isolated opposition journalists like Mata and Cabrera were becoming aware that Sarabia, Ricardo Flores Magón, and other young radicals who joined the Arriaga Liberal Club movement in the early 1900's were the wave of the future. They recognized their own role as one of publicizing the activities of these younger men, and they performed it admirably.[58]

Librado Rivera

Librado Rivera (1864–1932), except for his close association with Ricardo Flores Magón, is scarcely ever mentioned among the Precursors. Rivera himself invited neglect by his undemonstrative and retiring behavior. His very reticence, reflected in his reading of books even in crowded rooms or jail cells, earned him the nickname of "el fakir" for his powers of concentration.[59] Yet Rivera was a thoroughgoing, hardworking revolutionary, who at times edited the PLM weekly *Regeneración* single-handedly and who was always at the forefront of the PLM movement.[60]

Son of a struggling, small landholding farmer in the municipality of Rayón, not far from either Cárdenas or Río Verde, rail and agricultural centers of central San Luis Potosí, Librado Rivera grew up in the shadows of the state's large haciendas. He might never have left his rural home, with its close family ties and fierce land hunger, had it not been for the inspiration provided him by schoolteacher Jesús Sáenz, who taught in the open air on the "La Estancita" estate of Pablo Verástegui, a large landholder of the region. After classes, Sáenz would walk with

58 The best biography of Mata is Luis I. Mata, *Filomeno Mata: su vida y su labor*.

59 Interview with Nicolás T. Bernal, December 28, 1964, who noted that Rivera did not even look up when Sarabia, Arriaga, or other cellmates threw things at him. The Flores Magón letters collected by Manuel González Ramírez (ed.) in *Epistolario y textos de Ricardo Flores Magón* often contain references to "el fakir."

60 Maqueo Castellanos, interview, *El Demócrata*, September 12, 1924 (Maqueo Castellanos was the judge who sentenced Juan Sarabia to prison).

the taciturn, bookish farm boy and fill him with ideas about Juárez, Liberalism, social reform, and the poverty of the peasantry.[61]

Intellectually awakened, Rivera finished his schooling at the municipal school of Rayón, of which Luis Barragán was principal. Rivera's intellectual inclinations attracted the eye of the estate owner Verástegui, who obtained from the state government a scholarship for him to study at the Escuela Normal de Maestros (Normal School) in San Luis Potosí. This was the start of a career that would carry the lad far from the hard work of the farmstead.

Librado Rivera graduated from the Escuela Normal with honors in 1888. From 1888 to 1892, he taught at and directed the Escuela "El Montecillo" of San Luis Potosí. In 1890 he married Concepción Arredondo. By 1895, Rivera was back at the Escuela Normal, where he taught history and geography full-time, and, on the side, tutored the sons of San Luis Potosí elite families, including those of the *jefe político* and the state governor. His presence in the homes of the elite provided Rivera an opportunity to contrast the wealth and leisure of the urban rich with the poverty and labor among small farmers and workers of the countryside. He slowly advanced himself to the top of his profession, becoming director of the Escuela Normal. Such respectable social status as community educator, however, merely heightened his influence as classroom agitator and social rebel. Among those students who were affected by his tutelage at the Escuela Normal was Antonio I. Villarreal, with whom he later helped organize and lead the PLM from U.S. exile.[62]

When Rivera answered Arriaga's call and attended the First Liberal Congress in San Luis Potosí in February, 1901, he was responding as a medium-status intellectual who, as director of San Luis Potosí's Escuela Normal, had already achieved as high a status as he was likely to obtain in his career. Like Díaz Soto y Gama, he was cut off from further ad-

---

[61] Alicia Pérez Salazar, *Librado Rivera; un soñador en llamas*, p. 12. Her account of Rivera's life checks quite closely with Rafael Ramos Pedrueza, "Librado Rivera," *El Popular*, May 4, 1942, and Víctor A. Monjaras, "Librado Rivera," *El Nacional*, March 11, 1932. All three accounts are drawn upon here.

[62] Díaz Soto y Gama, interview, January 23, 1965; Fortunato Lozano, *Antonio I. Villarreal: vida de un gran Mexicano*, pp. 5–6.

vance. Even if he had not suffered the degree of social frustration or economic decline as that which affected Arriaga, Juan Sarabia, and Díaz Soto y Gama, Rivera was perfectly aware that what advance had been permitted a bright farm boy like himself had depended upon the paternalistic attention of rich estate owners and political bigwigs. In the inner circles of political power of San Luis Potosí, of which Rivera had caught a glimpse from his position as family tutor, life went on in the same spirit of hierarchical rank and status that he had observed on Rayón's haciendas.

Other schoolteachers might have rested content with the kind of status Rivera had achieved. There is certainly no necessary causal relationship between barred advancement and revolutionary behavior. Nevertheless, the correlation is relevant, and Rivera's later revolutionary acts would be unintelligible in the absence of knowledge about his upbringing and blocked social advancement. Consciously or not, Rivera responded by committing himself to the overthrow of the rigid social structure which separated him and those he knew best from a share in a fuller life.

At the First Liberal Congress, it was natural for Rivera to become a friend of Ricardo Flores Magón and Antonio Díaz Soto y Gama, with whom he had corresponded or conversed earlier. All three men were enthusiastic about Anarchist ideas and made good use of Arriaga's library collection.[63] Rivera, writing about the 1912 betrayal of at least his and Ricardo Flores Magón's brand of Anarchism by Europe's leading Anarchists, recalled this 1900–1901 period in the following terms:

Already in 1900 Ricardo was familiar with Peter Kropotkin's "The Conquest of Bread" and "Anarchist Philosophy." He had read Bakunin, the works of Jean Grave, Enrico Malatesta, and Gorki. He also knew the works of other authors, less radical, like Tolstoi and Vargas Vila. But it was for the former authors that he held his highest esteem as his teachers and for whom he maintained a special preference, and it might be said that because

[63] Díaz Soto y Gama, interview, January 23, 1965; Pérez Salazar, pp. 14–16; Enrique Flores Magón, "La vida de los Flores Magón," *Todo*, January 30, May 8, 1934; Bernal, interview; Duffy Turner, pp. 21–36; Cravioto, interview, *El Demócrata*, September 2, 1924; Anonymous, "El informe secreto de la 'Pinkerton,'" *El Demócrata*, September 4, 6, 1924; Pedro María Anaya Ibarra, *Precursores de la Revolución Mexicana*, pp. 22–23.

of this, and thanks to the opportune intervention of Peter Kropotkin, Ricardo controlled himself and did not denounce Jean Grave in the rough manner he was capable of . . . for Grave's insidious criticisms of the Mexican Social Revolution, which Ricardo had inspired and sought to bring to fulfillment at the very moment those European comrades were being duped by the radicalisms of Venustiano Carranza, whom Ricardo attacked without mercy.[64]

In general, there has been a most unfortunate neglect of innumerable primary schoolteachers who, however quietly and inconspicuously, played vital roles in the outbreak and development of the Mexican Revolution. Most of them, like Rivera, either failed or remained unknown at the national level. Schoolteacher Plutarco Elías Calles, on the other hand, became the nation's President and President-maker for ten years (1924–1934). Here again, local research and regional history may turn up overwhelming evidence on the pivotal role of intellectuals—in this instance primary schoolteachers—in forging the Mexican Revolution. In the case of San Luis Potosí, at least, schoolteachers, like journalists, were very important. Combining their teaching with political agitation, some teachers met early deaths, while others were driven into exile. A

[64] Librado Rivera, "Prólogo," *in* Diego Abad de Santillán, *Ricardo Flores Magón: el apóstol de la Revolución Social Mexicana*, p. ix. Pages 92–94 of this same work explain Rivera's comments about Kropotkin's intervention—the gentleman wrote a long letter to Grave's *Les Temps Nouveaux*, patiently explaining the need for all Anarchists to understand Mexican conditions and appreciate the gallant effort of Ricardo Flores Magón, Rivera, and the PLM; however, this was in 1912, and Rivera seems to have confused Carranza with Madero. Jean Grave (1854–1939) was a French Anarchist who had helped found Paris' *La Révolte* (1887) and its successor, *Les Temps Nouveaux* (1895–1914). Originally an Anarchist-communist influenced by Kropotkin, Grave later became an Anarcho-Syndicalist, believing that labor unions would provide the communal basis of a new social organization. He wrote, among other works, *La société au lendemain de la révolution, La société mourante et l'anarchie, Reformes, Révolution,* and *Terre libre.* Enrico Malatesta (1853–1932) was an Italian Anarchist who helped advance the general strike of Barcelona, Spain, in 1902. Opposed to overemphasis of Syndicalist tendencies in the Anarchist movement, Malatesta wrote such works as *En tiempo de elecciones, Entre campesinos,* and *La anarquía.* The works of Maxim Gorki (1868–1936), famous Russian novelist, were translated into many languages between 1895 and 1917. In 1917, Gorki sided with the Bolsheviks and Lenin. José María Vargas Vila (1860–1933) was a Liberal Colombian novelist, whose books attacked all dogmas. He spent much of his life in political exile. In 1903, while in New York, he founded *Némesis,* a polemical magazine with Anarchist tendencies.

number rose to significant political or military rank, expressing radical viewpoints in the Aguascalientes Convention of 1914 and the Querétaro Constitutional Convention of 1916–1917. After the fighting was over and the 1917 Constitution drafted, these teachers usually returned to their profession and were generally forgotten. Among those from San Luis Potosí were, besides Rivera, the following: Luis Toro, David G. Berlanga, Cándido Navarro, Luis G. Monzón Teyatzin, Graciano Sánchez, and Albert Carrera Torres.[65]

Ricardo Flores Magón

When Arriaga gaveled the First Liberal Congress to order in 1901, fellow Potosinos Díaz Soto y Gama, Juan Sarabia, and Rivera were all present, in the front ranks of a nascent political movement, eager in varying degrees to make their Anarchist and Socialist ideals a reality. Also present, although not yet the principal leader of the Precursor Movement, was a somber, Indian-looking former law student and rebellious journalist named Ricardo Flores Magón (1874–1922).

Ricardo's father was a soldier who had fought with Díaz in the revolt of 1876 and who subsequently had been promoted to the rank of lieutenant colonel. Ricardo's mother, like his father, had considerable Indian blood. In the rural household of San Antonio Eloxochitlán, Oaxaca, where Ricardo was raised with his two brothers, Jesús and Enrique, traditional communal Indian customs were stubbornly maintained in the face of social change. Ricardo's mother nevertheless insisted that the boys be educated in Mexico City—had not the Oaxacan Indian Benito Juárez advanced himself in that manner? Obtaining an education was not easy for the Flores Magóns, however. Enrique had to work as a carpenter's assistant. Only Jesús finished his legal training. Ricardo dropped out of Mexico City's Escuela de Jurisprudencia after three years.

After being arrested during the student demonstrations of 1892, Ricardo remained politically inactive until August 7, 1900, when *Regeneración* was founded by his brother Jesús. Ricardo contributed articles to the newspaper which were mildly critical of public magis-

65 James D. Cockcroft, "El maestro de primaria en la Revolución Mexicana," *Historia Mexicana*, XVI, No. 4 (April–June, 1967), 565–587.

trates. As Ricardo's biographer has stated: "An external stimulus was needed to change the orientation of *Regeneración*. That stimulus was already taking shape in San Luis Potosí. . . . It is very noteworthy that Ricardo became more audacious in his articles after receiving Arriaga's manifesto announcing the First Liberal Congress."[66] On December 31, 1900, *Regeneración* added to its masthead the words "Independent Newspaper of Combat." The newspaper's staff turned their eyes toward San Luis Potosí, "the Jerusalem of our democratic ideals," as Ricardo put it.[67]

Résumé

Thus, as early as 1900, there were significant trends of dissent among intellectuals of diverse social backgrounds who were willing to form new political coalitions involving different classes to oppose Porfirio Díaz and bring about political and social reforms. Insofar as Arriaga, Díaz Soto y Gama, Juan Sarabia, and Rivera, all of San Luis Potosí, and Ricardo Flores Magón, originally of Oaxaca, were representative of certain types of intellectuals, they formed not only the nucleus of the Precursor Movement but also a symbol of the kind of participation which the Revolution later commanded from other dissenting intellectuals.

In terms of a tentative sociological typology of revolutionary intellectuals, Arriaga (and later, Madero) represented the dissent of a small number of elite families' younger and middle generations. Removed from the problems of the masses, these high-status intellectuals were professional men and businessmen who, reflecting the economic crises and social tensions affecting their class, sought new political coalitions to introduce Liberal democracy into Mexico. Díaz Soto y Gama, Juan Sarabia, Rivera, and Ricardo Flores Magón represented a more widespread dissent among petty-bourgeois "out" intellectuals, who were either blocked toward further advance in their personal careers or else were declining in status. Familiar with the problems of the majority of Mexicans and influenced at first by the Anarchist and Socialist books

[66] Duffy Turner, pp. 23–24. This is the best source of biographical data on Ricardo Flores Magón.
[67] *Regeneración*, January 31, 1901.

of Arriaga's library, these particular low-status intellectuals advocated forming coalitions with other classes which might eventually bring into the political arena revolutionary groups of workers and peasants. Their impact as part of the Precursor Movement was extended in various ways after 1910 by other students, lawyers, journalists, and primary schoolteachers, who made important, if frequently overlooked, contributions to the Mexican Revolution.

PART TWO

Intellectuals as Precursors, 1900–1910

CHAPTER FOUR

San Luis Potosí and the Nation: Liberal Clubs and Broadening Coalitions, 1900–1903

W HEN ON AUGUST 30, 1900, Camilo Arriaga issued his manifesto "Invitation to the Liberal Party," denouncing resurgent clericalism under Porfirio Díaz, he had little idea that he was beginning a process of political opposition among various classes which would culminate in the overthrow of the dictator in 1911. Yet the content of his manifesto and the situation which produced it suggested, in however small a degree, certain larger social, economic, and personal forces which underlay and fed this process.

Initially, the 1900 conflict concerning the Catholic Church in San Luis Potosí was local and relatively unpublicized. When compared to some other state governments during the Díaz period, civil authorities in San Luis Potosí were especially lenient in their enforcement of the anticlerical Reform Laws of 1855–1862; Catholic discontent, like that represented by the newspapers *El Tiempo* and *El País* in Mexico City or by journalist Trinidad Sánchez Santos, was not significant. Priests were observed to have worn in public their elaborate sacerdotal vestments of satin and gold. Catholic schools were allowed to function in some parts of the state. Local Liberals became increasingly incensed at these open defiances of the 1857 Constitution and the Reform Laws.

In the summer of 1900, Liberals formally accused the Bishop of San Luis Potosí, Ignacio Montes de Oca y Obregón, of illegal real-estate manipulations. As might be expected, the local judiciary exonerated the Bishop (twelve years later the decision was reversed). Implicit in the Liberals' charges against the Bishop was a widespread feeling that the Church had regained a stature in San Luis Potosí reminiscent of Church power prior to the Reform Laws. So serious had the renewal of old Liberal-Conservative tensions become in 1900 that the Catholic daily *El Estandarte* reported Liberals to be arming themselves in Tamazunchale. The newspaper, indignantly denying Liberal charges that an abandoned monastery in the state had been converted into a convent for nuns, angered Liberals by stating that the building was instead being used as "a Catholic school for girls." Any further spark threatened to ignite the Liberal-Conservative conflict into conflagration.[1]

Bishop Montes de Oca y Obregón provided such a spark in a speech on June 6, 1900, to fellow prelates in Paris at the General Assembly of the International Congress of Catholic Agencies. In the absence of the tensions back home in San Luis Potosí, it is unlikely that the Bishop's remarks would have caused much furor. However, in San Luis Potosí, Liberals were infuriated when they read the speech in the August 7, 1900, issue of *El Estandarte*. The Bishop, who thirteen years earlier had warned Catholics that "better times" were a thing of the past, now asserted that, under the benevolent leadership of President Díaz and

---

[1] *El Estandarte*, August 30, September 22, 1900, January 4, 1901; Francisco Vázquez, "Asuntos graves de justicia," *El Contemporáneo*, September 30, 1900; Elpidio Rodríguez, *El crimen y su expiación Monseñor Pirene Obispo de Peregrina, Drama moral y religioso en prosa y tres actos* (pamphlet); Arturo A. Amaya, *Ignacio Montes de Oca y Obregón versus Elpidio Rodríguez. Juicio Sumario* (pamphlet); Karl M. Schmitt, "The Díaz Conciliation Policy on State and Local Levels, 1876–1911," *Hispanic American Historical Review*, XL, No. 4 (November, 1960), 523, and "Catholic Adjustment to the Secular State: the Case of Mexico, 1867–1911," *The Catholic Historical Review*, XLVIII, No. 2 (July, 1962), 196, 200–201; Juan Sarabia "Don Blas antiporfirista," *El Demófilo*, June 29, 1902, cited in Eugenio Martínez Núñez, *Juan Sarabia, apóstol y mártir de la Revolución Mexicana*, I, 77.

with the support of Mexico's women, the Church in Mexico had achieved "the prosperity it enjoys today." So far as some irascible Liberals were concerned, the Bishop had conceded and even boasted that an overlapping control of clerical, economic, and political elites had been re-established in Mexico. The Reform Laws, declared the Bishop, were so much dead wood.[2]

Arriaga, backed by other enraged Liberals of San Luis Potosí, promptly issued his manifesto, calling for the organization of Liberal Clubs, which would hold a national convention at San Luis Potosí in February, 1901. The aim of such a meeting would be ". . . to discuss and decide upon means to effect the unification, solidarity, and force of the Liberal Party, with the end of containing the advances of clericalism and of achieving, within law and order, an effective application of the Reform Laws." Although he limited his manifesto to these nineteenth-century issues, Arriaga described the evils of clericalism in a manner appealing to fellow Liberals of the upper and middle classes who might, like himself, harbor further complaints about the nature of political and economic power and its distribution in Mexico: "The clergy is strong because of its capital, its aristocracy, its conservative elements in public positions, its press, its pulpit, its lies, its immoral confessional." Viewing the Díaz government as inadequate to the tasks facing true Liberals, Arriaga ended his manifesto with a call for democratic reform, to be started by "private initiative, which should be seconded and extended until made into collective action."[3]

The language of "collective action" broadened the manifesto's appeal to take in the Mexican masses. Nevertheless, in his haste to circulate the manifesto, Arriaga collected few signatures other than those he obtained from people in the upper and middle classes of the city of San Luis Potosí. The manifesto showed 126 signatures, including those of 12 Army officers (mostly junior officers), 7 engineers, 7 doctors, 5 lawyers, 3 schoolteachers, and such elite-family names as Ipiña, Ca-

---

[2] González Ramírez (ed.), *Fuentes para la historia de la Revolución Mexicana,* IV, 108–111; original source is *El Estandarte,* August 7, 1900; cf. Schmitt, "The Díaz Conciliation Policy," p. 529.

[3] Camilo Arriaga et al., *Invitación al Partido Liberal* (pamphlet); photocopy in *Letras Potosinas,* VII, No. 83–84 (November–December, 1949), 13; Florencio Barrera Fuentes, *Historia de la Revolución Mexicana: la etapa precursora,* pp. 29–33.

brera, Rentería, and Espinosa. Through his friendship with student leader Díaz Soto y Gama, Arriaga obtained a score of student signatures. Among an indeterminate number of journalists signing were José de la Vega y Serrano, founder of *El Contemporáneo*, and Vélez Arriaga, Arriaga's cousin.[4] Porfirio Díaz, presumably angered by the large number of Army signatures, had General Jesús Camargo removed from the command post of the San Luis Potosí Military Zone two weeks after the appearance of the manifesto.[5]

In response to Arriaga's manifesto, Liberals in thirteen states and the Federal District organized some fifty Liberal Clubs. By the end of 1900, the states of Hidalgo and San Luis Potosí accounted for the most clubs, although there was a strong response from the rest of north-central Mexico (Chihuahua, Coahuila, Tamaulipas, Durango, Zacatecas, Nuevo León) and Michoacán, Puebla, and Veracruz. In this way, a highly localized situation, nurtured by traditional Liberal-Conservative animosity, was gaining national significance.[6]

From the start, Arriaga was receptive to the idea of broadening the political and national base of his Liberal Club movement. San Luis Potosí students, led by Díaz Soto y Gama, acted upon his initiative. On September 13, 1900, they helped launch San Luis Potosí's Club Liberal "Ponciano Arriaga," named after the prominent Liberal of the 1850's. Next day, Díaz Soto y Gama presided over a meeting of the Student Liberal Committee, where José María Facha excoriated the nation's "intriguing clerics and usurious capitalists." On November 11, 1900, with the backing of club president Arriaga, Juan Sarabia began publication of the club's newspaper, *Renacimiento*.[7] In Mexico City, Club Liberal "Ponciano Arriaga" evoked an enthusiastic response from Ri-

---

[4] Lyle C. Brown, "The Mexican Liberals and Their Struggle Against the Díaz Dictatorship," *Antología MCC, 1956*, p. 319; Primo Feliciano Velázquez, *Historia de San Luis Potosí*, IV, 175–177; Antonio Díaz Soto y Gama, interviews; Santiago R. de la Vega, "Los precursores de la Revolución," *El Universal*, November 20, 1932; Manuel Ramírez Arriaga, "Camilo Arriaga," *Repertorio de la Revolución*, No. 4 (May 1, 1960), p. 16; Joaquín Meade, *Hemerografía potosina, historia del periodismo en San Luis Potosí, 1828–1956*, p. 17.

[5] *El Contemporáneo*, September 16, 1900.

[6] Barrera Fuentes, p. 39; Brown, p. 319; Martínez Núñez, *Juan Sarabia*, I, 21.

[7] *El Contemporáneo*, September 20, 1900; Martínez Núñez, *Juan Sarabia*, I, 19–20.

cardo Flores Magón and the staff of *Regeneración.* The Flores Magón brothers looked forward to the First Liberal Congress where they might be able to convert "plain 'priest-baiters' into anti-Díaz militants." As Enrique Flores Magón later recalled: "Camilo Arriaga's initiative excited Ricardo and me . . . the formation of Liberal Clubs provided a basis for socialist organization."[8]

For the inaugural session of the First Liberal Congress, held on February 5, 1901, forty-fourth anniversary of the 1857 Constitution, San Luis Potosí's Teatro de la Paz was "filled to overflowing." Outside the theatre, the Army's 15th Battalion patrolled the streets—an indication of the government's fear of the congress' revolutionary political potential. Attending the congress were more than fifty delegates, including nine journalists, six lawyers, four engineers, four doctors, two teachers, and an indeterminate number of students.[9] Juan Sarabia delivered the keynote address. Díaz Soto y Gama read his law thesis and called for the elimination of the *jefe político* system. Camilo Arriaga presided over the meetings. These three Potosinos, with Ricardo Flores Magón, were later called "the main figures of the congress."[10]

Although fanatical anticlerical speeches dominated the six-day congress, the political high point was reached when Ricardo Flores Magón exclaimed: "Díaz' Administration is a den of thieves!" Many of the delegates, traditional Liberals of the upper class who supported the Reform but had not anticipated attacks against Díaz, hissed in protest. Incensed, Ricardo repeated the assertion. As the delegates began clamoring with cheers, hisses, "ayes" and "noes," Ricardo bellowed his statement a third time. The assembly broke into frenzied applause. Camilo Arriaga later recalled that some of the delegates were afraid that Ricardo's brazen statements might cause the federal troops outside to close down the congress prematurely. Arriaga wondered, "Where is this man taking us?"[11]

[8] Enrique Flores Magón, "La vida de los Flores Magón," *Todo,* January 30, February 6, 1934.

[9] *El Contemporáneo,* February 7, 1901; Martínez Núñez, *Juan Sarabia,* I, 21; Brown, p. 319; Barrera Fuentes, pp. 43–53.

[10] De la Vega; Martínez Núñez, *Juan Sarabia,* I, 23.

[11] De la Vega; Martínez Núñez, *Juan Sarabia,* I, 24; Díaz Soto y Gama, interviews; Samuel Kaplan, *Combatimos la tiranía (conversaciones con Enrique Flores*

Resolutions of the First Liberal Congress, however, did not go beyond the theme of militant anticlericalism. The congress' political program was founded essentially on formalistic liberties and political democracy not related to the social and economic sufferings of the Mexican people. Prolabor proposals merely endorsed the nineteenth-century form of labor organization known as "mutualism." A free press and a free, effective vote were encouraged. *Jefes políticos* were condemned. The delegates extended a vote of support to the Boer Republics, then fighting for independence against Great Britain. Otherwise, the congress failed to specify any demands beyond what might be expected from discontented elements of the upper and upper-middle classes, which dominated the meetings. The most radical statement the delegates could muster was one "rejecting policies of conciliation" and "creating Commissions of Public Health" to insist upon "the administration of justice in the nation."[12] As it turned out, the delegates' insistence upon the proper administration of established legal codes, or "justice"—when interpreted to mean social and economic justice—was an opening wedge for younger intellectuals like Ricardo Flores Magón, Juan Sarabia, Díaz Soto y Gama, and Rivera, who used it to extend the appeal of the Liberal Club movement to the middle and lower classes.

Arriaga later recalled the spirit of these younger men by describing a visit of Ricardo Flores Magón to his library during one of the recesses of the congress. Ricardo pointed to a copy of the 1857 Constitution and said: "Look, Camilo. What a beautiful thing! But it's a dead letter. . . . We'll have to take up arms to oppose Porfirio Díaz, because the old man won't give up power voluntarily, and even if he wanted to, the clique that surrounds him wouldn't let him." Arriaga, who was to retain a high respect for Ricardo Flores Magón even after they divided politically in 1904–1905, was impressed by Ricardo's acute political vision: "Ricardo's subsequent admonitions and warnings too were an extension of his apprehension in 1901 that the Revolution

---

Magón y el Partido Liberal Mexicano, pp. 31–34, based on interviews with Nicolás T. Bernal, who in turn drew this material from interviews with Camilo Arriaga (confirmed by this author in interview with Bernal, December 28, 1964).

12 *Regeneración*, February 28, 1901; Barrera Fuentes, pp. 53–62.

would prove profitable for scoundrels. I never ceased admiring and liking Ricardo. But what a barbarian!"[13]

Whatever his reservations about Ricardo's uncompromising radicalism, Arriaga himself apparently felt a need to broaden the appeal of the Liberal Club movement, for he helped take the first step toward the radicalization of Liberal Clubs—that is, a move toward the political Left, appealing to the middle and lower classes. In March, 1901, San Luis Potosí's Club Liberal "Ponciano Arriaga," in its capacity as the "Directorate" (*Centro Director*) of all Liberal Clubs, issued a "Manifesto to the Nation," signed by Arriaga as club president and Díaz Soto y Gama as vice-president. This manifesto went beyond the anticlericalism of the earlier congress to place the conflict squarely in the political arena. It attacked "the dominating dictatorship," "the semi-official press," and "the personalist, undemocratic, and inappropriately named Científico Party." The manifesto called for the formation of "a truly national party" which should expose "the traitors and puppets in today's Government" and replace Díaz with "a generous, able, and progressive man." In defiance of Mexico's elites, the signers of the manifesto vowed that the Liberals would overcome "the fury of the aristocrats" because the people would be "strong and sound." The Liberals would not be intimidated by "clerical sentences of excommunication or the threats of power." Bishop Montes de Oca y Obregón already had excommunicated the delegates to the First Liberal Congress. Now, led by the San Luis Potosí signatories of the March, 1901, manifesto, Mexican Liberals willing to do more than simply "bait the priests" were issuing a direct challenge to the Díaz regime.[14]

In support of this new lead, Ricardo and Jesús Flores Magón met with other Mexico City Liberals at the home of lawyer Diódoro Batalla in early April, 1901, to form the Asociación Liberal Reformista. The group's two principal aims were to "express a vote of solidarity with the Club Liberal 'Ponciano Arriaga' of San Luis Potosí" and to "issue a manifesto analyzing the political and social conditions of the country." In May, Porfirio Díaz, alerted to this rising political opposi-

[13] Duffy Turner, pp. 31–34; interview with Bernal.

[14] *Regeneración*, March 31, 1901; Barrera Fuentes, pp. 65–69; Duffy Turner, p. 35; Martínez Núñez, *Juan Sarabia*, I, 22.

tion by the public manifestoes of three successive months, sought to deflate the movement by ordering the arrest of Ricardo and Jesús Flores Magón. Liberal Clubs already had been shut down throughout the nation. With the removal of the two Flores Magón brothers, President Díaz apparently hoped that the movement would lose momentum and die a quiet, if not natural, death.[15]

However, on July 18, 1901, in Pinos, Zacatecas, Antonio Díaz Soto y Gama reinvigorated the Liberal movement and further radicalized it with a public speech which, resounding with Mexican nationalism, severely criticized Porfirio Díaz. Without revealing his Anarchist tendencies, the young San Luis Potosí lawyer sought to extend to the middle and lower classes the appeal of the burgeoning opposition movement. Díaz Soto y Gama's main theme was that Mexico was ruled by a narrow, unpatriotic, dictatorial clique, which catered to the interests of foreigners and especially the Catholic Church, whose fanatics were conspiring to take over the nation and destroy every last remnant of earlier revolutionary reforms (e.g., the 1857 Constitution).

Occasionally, Díaz Soto y Gama employed irony to communicate this: "We are at peace with the Clergy, even though it conspires and prostitutes; at peace with the foreigner, even though he humiliates and exploits us." Most of the time, however, he used bristling rhetoric, exhorting Liberals to take an intransigent stand against the Church in the tradition of "the guillotine of the French Revolution" and of Benito Juárez. "No compromise with the obstinate foe, war without quarter for the eternal conspirator . . . That is how Juárez fought and that is how he won . . . by decreeing the destruction of every last pile of riches amassed with the sweat and blood of the people . . . the wretched misery of the disinherited classes." The ultimate target of Díaz Soto y Gama's attack was Porfirio Díaz: "the *Caudillo* who betrayed democracy. . . [and who] holds the horseman's spur in higher regard than the hallowed Constitution of '57, that spur which today lacerates his horse and tomorrow disembowels the people."[16]

Díaz Soto y Gama was ahead of his time. Not even Madero, in his

15 *Regeneración*, April 7, 1901; Barrera Fuentes, pp. 74–77; Duffy Turner, p. 37.
16 *Regeneración*, August 31, 1901; Barrera Fuentes, pp. 84–90; Díaz Soto y Gama, interviews.

Presidential campaign against Díaz nearly a decade later, would express such violent dissent. In 1901, there was only one place fit for such a man. Porfirio Díaz had Díaz Soto y Gama seized in Zacatecas the next day, held until August 22, and then thrown into Mexico City's Belén Prison, "a musty old convent which was turned into a prison by the simple act of herding some thousands of persons within its walls." There the young lawyer remained until the end of 1901.[17]

When the imprisoned Flores Magóns received word of Díaz Soto y Gama's inflammatory speech, they asked their friends on the staff of *Regeneración* to publish it. The August 31, 1901, issue of *Regeneración* carried the full text of the talk, and a month later the government suppressed the newspaper. Before it was closed down, *Regeneración* issued a demand that President Díaz resign. This was coupled with an appeal to Mexican industrialists and small businessmen, then experiencing resentment because of monopolizing foreign economic interests and high local, state, and federal taxes. Wrote *Regeneración*: "The foreign-owned railroad companies kill all industry and business, because they use their high freight fares to skim off those profits that otherwise might be made by the merchant or industrialist. . . . Within the states, taxes are exasperating. The 30 per cent federal import tax kills any business whatsoever." This was the Precursor Movement's first detailed expression of economic nationalism, the appeal of which would prove even more attractive to Mexico's bourgeoisie during the next ten years.[18]

A climax to the Liberal movement's radicalization in 1901 came on November 4, with the issuance of a manifesto by Club Liberal "Ponciano Arriaga." This manifesto, signed by Camilo Arriaga and José María Facha and published in Juan Sarabia's *El Porvenir* and *Renacimiento,* introduced for the first time the agrarian problem, the need for social reform. Among six subjects to be discussed at the Second Liberal Congress, scheduled for February 5, 1902, the manifesto listed "legal and effective means to favor and improve the condition of farm workers and to resolve the agrarian problem." The manifesto also exposed

---

[17] John Kenneth Turner, *Barbarous Mexico,* p. 153 (quoted here); Barrera Fuentes, p. 90; Martínez Núñez, *Juan Sarabia,* I, 33–34.

[18] *Regeneración,* August 7, 1901; Barrera Fuentes, pp. 91–93.

the Díaz regime's forced draft of Yaqui Indians from Sonora to harvest tobacco crops in the Valle Nacional, Oaxaca. It intensified the attack against foreigners, "the privileged classes," and Díaz' "despotism." In its ideological impact, the manifesto completed a transition from traditional anticlericalism appealing mainly to the upper classes, to militant political opposition and nascent social reformism appealing to a far broader audience. As a result of their temerity, the signers of the manifesto were eventually convicted of "libel," Arriaga being sentenced to eleven months in jail and a one-thousand-peso fine and Facha to nine months and a five-hundred-peso fine.[19]

The suppression of Liberals by the Díaz regime served, in effect, to speed, rather than to impede, the radicalization of the movement. The First Liberal Congress of February, 1901, was, significantly, the last. Soon after the first congress adjourned, Liberal Clubs in at least six states (San Luis Potosí, Hidalgo, Durango, Coahuila, Oaxaca, and Chiapas) were shut down by the military or police. The reasons such repression did not occur during the congress itself derived in part from the prestige of Camilo Arriaga and other delegates. More importantly, so many states were represented at the congress that to suppress it might have caused national disturbances.[20]

Representative of reprisals on the local level against Liberals who attended the congress was the arbitrary dissolution of the Liberal Club in Lampazos, Nuevo León, during Holy Week of April, 1901. Military and police spies had failed to turn up incriminating evidence on leading Lampazos Liberals, even after maintaining twenty-four-hour watches on their homes. When an effigy of Judas was burned in the streets a day ahead of the scheduled ceremony, local authorities used the incident as a pretext for arresting a number of Liberals on the charge of "social delinquency." Three of the detained Liberals—César E. Canales, Carlos Zertuche, and Ernesto Bravo—were sentenced to two years' imprisonment for "sedition," although an appeals court

19 De la Vega; Martínez Núñez, *Juan Sarabia*, I, 47, 63; Barrera Fuentes, p. 97; Duffy Turner, p. 40; *El Estandarte*, September 24, 1902; Camilo Arriaga and José María Facha, *Petición de amparo*.

20 Diego Abad de Santillán, *Ricardo Flores Magón: el apóstol de la Revolución Social Mexicana*, p. 9; Barrera Fuentes, p. 73; Martínez Núñez, *Juan Sarabia*, I, 22, 27; *El Estandarte*, February 12, 1901.

two months later declared the men innocent. The president of the Liberal Club of Lampazos was jailed for nine months, twelve other Liberals for five months. An April, 1901, manifesto of Club Liberal "Ponciano Arriaga" accused General Bernardo Reyes, the Minister of War, of ordering such reprisals throughout the nation. In addition, protested the manifesto, "the homes of the town's leading Liberals were searched, their most personal mail was read, and the peace of their hearths was rudely disturbed."[21]

These repressive techniques had the effect of drawing political lines more sharply. Moderates from the upper class and traditional anticlericals, Protestants, and Masons[22] soon began to withdraw from the movement. Nevertheless, the number of Liberal Clubs in Mexico multiplied rapidly. A wave of indignation at the dictatorial methods of the Díaz regime swept the country, and new recruits joined the movement faster

[21] Martínez Núñez, *Juan Sarabia,* I, 31, from his personal archive. Martínez Núñez' account is supported with articles from Mexico City's *El Tiempo* and *El Hijo del Ahuizote* (other histories treat the event in less detail).

[22] Díaz Soto y Gama, interview, March 19, 1965; Martínez Núñez, *Juan Sarabia,* I, 34, 71–72, 94, 109, 120. The role of Masons in Mexican politics should not be underestimated. Porfirio Díaz was head of the Masons' Scottish Rite, which, after 1890, encompassed nearly all Mexican lodges, including the Valley of Mexico Grand Lodge. In 1909, General Bernardo Reyes rallied some schismatic lodges around his short-lived political campaign. Numerous Masons detested the intellectual and administrative monopoly of the Científicos. Many Maderistas were Masons, including Madero, who in 1911 achieved the highest rank (thirty-third degree of Free Masonry) in the Scottish Rite (R. Y. Guzmán "33," Gran Secretario General del Rito Escocès, to Madero, October 14, 1911, in Isidro Fabela [ed.], *Documentos históricos de la Revolución Mexicana,* VI, 161–162). Of the delegates attending the 1916–1917 Querétaro Constitutional Convention, a large number were Masons. However, Mexican Masons were divided in 1910 by the taking over of the Valley of Mexico Grand Lodge by American, Canadian, and British Freemasons. Politically, some Masons sided with Díaz. Masonic influence in the Revolution was uneven, although through the contribution of individuals and a generally Liberal, nationalistic, anticlerical, and democratic spirit, Masons played an important role. In the Precursor Movement, Masonic lodge quarters were often used for political meetings; however, PLM member César E. Canales warned in 1908 that the lodges were rife with Díaz spies (*El Demócrata,* September 13, 1924). The best discussion in English on these questions is Frank R. Brandenburg, *The Making of Modern Mexico,* pp. 191-204. In Spanish, consult: Rito Escocès Antiguo y Aceptado, *Código penal masónico* (pamphlet); Luis J. Zalco y Rodríguez, *Apuntes para la historia de la masonería en México;* Félix Navarrete, *La masonería en la historia y en las leyes de México.*

than older, more traditional Liberals could leave it. Even the pro-Díaz clerical press had to admit that by October of 1901 there were at least 150 Liberal Clubs operating in the open and two or three times as many clandestine ones.[23]

Much of the government's repression was aimed at the opposition press. When Filomeno Mata's printing presses were shut down in Mexico City, Arriaga had his cousin in San Luis Potosí publish *Diario del Hogar* from June to September, 1901. For this and earlier actions, Arriaga was jailed in San Luis Potosí.[24] In 1901 and 1902, at least forty-two anti-Díaz newspapers were closed down. More than fifty journalists were jailed throughout the nation, not counting the detention in Belén of Mexico City journalists from *Regeneración, El Hijo del Ahuizote, El Alacrán, Diario del Hogar,* and *El Paladín,* all of which newspapers were periodically closed down. During the same 1901–1902 period, two journalists were murdered by Díaz henchmen. In addition, there were innumerable beatings and attempted murders of opposition journalists.[25] As fast as old opposition newspapers were closed down, new, more militant ones opened up. Thus, for example, on June 15, 1901, Juana B. Gutiérrez de Mendoza and schoolteacher Elisa Acuña y Rosete founded the outspokenly anti-Díaz weekly *Vésper;* from *Vésper's* presses came hundreds of copies of Kropotkin's *La conquista del pan.*[26]

However, neither the press nor the Liberal Clubs were the government's main concern in 1901 and early 1902. Rather, as a leading historian of this period has noted, "the government worried most about the nucleus of San Luis Potosí and toward it focused its repression."[27]

[23] *El Estandarte,* October 4, 1901.

[24] Arriaga and Facha, p. 5; Alfonso Arciniega Soria to Esteban B. Calderón, no date, in personal collection of Ethel Duffy Turner.

[25] Martínez Núñez, *Juan Sarabia,* I, 42–45, 57–61; Barrera Fuentes, pp. 98–99; Ricardo Flores Magón showed John Kenneth Turner in 1908 a list of fifty newspapers founded and suppressed during 1901 and 1902 and of a hundred journalists jailed for their support of Liberal Clubs (Duffy Turner, p. 370). The newspapers *El Alacrán* and *El Paladín* are not listed in the Bibliography because copies are not available in the appropriate archives.

[26] Martínez Núñez, *Juan Sarabia,* I, 119; José C. Valadés, "El hombre que derrumbó un régimen: Ricardo Flores Magón," *Todo,* March 26, 1942.

[27] Barrera Fuentes, p. 101.

Camilo Arriaga must have sensed the coming crisis when, on the afternoon of January 24, 1902, twelve days prior to the scheduled opening of the Second Liberal Congress, he received in his home national Congressman Heriberto Barrón and Army Lieutenant Amado Cristo. Barrón had supported the Liberal Club movement until October, 1901, when he wrote a letter criticizing *Regeneración* and the movement in general. Mexico City's *El Popular* published Barrón's letter on October 10, and *El Estardarte* reprinted it on October 30. Lieutenant Cristo had signed Arriaga's first manifesto, that of August, 1900. Arriaga gave these two visitors the three copies of *Renacimiento* which they requested, and agreed to let them visit a public meeting of Club Liberal "Ponciano Arriaga" scheduled for 8:30 that evening in Arriaga's Hotel Jardín, across the street from the Teatro de la Paz.

At about 6:00 P.M., Arriaga noticed that from forty to fifty policemen had gathered outside the Teatro de la Paz, where they were conferring with the city's *jefe político*. When the club's public session opened at 8:30, an enormous crowd swarmed into the hotel salon. From the head table, president Arriaga and secretaries Juan Sarabia and Librado Rivera looked out into the audience and recognized not only Lieutenant Cristo but also Army Sergeant Emilio Penieres, among a group of sergeants from the 15th Battalion disguised in sombreros and serapes as common folk. Arriaga's worst suspicions were confirmed. Nevertheless, he introduced the evening's speaker, schoolteacher Julio B. Uranga, who delivered a militantly anticlerical address. After Uranga's speech, Congressman Barrón rose in the audience and accused the speaker of having soiled the nation's honor by assailing its President (Díaz) and War Minister (Reyes). Then Barrón shouted, "¡Viva el general Díaz!," Lieutenant Cristo joined in, and the disguised sergeants heaved their chairs over the heads of assembled delegates and visitors. The Liberals, reluctant to give the police stationed across the street an excuse to intervene, ducked, but did not fight back. Not to be outschemed, Barrón pulled out a pistol and fired.

This produced instantaneous results. As the sergeants whipped out their weapons, some fifty club-wielding policemen poured into the hotel with the *jefe político*, followed shortly by the city mayor and General Kerlegand, whose federal troops invested the downtown area around the hotel and Teatro de la Paz. Bullets ricocheted from the ceiling above the head table. As Arriaga raised his arm against a sergeant brandishing a pistol at him, Carlos Uranga, the speaker's brother, jumped between them, disarmed the sergeant, and then fell from a gun-blow on top of his head. Arriaga and Rivera slipped out the back door and dashed to Arriaga's home behind the hotel. About twenty-five other club members were less fleet—policemen herded them into a waiting van which took them to the local jail.

There they were crammed into "a disgusting, noxious, filthy room," as a manifesto of Club Liberal "Ponciano Arriaga" expressed it four days later. At about midnight, according to the manifesto, Juan Sarabia had to fight off an assassin who had been put in the prisoners' cell under the guise of a harmless drunk. Next day, upon request by their lawyers, the prisoners were transferred to somewhat safer quarters in the state penitentiary.

Meanwhile, Arriaga and Rivera found themselves surrounded by *Rurales* (Díaz' crack rural police force of "rehabilitated" bandits and outlaws), soldiers of the 15th Battalion and 2nd Regiment, and various special agents who occupied the hotel, the gardens, the grounds, and even the kitchens of Arriaga's property. Reluctantly, Arriaga permitted the soldiers to search his home. The soldiers seized Librado Rivera and took him to the state penitentiary. Two hours later, "Don Camilo" was courteously invited to join his colleagues there. Four days later, all except three prisoners were released. Left in jail for almost a year were three of the San Luis Potosí "nucleus": Arriaga, Sarabia, and Rivera. Their alleged crime was having "obstructed public officials in the exercise of their duty."

However, there still remained free one member of the San Luis Potosí nucleus: Díaz Soto y Gama, who had himself only recently completed a jail term, the result of his July, 1901, Zacatecas speech. Díaz Soto y Gama took up the defense of his three companions. He was assisted later, when the two Flores Magón brothers were released from Belén (April 30, 1902), by lawyer Jesús Flores Magón. The facts in the case were perfectly clear. When the prisoners gained their release in late 1902, it was because of lack of evidence in support of the accusations. By then, they were four prisoners, not three. Díaz Soto y

Gama had been thrown in with them—the San Luis Potosí "nucleus" had been put in the cell.[28]

For most of the rest of 1902, the leaders of the Liberal Club movement were in jail. A dying opposition press carried on a flanking attack against the Díaz government, hitting, pulling back, and often being suppressed. In San Luis Potosí, the printing presses of *El Porvenir* and *Renacimiento* were seized by court order right after the jailing of their editor (Juan Sarabia) and the rest of the San Luis Potosí nucleus.[29]

On April 6, 1902, the jailed Potosinos, without the support of Facha, who withdrew from the movement for personal reasons in May,[30] founded one of the most important opposition newspapers of this period, *El Demófilo*. Arriaga, Sarabia, Rivera, and Díaz Soto y Gama launched *El Demófilo* "as a political and Anti-reelectionist newspaper" on behalf of "workers who are victims of injustices . . . the humble and exploited classes."[31] Arriaga's cousin printed the newspaper on his presses in San Luis Potosí.

The founding of such a radical newspaper by the four jailed Potosinos indicated more than defiant, almost foolhardy bravery on their part. It showed the willingness of Camilo Arriaga to postpone latent

[28] Arriaga and Facha; Club Liberal "Ponciano Arriaga," manifesto of January 28, 1902, in Barrera Fuentes, pp. 101–108, and Martínez Núñez, *Juan Sarabia*, I, 48–53; Librado Rivera, "La mano férrea de la dictadura y el Congreso Liberal de San Luis," *Gráfico*, December 12–14, 1930; Díaz Soto y Gama, interviews; also, on the basis of Arriaga–Bernal interviews, Duffy Turner, pp. 41–43. Barrón later admitted having ties with War Minister Reyes, although he did not refer directly to this incident (letter to *Gráfico*, November 26, 1930; Duffy Turner, p. 41). An example of pro-Díaz press coverage of the Barrón goon-squad affair is *El Estandarte*, which during the last week of January, 1902, provided many of the facts used here; however, the February 1, 1902, issue began to whitewash the government of all responsibility in the affair. On February 27, 1902, a group of San Luis Potosí women, unaffiliated with the Liberal Club movement, distributed a broadside which confirmed the Liberals' version of the incident and protested the gross injustices involved (*El Hijo del Ahuizote*, March 16, 1902; Martínez Núñez, *Juan Sarabia*, I, 53–56).

[29] Martínez Núñez, *Juan Sarabia*, I, 63.

[30] José María Facha to Antonio Díaz Soto y Gama, May 27, 1902, in *El Contemporáneo*, July 6, 1902, and *El Estandarte*, July 3, 1902.

[31] *El Demófilo*, April 6, 1902, and later issues, cited in Martínez Núñez, *Juan Sarabia*, I, 64–83.

conflicts with Anarchists like Ricardo Flores Magón by agreeing to a stepped-up radicalization of the Liberal movement. How aware at this time Arriaga was of these latent conflicts, or to what extent he consciously encouraged the movement's radicalization, is difficult to assess. However, the Díaz government's suppression of his dissent, combined with the ultimate threat to his leadership by more radical intellectuals prominent in the movement, undoubtedly had some effect on Arriaga's behavior. His own frequent jailings, as well as prison discussions with Díaz Soto y Gama, Rivera, and Sarabia, ostensibly had contributed to Arriaga's willingness to move Left. By giving his consent, actively or passively, to such a move, Arriaga was in effect able to maintain a high degree of personal control over the movement he had founded a year and a half earlier. In addition, he may have felt that more moderate political positions were doomed to failure, since the Díaz government already had shown its determination not to let any public opposition go unpunished. This was a lesson that Madero, and other dissident intellectuals who had not yet awakened politically, would learn the hard way during 1909–1910.

While Arriaga and Rivera treated social questions in *El Demófilo*, Díaz Soto y Gama wrote the legal articles. Juan Sarabia contributed a series of satiric verses against clericalism, bossism, and police brutality. *El Demófilo* exposed the Díaz regime's use of the *leva* (forced military conscription) as a kind of slave-labor system. The newspaper criticized the abuses of caciques and *hacendados* in the Huasteca, while at the same time it denounced the disproportionately high taxes on commerce, small businesses, and new industries.[32]

On the eve of San Luis Potosí's gubernatorial elections, the printing press of *El Demófilo* was confiscated (July 30, 1902). It was returned after the elections, but the newspaper appeared in print only once again, on August 10, 1902. Further precautionary steps taken by the government at this time included the jailing of the printer, Arriaga's cousin. Arriaga, Sarabia, Rivera, and Díaz Soto y Gama were placed in separate cells, incommunicado, for two months. Federal troops sur-

---

[32] *Ibid.*; for further examples, see *El Hijo del Ahuizote*, July 27, 1902.

rounded the state penitentiary and extra guards stationed themselves in front of the cells of the four Liberal leaders.[33]

Meanwhile, as stated earlier, Ricardo and Jesús Flores Magón had been released from Belén on April 30, 1902. Jesús disapproved of the radicalization of the Liberal movement. About to be married, he was concerned about the effect of radical politics upon his career as a professional lawyer. Therefore he ceased active participation in the movement except to give legal consultation to the Precursors from time to time.

Ricardo, on the other hand, delighted by the movement's radicalization and anxious to exploit it, rented the Mexico City opposition weekly *El Hijo del Ahuizote* from its ill and imprisoned founder (1885), Daniel Cabrera. Ricardo's first issue of *El Hijo del Ahuizote*, July 16, 1902, launched a series of articles against President Díaz and General Bernardo Reyes. The newspaper's criticisms were strengthened by the cartoons of Jesús Martínez Carrión, the most prominent of the Precursor Movement's many cartoonists who made significant contributions as revolutionary intellectuals.[34] General Bernardo Reyes' Second Military Reserve, newly founded as a potential military arm for the General's rumored Presidential campaign of 1904, was ridiculed by *El Hijo del Ahuizote*. This led to the confiscation of the newspaper's presses and office equipment and the jailing of its staff on September 12, 1902, upon order of a military judge. Ricardo and Enrique Flores Magón were held incommunicado in the military prison of Santiago Tlatelolco for thirty-four days. Even Cabrera, legal owner of the newspaper, in spite of his failing health, was returned to jail. The Supreme Court later cleared Daniel Cabrera, and all prisoners in the case had been released by January 23, 1903.[35]

---

[33] *El Hijo del Ahuizote*, August 3, 1902; Martínez Núñez, *Juan Sarabia*, I, 90–105; Díaz Soto y Gama, interview, January 23, 1965.

[34] Barrera Fuentes, pp. 110 ff.; Duffy Turner, pp. 47–48; Kaplan, p. 58. There are two excellent collections of political cartoons covering the Porfiriato, both of which confirm the revolutionary role of cartoonists: González Ramírez (ed.), *Fuentes*, II (*La caricatura política*), and Salvador Pruneda, *La caricatura como arma política*.

[35] *El Hijo del Ahuizote*, November 23, 1902, November 23, 1903; *El País*, November 20, 1902; De la Vega; Alfonso Cravioto, interview, *El Demócrata*, September

By mid-September, 1902, all recognized leaders of the Liberal movement were in jail, most of them incommunicado. However, by the end of the month, Juan Sarabia, Rivera, and Díaz Soto y Gama had been released, and Arriaga had been transferred to Belén Prison in Mexico City. When San Luis Potosí officialdom still persecuted them, Juan Sarabia and Díaz Soto y Gama left for Mexico City. Knowing this, Arriaga persuaded Ricardo and Enrique Flores Magón, Cabrera, and other leading figures of the capital's opposition press that Juan Sarabia should become editor of *El Hijo del Ahuizote*, which had not been published since September 7, 1902.[36]

On November 23, 1902, *El Hijo del Ahuizote* reappeared under twenty-year-old Sarabia's direction. Besides publicizing the repression of all opposition by the Díaz regime, which had reached new peaks during the 1901–1902 period, *El Hijo del Ahuizote* now renewed the attack on Díaz and Reyes. It was at this time that Manuel Sarabia, Juan's cousin, joined the movement. The Sarabias, Díaz Soto y Gama, and lawyer-writer Alfonso Cravioto, among others, worked full-time on the newspaper.[37]

Momentarily tolerating this new threat from the opposition press, the Díaz Administration now shifted its attack to what it hoped might be a weak link in the burgeoning opposition movement: the President's old friend, Camilo Arriaga. In mid-December, 1902, Pablo Macedo and Joaquín D. Casasús, two of the nation's most famous Científicos, approached Arriaga in his Belén cell with an offer from Díaz: Cease your attacks on the President and go free. Arriaga answered: "In that case, it would be far better that I not go free."[38]

Nevertheless, Arriaga was released from Belén on January 10, 1903. He immediately set about reorganizing Club Liberal "Ponciano Arriaga" to incorporate leading Liberals and opposition journalists from

2, 1924; Federico Pérez Fernández, interview, *El Demócrata*, September 3, 1924; articles by Enrique Flores Magón listed in Section II–D of the Bibliography; Barrera Fuentes, pp. 110–112; Duffy Turner, pp. 47–50; Martínez Núñez, *Juan Sarabia*, I, 120–122; Kaplan, pp. 65–76.

36 Martínez Núñez, *Juan Sarabia*, I, 109–129.

37 *Ibid.;* Alfonso Cravioto, interview, *El Demócrata,* September 2, 1924, and his "Algunos recuerdos de Belén," *El Nacional,* March 22, 1933.

38 *Ibid.* (Cravioto's work and Martínez Núñez, *Juan Sarabia,* I, 11, 124.)

other parts of the nation, all of whom had fled local harassment to take up the struggle in Mexico City. The new club was officially installed on February 5, 1903, with half the membership and most of the top leadership still from San Luis Potosí. By force of circumstances, all the club members, no matter what their earlier careers, were by now active journalists. Club president Arriaga was the only high-status intellectual in the leadership. The others were petty-bourgeois, low-status intellectuals like vice-president Díaz Soto y Gama, first secretary Juan Sarabia, and second secretary Ricardo Flores Magón.[39]

The first manifesto of Club Liberal "Ponciano Arriaga" in 1903—that of February 23—accused the Díaz regime of "having left the people in the saddest possible political orphanage, without a guarantee to protect them, a liberty to elevate them, or a right to dignify them."[40] On February 5, Constitution Day, twelve journalists of *El Hijo del Ahuizote,* six of them from San Luis Potosí, appeared with bowed heads on the newspaper office's balcony, which was draped with a giant black banner reading: "THE CONSTITUTION HAS DIED." As *El Hijo del Ahuizote* explained: "We solemnly censure the assassins of the Constitution who, as if in bloodstained mockery of the people they have scoffed, celebrate this day with demonstrations of merriment and pleasure."[41]

On February 27, 1903, Club Liberal "Ponciano Arriaga" issued a manifesto which declared in strong terms the movement's new emphasis on social and economic injustices and the need for radical reform. The manifesto excoriated "the capitalist, the priest, and the high official,

[39] Other officers were: treasurer, Benjamín Millán (Potosino); third secretary, Santiago de la Hoz; fourth secretary, Enrique Flores Magón; committeemen, Juana B. Gutiérrez de Mendoza and Elisa Acuña y Rosete (of *Vésper*), Evaristo Guillén, Federico Pérez Fernández, Alfonso Arciniega, and Potosinos Rosalío Bustamante, Cravioto, Macías Valadés, María del Refugio Vélez, and Tomás Sarabia (another of Juan's cousins). See the signatories of the club's February 23 and 27, 1903, manifestoes, or, for only slight variation, Barrera Fuentes, p. 116, Duffy Turner, p. 43, and Martínez Núñez, *Juan Sarabia,* I, 132.

[40] *El Hijo del Ahuizote,* February 15, 1903; Barrera Fuente, pp. 115–119; Martínez Núñez, *Juan Sarabia,* I, 132–137.

[41] *El Hijo del Ahuizote,* February 8, 1903; Barrera Fuentes, p. 119; Martínez Núñez, *Juan Sarabia,* I, 129–131; Kaplan, pp. 91–95; and, for a photograph of the memorable scene, Agustín Casasola (ed.), *Historia gráfica de la Revolución Mexicana,* I, 68.

civilian or military." Asking that "the proletariat be given dignity," it condemned the predominance of "money, power, priest, and foreigner" and the influence of monopolies in "raising the cost of living while lowering wages." It protested the *leva*, the company store (*tienda de raya*), and the peasant slave trade to Valle Nacional and Yucatán. The manifesto went on to condemn land monopolization, especially by "Yankees" and the Church, and to lament the wretched conditions among the peasantry. It mourned the death of the Constitution, of freedom, and of suffrage ("a corpse"). It denounced the absence of commercial prosperity or honesty in business and government. It also criticized the Jesuits for increasing Church control of education. Repeating all earlier charges against the Díaz regime, the manifesto concluded that there was no longer any respect "for human life." Although th₂ February 27, 1903, manifesto denied that it was calling for a revolution, its last paragraphs came perilously close to doing just that:

The Club Liberal "Ponciano Arriaga" . . . summons you today before the altar of everyone's duty to fight for the regeneration of the Fatherland! Countrymen! "The world marches on," Pelletan has said: let us all march together! . . .

In another century, the French gave of their blood to teach all tyrants a lesson: in the twentieth century, let us give of all the energies of our minds for the sacred cause of humanity!

Above the oppression of tyranny, the intrigue of the Clergy, and the greed of capital and the military, there rises up the great edifice of national brotherhood, democracy, and grandeur! Reform, Union, Liberty.[42]

By mid-March of 1903, the leaders of Mexico's Liberal opposition were already beginning to discuss tactics for a revolution they all envisioned as ultimately necessary. Three important additions were now made to the leadership group: schoolteacher Librado Rivera from San Luis Potosí; twenty-one-year-old former law student and first president

---

[42] *El Hijo del Ahuizote*, March 1, 1903; Barrera Fuentes, pp. 120–127; González Ramírez (ed.), *Fuentes*, IV, 100–106. Camilo Pelletan (1846–1915) was a French polemicist and journalist of the Left who supported broad alliances with the Socialists. He wrote for the French left-wing newspapers *La Justice*, *La Lanterne*, and *La Dépêche* (Toulouse). His books include *Questions d'histoire: le Comité central et la Commune* (1879), *Les guerres de la Révolution* (1884), *Histoire contemporaine* (1902), and *Victor Hugo, Homme politique* (1905).

of Veracruz' Liberal Club (1901) Santiago de la Hoz; and eighteen-year-old Monterrey author, cartoonist, and journalist Santiago R. de la Vega—all low-status intellectuals. As soon as they arrived in Mexico City, Rivera and De la Vega went straight to the offices of *El Hijo del Ahuizote,* where they encountered Arriaga, Díaz Soto y Gama, Juan Sarabia, Ricardo Flores Magón, and others discussing Kropotkin's *La conquista del pan.*[43]

De la Hoz sparked the founding of the Mexico City Club Redención and its newspaper *Excélsior,* the aim of which was to guide the revolution along strictly Anti-reelectionist lines. Porfirio Díaz' followers were already preparing for the *caudillo*'s sixth re-election in 1904. There was considerable overlap in membership between Club Redención and Club Liberal "Ponciano Arriaga" (e.g., Juan Sarabia, Manuel Sarabia, Ricardo and Enrique Flores Magón, and Cravioto).[44]

The tactic of Anti-reelectionism, endorsed by those members of Club Liberal "Ponciano Arriaga" who had joined Club Redención, became the subject of intense debate at a meeting of Club Liberal "Ponciano Arriaga" on March 16, 1903. No one favored Díaz' re-election, but Arriaga and Díaz Soto y Gama protested that Club Liberal "Ponciano Arriaga" now could justifiably be accused of political "ambitiousness" and "personalism," since some of its members had decided to enter the 1904 political campaign. Juan Sarabia countered that Díaz Soto y Gama was behaving childishly by presenting a favorite argument of the club's

---

[43] Rivera joined fellow Potosino Macías Valadés and Enrique Flores Magón as part of the administrative team of *El Hijo del Ahuizote* (Martínez Núñez, *Juan Sarabia,* I, 144–146; Barrera Fuentes, p. 116; De la Vega; Díaz Soto y Gama, interview, January 23, 1965). According to Enrique Flores Magón, Rivera was in Mexico City as early as January, 1903, and helped conceive the "The Constitution Has Died" idea (Kaplan, p. 91); however, Enrique's memory was often confused in his writings. Since Rivera was, as a rule, so inconspicuous, no chroniclers have succeeded in tracing his whereabouts consistently during the Precursor period. Documents in Relaciones, L-E-920–926, indicate nevertheless that Rivera—in spite of his complicated escape from Pinkerton agents in Missouri and Texas to Los Angeles, California—was, next to Ricardo Flores Magón, the principal planner of the 1908 PLM revolt during the October, 1906–June, 1907, phase of planning.

[44] *El Hijo del Ahuizote,* March 22, 1903. Barrera Fuentes (p. 115) asserts that Club Redención and *Excélsior* (unrelated to today's newspaper of the same name) were founded in January, 1903; however, the evidence is lacking, and Martínez Núñez (*Juan Sarabia,* I, 146–148) and Cravioto disagree.

enemies. There followed some stormy exchanges, before Cravioto intervened to propose compromise, leaving Club Redención as Anti-reelectionist and Club Liberal "Ponciano Arriaga" as open to all ideas. Díaz Soto y Gama agreed to the compromise, repeating that "those Anti-reelectionist jobs are not of the club [Club Liberal "Ponciano Arriaga"] but of a group of its members who do them on their own personal account."[45] Subsequent developments would make the issue academic, although by 1910 all Mexico would again be enveloped in the questions of tactics: Anti-reelectionism alone, or violent revolution too? political reform, or socio-economic reform too? Within months of the club's 1903 dispute, however, there was only minimal disagreement among the Liberal leadership as to the need for violent revolution and some kind of social reform.

The events which climaxed the Liberal Club movement's evolution by committing its leadership to a radical program of revolution were the final and decisive acts of represssion executed by the Díaz regime. The issue was drawn in the first sixteen days of April, 1903. On April 2, while a public demonstration in honor of Porfirio Díaz' victory at Puebla against the French in 1867 was taking place in Mexico City, a large number of counterdemonstrators appeared carrying "NO RE-ELECTION!" banners and shouting "Death to re-election!" The counterdemonstrators marched to the National Palace and demanded the appearance of the President. After an hour, Díaz did appear, but he was received coldly by the assembled public. The anti-Díaz demonstration concluded enthusiastically outside the downtown offices of *El Hijo del Ahuizote.*[46]

A more serious protest occurred in Monterrey, where a reported ten thousand persons had gathered to denounce General Bernardo Reyes' effort to have himself re-elected governor of Nuevo León. General Reyes' troops opened fire on the crowd, killing fifteen, wounding many

---

45"Nota Club Liberal 'Ponciano Arriaga.' Acta," *El Hijo del Ahuizote,* March 22, 1903; Barrera Fuentes, pp. 128–131; Duffy Turner, pp. 54 ff.

46 The counterdemonstration was Juan Sarabia's idea, according to Enrique Flores Magón (Kaplan, pp. 96–105). Cf. *Excélsior,* April 2, 1903; Martínez Núñez, *Juan Sarabia,* I, 148–160; Barrera Fuentes, pp. 131–137; and Juan Sarabia, "El 2 de abril," *El Hijo del Ahuizote,* April 5, 1903.

others, and causing a general panic. More than eighty were arrested.[47] The Directorate of Club Liberal "Ponciano Arriaga" promptly submitted to the Mexican Congress a legal brief[48] demanding that General Reyes be punished for his infractions against free assembly, free expression, and free suffrage, and his alleged crimes of arbitrary arrest and collective murder. Díaz' *caballada,* or "herd of tame horses" as the President called his Congress, cleared Reyes of all charges and accused the signers of the club's protest of "false accusation." Arriaga and Díaz Soto y Gama, their lives now threatened by General Reyes, had no alternative but to flee Mexico. They sought refuge in the United States. From El Paso, Texas, in June, 1903, Arriaga and Díaz Soto y Gama summed up the miserable affair in a written statement titled "The Lawsuit of General Bernardo Reyes," which observed that "the indecent farce has now been consummated."[49] Two of the San Luis Potosí nucleus were thus again removed from the scene of action.

The other half of the Potosino nucleus, Rivera and Juan Sarabia, was also being harassed by the Díaz regime. Sarabia and the Flores Magóns, however, joined by De la Hoz and other members of Club Redención, succeeded in issuing one more manifesto on April 11, 1903. This one called for all Liberal Clubs to campaign for a Liberal candidate against Díaz in 1904. Although emphasizing "no re-election," the manifesto maintained the broad appeal to different classes. It protested the conversion of Mexicans into "the servants of foreigners, who are the ones exploiting the wealth of our country." It criticized the use of "forced labor in a multitude of towns and farms." And it blamed the Díaz government for having "produced the supremacy of capital . . . the

---

[47] *El Hijo del Ahuizote,* April 12, 1903; Martínez Núñez, *Juan Sarabia,* I, 160–164; Barrera Fuentes, pp. 137–138; Duffy Turner, p. 56; various articles listed in Section II-D of the Bibliography.

[48] Reprinted in *Diario del Hogar,* August 17, 1911.

[49] Reprinted in *Diario del Hogar,* August 21–31, 1911. See also, *El Hijo del Ahuizote,* April 19, 1903; Martínez Núñez, *Juan Sarabia,* I, 161–164, 192; Ramírez Arriaga, pp. 20–21; Bernardo Reyes, *La declaratoria de absolución en favor del Sr. Gral. Reyes, ante la opinión pública nacional* (n.d.) (pamphlet), in the Biblioteca de México. General Reyes may not have been as directly responsible for the bloodshed at Monterrey as Liberals assumed, judging from the findings of E. Victor Niemeyer, Jr., "The Public Career of General Bernardo Reyes" (Ph.D. dissertation), pp. 177–186.

decline of work, general discontent, and a veritable malaise among all classes of society." Finally, the manifesto again implied that, failing the removal of Díaz from office, a violent revolution was the only viable alternative for Mexico.[50]

Five days later—April 16, 1903—police invaded the offices of *El Hijo del Ahuizote* and confiscated all equipment. Arrested on the trumped-up charge of "contempt of public officials in the exercise of their duty" were Juan and Manuel Sarabia, Ricardo and Enrique Flores Magón, Rivera, De la Vega, Cravioto, Macías Valadés, Rosalío Bustamante, and Federico Pérez Fernández, among others. At the time of the attack, *El Hijo del Ahuizote* claimed a circulation of twenty-four thousand. The prisoners were held incommunicado in Belén for two and one-half months. Some were released, including apparently Rivera, who went underground. Juan Sarabia, Ricardo and Enrique Flores Magón, Cravioto, and De la Vega remained in Belén until October of 1903.

With the San Luis Potosí nucleus thus removed, the Díaz regime finished jailing and driving into exile all remaining Liberal opposition journalists in Mexico City. The presses of *Vésper, Excélsior, El Padre del Ahuizote, El Nieto del Ahuizote,* and *La Voz de Juárez* were confiscated, and their editors and chief writers were jailed. Paulino Martínez, editor of *La Voz de Juárez,* escaped into U.S. exile. All the journalists involved were threatened, at least indirectly, with death if they tried to publish again. A decree dated June 9, 1903, forbade publication of any article written by those journalists of *El Hijo del Ahuizote* who had been jailed on April 16, 1903.[51]

In Belén Prison, Juan Sarabia, Ricardo and Enrique Flores Magón, Cravioto, De la Vega, De la Hoz, Rosalío Bustamante, and Macías Valadés—that is, eight of the prisoners, half of them from San Luis Potosí—laid plans for a revolution against Porfirio Díaz, checking whenever possible for the views of their colleagues in other jails,

50 *El Hijo del Ahuizote,* April 19, 1903; Barrera Fuentes, pp. 138–142; Martínez Núñez, *Juan Sarabia,* I, 165.

51 De la Vega; interviews with Cravioto and Pérez Fernández, *El Demócrata,* September 2–3, 1924; articles by Enrique Flores Magón in Section II-D of the Bibliography; Martínez Núñez, *Juan Sarabia,* I, 165–190; Barrera Fuentes, pp. 145–146; Duffy Turner, pp. 56–59.

underground, or exile. All agreed to conceal their "revolutionary Socialism," derived from Bakunin. They decided that the words "Socialism" and "Anarchism," so unfavorably distorted by the mass media, should not be used in the revolution's program, which at first would have to be general and not too threatening in its labor and agrarian sections. The appeal to Liberals would be maintained. Upon release from prison, the revolutionaries would go to the United States, renew publication of *Regeneración,* form a "recruitment board" (*junta organizadora*) for the Partido Liberal Mexicano (PLM), and write a revolutionary program with social and economic substance for labor and the peasantry. They would then organize trusted PLM members into armed revolutionary cells. "In case of failure in the first uprising," they agreed "to keep repeating the attempts until the movement spreads." Finally, they decided that their group would evolve more and more openly toward "libertarian Socialism," without the need for a transitional phase of "state Socialism." This constituted an important concession to the Anarchism of Ricardo Flores Magón, who already was emerging as a prominent leader of the movement.[52]

Although Enrique Flores Magón, not always a trustworthy or consistent source, reported the radical nature of the prisoners' plotting some twenty years after the fact, two letters of Díaz Soto y Gama to Ricardo Flores Magón in the autumn of 1903 confirm the general plan of attack along such lines. The only difference is that Díaz Soto y Gama envisioned, in one form or another, the continued leadership of Arriaga. On October 15, 1903, Díaz Soto y Gama wrote to Ricardo from his Texas exile: "Your idea of going to New York to found a newspaper delights me . . . and there is no better impetus than that which Camilo can give to all the movement." When Ricardo answered on October 23, describing the program he and his companions in jail had conceived, Díaz Soto y Gama replied, on November 3, that "more

---

[52] Enrique Flores Magón, "Notas breves de un viejo revolucionario en defensa del Partido Liberal Mexicano, iniciador de la Revolución Social Mexicana," *Gráfico,* January 19, 1931, and "La vida de los Flores Magón," *Todo,* May 8, 1934. Flores Magón's memories of this plotting are not contradicted in any substantial way by those of other participants. The newspapers *El Padre del Ahuizote, El Nieto del Ahuizote,* and the Mexico City version of *La Voz de Juárez* are not listed in the Bibliography because copies are not available in the appropriate archives.

than anything, we must dedicate ourselves to the regeneration of the oppressed classes, those suffering the exploitation of the artful and sybaritic bourgeois." He affirmed to Ricardo that he was "a convinced socialist, or better said, a communist through and through." As such, he supported the goals of "labor's regeneration, punishment of the unscrupulous exploiter, profound reforms that shake to the roots our ancient social organization . . . triumphs more genuine for the cause of the poor, the worker, the modern victim." In the same letter, Díaz Soto y Gama reiterated his previous offer to procure funds for the revolution from the sale of Camilo Arriaga's property in San Luis Potosí. Arriaga, in earlier correspondence with Ricardo, had conceived the idea.[53]

Thus, as 1903 drew to a close, there was a striking similarity to the closing months of 1901 and 1902 insofar as the San Luis Potosí "nucleus" was concerned: it was, at least metaphorically, still in the "cell." Arriaga and Díaz Soto y Gama were in U.S. exile, where they shortly would be joined by Juan Sarabia. Rivera was underground in Mexico. In spite of the ideological and tactical transformation within the Liberal Club movement since its 1900 inception, all four men remained united on essentials. Indeed, all four, no matter how different their reasons and social backgrounds, had agreed and contributed to the radicalization of the movement far beyond its initial anticlericalism. All now aspired to launch and maintain a national revolutionary movement to overthrow Díaz and to introduce profound social and economic reforms. Curiously, not one of the four Potosinos realized that such a revolutionary movement had already been launched and had been developing its own momentum, with themselves in the lead, since August of 1900.

[53] Originals in Relaciones, L-E-918; cf. Martínez Núñez, *Juan Sarabia*, I, 192–199.

CHAPTER FIVE

Exile, Division, and the PLM Program, 1904–1906

THREATENING THE durability of the Precursors' political coalition against Díaz were certain personal, ideological, and social forces, which became increasingly divisive during the 1904–1906 period of exile. Basic differences in social background and political conviction began to divide the Precursors at the very time they were organizing the PLM, formulating its program, and preparing for the 1906–1908 revolts.

For a month or two these differences remained submerged, as Camilo Arriaga continued to be a prominent leader of the Precursor Movement. Arriaga paid most of the travel expenses of Ricardo and Enrique Flores Magón, Juan and Manuel Sarabia, De la Vega, De la Hoz, and other opposition journalists who left Mexico at the end of 1903 and arrived in Texas in early 1904. On February 5, 1904—forty-seventh anniversary of the 1857 Constitution—the exiles assembled in Laredo under the auspices of the Directorate of Club Liberal "Ponciano Arriaga." There they laid plans for collecting funds to re-establish *Regeneración,* to found a political party, and to launch a revolution. Left in Mexico City to assist in the fund-raising project were Cravioto, Pérez Fernández, and other journalists, who founded in March, 1904, *El Colmillo Público*, a weekly publication concealing its political purpose under the guise of cartoons allegedly aimed at no more than "frivolity and entertainment." When eight hundred pesos had been raised, Manuel Sarabia went to San Antonio, Texas, to contract for a printing press for *Regeneración*. However, Manuel's collaborator spent the money on an apartment for a paramour.[1]

By this time, Camilo Arriaga was beginning to recognize an emerging threat to his leadership in the person of Ricardo Flores Magón. In March of 1904, Arriaga quarreled with Ricardo on the specific issue of leadership. Some of the exiles found themselves taking sides along strictly personal lines. De la Vega accompanied Arriaga to San Antonio, leaving Ricardo in Laredo. Also siding with Arriaga were Juana B. Gutiérrez de Mendoza and Elisa Acuña y Rosete, who went to San Antonio to re-establish *Vésper*. Sara Estela Ramírez, editor of the exile weekly *La Corregidora* who had maintained a long, friendly correspondence with Ricardo since 1901, wrote from San Antonio a letter to him explaining her reluctant decision to side with Arriaga.

Ramírez' letter reflects the personal nature of the leadership struggle: "I've become sad and weary, Ricardo, of so many personal antagonisms. I tell you frankly, I am disillusioned with everything, absolutely everything. . . . I don't want to analyze the causes of your quarrels with Camilito. I believe you both are right and both to blame." So far as Ramírez was concerned, the tragedy of the dispute was that "we don't know how to forgive one another's shortcomings, to help each other out like true brothers. We criticize each other and tear ourselves

1 Pérez Fernández, interview, *El Demócrata*, September 3, 1924. Footnotes covering the remainder of the 1904–1910 period will provide only for occasional discrepancies in primary and secondary sources, or for especially useful references and primary sources. In varying degrees, facts presented here are confirmed by all accounts of the Precursor Movement, as well as by this author's interviews listed in Section II–G of the Bibliography and much repetitive archival material, of which a portion is cited here. About fifteen linear feet of boxes of pertinent documents are housed by the U.S. Government in its General Archives, especially the Department of State and Justice Department, and by the Mexican Government in its General Archive, Secretaría de Relaciones Exteriores.

apart instead of inspiring one another and mending our fences." She could only hope that "by working in groups apart, separately and in different places, we will get along better and gain a new harmony."[2]

Although deep ideological and social differences underlay the division between Arriaga and Ricardo Flores Magón, apparently neither of the men wanted these points to be emphasized at such an early stage of the struggle against Díaz. Unity, even in the face of their own personal quarrel, seemed preferable. Other exiles tried to bring the two men back together. Crescencio Villarreal Márquez, editor of the Liberal newspaper *1810* (Laredo, Texas), urged Ricardo Flores Magón and Juan Sarabia "to be indulgent with Arriaga."[3]

On the other hand, San Luis Potosí individuals involved in the dispute did not unite in an effort to maintain their earlier hegemony, but rather divided for personal and only partly ideological reasons. Both Díaz Soto y Gama and Rivera were in sympathy with Ricardo Flores Magón's Anarchism, but Díaz Soto y Gama admired Arriaga too much to leave him. Rivera, on the other hand, had formed a close friendship with Flores Magón and so sided with him. Juan Sarabia leaned toward the Socialism of De la Vega, who had already declared his support for Arriaga. Yet Sarabia stayed with his cousin to help Flores Magón edit *Regeneración*, when it finally reappeared in San Antonio, November 5, 1904.[4]

Despite these quarrels, Arriaga sought to assist all the exiles, including Flores Magón, in their common effort to launch a revolution against Díaz. He played a pivotal role in financing the renewed publi-

---

[2] Sara Estela Ramírez (San Antonio, Texas) to Ricardo Flores Magón (Laredo, Texas), March 9, 1904, in Relaciones, L–E–918, which also has her earlier letters going back to 1901. The newspaper *La Corregidora* is not listed in the Bibliography because copies are not available in the appropriate archives.

[3] C. V. Márquez (Laredo, Texas) to "Sres. Flores Magón y Sarabia," July 28, 1904, in *ibid.* The newspaper *1810* is not listed in the Bibliography because copies are not available in the appropriate archives.

[4] Antonio Díaz Soto y Gama, interviews; Santiago R. de la Vega, "Los precursores de la Revolución," *El Universal*, November 20, 1932. Juan Sarabia at first stayed in Laredo with Ricardo Flores Magón, but commuted to San Antonio to procure funds from the still amiable Arriaga (Sarabia to Ricardo Flores Magón, March 12, 1904, in *ibid.*); later, in May, 1904, the Sarabias and Flores Magóns moved to San Antonio where they were welcomed by Arriaga.

cation of *Regeneración,* for which he also wrote some articles. He helped finance the Socialist weekly *Humanidad* (named after Jean Jaurès' publication) edited in San Antonio by De la Vega. Arriaga was essentially striving to preserve at least nominal unity in the movement and, at the same time, his own leadership position as co-ordinator and financial backer of the various newspapers involved.[5]

In retrospect, it seems that at stake in this struggle was the role of high-status intellectuals in the Precursor Movement—men like Arriaga and Madero. In early 1905, Arriaga succeeded in obtaining an advance of $2,000 (U.S. dollars) from Madero, using as collateral Arriaga's San Luis Potosí properties, to help finance the publication of *Regeneración.* Madero, awakened politically by the 1903 Monterrey massacre, wrote Ricardo Flores Magón that he found "all your ideas congenial" and believed that *Regeneración* would assist in the "regeneration of the Fatherland by arousing Mexicans in noble indignation against their tyrants." Madero asked Flores Magón to assist him in drafting a manifesto to urge citizens of Coahuila to exercise their right to vote in the summer gubernatorial campaign of 1905. Flores Magón readily agreed. Such collaboration, however, was destined to founder on the rocks of ideological and social differences.[6]

In February of 1905, Arriaga, Juan Sarabia, and Ricardo and Enrique Flores Magón fled harassment in Texas and took up residence in St. Louis, Missouri. Life had become impossible in San Antonio. The offices of *Regeneración* had been kept under surveillance by Díaz

[5] De la Vega; José G. Escobedo and Rosendo Salazar, *Las pugnas de la gleba,* 1907–1922, I, 56–57; *El Colmillo Público,* August 13, 1905. Jean Jaurès (1859–1914) was a prominent figure in the French Socialist Party who founded, earlier in 1904, *L'Humanité,* principal voice of French Socialists. The newspaper *Humanidad* is not listed in the Bibliography because copies are not available in the appropriate archives.

[6] Francisco I. Madero to Ricardo Flores Magón, January 17, 1905, in Madero, *Archivo de Francisco I. Madero: Epistolario (1900-1909),* pp. 109–110; Ricardo Flores Magón to F. Y. (*sic*) Madero, March 5, 1905, in private collection of José C. Valadés, cited in Stanley R. Ross, *Francisco I. Madero: Apostle of Mexican Democracy,* pp. 42–43. Cf. Valadés, "El hombre que derrumbó un régimen: Ricardo Flores Magón," *Todo,* April 16, 1942. There are discrepancies in the amount of money Madero is said to have advanced, but $2,000 is the sum usually given.

agents, one of whom had attacked Manuel Sarabia with a knife.[7] Enrique Flores Magón had been arrested by four Pinkerton detectives and sentenced to three months' imprisonment on a trumped-up charge.[8] The U.S. Post Office had insisted that *Regeneración* be mailed as second-class mail instead of fourth-class, thereby doubling the cost.[9]

In St. Louis, differences between Arriaga and Ricardo Flores Magón became aggravated when Ricardo, Rivera, Juan Sarabia, and Antonio I. Villarreal engaged in frequent conversations with Chicago Anarchist Emma Goldman and Spanish Anarchist Florencio Bazora. Goldman and Bazora were both friends of Errico Malatesta, an Anarchist leader in Europe who subsequently was to be a prominent figure at the 1907 Amsterdam Congress.[10] These talks, by leading Ricardo Flores Magón into an ever more open avowal of his Anarchism, brought out the ideological differences underlying the earlier leadership dispute between him and Arriaga. Arriaga, joined tentatively by Juan Sarabia, tried to have Ricardo "tone down" his views when printing them for the public. He was afraid that part of the growing Mexican readership might be alienated by the mass media's labeling of the movement as "Anarchist"—a word falsely associated in many people's minds with "mad bombers." Arriaga, but not Sarabia, broke with Ricardo on the

---

[7] Eugenio Martínez Núñez and Enrique Flores Magón (Samuel Kaplan, *Combatinos la tiranía* [*conversaciones con Enrique Flores Magón*], p. 135, and various articles) agree that Manuel Sarabia was the intended victim. However, Ricardo Flores Magón (Fort Leavenworth, Kansas) to Harry Weinberger (New York), May 9, 1921 (Manuel González Ramírez [ed.], *Epistolario y textos de Ricardo Flores Magón*, pp. 39–240), asserts that Ricardo was the victim of the attack, and Florencio Barrera Fuentes, Ethel Duffy Turner, and Diego Abad de Santillán, using this letter as evidence, agree. For once, because of an uncharacteristic consistency in his articles on this point, Enrique's judgment, which usually provided Ricardo whatever glory possible, may be accepted.

[8] Relaciones, L-E-918, includes a receipt for a fine Enrique Flores Magón had to pay in the case.

[9] *Ibid.* provides relevant correspondence of December, 1904, and January, 1905, between U.S. postal authorities and *Regeneración*, as well as duplicates of second-class mailing permits.

[10] Eduardo Blanquel, "El pensamiento político de Ricardo Flores Magón, precursor de la Revolución Mexicana" (unpublished Master's thesis), pp. 66–85; George Woodcock, *A History of Libertarian Ideas and Movements*, pp. 265–267.

issue, returning to San Antonio with De la Vega to write for *Humanidad*.

Madero and other Precursor elements from the upper class now, and over the next few years, pulled back from plans for armed revolution being drawn up by Ricardo Flores Magón, Juan Sarabia, Villarreal, Rivera, and the group from *Regeneración*. Arriaga, by his own testimony, had told Flores Magón of Madero's desire to have the $2,000 advance for *Regeneración* returned. At the same time, Arriaga's personal funds were running low.[11] Ricardo Flores Magón was distressed at Madero's withdrawal of support, because, as he wrote in 1907, he thought that Madero, "with the money that he could give, might save the situation today." In these initial, relatively mild phases of the Flores Magón–Madero controversy, which was to become ever more exacerbated over the next few years, Arriaga apparently sought to keep the peace. According to Ricardo Flores Magón, however, Arriaga was to blame for the split with Madero: "Madero and I were good friends until that miserable turncoat Arriaga started slandering me."[12]

Madero thought otherwise. He washed his hands of the Flores Magóns, who upset him not only by their revolutionary politics but also by their "insulting everyone," especially "spotless Liberals like Engineer Camilo Arriaga."[13] Even if the Díaz government was bad, Madero later wrote his grandfather, in a letter meant to reassure his family about his political sentiments, at least the country was "progressing, even if not as rapidly as desirable." A revolution would cause "more evil to the country than the bad government we have." Looking back on the 1906 PLM revolt, Madero concluded that it was "a useless shedding of blood causing untold harm to the nation."[14]

11 Arriaga, in statements to De la Vega and Bernal, both of whom recounted them to Ethel Duffy Turner (*Ricardo Flores Magón y el Partido Liberal Mexicano*, pp. 74, 372); cf. Manuel Ramírez Arriaga, "Camilo Arriaga," *Repertorio de la Revolución*, No. 4 (May 1, 1960), p. 21; Madero's letters in Madero, *Archivo*, pp. 139–172; Ross, p. 43; Charles C. Cumberland, *Mexican Revolution: Genesis under Madero*, pp. 45–46.
12 Ricardo Flores Magón to Antonio de P. Araujo, June 6, 1907, in González Ramírez (ed.), *Epistolario*, pp. 107–110.
13 Madero to C. V. Márquez, August 17, 1906, in Madero, *Archivo*, pp. 165–166.
14 Madero to Evaristo Madero, October 1, 1906, *ibid.*, pp. 172–173.

Arriaga thus found himself unable to maintain the coalition he had so assiduously put together during the previous years. Heretofore co-operating upper-class elements, not yet hit by the 1907–1911 economic crisis, were retreating from the revolutionary brink. Lower-class elements, on the other hand, responding to left-wing exhortations of their petty-bourgeois intellectual mentors, were beginning to organize themselves for the 1906–1908 strikes and revolts which were to plague the Díaz Administration from 1906 on.

Arriaga's San Luis Potosí friends, although greatly upset by the increasing indications of disintegration of the broad-based coalition, did not view the split between the Flores Magóns and Arriaga and Madero as sufficient cause for their withdrawal from the PLM. On the contrary, they preserved part of the earlier San Luis Potosí hegemony by joining Ricardo Flores Magón in September, 1905, to found the PLM Recruitment Board (*Junta Organizadora*). Four of the board's seven members were from San Luis Potosí: Juan and Manuel Sarabia, Rivera, and Rosalío Bustamante.[15] Díaz Soto y Gama was no longer able to assist directly, having had to return to San Luis Potosí in 1904 to help support his family. He had done this only after vainly attempting to publish a newspaper in San Antonio with Arriaga's assistance and then collaborating with the El Paso anti-Díaz newspaper *La Reforma Social.*[16] In spite of this dispersal of his San Luis Potosí following, Arriaga persisted in his efforts to moderate the Precursor Movement and preserve its broad appeal by joining with Díaz Soto y Gama and Juan Sarabia in arguing against Flores Magón and Rivera for less radical, more diverse ideological appeals in the PLM's program, then in the first stages of drafting.

Arriaga was unable to commit himself entirely to the kind of workers' and peasants' revolution envisioned by PLM Recruitment Board

[15] *Regeneración,* September 30, 1905; *El Colmillo Público,* October 5, 1905; Eugenio Martínez Núñez, *Juan Sarabia, apóstol y mártir de la Revolución Mexicana,* I, 267–268.

[16] De la Vega, who observed that in 1904 the Precursor Movement lost both its "mystic" (Díaz Soto y Gama) and its "poet" (De la Hoz, who drowned accidentally on March 22, 1904); Díaz Soto y Gama, interviews. The newspaper *La Reforma Social* is not listed in the Bibliography because copies are not available in the appropriate archives.

president Ricardo Flores Magón. For the moment, he saw his role as one of moderation and cautious support for the PLM. His break with Flores Magón, however, was irreparable. In an article published by *El Colmillo Público* in October, 1905, Flores Magón excoriated Arriaga as a virtual traitor:

> Today, Camilo resides at the Consulate in St. Louis, Missouri, sits at the same table as the Consul. . . . He has chosen to abandon his ideals, to turn his back on the Liberals, and to meekly beg of the Powers That Be whatever scrap of bread or sliver of meat they deign to toss him, in exchange for confidential services that no word in the lexicon of honor can describe.[17]

Other San Luis Potosí figures regretted this ungrateful attack on Arriaga, but did not break their relationships with Flores Magón. Juan Sarabia, for example, became vice-president of PLM. In his letters from prison in 1910, Sarabia had only the fondest of memories and highest of admiration for Ricardo Flores Magón.[18]

In spite of the difficulties with Arriaga and Madero, and in defiance of continued harassment by Díaz agents, Ricardo Flores Magón and his followers began to succeed in their political campaign to organize the PLM and launch a revolution. Employing a political smuggling network of small shopkeepers stationed along the U.S.–Mexican border and railroad workers inside Mexico, the exiles sent thousands of copies of *Regeneración* into Mexico. Among those receiving the newspaper were such future heroes of the Mexican Revolution as Socialist Governor of Yucatán (1915–1918) Salvador Alvarado, President (1911–1913) Madero, President (1914–1915) Eulalio Gutiérrez, President (1924–1928) Plutarco Elías Calles, and Sonoran revolutionary commanders José María Maytorena and Adolfo de la Huerta. In addition, large numbers of small shopkeepers, merchants, artisans, workers, and peasants read the weekly with surprising regularity. *Regeneración's* circulation rose from eleven thousand to twenty thousand by September, 1905, and to thirty thousand in 1906.[19]

17 *El Colmillo Público*, October 8, 1905.

18 Juan Sarabia (San Juan de Ulúa Prison) to Manuel Sarabia (Los Angeles, California), August 10, 1910, and to Antonio I. Villarreal (Los Angeles, California), September 29, October 26, 1910, in Martínez Núñez, *Juan Sarabia*, I, 499–530.

19 Valadés, "El hombre que derrumbó un régimen: Ricardo Flores Magón," *Todo,*

In *Regeneración*'s offices, Juan Sarabia, Ricardo Flores Magón, De la Vega, Rivera's former student Villarreal, and, in the early phases, Arriaga handled all major articles and correspondence, while Rivera, Bustamante, and Enrique Flores Magón ran administrative matters. Pinkerton detective Thomas Furlong reported that "the revolutionary fanatics" Ricardo Flores Magón, Juan Sarabia, and Villarreal formed the core leadership of the movement.[20]

On September 28, 1905, the seven-man Recruitment Board of the PLM issued the party's founding statutes in a manifesto to the Mexican nation. The "Bases for Unification of the Mexican Liberal Party" were as follows: *Regeneración* as PLM's official newspaper; formation of secret PLM cells inside Mexico; a membership drive guaranteeing the secrecy of all names involved; and financial backing of oppositionist newspapers and impoverished or persecuted Liberals inside Mexico.[21]

Two weeks later—October 12, 1905—agents of the Pinkerton Detective Agency, acting without warrants and not having been deputized, invaded the St. Louis offices of *Regeneración,* confiscated the presses, files, and equipment, and detained Juan Sarabia and the Flores Magóns. The three men were charged with "libel and defamation" by Manuel

May 21, 1942; Enrique Flores Magón, "El Partido Liberal (acción e ideología)," *El Nacional,* January 18, 1954, and "La vida de los Flores Magón," *Todo,* May 15, 1934; Martínez Núñez, *Juan Sarabia,* I, 46. Relaciones, L-E-918–954, provides hundreds of letters of contribution and lists of names running into the thousands, relating to *Regeneración;* many of the letters from working-class supporters are semiliterate. J. Pérez Fernández (Mexico City) to Antonio Y. (*sic*)Villarreal (St. Louis, Missouri), November 10, 1905, reveals that Luis Cabrera, later chief intellectual adviser to Carranza, contributed eighteen dollars. Armando de María y Campos (*Música, crónica biográfica,* p. 20) points out that Francisco J. Múgica, later a leading "Jacobin" at the 1916–1917 Querétaro Constitutional Convention, read *Regeneración* faithfully. Silva Herzog and Aurelio Manrique, Jr., in interviews with this author, stated that San Luis Potosí artisans shared with them their copies of *Regeneración* often. Circulation of *Regeneración* inside Mexico was still as high as twenty thousand by 1910, in spite of the Díaz regime's suppression and control of the mails, according to U.S. Consul Luther T. Ellsworth (Cd. Porfirio Díaz, Coahuila) to U.S. Secretary of State, September 20, 1910, in U.S. Department of Justice Archives, file number 90755 (hereafter referred to as Justice, followed by file number).

[20] Anonymous, "El informe secreto de la 'Pinkerton,'" *El Demócrata,* September 4, 6, 1924.

[21] *Regeneración,* September 30, 1905; *El Colmillo Público,* October 5, 1905; Martínez Núñez, *Juan Sarabia,* I, 267–268.

Esperón y de la Flor, a Oaxacan cacique whom *Regeneración* had attacked in past issues. Esperón y de la Flor, according to a circular of the PLM's Recruitment Board thanking Mexican Liberals for their financial aid in posting bond for the prisoners, had been sent to St. Louis by Porfirio Díaz specifically to press these "trumped-up" charges. The three PLM leaders were held in jail until mid-December, 1905, when they succeeded in posting a $10,000-bond, raised in large part during an intensive campaign inside Mexico by *El Colmillo Público,* as well as in the United States by various Socialists and Anarchists and the St. Louis *Post-Dispatch* and St. Louis *Globe Democrat*.[22]

U.S. left-wing support of the PLM built up during the next few years. The American Left and PLM were natural allies. Pinkerton detectives played a critical role not only in the persecution of PLM exiles but also in the arrest of U.S. radicals, as in the Haywood–Moyer case of 1905–1907. "Big Bill" Haywood and Charles Moyer were leaders of the extremely militant Western Federation of Miners, largest union behind the founding of the Industrial Workers of the World (IWW). Agitators from the Western Federation of Miners assisted PLM labor organizers in southern Arizona and northern Sonora in developing militancy among Mexican copper miners employed by Colonel William C. Greene. Their results would be manifested in part during the Cananea strike and PLM revolt of 1906. Prior to that, however, Haywood and Moyer were falsely accused of the murder of Idaho Governor Frank Steunenberg. This case became a national storm center involving President Theodore Roosevelt, the trade-union movement, and the press (workers everywhere picked up the chant, "If Moyer and Haywood die, if Moyer and Haywood die, Twenty million workingmen will know the reason why!"). Haywood and Moyer, after a stormy and

22 Junta Organizadora del Partido Liberal Mexicano (St. Louis, Missouri) circular to "Estimado correligionario," December 8, 1905, in González Ramírez (ed.), *Epistolario,* pp. 58–59. *El Colmillo Público,* December 31, 1905, reproduced an article from the St. Louis *Star Chronicle* of October 15, 1905, which reported the Liberals' version of the affair as fact, even though the *Star Chronicle* did not support the fundraising campaign. *El Colmillo Público,* December 24, 1905, and January 14, 1906, provided further details on the case, as well as reports of the success in raising funds, which came from all over Mexico, including the "Sociedad Hidalgo" of Cananea's mining community. For accounts in St. Louis newspapers, consult Relaciones, L-E-942–944, and Justice, 90755.

lengthy trial that rallied left-wing support from coast to coast, were acquitted in late 1907.

Their case set the pattern for subsequent IWW, Syndicalist, Anarchist, and Socialist campaigns in the United States in defense of jailed companions, including Mexicans from the PLM. Thus, when Rivera, Ricardo Flores Magón, and Villarreal, arrested by Pinkerton detectives, were kept in jail from 1907 to 1910, American Socialist lawyers Job Harriman and A. R. Holston provided an eloquent, if vain, legal defense of the men. Socialist leader Eugene V. Debs, who contributed to *Appeal to Reason* (Girard, Kansas) articles in defense of the PLM leaders, made their jailing an issue in the United States' 1908 Presidential campaign. Socialists Harriman, Primrose D. Noel and Frances Noel, John Murray, James ("Jimmy") Roche, John Kenneth Turner, Ethel Duffy Turner, and Boston heiress Elizabeth Darling Trowbridge spent months and years propagandizing for the PLM through *The Border* (Tucson, Arizona), *Appeal to Reason*, and other periodicals. With the assistance of Lázaro Gutiérrez de Lara, a PLM Socialist from Cananea, Sonora, John Kenneth Turner made trips to Mexico to collect material for his book *Barbarous Mexico*. Its publication in the form of articles in *The American Magazine* (New York) during the autumn of 1909 caused an uproar among Díaz supporters throughout the world, including Stanford University's progressive educator David Starr Jordan.[23]

From late 1905 on, an international system of persecution of the

[23] Ray Ginger, *Eugene V. Debs: A Biography*, pp. 261–273; Ambassador Enrique Creel to Secretario de Relaciones Exteriores, October 31, 1908, in Relaciones, L-E-944; González Ramírez (ed.), *Epistolario*, p. 222; U.S. Supreme Court, *In the Matter of the Application of R. Flores Magón, Antonio I. Villarreal and Librado Rivera, for a Writ of Habeas Corpus;* U.S. House of Representatives, *Hearings on House Joint Resolution 201 Providing for a Joint Committee to Investigate Alleged Persecutions of Mexican Citizens by the Government of Mexico;* documents in Relaciones, L-E-942–944, State, 100, and Justice 43718, 90755; David Starr Jordan, *The Days of a Man, Being Memories of a Naturalist, Teacher and Minor Prophet of Democracy,* I, 639–645. The impact of Turner's articles is not to be underestimated. See Manuel González Ramírez, *La revolución social de México: las ideas—la violencia,* pp. 107–111; Librado Rivera, "La mano férrea de la dictadura y el Congreso Liberal de San Luis," *Gráfico,* December 14, 1930; Alejandro Carrillo, "Una historia de amistad yanqui-mexicana," *Mañana,* April 10, 1954.

PLM was developed. Co-operating in this system were the Pinkerton Detective Agency; the Mexican Embassy in Washington, D.C.; Mexican consulates throughout the United States; the Secretariat of Foreign Relations in Mexico City; the U.S. Embassy in Mexico; the U.S. Departments of State, War, Treasury, Commerce, Labor, Justice, and Immigration; both nations' Presidents; and such leading foreign businessmen in Mexico as William C. Greene, mining magnate of Cananea. The Mexican Government paid for private-detective service in the United States; it also paid stipends and gave "gifts" to various of the U.S. officials who co-operated. A heavy correspondence between the governmental and private institutions involved indicates large-scale collaboration in keeping watch over the Mexican exile community.[24]

24 Archival materials in the Bibliography, II-A. A good summary is Mexican Consul M. E. Diebold (St. Louis, Missouri) to Secretario de Relaciones Exteriores (Mexico City), November 1 and 13, 1906, in Relaciones, L-E-920, and February 17, 1909, in González Ramírez (ed.), *Epistolario,* pp. 171–177. The Consul boasted of extensive co-operation from U.S. authorities and, among other details, noted that more than three thousand PLM letters had been intercepted (at least that many can be found in Relaciones). See also, Anonymous, "El informe secreto de la 'Pinkerton,' " *El Demócrata,* September 4 and 6, 1924, a report made by Pinkerton detective Thomas Furlong in the summer of 1906 and delivered to Governor Enrique Creel of Chihuahua (later Mexican Ambassador to the United States), who on October 28, 1906, submitted it to President Díaz. Mexican payment of Pinkerton detectives was confirmed by: Mexican Secretary of Foreign Relations to Mexican Embassy in the United States, November 4, 1906 (Relaciones, L-E-920); Mexican Embassy to U.S. Department of State, November 6, 1906 (State, 1730); Furlong's testimony in U.S. Supreme Court, *In the Matter,* pp. 203–205. Specific examples of the Mexican–U.S. Pinkerton surveillance system follow. On "Operative Joe Priest" of the Secret Service Division of the U.S. Treasury Department: Acting Secretary of Treasury to Attorney General, August 29, 1906, in Justice, 43718. On William C. Greene's participation: Consul Diebold's letters and Greene to Acting Secretary of State Robert Bacon, September 12 and 13, 1906, in State, 100, and Justice, 43718. On the kidnaping of Manuel Sarabia (*q.v.* in Section II–D of the Bibliography): Phoenix (Arizona) Consul Augustín Pima to Secretario de Relaciones Exteriores, July 3, 1907, in Relaciones, L-E-926. On the August, 1907, arrest of Ricardo Flores Magón, Rivera, and Villarreal: Los Angeles Consul Antonio Lozano to Secretario de Relaciones Exteriores, September 1, 1907, in González Ramírez (ed.), *Epistolario,* pp. 122–127, and U.S. Attorney General to U.S. Attorney in Los Angeles, August 28, 1907, in Justice, 90755. On Phoenix Consul Arturo M. Elías' crediting U.S. Attorney J. L. B. Alexander with the PLM leaders' conviction and giving Alexander a five-hundred-dollar ring purchased by the Mexican Government as a token of its gratitude: Elías to Secretario

In March, 1906, Juan Sarabia and the Flores Magóns, suspecting that the Mexican Government might succeed in arranging for their extradition to Mexico, forfeited their bond and fled to Toronto, Canada. In Canada the three PLM leaders were again harassed by Pinkerton agents; $20,000-rewards were offered by the Mexican Government for the capture of each one. In May, 1906, they fled from Toronto to Montreal.

Left behind in St. Louis in charge of *Regeneración* were Rivera, Villarreal, and Manuel Sarabia. *Regeneración* had renewed publication on February 1, 1906, in spite of a new U.S. postal regulation designating it as first-class mail. Parts of the PLM Program were already drafted, and the final version, though dated St. Louis, July 1, 1906, was probably written from points as distant from St. Louis as Toronto, Montreal, and Ciudad Juárez. (Villarreal had gone to this last-named border town to oversee the formation of armed revolutionary units scheduled to revolt for the PLM in September of 1906.) Villarreal was responsible for the education and debt-peonage sections of the PLM Program, and Juan Sarabia wrote those pertaining to peasants and workers. Cananea's labor-union leaders also played an important role in drafting the labor code. Ricardo Flores Magón drafted an accompanying "expository" section for the PLM Program. Innumerable Mexicans of all classes were consulted through the mails and by word of mouth.[25]

Juan Sarabia "edited" the entire Program and, with the assistance of Arriaga and others, was able to moderate the Flores Magóns' and Rivera's Anarchist predilections. One of Ricardo Flores Magón's biographers has asserted that the program "owes a great deal to Sarabia." In spite of Sarabia's important editing role, however, it appears that, as Sarabia's biographer has asserted, the PLM Program was not the work

de Relaciones Exteriores, May 19, 1909, and March 10, 1910, in González Ramírez (ed.), *Epistolario*, pp. 157–161. On Mexican payment of U.S. sheriffs: various bills and receipts in Relaciones, e.g., Elías to Secretario de Relaciones Exteriores, September 19, 1908, in L-E-941.

[25] There are no discrepancies in the sources on these points, but conclusive evidence can be found in Manuel González Ramírez (ed.), *Fuentes para la historia de la Revolución Mexicana*, III, 111, and his *La revolución social*, p. 57.

of any "single" hand, but rather was the product of years of collaboration between the Precursors and consultation through the mails.[26]

The February 20, 1906, issue of *Regeneración* already had invited readers to mail in recommendations for the PLM Program and future political action. Those correspondents who came out in favor of violent revolution were immediately recruited to head PLM armed units.

The stage was now set for the launching of PLM's revolutionary program. Its impact was to have repercussions for years to come. Dated July 1, 1906, the Program's radical social content was to be imitated, though never equaled in its entirety, by revolutionary proclamations throughout the 1911–1917 period. Its labor platform would be adopted in great part by the major labor movement of the Mexican Revolution. Its socio-economic proposals formed a basis for many of the innovations of the 1917 Constitution.[27] If the PLM Program was the first to present publicly and nationally the major socio-economic ideas of the Mexican Revolution, it also was the only public document to go beyond the 1917 Constitution in various progressive aspects—in spite of the fact that the authors of the PLM Program deliberately toned down their statement in order not to alienate sympathetic but conservative upper-class elements, while drafters of the 1917 Constitution, by means of "Jacobin" majorities, deliberately radicalized their statement in order to meet the demands of an aroused peasantry and working class which had fought the Revolution.[28] As a Precursor document, the PLM Program remains without parallel.[29]

The longest section of the PLM Program was the "Exposition,"

---

[26] Diego Abad de Santillán, *Ricardo Flores Magón, el apóstol de la Revolución Social Mexicana*, p. 19; Martínez Núñez, *Juan Sarabia*, I, 324–325. Díaz Soto y Gama wrote letters supporting strong municipal and agrarian sections and urging a war against middlemen and moneylenders (interview, March 19, 1965).

[27] Since many of these innovations were "in the air" throughout the post-PLM Program period, historians have agreed that the PLM document itself may not have been used directly during the 1916–1917 Querétaro Constitutional Convention, but that, in any case, the similarities between the PLM Program and the Constitution are striking.

[28] Djed Bórquez, *Crónica del constituyente;* Gabriel Ferrer Mendiolea, *Historia del Congreso Constituyente de 1916–1917.*

[29] Appendix A provides the fifty-two points of the PLM Program and a point-by-point analysis comparing it with the 1917 Constitution.

which preceded and explained the fifty-two points. The Exposition was intended to appeal to all Mexicans, to workers and peasants especially, but also to businessmen, industrialists, and even large landholders. Specific appeals were addressed to the rank-and-file of the military; to anticlericals (one-seventh of the Exposition); to workers (one-fifth); to peasants (one-fifth); to nationalistic, profit-minded businessmen; to productive *latifundistas;* and to Yankeephobes from all classes.

Point 4 of the Program, by appealing to draftees and a potential popular militia rather than to the officers of Mexico's Army, reflected PLM's concern for the lower classes. It was the opposite of Article 9 of Presidential candidate Madero's April 20, 1910, political platform, which appealed essentially to the military elite.[30] As the PLM Program's Exposition stated: "The Army of the future must be one of volunteers, not of people forced against their will, and, for that purpose, the Nation must offer its soldiers a decent wage and must eliminate from the military system that cruel brutality and inflexibility which now insult and crush human dignity."

Points 10–14 emphasized the need for universal, free, secular education. The Exposition further devoted an impassioned, long paragraph proposing substantially higher wages for Mexico's underpaid, overworked primary schoolteachers, many of whom were destined to play such an important role in the Revolution.

The PLM Program included advanced and, for its time, radical provisions in its "Capital and Labor" section (Points 21–33). It provided, among other things, for an eight-hour work day, a minimum wage, abolishing child labor, guaranteed job safety and hygienic work conditions, accident indemnization, Sunday rest, cash wages, abolishing company stores, and the canceling of debts. Despite this broad program, the Exposition admitted that the labor section was inadequate, a mere "first step." Because of their anticipation of government suppression of strikes, Cananea's labor leaders had been deliberately cautious in their recommendations for the Program's labor code. Nevertheless, Cananea schoolteacher and labor leader Esteban Baca Calderón envisioned a strong labor movement which would provide the PLM with

[30] For text of Madero's Article 9, see Jesús Silva Herzog, *Breve historia de la Revolución Mexicana,* I, 74.

mass revolutionary support. Writing two months prior to the Cananea strike of June, 1906, Baca Calderón told PLM secretary Villarreal:

A Miners Union must be organized right away, without a hostile stance or political manifesto, at least for now. Later, we should invite all miners in the Republic to found their respective unions so that we might all then merge into the Liga Minera de los Estados Unidos Mexicanos ... which in turn will provide mass and militant support for the Liberal Party.[31]

Scattered throughout the Program and its Exposition were indirect reminders of the Mexican Government's military suppression of, and the armed intervention of the United States in, the Cananea strike (discussed in the following chapter). An appeal to workers and peasants implicitly recalled this, while at the same time reminding the lower classes of the Marxist dictum that "the worker is the producer of all wealth," yet "the sovereign capitalist" enjoys the worker's produce.

The program also tried to attract energetic Mexican businessmen to agrarian reform by noting the potential expansion of internal markets:

When the millions of pariahs now vegetating in nakedness and starvation begin to eat better, wear clothes and shoes, and have more than the palm-mat which now constitutes their only piece of furniture, demand for a thousand kinds of goods, which today is insignificant, will increase until it reaches colossal proportions.

On the tacit assumption (Points 34–37, 50) that uncultivated lands, government lands, lands "robbed" by the Porfiristas, and *ejidos* that had been broken up or seized would suffice to provide land for all peasants, and that an agrarian bank would protect the interests of poorer peasants, the Program tried to combine sweeping guarantees to the Mexican peasantry with an assurance for productive large landholders, given in the Exposition: "Those lands which are planted and cultivated, or used as pasture for cattle and so on, are not going to be taken away, but only those that are unproductive or abandoned by the landowners themselves and that in fact do not bring them any yield."

31 Baca Calderón to Villarreal, April 6, 1906, in González Ramírez (ed.), *Fuentes,* III, 9–10. On the Cananea labor leaders' caution, see other letters in *ibid.,* 109, and José C. Valadés, "El hombre que derrumbó un régimen: Ricardo Flores Magón," *Todo,* May 21, 1942.

All these points, especially nationalism and the "anticapitalist" appeal to labor and the peasantry, were accented in the impassioned manifesto concluding the PLM Program:

Everything will change in the future.
Public offices will not be for lackeys and intriguers. . . .
No longer will there be present the Dictatorship, always at hand to advise the capitalists who rob the worker or to use the Armed Forces as protection for foreigners who reply to peaceful petitions of Mexican workers with showers of bullets. . . .
Mexicans! Between the offerings of despotism and those of the Liberal Party's Program, make your choice! If you want to be bound with fetters, misery, humiliation at the feet of the foreigner, and the gray existence of a debased pariah, then choose the Dictatorship which provides you all that; but if you prefer freedom, economic betterment, the dignity of a Mexican citizen, and the proud existence of a man who is master of himself, then join the Liberal Party . . .
Reform, Liberty, and Justice.[32]

---

[32] Text in Silva Herzog, *Breve historia,* I, 76–107. According to Librado Rivera ("La mano férrea de la dictadura ye el Congreso Liberal de San Luis," *Gráfico,* December 14, 1930), 250,000 copies of the PLM Program were printed, many of which reached Mexico via the "underground" railroad. After publication of the Program, the San Luis Potosí four-to-three majority on PLM's Recruitment Board ended, as Rosalío Bustamante withdrew from the movement—perhaps because he opposed the use of violence, although his subsequent testimony was ambiguous on the point (letter from Tampico, September 11, 1924, in *El Demócrata,* September 16, 1924).

CHAPTER SIX

PLM Strikes and Revolts,
1906–1908

THOUGH IN EFFECT serving diverse and often conflicting ambitions of different individuals, groups, and classes, the PLM Program was strongly oriented toward labor. This labor orientation reflected the emergence in Mexico of a strong labor movement in the first decade of the twentieth century.

From 1906 to 1908, large-scale strikes occurred in Cananea (Sonora), Río Blanco (Veracruz), San Luis Potosí, and various mining and industrial centers in northern Mexico. The main political force behind these strikes was the PLM. As early as mid-1906, a Pinkerton detective linked "the working class" with the PLM when he reported that *Regeneración* was financed almost entirely by small donations from workers throughout Mexico.[1]

Labor strikes not only reflected nationwide antiforeign sentiment and antiemployer resentment among workers, but also served to alert

[1] Anonymous, "El informe secreto de la 'Pinkerton,' " *El Demócrata*, September 4, 1924.

advisers of President Díaz to a groundswell of revolt from below, among the lower classes. In addition, the strikes provided impetus, or at least rhetoric, for PLM revolts in 1906 and 1908. That these strikes were considered a serious threat to the economic and political system of the Porfiriato is suggested by the swiftness with which Mexican federal troops and U.S. "volunteers" rushed to suppress them.

The first major disturbance occurred at Cananea on June 1, 1906, when thousands of workers struck at William C. Greene's Cananea Consolidated Copper Company, a subsidiary of Anaconda. Reacting to a wage increase granted Americans but not Mexicans, the workers walked out in demand of an eight-hour day, a minimum wage, and the introduction of the merit system to displace discriminatory hiring practices. A shooting incident at the company's lumber yard, in which 3 Mexicans and 2 Americans were killed, provoked two days of rioting. During these first forty-eight hours, Mexican *Rurales,* gendarmes, and soldiers rushed from their distant garrisons toward the northern border and Cananea. Responding to Greene's urgent telephone appeals, some 275 armed U.S. volunteers from across the border at Naco, Arizona, arrived first. They were under the nominal command of Captain Thomas Rynning and 5 other Arizona Rangers. The United States Government learned of this intervention after the volunteers had arrived in Mexico. Territorial Governor Joseph H. Kibbey of Arizona telegraphed Captain Rynning that territorial officials should not enter Mexico and that civilian volunteers would do so at their own risk. However, these actions came too late to restrain Rynning and his group.

Established U.S. policy during the 1906–1910 period was to patrol all border areas carefully, but not necessarily to enter Mexican territory. Nevertheless, on June 2, 1906, Secretary of State Elihu Root wired U.S. Ambassador David E. Thompson the following instructions: "Ascertain whether, discreetly, Mexican Government would welcome or acquiesce in assistance of United States troops to preserve order in this emergency, special, pending arrival of Mexican troops." Thompson informed Root on June 3 that President Díaz, who viewed the Cananea disturbance as part of a PLM revolution, would "be glad to have federal soldiers' assistance," but only if the situation worsened, "which he

thinks not likely." Four troops of U.S. Cavalry were dispatched from
Fort Huachuca to Naco but did not cross the border. The main purpose
of dispatching armed American volunteers to Cananea, so far as
Greene and worried Mexican officials were concerned, was to provide
a quick show of strength, since the *Rurales* would not be able to arrive
from their headquarters in Magdalena for at least twenty hours. This
aim was accomplished, as the volunteers marched up and down Cananea's streets without, according to Arizona newspaper accounts, firing
a shot. When the *Rurales* arrived, the volunteers returned to the U.S.
side of the border. They had spent only about twelve hours in Cananea,
but the scandal of "Yankee intervention" has not subsided in Mexico
to this day.

Until June 5 or 6, intermittent shooting continued at Cananea.
About 2,000 Mexican troops finally put down the strike, leaving a toll
of from 30 to 100 Mexican dead, 6 American dead, and countless
wounded. On January 6, Sonora's Military Governor threatened to
draft 2,000 striking Mexican miners into the Army and send them to
fight rebellious Yaqui Indians in southern Sonora if they did not return to work. Within a few days, the strike ended.[2]

Sonoran Governor Rafael Izábal wired Vice President Ramón Corral
information about PLM involvement in the affair. Because of the widespread publicity given PLM's role in "inciting the workers to violence,"
PLM secretary Villarreal found it politic to state: "This is purely a labor
fight, not a revolution, so far as we are concerned. Our great purpose
is to overthrow Díaz . . . But we do not hold ourselves responsible for
the riot and bloodshed."[3]

[2] Root to Thompson, June 2, 1906, and Thompson to Root, June 3, 1906, in
Department of State, *Despatches from United States Minister to Mexico, 1823–1906*,
Vol. 183, No. 79. Naco was not only closer to Cananea than was Magdalena, but it
was located on the area's only railroad line, which had been built by Anaconda to
connect Cananea with Naco, Douglas, and other mining centers in southern Arizona.
Best accounts in English are Lyle C. Brown, "The Mexican Liberals and Their Struggle Against the Díaz Dictatorship," *Antología MCC, 1956*, and Herbert O. Brayer,
"The Cananea Incident," *New Mexico Historical Review*, XIII, No. 4 (October,
1938), 387–415. The best source remains Manuel González Ramírez (ed.), *Fuentes
para la historia de la Revolución Mexicana*, III, which contains only primary materials.
[3] Izábel to Corral, June 5, 1906, in Manuel González Ramírez (ed.), *Epistolario*

Nevertheless, there can be little doubt that PLM agitation did play a determinant role. For months prior to the disturbance, Cananea's Unión Liberal Humanidad, founded by strike leaders Baca Calderón, Manuel M. Diéguez, and Francisco M. Ibarra to support the PLM, had distributed PLM propaganda and contributed to an atmosphere of growing worker unrest. Following the strike, Baca Calderón, Diéguez, and Ibarra were singled out by the Díaz regime for the severest penalties delivered in the case: fifteen years of forced labor in the military fortress prison of San Juan de Ulúa. Up to the eve of the strike, Baca Calderón, seeking Army support for "the people," was placing military officials in touch with Ricardo Flores Magón.[4] PLM's *Regeneración* was the first newspaper to publicize American intervention, rushing to press a supplement to its June 1, 1906, issue which headlined: "Invasion of National Territory! . . . Treason! The Dictator has asked that the feet of foreign legions trample our soil and crush our brethren!"[5]

An immediate consequence of the Cananea strike was the Díaz regime's increased alertness for future disturbances. The United States was also advised of the possibility of continuing turmoil. Ambassador Thompson dispatched to the Department of State a series of messages urging swift suppression in the United States of the PLM and *Regeneración*; this did, in fact, occur prior to the PLM revolt of September, 1906. Newspaper rumors that a revolution would take place in September, wrote the Ambassador, were harming U.S. business interests and "worrying" President Díaz. *Regeneración*, the Ambassador added, was propagandizing for nothing less than "Anarchism" and revolution. In response, U.S. Cavalry troops were dispatched to the Sonora–Arizona border and held there until after the 1906 revolt.[6]

---

y textos de Ricardo Flores Magón, p. 76, and June 6 and 8, 1906, in *Fuentes*, III, 78–79, 92–94; Los Angeles *Times* (AP), June 6, 1906, enclosed by Thompson to Root, June 19, 1906, in Justice, 43718.

[4] González Ramírez (ed.), *Fuentes*, III, 3, 7–10, 110–111, 131–137, *passim*; cf. Cananea donations to PLM listed in Relaciones, L-E-18. Of Cananea's labor spokesmen, Baca Calderón seemed to be the most outspoken, attacking as early as January of 1906 "the blond-haired, blue-eyed capitalists" (pp. 110–111).

[5] Thompson to Root, June 19, 1906, in Justice, 43718.

[6] *Ibid.*; Thompson to Acting Secretary of State, August 28, 1906, in Justice, 43718; Thompson to Root, September 1, 5, 1906, in State, 100; cf. documents in

The impetus provided by the PLM Program, *Regeneración*, and Cananea's strike stimulated the recruitment of thousands of industrial workers to PLM ranks during the rest of 1906. The 1906–1907 nationwide textile strike, known as the Río Blanco (Veracruz) strike because of incidents occurring there, reflected this growing strength in the labor movement. In Orizaba, Veracruz, Manuel Avila showed textile workers the PLM Program. Río Blanco labor agitator José Neira, a personal friend of Camilo Arriaga, maintained contact with PLM. Neira helped found the Río Blanco textile workers' weekly *La Revolución Social*. Collaborating with Neira were the editors of Mexico City's *El Colmillo Público*, who, in July of 1906, were jailed on charges of "inciting to rebellion."[7]

When cotton producers reduced wages in November, 1906, on the grounds that cotton prices were down, textile workers in Puebla and Tlaxcala went on strike (December 4, 1906). This movement was supported by the Círculo de Obreros Libres in the Orizaba–Río Blanco area, where Avila and Neira continued to agitate for goals announced in the PLM Program. On December 7, 1906, worker Abraham Trujillo sparked a Puebla demonstration by proclaiming the need in Mexico for a third revolution (besides Independence and Reform) : "Labor versus Wealth." Two days later, Puebla workers drew up a detailed labor code which clearly reflected the influence of the PLM Program.[8]

State, 283. That U.S. business interests did suffer from rumors of revolution has been fully documented by Brown, pp. 350–353.

7 Two of *El Colmillo Público*'s editors—Jesús Martínez Carrión, the famed cartoonist, and Dr. Juan de la Peña—were infected with tuberculosis while in jail and, shortly after their release, died (Pérez Fernández' *El Demócrata* interview, and Eugenio Martínez Núñez, *Juan Sarabia, apóstol y mártir de la Revolución Mexicana*, I, 342–344). On Neira, see Manuel Ramírez Arriaga, "Camilo Arriaga," *Repertorio de la Revolución Mexicana*, No. 4 (May 1, 1960) p. 23; Ricardo Flores Magón to Enrique Flores Magón, June 7, 1908, in *El Estandarte*, August 8, 1908. For the story of the Río Blanco strike, consult: Pérez Fernández' *El Demócrata* interview; Florencio Barrera Fuentes, *Historia de la Revolución Mexicana: la etapa precursora*, pp. 213–223; Ethel Duffy Turner, *Ricardo Flores Magón y el Partido Liberal Mexicano*, pp. 119–123; and Fernando Rodarte, *7 de enero de 1907. Puebla–Orizaba*. The newspaper *La Revolución Social* is not listed in the Bibliography because copies are not available in the appropriate archives.

8 Text in Rodarte, pp. 11–17, or Barrera Fuentes, pp. 215–217.

Employers retaliated on December 22, 1906, by laying off between twenty thousand and thirty thousand workers in the Orizaba area. Four days later, workers' representatives conferred with President Díaz in Mexico City. On January 4, 1907, Díaz ordered that no more strikes be allowed in Mexico, and that all workers in Puebla, Veracruz, Tlaxcala, Querétaro, Jalisco, and the Federal District return to their jobs by January 7.[9]

Workers obeyed this order. However, in Río Blanco, an incident occurred at the company store (*tienda de raya*) and, during a scuffle, enraged workers killed a clerk. Seconds later, the store was in flames. Federal troops rushed to the scene and fired upon a handful of workers occupying the municipal palace. Many workers fled to nearby Nogales (Veracruz; not to be confused with Nogales, Sonora), where they were again assaulted by troops. U.S. Consul General Cottschalk in Mexico City wired the Department of State:

The situation at Orizaba, according to reliable private reports which I am receiving, is growing daily more grave. Forty-nine persons are reported to have been killed there yesterday. The Subsecretary of War has been ordered to the spot and a large force of Federal troops are said to be on their way to the scene of the disturbance. The press here, which is subsidized almost in its entirety, has received specific instructions to give no news on the subject of the increased seriousness of the situation.

The Consul General prophetically pointed out that labor unrest was "nationwide" and that "violence" was bound to occur, especially after the passing of Díaz from power, "a matter of a few years only in view of the Executive's advanced age."[10]

The Río Blanco workers, finding themselves harassed in Nogales and hearing of the heavy death toll in Río Blanco, decided to return to Río Blanco to collect the bodies of their dead. They were met on the road by federal reinforcements under the command of Colonel Rosalino Martínez, who ordered his troops to shoot the advancing workers. An indeterminate number were killed in the bloodiest single massacre of the Díaz regime.

[9] Text in Rodarte, pp. 20–23, or Barrera Fuentes, pp. 218–221.
[10] Cottschalk to Assistant Secretary of State Robert Bacon, January 8, 9, 1907, in State, 3916.

As U.S. Consul in Veracruz William W. Canada later reported the event: "Rumor has it, and all indications point that way, that over 100 persons were killed. Military executions were frequent; no unnecessary time was spent on men caught in the act, and many more were sent to the Valle Nacional or to Yucatán, where the Federal Government has penal colonies from whence but few return." Consul Canada emphasized that the "riots" were directed against foreigners, most of the millowners being Spaniards; citizens were hanging Mexican flags out their windows to avoid being attacked by workers. The Consul thought that the violent suppression of the strike was justified: "These measures, harsh as they seem to others, offer however the only means for subduing the unruly natives, who, when excited by cheap and fiery liquors and inflamed by the incendiary harangues of their so-called labor leaders, are more like savages than quiet citizens and absolutely fearless of consequences."[11]

Among those strike leaders at Orizaba and Río Blanco not killed in action were Arriaga's friend José Neira, and Veracruz' left-wing Revolutionary hero Heriberto Jara (who was still influential in Mexican politics in the mid-1960's). The Río Blanco-Orizaba area, like Cananea, continued to be a center of PLM agitation and revolutionary plotting, although strong government surveillance prevented any further outbreaks of violence during the Precursor period.

A third area of strike agitation influenced by PLM was that of the nation's railroads, especially in San Luis Potosí and the North. This agitation was led by the Gran Liga Mexicana de Empleados de Ferrocarril, which had its headquarters in San Luis Potosí. Labor historian Roberto de la Cerda Silva, Precursor journalist Luis F. Bustamante, PLM member Enrique Flores Magón, and historian-economist Jesús Silva Herzog have all placed these railroad workers as historically among the first in Mexico to agitate for Socialism and Syndicalism.[12]

11 Canada to Bacon, February 2, 1907, in State, 3916. Cf. El Paso *Times*, January 12, 1907, in State, 1730–1750.

12 Roberto de la Cerda Silva, *El movimiento obrera en México*; Luis F. Bustamante, *Savia roja (socialismo mexicano)*, p. 74; Enrique Flores Magón, "Sindicalismo revolucionario," *Todo*, June 18, 1953; Jesús Silva Herzog, *Breve historia de la Revolución Mexicana*, I, 43. Syndicalism, especially influential in France during the first decade of the twentieth century, envisioned the workers' "expropriation'" of the capi-

The Gran Liga was all-Mexican, the American railworkers having their own organization. By 1908, it claimed a membership of ten thousand. One of its main complaints was that Mexicans were relegated to the worst possible jobs, with high- and middle-level positions reserved for "Americans only." An antiforeign sentiment lay at the core of the railworkers' movement from its inception, even as earlier had been the case at Cananea and Río Blanco.[13]

A nationwide general rail strike in 1908 was but the logical climax of earlier resentments and confrontations which had received the sympathetic attention of even the Conservative press. For example, rail strikes in San Luis Potosí and Nuevo León in 1903 had provoked *El Estandarte* to comment: "It is only just that the worker should share in the abundant profits that foreign concerns, among them the railroad companies, are making in our country." *El Estandarte* had praised the railroad strikers for proving to the Americans "what the rebelling Mexican worker is capable of."[14] Later, in July and August of 1906, more than three thousand railworkers, led by Mexican mechanics, had gone on strike in San Luis Potosí, Nuevo León, Aguascalientes, and Chihuahua, thereby crippling the northern rail network. In October, 1907, a fight broke out between American and Mexican railroad employees in Cárdenas, San Luis Potosí. According to unconfirmed reports, eighteen men were killed, the Mexican flag was sullied, and many Mexicans were arrested. As a consequence, more than two thousand men in San Luis Potosí and surrounding states launched what *El Estandarte* called "one of the most serious strikes ever registered in our country."[15]

President Díaz often had to intervene to settle these affairs. During the 1906 rail strike, for example, the President was reported to have reassured the workers "that they were on a reasonable road to the realization of their just rights."[16] Díaz' policy on labor unrest seemed

---

talist class by means of a general strike, with the trade union as the foundation of future social organization.

[13] Turner, pp. 206–207; Silva Herzog, *Breve historia*, I, 43.
[14] *El Estandarte*, September 23, 27, 1903.
[15] *Ibid.*, August 2, 14, 22, 1906; October 31, November 1, 1907.
[16] *Ibid.*, August 22, 1906.

to be one of peaceful mediation, as in the case of the 1906 rail strike, followed by violent repression if mediation failed, as at Río Blanco. Evidence like Rafael de Zayas Enríquez' special report in 1906 on the imminence of a "socialist" revolution and Díaz' 1908 "Creelman interview" confirms that the President was not unaware of the need for some political adjustment to ward off a rising revolt from below in Mexico.

The most important of all the rail strikes occurred in the spring of 1908. Gran Liga president Félix C. Vera later described the strike to John Kenneth Turner, the American journalist sent to Mexico by PLM exiles in 1908 "to see and report the truth." According to Turner's transcription of Vera's account, more than three thousand railroad workers went on strike because "the bosses at San Luis Potosí began discriminating against union men, both in the shops and on the trains." The strike brought traffic to a standstill for six days and "tied up every foot of the Mexican National Railroad, consisting of nearly 1,000 miles of road running from Laredo, Texas, to Mexico City." The Governor of San Luis Potosí informed Vera "that if the men did not return to work forthwith they would all be rounded up and thrown in jail and prosecuted for conspiracy against the Government." The union leader was shown a telegram from President Díaz "which in significant terms reminded Vera of the massacre at Río Blanco." Vera asked that the workers be fairly treated since they "were keeping perfect order." His pleas went unheeded. Not wanting his workers shot down the way those at Río Blanco had been, Vera conferred with the union's executive board. It was decided that the strike should be called off.

Railroad workers did return to their jobs, but those who had struck were discharged "one after another at convenient times." Vera's resignation from the presidency of the Gran Liga was not accepted: "He still remained the nominal head of the organization, but there was nothing he could do."[17] For a brief spell, another president served, but

---

17 Turner, pp. 208–209. There is nothing in other accounts to contradict Turner; see, for example, Moisés González Navarro, *Historia moderna de México. El Porfiriato: la vida social*, p. 339, and *El Estandarte*, April 24, 1908.

the Gran Liga never recovered.[18] Vera claimed he always avoided anything political, yet in 1909 he became a newspaper correspondent and was arrested in Guadalajara, presumably because of his articles' outspoken criticism of Díaz. Without formal charge, he was locked up in Mexico City's Belén Prison.[19] In rather ironic contrast to the failure of Mexican railworkers to achieve their aims, American rail employees struck in 1909 to protest the new Mexican management's vain efforts to promote Mexican workers on the basis of merit—and the Americans won.[20]

In spite of their many setbacks, striking Mexican workers in critical industries like mining, textiles, and rails had shown that they were politically conscious and receptive to PLM ideals. Three strikes (Cananea, Río Blanco, and San Luis Potosí) had dealt a psychological blow to the Díaz regime. The nation's press, in spite of its loyalty to Díaz, expressed grave concern about "American intervention" and "excessive bloodshed." For the PLM, as for Madero three years later when he referred to Cananea's "martyred" workers, an important source of revolutionary propaganda had been established.[21] In a literal sense, Mexico's modern labor movement had received its "baptism of fire." A significant number of workers remained in a state of revolutionary anticipation after the 1906–1908 strikes. The rash of strikes that was to break out in Mexico following Díaz' downfall and the Anarchist-dominated founding of the Casa del Obrero Mundial in 1912 would confirm that a strong labor movement had been born, not killed, during 1906–1908.

A revolution, too, was born during this 1906–1908 period. Both in terms of ideology and in terms of military preparedness, PLM now made critical contributions to the development of the 1910–1917 Revolution. While not succeeding in the overthrow of Porfirio Díaz, PLM's revolts did help to undermine his regime. The ideas of the PLM Program began now to receive a new, more militant emphasis on bene-

[18] *El Estandarte,* July 23, 1908.
[19] Turner, p. 210.   [20] González Navarro, p. 340.
[21] Brown, p. 361; Francisco I. Madero, *La sucesión presidencial en 1910,* pp. 219–221.

fiting the working class. In addition, members of PLM's armed units gained valuable battlefield experience which would prove useful in the fighting against Díaz that erupted in late 1910.

In terms of ideology, the 1906 and 1908 revolts sought to implement the PLM Program, with special emphasis upon the labor code and the restoration of *ejidos* and private landholdings to deprived peasants. In response to initial setbacks during the 1906 revolt, PLM issued revised orders for the remainder of the 1906 revolt and all of the 1908 revolt which introduced two new ideological variations. First, rebels were not to lay down their arms "until the triumph of the revolution." Insistence upon this condition was highly significant and would be used, for example, in 1911 to justify the refusal of followers of Zapata and of PLM to surrender their arms to a Madero-backed interim government they felt was betraying the Revolution. Second, labor and agrarian reforms outlined in the PLM Program would be implemented by decree during the course of the revolution, without waiting for corresponding legislative action.[22] The PLM, by pressing for these socio-economic goals of the Mexican Revolution from the start, was forcing the terms of subsequent factional polemics, such as those of 1910–1917.

Although nationalist in its 1906–1908 propaganda, PLM issued circulars guaranteeing protection of foreign property. It also instructed its followers to issue redeemable receipts for all "funds and elements" taken from government offices or, in emergencies, from private individuals. When these circulars were intercepted by government officials in 1906, much publicity was given the allegation that PLM had ordered the execution of any member who failed to revolt on the appointed day. However, PLM denied that this clause had been included in its instructions, citing Point 6 of its Program, which called for abolition of the death penalty except for traitors. Moreover, captured 1908 instructions of PLM made no mention of the death penalty for those failing to revolt. The 1908 instructions paralleled those of 1906 in every other respect, although they were more explicit in their attacks on capitalism and in warning against revolutionary pillage. In 1908, PLM mem-

---

22 PLM, "Proclama a la nación," September, 1906, in personal archive of Martínez Núñez, or Barrera Fuentes, pp. 201–203; October 15, 1906, instructions to PLM affiliates in González Ramírez (ed.), *Epistolario*, pp. 64–66.

bers were instructed to seize "the properties of enemies of the people, of private slave traders who have accumulated enormous riches at the cost of the proletarian's blood, and of corrupt officials and their lackeys, well known as wicked exploiters." Members were warned against "inflicting outrages of any kind upon peaceful residents." Anyone committing pillage or other "acts which violate the spirit of justice characterizing the Revolution" would be swiftly punished.[23]

In terms of military preparedness, the 1906 and 1908 revolts were planned for most of the states of the Republic. PLM "cells" were widespread, although their strength varied. The PLM issued commissions to individual leaders in key trouble spots like Cananea, Yaqui Indian areas in Sonora, labor and Indian centers in Veracruz and Oaxaca, and military barracks in numerous cities and provinces. Specific targets and "military zones" were established throughout the Republic.

During these years, PLM popularity was spreading, not declining. As early as June 3, 1906, President Díaz had confided to U.S. Ambassador Thompson "that the little party of about twenty revolutionists at Cananea were only a handful of those who hold the same sentiments in other places." According to Thompson, "It seems plain the President is fearful that this Cananea affair may not be the last one and it was clearly because of this fear that he said if further serious disturbances were to arise he might be pleased to have American assistance."[24] In 1907, U.S. Attorney C. A. Boynton confirmed that PLM memberships and the circulation of PLM publications were on the increase. In the words of Captain W. S. Scott, commander of U.S. Army troops sent to patrol the border at Ambassador Enrique Creel's request, "There exists, particularly in the northern states of Mexico, much discontent with present conditions, and a strong leader would receive a large following in case of a revolutionary outbreak."[25]

The revolt of 1906 failed because the Díaz Government learned of

---

[23] *Ibid.;* 1908 PLM instructions in Relaciones, L-E-944.

[24] Thompson to Root, June 5, 1906, in Department of State, *Despatches from United States Ministers to Mexico, 1823–1906*, Vol. 183, No. 79.

[25] Boynton to U.S. Attorney General, April 23, 1907, in Justice, 90755; Scott to U.S. Army Adjutant General, August 26, 1907; Ambassador Creel to Assistant Secretary of State Bacon, June 21, 1907; U.S. Adjutant General to Root, September 14, 1907, in State, 5028.

PLM plans before action was taken. The government capitalized on an efficient spy system that included use of Pinkerton detectives, raids on PLM headquarters, and St. Louis Consul M. E. Diebold's steady interception of PLM mail (in collaboration with U.S. postal authorities). The revolt was initially planned for Independence Day—September 16 —but was postponed when PLM leaders realized that the Díaz Government knew of the date. When no revolt occurred as scheduled, Cananea Consolidated Copper Company shares and Mexican bonds led a sharp advance on the U.S. Stock Exchange.[26] Also setting back the date of the 1906 revolt was the arrest of Librado Rivera (September 12), on charges brought by Cananea's William C. Greene. This development, together with the smashing of *Regeneración* in St. Louis (September 15–October 1) by the combined forces of the U.S. Justice Department and Immigration officers and Pinkerton detectives, interrupted the execution of PLM plans.[27]

Arizona, Texas, and Veracruz were the major centers of PLM preparations for the 1906 revolt. For many weeks prior to the revolt, Plácido Ríos and Gabriel Rubio, veterans of the Cananea strike, smuggled arms into Mexico's northwest. They were assisted by Arizona's PLM nucleus of Lázaro Puente, Antonio de P. Araujo, Tomás D. Espinosa, Luis A. García, Bruno Treviño, Callis Humbert, Leonardo Villarreal, and schoolteacher Luis G. Monzón Teyatzin. Douglas and the mining camps of Mowry and Patagonia, north of Nogales (Sonora), formed the base of the PLM's Arizona-Sonora operations. Mexican laborers living in the area, most of whom worked in copper pits and smelters owned by William C. Greene, comprised the bulk of membership in the PLM's Club Liberal Libertad in Douglas. On behalf of PLM, Ricardo Flores Magón wrote these rebels instructions to arm Cananea's workers, confiscate Greene's weapons, seize customs houses at Agua

26 *Mexican Herald* (Mexico City), September 18, 1906, in Brown, p. 352; archival documents.

27 Consul M. E. Diebold (St. Louis, Missouri) to Secretario de Relaciones Exteriores, November 13, 1906; Librado Rivera (Fort Leavenworth, Kansas) to Mexican Embassy (Washington, D.C.), June 12, 1921, in Diego Abad de Santillán, *Ricardo Flores Magón, el apóstol de la Revolución Social Mexicana*, pp. 25–26, and Martínez Núñez, *Juan Sarabia*, I, 353–354; cf. documents and clippings in Relaciones, L-E-921.

Prieta and Nogales, confer with Yaqui chiefs, and win over military men.

However, on September 4, 1906, Arizona Rangers raided the homes of PLM members in Douglas, Mowry, and Patagonia. The Rangers confiscated the PLM newspaper *El Demócrata*, seized caches of arms, and arrested fifteen persons. These prisoners were turned over to Mexican authorities and sent to San Juan de Ulúa Prison. The U.S. Department of State reassured Ambassador Thompson in Mexico City: "All the Arizona Ranger force is concentrated at the line. Federal and local officers advised and alert."[28]

In spite of the Arizona group's setback, in Texas and Veracruz the PLM continued its preparations for revolt. On September 2, 1906, Juan Sarabia and Ricardo Flores Magón arrived at El Paso, Texas, after an exhausting sixty-hour trip from Canada. In El Paso, they co-ordinated plans for the revolt with Antonio I. Villarreal, César E. Canales, Prisciliano G. Silva, schoolteacher Lauro Aguirre, and other PLM members operating along the border.[29] The first attack was engineered by the Texas group on September 26, 1906. Juan José Arredondo y de León Ibarra and about thirty others seized the main plaza of Jiménez, Coahuila, cut all major telephone wires, and sacked the town treasury. However, federal troops rushed to the scene and dispersed the rebels in the revolt's first bloodshed. Co-ordination with other PLM rebels in Coahuila was faulty, although uprisings did occur in Zaragoza, Monclova, Ciudad Porfirio Díaz, and other Coahuilan towns. In spite of newspaper and government allegations of no more than sporadic banditry and smuggling, the Mexican Government immediately asked U.S. authorities to arrest and extradite, on the charge of "robbery and mur-

---

[28] Bacon to Thompson, September 7, 1906, in State, 100; Ricardo Flores Magón to Gabriel Rubio, July 27, 1906, to Tomás D. Espinosa, August 2, 1906, and to Bruno Treviño, August 18, 1906, in Justice, 90755; Djed Bórquez, *Monzón: semblanza de un revolucionario*; González Ramírez (ed.), *Fuentes*, III, 141–145; Brown, pp. 347–349; Teodoro Hernández, *Las tinajas de Ulúa*, pp. 39–42 (Luis A. García's account); Thompson to Root, September 4, 1906, in Justice, 43718.

[29] Canales was a veteran of the Liberal Club of Lampazos, Nuevo León, and had been arrested when that club was smashed in April, 1901; Aguirre was the editor of El Paso's *La Reforma Social*, for which Díaz Soto y Gama had written in 1904; Silva already had two hundred armed men at his command (archival documents).

der committed in Coahuila," at least sixty-five PLM members involved in the action.[30]

The second major attack occurred in the Acayucán region of Veracruz, from September 30 to October 3, 1906. More than a thousand men rose up in arms. PLM commander Hilario C. Salas led the first charge on Acayucán, with some three hundred Indians behind him. Salas was wounded in the leg and forced to pull back with his troops. Nearby, similar attacks, to the cries of "Death to Porfirio Díaz!" and "Long Live the Liberal Party!," were launched by PLM members and Indian peasants against Chinameca, Minatitlán, and Ixhuatlán, but they too were repulsed by federal troops. Those rebels not captured, killed in battle, sent to San Juan de Ulúa, or executed, fled to the Sierra de Soteapán to regroup.[31]

A third PLM uprising in 1906 occurred near Camargo, Tamaulipas, in mid-October, when Jesús M. Rangel and other members fought Army Reserve troops and *Rurales*. The PLM was again turned back, and Mexican troops proceeded to string out along the entire Texas-Tamaulipas border.[32]

The PLM's major target in 1906, however, was Ciudad Juárez, Chi-

30 The Mexican Consul in Eagle Pass, Texas, informed the Secretaría de Gobernación as early as September 27, 1906, that the Coahuila disturbances were part of a PLM revolution (González Ramírez [ed.], *Epistolario*, pp. 68-69). U.S. Attorney General to Secretary of State, November 22, 1906, reviewed the series of requests for extradition, starting from Mexico City in early October and being relayed through the Mexican Embassy in Washington to State and Justice; for further correspondence on the subject between the United States and Mexican Governments, consult documents in Justice, 90755, State, 1730-1750, and Relaciones, L-E-920 ff.

31 Governor Teodoro A. Dehesa (Veracruz) to Secretaría de Gobernación, October 13, 30, 1906, in González Ramírez (ed.), *Epistolario*, pp. 69-75. For accounts by PLM participants, see Abel R. Pérez, "El brote revolucionario de septiembre de 1906 en Minatitlán y Acayucán," *Excélsior*, June 9 through July 8, 1935; Cándido Donato Padua, *Movimiento revolucionario 1906 en Veracruz*, pp. 23-25; and the material by Teodoro Hernández listed in the Bibliography.

32 Consul P. Merrill Griffith (Matamoros, Tamaulipas) to Assistant Secretary of State Bacon, October 18, 1906, in Justice, 43718; Antonio de P. Araujo (Waco, Texas) to Ricardo Flores Magón, October 11, 1906, in Relaciones, L-E-919; Casmiro H. Regalado (Waco, Texas) to Ricardo Flores Magón, June 26, 1906, in L-E-918— Regalado anticipated a PLM armed force of six thousand men for the Tamaulipas campaign alone.

huahua. Capture of this border city four and one-half years later was to precipitate Porfirio Díaz' flight from Mexico. Now the PLM planned to paralyze the defense of Ciudad Juárez by blowing up the local Army barracks; however, secret agents informed Governor Enrique Creel of the plot. On October 5, 1906, President Díaz wired Creel a promise of four times the number of soldiers Creel had requested.[33] As tension mounted in Ciudad Juárez, Second Lieutenant Zeferino Reyes of the local garrison, a former schoolmate of Juan Sarabia and one-time member of San Luis Potosí's Club Liberal "Ponciano Arriaga," lured Sarabia, Canales, and Vicente de la Torre into a government trap. All three men were arrested on October 19, 1906.[34] At the same time, across the border in El Paso, U.S. Immigration authorities and Pinkerton detectives arrested Antonio I. Villarreal, Lauro Aguirre, José Cano, and a score of other PLM conspirators. Ricardo Flores Magón and Modesto Díaz, after barely escaping El Paso, fled to Los Angeles, California. As a result of these developments, the Ciudad Juárez revolt never took place.

In El Paso, U.S. authorities raided PLM headquarters and seized many incriminating documents. In this way, names of PLM collaborators and recipients of *Regeneración* in practically every Mexican state were discovered and passed on to Mexican officials. Armed PLM cells in all of Chihuahua were now swiftly crushed or dispersed. A flourishing correspondence between Governor Creel and President Díaz reported continued arrests throughout Mexico.

Creel and Díaz next arranged for "loyal" judges and lawyers to "try" Juan Sarabia, who had been transferred to a prison at the state capital in Chihuahua on October 20. Even before Sarabia's "trial" began, considerable drama developed when PLM followers distributed leaflets reporting more than 250 arrests in Chihuahua and accusing Governor Creel of having threatened to kill Sarabia in jail. On the day

[33] The September, 1924, series of articles in *El Demócrata* reproduces this and other correspondence by government officials during October–November, 1906; cf. Juan Sarabia's testimony in Barrera Fuentes, pp. 227–240.

[34] Ironically, after the overthrow of Porfirio Díaz, Lieutenant Reyes was promoted (Martínez Núñez, *Juan Sarabia*, I, 361, 543–544).

of the trial, January 7, 1907, the courtroom was packed with people loyal to Sarabia. Outside, the Army's 18th Battalion and the gendarmes' 13th Regiment stood guard.

Rising to speak in his own defense, Sarabia asserted that he was being falsely accused. The charges of "murder, arson, and robbery" did not apply to him, because his acts had been strictly political and therefore fell outside the realm of "common crimes." As for the charge of "rebellion," Sarabia was proud to acknowledge his role in the PLM revolts. To a stunned and hushed courtroom, he stressed the importance of the PLM Program:

The object of the revolution we organized—after a thousand fruitless campaigns, after a thousand impulsions toward liberty, all choked by the iron hand of despotism—was to put into practice that very Program, the main points of which call for the dividing up of land for the benefit of the people and the improvement of conditions for the working class, by means of shorter work days and increased wages.

Therefore, Sarabia concluded, far from being a criminal act, revolution against Díaz was a constitutional duty:

In a word, when legality has been dragged down from its throne by that monstrous scourge of peoples known as Tyranny, rebellion must be viewed not as a political crime punishable by the Penal Code, but as a right granted to the oppressed by Article 35 of our thousand-times-sage Constitution.

Notwithstanding the eloquence of his defense, Sarabia was sentenced to seven years in San Juan de Ulúa. There, he became one of nearly a thousand PLM prisoners during the Precursor period, of whom five hundred died. At Ulúa, Sarabia suffered a heart attack and nearly lost his eyesight. His premature death in 1920 at the age of thirty-eight was a result of tuberculosis contracted while imprisoned in Ulúa's damp, dark dungeons.[35]

As in 1906, so in 1908, the Mexican Government learned of PLM's scheduled revolt ahead of time and, with U.S. help, moved to smash

---

[35] *Ibid.*, pp. 416–540; Barrera Fuente, pp. 227–240; Hernández, *Las tinajas de Ulúa.*)

it. The revolt was originally set for September, 1907. However, the arrest of Ricardo Flores Magón, Librado Rivera, and Antonio I. Villarreal in Los Angeles, in August of 1907, caused its postponement. PLM members agreed instead to devote their resources to the legal case for their jailed leaders, as well as to further collection of arms.[36] Judging from available archival evidence, the PLM, in spite of its many setbacks, entered the 1908 revolt with more arms, ammunition, major targets, and popular support than in 1906, but against stronger Mexican and U.S. border patrols and spy networks.

On the eve of the rebellion—June 23, 1908—U.S. authorities raided the El Paso home of Prisciliano G. Silva and seized more than three thousand rounds of ammunition.[37] Among papers removed from Silva's house was a long letter from Ricardo Flores Magón to his brother Enrique, dated June 7-9, 1908. This letter, given extensive publicity after the revolt's failure,[38] contained detailed plans for rebellion in almost every state of the Republic. In addition, it raised the subject of a "possible *gringo* invasion because of the revolution." Ricardo was convinced not only that the Americans would invade, but also that American liberals and Socialists would *not* rally to the support of the revolution. So far as he was concerned, the United States was "a nation of pigs," plagued by "stepped-up militarization" and repression of the Left. He was especially disillusioned with the American Federation of Labor, which "simply refuses to get upset by the government's outrages." Yet Ricardo could not help believing that an American intervention would ultimately backfire: "If they invade when the people

---

[36] Relaciones, L-E-926–929, e.g., Ricardo Flores Magón (Los Angeles, California) to Eulalio Treviño and Aurelio N. Flores (San Antonio, Texas), June 21, 1907, and I. J. Mendiola (San Antonio, Texas) to Jesús M. Rangel (Waco, Texas), September 18, 1907.

[37] At about the same time, more than a hundred men of the U.S. Cavalry rushed to Del Rio, Texas, across the border from PLM target area Las Vacas, Coahuila. U.S. Attorney Boynton (Del Rio) to U.S. Attorney General, July 20, 1908 (in Justice, 43718), provided a detailed account of these developments.

[38] Full text in Relaciones, L-E-937; partial text in Barrera Fuentes, pp. 254–260. Cf. *La Patria*, August 5, 1908; *El Estandarte*, August 8, 1908; *Mexican Herald*, August 6, 1908; Washington *Post*, August 24, 1908; *Arizona Daily Star*, September 9, 1908, and other newspaper clippings in Relaciones, L-E-933–941.

are in full rebellion against Díaz, they will precipitate the dictator's downfall, since the Mexican people will see clearly that Roosevelt, Díaz' ally in enslaving us, intends to take away our autonomy." Additional PLM plans, according to Enrique Flores Magón, were discovered in Casas Grandes, Chihuahua, because a Díaz spy bearing a remarkable physical resemblance to Antonio I. Villarreal won the confidence of PLM rebels. A government raid in Casas Grandes on June 18, 1908, bagged twenty PLM rebels and a score of incriminating documents. Such swift government action, repeated in other states of the Republic, prevented the PLM from making its rebellion nationwide.[39]

Nevertheless, as Mexican Ambassador Creel informed the U.S. Department of State, perhaps with some exaggeration, thousands of persons rose up in arms in late June of 1908 in the state of Coahuila and Chihuahua. The first uprising occurred on June 24 at Viesca, in southern Coahuila, when rebels launched an attack to the cries of "Long Live the Revolution!" and "Long Live the Liberal Party!" The rebels assaulted the offices of the municipal government, the house of the *jefe político,* and the branch office of the Bank of Nuevo León. For a brief spell, they ruled the town. To delay the arrival of federal reinforcements from Torreón and Saltillo, they ripped up the railroad tracks. Within a day or two, however, enough Army troops arrived to retake the town.

On June 26, a group of PLM rebels in Las Vacas (Coahuila) attacked the local Army garrison. After suffering heavy casualties, the rebels withdrew. Meanwhile, some fifty others rose up in Casas Grandes (Chihuahua), executed a series of feints, and then marched north toward Palomas in a vain effort to link up with PLM members planning an attack from across the border. On June 30 and July 1, the streets of Palomas crackled with gunfire, as soldiers from the local garrison and the rebels drew up their battle lines. The PLM was hopelessly outmanned. Those rebels not killed wandered into the nearby desert, where they walked for days before finding refuge in the United States.

<hr />

[39] U.S. Acting Secretary of State to Attorney General, July 25, 1908, in Justice, 43718; documents in Relaciones, L-E-935.

Similar setbacks were suffered by the PLM in Los Hornos, Matamoros, and La Sierra de Jimulco, Coahuila.[40]

In the West and South, PLM action was sporadic, at best. In Baja California, a small PLM contingent attacked Mexicali and then moved inland. Yaqui Indian rebels led by Fernando Palomárez in Sonora were generally confined to the mountains; Palomárez was later arrested. In the state of Veracruz, where so many peasants had risen two years earlier, PLM plans went completely awry. Government arrests foiled a revolt scheduled for Orizaba and other locations, although Juan Olivares did succeed in escaping. Because of reverses like these, communication between PLM members broke down throughout Mexico, and for a while general confusion reigned. The U.S. Attorney General ordered that the movement's top leaders—Ricardo Flores Magón, Rivera, and Villarreal—all in confinement in Los Angeles County Jail since late 1907, be held incommunicado.[41]

Although much of the nation's press ridiculed the PLM's efforts as insignificant or mere "banditry," the Mexican Government did not cease its intensive correspondence with U.S. officials on the subject of possible further revolt and the need to arrest "fugitives from the law." American Consul Luther T. Ellsworth informed the Secretary of State that there existed much concern about PLM press releases which alleged that twenty thousand rebels were waging guerrilla warfare against federal troops in central and southern Coahuila.[42] As of August, 1908, Ellsworth warned, the PLM had at least five separate armies prepared to invade Mexico "soon."[43] Consular officials of both the American and the Mexican Governments reported the Texas border area to be in-

---

[40] Ambassador Creel to Acting Secretary of State Bacon, July 11, 1908, in Justice, 90755. For newspaper and government accounts of the heavy fighting, see Relaciones, L-E-935–937.

[41] *Ibid.*; U.S. Attorney Oscar Lawler to U.S. Marshal Leo Youngworth, July 6, 1908, in Justice, 90755.

[42] Ellsworth (Cd. Porfirio Díaz, Coahuila) to U.S. Secretary of State, July 3, 20, 1908, in Justice, 43718, and State 5028, enclosing issues of the Del Rio (Texas) weekly *El Liberal*; Attorney Boynton to Attorney General, July 20, 1908, in Justice, 43718.

[43] Ellsworth to Department of State, August 12, 1909, January 29, 1910, in State, 5028.

fested with "socialists."[44] Commenting on Tomás Sarabia's sixteen-page defense speech of September, 1909, which eulogized the labor and agrarian-reform sections of the PLM Program, Consul Ellsworth observed that Sarabia "actually expresses the freely expressed sentiments of the majority of the educated Mexicans who earnestly desire the overthrow of all of the present administrators of Mexican affairs."[45]

U.S. troops were reinforced along the border from 1908 to 1910.[46] Such precautions, together with further arrests of PLM leaders inside Mexico, forced the rebels to defer future revolt plans and maintain underground and guerrilla warfare until their re-emergence as fighting units in the 1910 Revolution. On August 9, 1908, Jesús M. Rangel, who in 1906 had fought Army Reserves and *Rurales,* led a guerrilla ambush of federal troops in the Sierra del Burro of northern Coahuila, killing twenty soldiers. Ambassador Creel later reported some four hundred to five hundred rebels active in the "Burro and Toro mountains of Coahuila."[47]

In similar fashion, remnants of the Acayucán (Veracruz) revolutionists of 1906 kept up a guerrilla struggle, mainly defensive. On September 5, 1908, led by Hilario C. Salas and Cándido Donato Padua, they issued a revolutionary proclamation repledging their movement to the PLM and its Program.[48] While Padua stayed with the guerrilla troops in Veracruz, Salas traveled through the states of Oaxaca, Puebla, Tlaxcala, and Mexico, spreading PLM propaganda. In July of 1910, Santana

44 E.g., Ellsworth to Department of State, May 14, 1909, in State, 5028, and Consul A. V. Lomelí (El Paso, Texas) to Secretario de Relaciones Exteriores, June 30, 1909, in González Ramírez (ed.), *Epistolario,* pp. 226–227.

45 Ellsworth to Department of State, November 1, 1909, in State, 5028.

46 For 1908 and 1909, see documents in State, 5028; for 1910, see Justice, 90755. By 1910, there was concern about the Madero exile movement also, but clearly the PLM continued to be a major concern of both the Mexican and United States Governments (cf. Isido Fabela, *Documentos históricos de la Revolución Mexicana,* X, 105).

47 Ambassador Creel to Secretario de Relaciones Exteriores, September 10, 1908, in Relaciones, L-E-941; Antonio de P. Araujo (McAllen, Texas) to Jesús Maldonado (Rotan, Texas), August 21, 1908, and to Brígido Torres (Waco, Texas) August 22, 1908, in Relaciones, L-E-933; Ellsworth to Department of State, April 17, 1909, in State, 5028, linking a "bandit raid"at Viesca in April, 1909, with the PLM.

48 Text in Barrera Fuentes, pp. 265–267.

Rodríguez, also known as "Santanón," a prominent leader of Veracruz peasant revolutionaries, joined his forces with those of Padua. Together they led their men in battle in October, 1910, thus anticipating the November 20, 1910, revolt of Madero. Also helping to maintain the revolutionary impetus of 1906 and 1908 into the ultimately successful 1910 Revolution were the Valladolid (Yucatán) revolt, locally sponsored, and Gabriel Leyva's Anti-reelectionist revolt at Cabrera de Inzunza (Sinaloa), both in June of 1910.[49]

In support of the guerrilla movement, those PLM members not in jail maintained a steady propaganda effort. Poet-Anarchist Práxedis G. Guerrero issued a series of manifestoes in 1909, often addressed to "the workmen of all countries" and calling upon Mexican "comrades" to rise up in revolt.[50] The PLM's most effective weapon remained the press, even if an exile press, which included at least seven newspapers in five locations, all of which were suppressed from time to time.[51]

There can be little doubt that these propaganda efforts and the PLM-inspired strikes and revolts of 1906–1908 contributed to the undermining of the Díaz regime. Revolutionary impetus, especially among workers and peasants, had been enhanced by PLM manifestoes, strikes, revolts, and guerrilla warfare. Even before Madero made up his mind in October of 1910 that he and his followers would have to resort to

[49] Santanón was killed in the October, 1910, action. For details and relevant PLM documents, see: Padua; Enrique Flores Magón, "Histórica figura de Santanón," *Todo*, May 28, 1953; González Ramírez (ed.), *Fuentes*, IV, 164–167; Fabela, X, 99, 105; Martínez Núñez, *Juan Sarabia*, I, 534; Duffy Turner, pp. 192–194, 208–210, 382.

[50] Ellsworth to Department of State, October 1, 1909, February 22, 1910, and March 19, 1910, in State, 5028.

[51] Scattered among archival collections are the following publications: *Libertad y Trabajo* (organ of the PLM's Club Tierra, Igualdad y Justicia, edited by Cananea veteran Fernando Palomárez and Río Blanco veteran Juan Olivares [Los Angeles, California], May–June, 1908); *Reforma, Libertad y Justicia* (edited by Antonio de P. Araujo and Tomás Sarabia [Austin, Texas], June and September, 1908); *El Defensor del Pueblo* (Socialist weekly edited by Manuel Sarabia [Tucson, Arizona], 1908); *El Liberal* ([Del Rio, Texas], June–July, 1908); *El Progreso* (PLM [San Antonio, Texas], 1907–1908); *Punto Rojo* (Anarchist weekly, edited by Práxedis G. Guerrero [Del Rio, Texas], 1909); and *El Obrero* (Anarchist- and Socialist-oriented, edited by Antonio I. Villarreal's sister, Teresa [San Antonio, Texas], 1910).

violent revolution, the press was referring to a major uprising in San Luis Potosí's Huasteca in August, 1910, as a "Precursor revolt."[52] What this meant, in effect, was that a revolutionary movement of workers and peasants—abetted by the Precursor Movement, championed by the PLM, and directed against the Mexican bourgeoisie and foreign businessmen—already posed a serious threat, not only to the Díaz regime, but also to any other movement against Díaz (e.g., Madero's) not founded with worker or peasant support.

52 *El Estandarte,* August 7, 11, 12, September 2, 1910.

CHAPTER SEVEN

PLM-Madero Divisions and Coalitions, 1906–1910

DURING THE early phase of the Precursor Movement (1900–1903), the political rhetoric of Liberal democracy had helped to unify dissenters from various classes behind common goals: overthrow or modification of the Díaz system, reinstitution of the Reform Laws and formal democracy, and modest socio-economic reform. However, a more radical phase began with the founding of the PLM (1905), the publication of its Program (1906) and the launching of the strikes and revolts that it inspired (1906–1908). This phase constituted such a radicalization of the Precursor Movement—that is, an ideological move to the Left primarily aimed at satisfying worker and peasant demands, and a political move to the extreme Left incorporating the use of violence—that for many middle- and upper-class people the earlier coalition lost its appeal. The Arriaga–Flores Magón schism of 1904–1905 was the first serious Precursor division involving these ideological questions of radicalization to the Left and social questions of inherently conflicting interests of different classes (which otherwise shared some resentment against Díaz and the Científicos).

From 1906 to 1910, this process of division continued. The way to progressive social change in Mexico became marked by two outstanding, but quite distinct, alternatives: one of violent revolution for mainly socio-economic goals, and the other of nonviolent change for principally political goals. The first alternative was championed by PLM and, in general, by discontented elements of the lower and lower-middle classes. The second alternative was advocated by Madero and, in general, by dissatisfied members of the upper-middle and upper classes. Precursor veterans like Arriaga and some middle-class intellectuals, who favored broader political coalitions than those offered by either the PLM or Madero, came to straddle the two alternatives.

Madero, however, did not make his presence felt as a major figure on the national political scene until 1909. By then, PLM, by means of its earlier start and increasing left-wing radicalism, already had established many of the terms and conditions of political dispute. The highly explosive revolutionary threat posed by the coalition backing PLM affected not only Madero's initial opposition to the PLM but also his eventual decision to pursue a type of political action different from any of those offered by the PLM, Díaz' Científico braintrust, or the "Reyistas," as dissenting elements inside the Díaz Administration and occasional independents who supported General Bernardo Reyes were called.

Throughout the Porfiriato, the Madero family had been developing its economic interests in mining, farming, commerce, industry, and banking. At the time of the 1906 revolt, for example, Francisco I. Madero was advising his younger brother how to develop his capital into a "base for future businesses and the conquest of your true autonomy."[1] To friends he was writing about the financing of the Spiritist movement in Mexico.[2] Madero was busy with the cotton harvest and with founding a new guayule factory in Cuatro Ciénegas, Coahuila; for the latter project, he employed the counsel of an American rubber pro-

---

[1] Madero to Julio Madero, October 11, 1906, in Francisco I. Madero, *Archivo de Francisco I. Madero: Epistolario (1900–1909)*, p. 174.
[2] *Ibid.*, pp. 175 ff.

ducer at nearby Parras, Coahuila.[3] It is understandable that, under such circumstances, Madero was not interested in supporting violent revolution or directing his political energies to the development of a mass labor movement.

Prior to the 1906 revolt, Madero had informed PLM members that he opposed their plans. On September 24, 1906, he refused to furnish arms to Prisciliano G. Silva, claiming that "General Díaz is not a tyrant —a bit rigid, but not a tyrant . . . and even if he were a tyrant, I never would lend aid to make a revolution, for I have a veritable horror of bloodshed."[4] Madero explained to PLM member Crescencio Villarreal Márquez that, so far as he was concerned, fomenting revolution was "antipatriotic" and had "no plausible pretext."[5]

Although critical of the Díaz regime's methods of suppression, Madero had opposed the calling of the Río Blanco strike. In his eyes, labor-union leaders were to blame for having taken "the disastrous step of throwing ten thousand workers out on the street."[6] Only later—in 1909 and 1910—did Madero begin openly to court labor and peasant support, and then without nearly so much commitment and conviction as that manifested by the intellectuals of the PLM.

Madero believed that Mexico's problems were mainly political, not economic. During his 1910 campaign for the Presidency, he actually opposed the Reform Laws on the grounds that they violated political freedom and that religious interests were no longer a threat in Mexico. In this respect, Madero was not nearly so outspoken as the Liberals who initiated the Precursor Movement in 1900. At Orizaba and San Luis Potosí, two centers of the national labor movement, Madero told workers that he was not offering them reductions in work hours or increases in wages but "only freedom, because freedom will let you conquer bread. . . . the people do not ask for bread, they ask for freedom."[7]

---

[3] Madero to Evaristo Madero, October 1, 1906, *ibid.*, pp. 172–173.

[4] *Regeneración*, March 4, 1911; Stanley R. Ross, *Francisco I. Madero: Apostle of Mexican Democracy*, p. 43; Ethel Duffy Turner, *Ricardo Flores Magón y el Partido Liberal Mexicano*, pp. 102–103.

[5] Madero to C. V. Márquez, August 17, 1906, in Madero, *Archivo*, pp. 165–166.

[6] Madero to Francisco Sentíes, January 19, 1907, *ibid.*, p. 179.

[7] Jesús Silva Herzog, *Breve historia de la Revolución Mexicana*, I, 121–125, and interviews; Ross, p. 103.

An important element in the division between Madero and the PLM was the time factor. Major figures in PLM had begun their anti-Díaz fight in 1900 and underwent suppression ever more harsh at the hands of government troops, agents, and collaborators. Madero, on the other hand, starting his political career later and with greater caution, had not yet suffered total disillusionment with peaceful means of protest. The PLM, in its September, 1906, "Proclamation to the Nation," had demonstrated in detail how all peaceful means of satisfying fundamental rights under Díaz had been exhausted.[8] A number of reform leaders did not accept this interpretation of Mexican political realities. Many of them, stimulated by the PLM but not yet committed in 1906, later coalesced around Madero with the belief that reform could be achieved in Mexico by means of exercising one's right to vote. Only after experiencing in "Anti-reelectionist Clubs" (1909–1910) the kind of suppression that already had been experienced by PLM veterans in "Liberal Clubs" (1900–1903) would these Maderista reformers reach the same conclusion as the PLM: violent revolution offered the only road to substantial reform in Mexico.

Madero's differences with PLM coincided with the emergence in Mexico of a significant labor movement and the formation of a political alliance between workers and low-status intellectuals. As soon as these intellectuals lent their support to the labor movement, divisions between them and men like Madero were almost bound to occur. A process of radicalization of petty-bourgeois intellectuals affected people like Ricardo Flores Magón. In this process, certain intellectual leaders of the labor movement, who themselves were from other classes, were becoming increasingly "fanatic," in the words of German sociologist Karl Mannheim, as "a psychic compensation for the lack of a more fundamental integration into a [working] class and the necessity of overcoming their own distrust as well as that of others."[9] This occurred not only with petty-bourgeois intellectuals but also with occasional intel-

---

[8] Eugenio Martínez Núñez, *Juan Sarabia, apóstol y mártir de la Revolución Mexicana,* I, personal archive; Florencio Barrera Fuentes, *Historia de la Revolución Mexicana: la etapa precursora,* pp. 201–203.

[9] Karl Mannheim, *Ideology and Utopia,* p. 159; cf. Roberto Michels, "Intellectuals," *Encyclopedia of the Social Sciences,* VII, 118–124.

lectuals who came from the upper class, like Práxedis G. Guerrero. Unlike Madero and most high-status intellectuals, Guerrero transcended his class interest completely. Both Guerrero and Ricardo Flores Magón, as well as the majority of the PLM leadership, embraced Anarchism ever more openly during the 1906–1910 period.

The PLM's move to the Left had begun with its emphasis on labor in the 1906 Program and continued with its special instructions implementing the labor and agrarian portions of the Program at the time of the revolt of 1906. After the revolt's failure, Ricardo Flores Magón and Antonio I. Villarreal had issued a "Balance Sheet of Events in 1906" which, while maintaining PLM's pledge to revolution, established "anti-imperialism" and "anticapitalism" as pivotal terms of discourse for the Mexican Revolution. The PLM, Flores Magón and Villarreal asserted, represented "a danger for the development and strengthening of American imperialism in Mexico." Porfirio Díaz, they said, was "shamefully handing the nation over to American capitalists."[10]

On June 1, 1907, PLM began publishing *Revolución,* successor to *Regeneración,* in Los Angeles, California. There the rebels renewed their appeal to workers and peasants. From Sacramento, California, Ricardo Flores Magón contributed articles which were extremely romantic and moralistic in tone and uncompromising in their pledge to continue the 1906 revolution until the achievement of a "new, egalitarian, and happy society." In preaching the seizing of lands, antiparliamentarianism, the taking up of arms in revolution for the PLM Program, and a war of the poor against the rich, Ricardo's articles became increasingly explicit on the question of Anarchism: ". . . by means of rebellion will humanity one day be great and prosperous." As early as November of 1907, not long after Ricardo's imprisonment in Los Angeles, selections from Kropotkin were appearing regularly on the back page of *Revolución.*[11]

[10] Text in Barrera Fuentes, pp. 206–210, Diego Abad de Santillán, *Ricardo Flores Magón, el apóstol de la Revolución Social Mexicana,* pp. 34–38.

[11] *Revolución,* June 22, 1907, and November, 1907, *passim;* cf. Santillán, pp. 28–34, 40, *passim.* Principal editors of *Revolución,* of which a good collection can be found in Relaciones, L-E-926–933, were Librado Rivera, Antonio I. Villarreal, Práxedis G. Guerrero, Modesto Díaz, and Cananea veteran Lázaro Gutiérrez de Lara.

On the eve of the revolt of 1908, a majority of the PLM Board, led by Ricardo Flores Magón, Librado Rivera, Guerrero, and Enrique Flores Magón, agreed secretly to commit the movement to Anarchism and later to remove Villarreal and Manuel Sarabia from leadership ranks. At issue were revolutionary goals and tactics, and these four leaders, among others (e.g., Juan Olivares, Fernando Palomárez, Anselmo L. Figueroa), agreed that Anarchism offered the best solution. Prior to the PLM armed uprisings of 1908, letters were dispatched to various conspirators informing them that neither Villarreal nor Manuel Sarabia was to know of the dates of the revolt and that they were not to be considered part of the PLM Board. Juan Sarabia, on the other hand, was considered by the Anarchists to be "one of them."[12]

A letter by Ricardo Flores Magón to his brother Enrique and to Guerrero, dated June 13, 1908, best expressed the thinking of the majority of the PLM Board on the eve of the 1908 revolt: "All is reduced to a mere question of tactics," Ricardo wrote. "If we had called ourselves Anarchists from the start, no one, or at best a few, would have listened to us. Without calling ourselves Anarchists, we have been firing the people's minds with hatred against the owner class and governmental caste." Thus, he boasted, "There is no Liberal party in the world that has the anticapitalist tendencies of the one that is about to declare a revolution in Mexico." Ricardo went on to argue that lands, factories, and mines should be delivered into the hands of peasants and workers during the fighting of the revolution rather than afterward. "In addition," he wrote, "workers will be advised that they themselves have the arms to defend what the Revolution has given them against the assaults of the soldiers of tyranny and the probable attack of the *gringos* or other nations." Finally, Ricardo expressed hope that Spanish and Italian Anarchists would assist Mexican revolutionaries:

It is quite possible that our revolution will upset Europe's equilibrium and

12 For all this correspondence, involving mainly Rivera, his wife, Guerrero, and the Flores Magóns, consult Santillán, pp. 44–45; Barrera Fuentes, pp. 254–260; Manuel González Ramírez (ed.), *Fuentes para la historia de la Revolución Mexicana*, IV, 377 ff., and *Epistolario y textos de Ricardo Flores Magón*, pp. 170, 182–186, 191–193, 213, 229, 237–238; Isidro Fabela (ed.), *Documentos históricos de la Revolución Mexicana*, X, 86–88; archival materials.

that proletarians over there will do what ours are doing here. Perhaps, if we carry out what I am proposing, the European Powers will throw their weight against us, but that will be the final act of the governmental farce, because I am certain that our brothers on the other side of the sea will not let us perish.[13]

In accordance with this increasing emphasis on Anarchism, PLM newspapers like *Reforma, Libertad y Justicia* (Austin, Texas) published inflammatory articles on the eve of the 1908 revolt urging workers and peasants to "destroy the factory, block up the mine, devastate the farm, and resist the attack of the Cossacks with rifle bullets."[14] Discarding their earlier appeals to discontented elements of the upper class, PLM leaders were now calling for a revolution of workers and peasants against the bourgeoisie, that is, an anticapitalist revolution.

In the aftermath of the revolt of 1908, and in part because of the threat to the bourgeoisie represented by the PLM and a nascent worker-peasant coalition, Mexican politics underwent important changes. Some Científicos and Porfirista politicians, for example, began experimenting with hesitant, new political movements which might accede to power after Díaz' passing. The ostensible cause of the new political atmosphere was Díaz' interview with James Creelman of *Pearson's Magazine,* on February 17, 1908. The dictator told Creelman that he would retire at the end of his present term in office, when he would be eighty years of age (1910). Díaz welcomed an opposition party, he said, which, if "progressive," he would "support."[15] Perhaps the interview represented Díaz' response to PLM pressures, but the PLM was the last thing Díaz had in mind when he told Creelman he welcomed an opposition party. Talk of a new political party with Díaz' support mounted throughout the remainder of 1908.

Little opposition to Díaz appeared openly until after the failure of the 1908 revolt and Díaz' announcement on May 30, 1908, that he would, after all, accept another Presidential term. Even in the face of

[13] Text in González Ramírez (ed.), *Epistolario,* pp. 202–209. Ricardo was in touch with Italian Anarchists, whose newspapers published the PLM cause, according to U.S. Attorney General to Secretary of State, October 29, 1908, in State, 5028.

[14] *Reforma, Libertad y Justicia,* June 15, 1908, in Justice, 90755.

[15] James Creelman, "Interview with Porfirio Díaz," *Pearson's Magazine,* XIX, No. 3 (March, 1908), 241–277.

that retraction, moderates like Madero did not begin to emerge as leaders of a possible new opposition movement until about the end of 1908. Rather, Madero encouraged the formation of the Partido Democrático, a new political party dominated by Reyistas, elements from the military and lower bureaucracy, and other figures from inside Díaz' Administration itself.[16]

Madero, like others of the class from which he came, felt considerable conflict between the need for political change and a break in the nation's economic logjam, on the one hand, and the economic, personal, and political risks involved in such change, on the other. This feeling of ambivalence among some of Mexico's bourgeoisie plagued Madero, one of its most progressive spokesmen, throughout his political career. Madero clearly preferred nonviolent change through the electoral process, as evidenced by his 1910 Presidential campaign. If he had been permitted to succeed electorally, or if relatively progressive Porfiristas had merged with the Madero movement in order to provide political change and some kind of moderate social reform, it is possible that the Revolution would have been averted or at least postponed.[17]

By early 1909, Madero was beginning to realize that his potentially most important political allies—traditional, respected Liberals like Camilo Arriaga and Fernando Iglesias Calderón—were refusing to cooperate with him because, in Iglesias Calderón's words, "this so-called 'Democratic Party' . . . is a group of scheming Reyistas, protecting themselves with the names of some deceived independents." Heriberto Barrón, a Reyista who had masterminded the goon-squad attack on the Club Liberal "Ponciano Arriaga" in 1902, was a leading figure in the Partido Democrático.[18]

16 Charles C. Cumberland, *Mexican Revolution: Genesis under Madero,* pp. 44–54; Ross, pp. 46–52, 65–73.

17 A separate investigation of 1909–1910 politics from the perspective of the Porfiristas needs to be made if the failure of moderates like Madero and progressive Porfiristas (like Díaz' Development Minister) to coalesce and ward off violent revolution is to be understood fully.

18 Iglesias Calderón to Madero (n.d., but *ca.* January, 1909), in Alfonso Taracena, *Madero. Vida del hombre y del político,* pp. 155–159, and cited in Cumberland, p. 52. On Arriaga's rejection of Madero's overtures, on the same grounds, consult Manuel Ramírez Arriaga, "Camilo Arriaga," *Repertorio de la Revolución Mexicana,* No. 4 (May 1, 1960), pp. 22–23.

Despite criticisms from men like Arriaga and Iglesias Calderón, the Reyista movement gathered strength over the next year, incorporating a number of "Establishment" intellectuals, including occasional Científicos, who felt that a change in government was bound to occur if only because of Díaz' advanced age and failing health. Científico theorist Manuel Calero, distinguished novelist and Senator José López-Portillo y Rojas, lawyer Luis Cabrera, agrarian reformer Andrés Molina Enríquez, and Dr. Francisco Vázquez Gómez, Díaz' personal physician and later Madero's running mate for Vice President, were representative of important intellectuals endorsing the Reyista movement. Cabrera wrote at the time that many Científicos were beginning to consider Díaz as expendable. A large number of Científicos, on the other hand, viewed the Reyes movement as far more serious a threat to their hegemony than the subsequent Madero movement. Under whatever political guise—as Reyistas, Corralistas, or simply steadfast Porfiristas— the Científicos wished to perpetuate their power. Adding to the popular appeal of the Reyes movement was the General's record of having opposed the Científicos' ascendancy and having enacted, in Nuevo León, Mexico's first workmen's compensation law. In addition, a number of Masonic lodges threw their support to Reyes. The Reyes movement collapsed, however, in November of 1909, when Díaz exiled its figurehead, General Bernardo Reyes, on a military study assignment to Europe.

The exile of Reyes marked another significant failure by the Díaz regime to accommodate bourgeois Liberals in some kind of political coalition with Científicos willing to change official policy. Reyes himself may have invited the collapse of the movement by insisting, against the wishes of his followers, that the 1910 electoral ticket of Díaz and Corral be supported, instead of favoring the replacement by his own name of that of Vice President Ramón Corral. Aware of the disappointment he was causing his followers, Reyes told his son Rodolfo, "I am going to commit political suicide." In response to his son's objections, Reyes explained that the momentum generated by the Reyista movement threatened to plunge the country into revolution, which would mean Mexico's "ruin." Later, Reyes reportedly told a friend he was accepting exile "for the good and tranquillity of the country."

Most historians have agreed with his biographer's conclusion that Reyes "made a personal sacrifice of himself on the altar of loyalty" to Porfirio Díaz. President Díaz personally wrote Reyes his congratulations for having advised Reyistas to stop the movement, asserting that the General thereby had avoided "disturbances of the public peace which would be caused not by your candidacy but by the revolutionary cloak that two or three incrusted anarchists among your friends have tried to give it."

Yet there remain many unanswered questions. For example, were Reyistas granted anything in exchange for the General's exile? How far did Díaz swing over to the side of entrenched Científicos by ostensibly siding with them against Reyes? What went on in the inner councils of government that prevented an accommodation of some kind? What did Díaz think he could achieve by having himself re-elected in 1910 instead of some other figure loyal to him? Was the President even remotely aware that, in the words of one biographer of Madero, "by closing the door on Reyes whom he feared, he opened the door for Madero whom he at first regarded with disdain"? The answers to these and similar questions must remain in the area of conjecture until a thorough investigation of Díaz Administration policymakers is undertaken by historians.[19]

Madero, while desiring support from many of the intellectuals sympathetic to Reyes, did not want his movement to serve as a kind of front for the General. He remained somewhat aloof during the first nine months of the Reyista movement, although making clear his feeling that Mexico must be democratized in some fashion. Also, he made perfectly clear his rejection of the PLM and its 1908 revolt, which he debunked as a minor series of local disturbances insignificant even at the state level. In taking this position, Madero was asserting the same sentiments as those expressed by Vice President Corral. What remained at question in Madero's mind, however, was whether manifesting his

19 The most authoritative, if apologetic, account of Reyes remains Victor E. Niemeyer's dissertation, "The Public Career of General Bernardo Reyes," published in Spanish under the title *El General Bernardo Reyes*. Rodolfo Reyes, *De mi vida. Memorias políticas (1899–1913)*, I, 92–94; Díaz to Bernardo Reyes, September 10, 1909, in Niemeyer (dissertation), p. 264; Luis Cabrera (Lic. Blas Urrea), *Obras políticas*, pp. 1–139; Ross, p. 73.

political opposition too strongly at this time might not be premature and unwise.[20]

Indeed, only in early 1909 did subsequent revolutionary heroes like Madero and Luis Cabrera begin to publish oppositionist articles. Madero's major effort consisted of a very cautious book titled *La sucesión presidencial en 1910*. At best, Madero foresaw development of an Anti-reelectionist political party which would seek to win not the Presidency but the Vice Presidency. It was hoped that this would be done by running an Administration figure—someone like Científico Finance Minister Limantour. In an effort to disengage himself from Reyistas, Madero enlisted the support of such men as Toribio Esquivel Obregón, who represented credit-shy, economically pressed large landholders in Mexico.[21] Yet later, in November, 1909, Madero sought Reyista support.[22]

In such instances as these, the conflicts in Mexico's bourgeoisie on the eve of the Revolution were being manifested by the behavior of the Revolution's first President, Francisco I. Madero. Also, a shrewd and often complicated political maneuvering by leading bourgeois spokesmen was evidenced by this search of Madero's—presumably a not unconscious search—for a viable political coalition which might achieve some kind of accommodation with the Díaz regime and thereby avoid a violent social upheaval, destructive not only of the Porfirista Establishment but also of a number of vested economic interests, including Madero's own.

As Porfiristas, Reyistas, Corralistas, and, finally, Maderistas preened themselves in political anticipation of 1910, a number of Precursor veterans, who considered the PLM too radical in its revolutionary phase, found themselves to the Left of Madero but to the Right of PLM. Typical of these men was Camilo Arriaga, who, after vainly trying to found an opposition newspaper in San Antonio, Texas,[23] returned to

[20] Madero to Rafael L. Hernández, July 9, 1908, in Taracena, p. 73; other Madero letters of July, 1908–April, 1909, in Taracena, pp. 50–160, and Madero, *Archivo*, pp. 213–325.

[21] Francisco I. Madero, *La sucesión presidencial en 1910;* Madero's letters in Taracena, pp. 118–220, and Madero, *Archivo*, pp. 213 ff.; Cumberland, p. 53.

[22] Cumberland, pp. 85–90; Ross, pp. 84–94.

[23] Práxedis G. Guerrero (Los Angeles, California) to A. G. Hernández (Austin,

San Luis Potosí in the summer of 1908 to look after his real-estate interests in the state capital and near Río Verde. Arriaga was jailed but later released. He proceeded to Mexico City to confer with Porfirio Díaz, who agreed to assist him in his financial problems and urged him in return to cease his oppositionist political activities. Arriaga politely refused. In Mexico City, he obtained some credits to see him through his financial crisis and then renewed political contacts with such friends as Río Blanco strike agitator José Neira. He rejected all Madero's overtures for a political alliance. According to Arriaga, Madero's policies were too moderate, and the Madero movement was playing into the hands of the Precursors' old foe, General Reyes.[24]

Arriaga could not, on the other hand, endorse the PLM. His earlier quarrels with Ricardo Flores Magón, who had since emerged as the main leader of PLM, together with his disapproval of overt Anarchism, made collaboration with the exiles unfeasible. Instead, Arriaga remained in Mexico City to develop further political opposition against Díaz. He was not alone. Other Precursor veterans, like Alfonso Cravioto, were also groping for a viable political alternative to the aging but entrenched Díaz system. Cravioto and José Vasconcelos became prominent leaders of the Ateneo de la Juventud when it was founded in November of 1909.[25]

Even as the PLM's move to the Left coincided with the emergence of the labor movement and the 1906–1908 strikes and revolts, so did the various attempted political alliances after 1908 reflect the pressures affecting diverse individuals, groups, and classes at the time, especially elements of the bourgeoisie hard hit by the 1907–1911 economic crisis. The bourgeoisie, however, was not united. Many opposed the perpetuation of the Díaz system, including bourgeois spokesmen outside the government and some from within the Establishment itself. However, those outside the government could not agree among themselves, as exemplified by Arriaga's refusal to co-operate with Madero. Nor could they reach agreement with possible allies inside the govern-

Texas), May 1, 1908, in Relaciones, L-E-954, and Tomás Sarabia (Austin, Texas) to Guerrero (Los Angeles, California), May 12, 1908, in Relaciones, L-E-932.
24 Ramírez Arriaga, 22–23; Cabrera, pp. xvi–xvii.
25 José Vasconcelos, *Ulises criollo* in *Obras completas*; Ateneo de la Juventud.

ment, such as General Reyes. Disagreement was rife within the Administration as well. Not only was President Díaz failing in his personal pleas to Arriaga and Madero for co-operation—he could not even keep his own team united, as shown by his exiling of General Reyes.

In brief, divisions among bourgeois elements inside and outside the government contributed to the failure of the bourgeoisie to achieve a peaceful accommodation and avoid a revolt from below. In addition, these divisions paved the way to Madero's eventual decision to resort to violent revolution in order to replace Díaz and his aides with a more flexible political leadership.

As the year 1910 approached, Mexico's intellectuals faced some difficult political choices. Precursor moderates, like Arriaga, and a number of restless middle-class intellectuals, like Vasconcelos,[26] found inadequate each of the two clear-cut choices offered Mexico by the most viable opposition movements: violent socio-economic revolution (PLM), or nonviolent political change (Anti-reelectionists). By deciding to straddle the two alternatives and to seek broader political coalitions between classes than those offered by the PLM or Madero, Arriaga and intellectuals like him were anticipating a third grouping, which would emerge more clearly in early 1911. That would be a loose coalition led by the moderate minority wing of PLM and the left wing of the Madero movement. This new grouping would encourage violent revolution to overthrow Díaz, but then would defend the Ciudad Juárez peace treaties in order to make possible a fair Presidential election and eventual socio-economic reform by legislative action.

[26] Vasconcelos; Cumberland, p. 87; Ross, pp. 86–87; Richard B. Phillips, "José Vasconcelos and the Mexican Revolution of 1910" (Ph.D. dissertation).

PART THREE

Intellectuals as Revolutionaries,

1910–1917

CHAPTER EIGHT

Divisions and Polemics,
1910–1911

CONTRARY TO popular belief, the aims of the Mexican Revolution were not well defined in 1910. Except for the overthrow of Porfirio Díaz, major revolutionary groupings held few goals in common and many in direct contradiction. As we have seen, the PLM, at least as represented by its exiled leadership and its armed units in northern Mexico in 1910 and 1911, wished to spread a violent, anticapitalist revolution of workers and peasants which, it hoped, would achieve the aims of a social revolution—"Land and Liberty" was PLM's battle cry. The pro-Madero Anti-reelectionists, on the other hand, reflecting the attitudes of their coalition of discontented elements from the upper and upper-middle classes, advocated political democracy with their slogan of "Effective Suffrage and No Re-election." In part to offset the appeal of the PLM and in part to gain armed support from some of the lower classes, the Maderistas made vague promises to the peasantry a few weeks prior to the day set for their revolt, November 20, 1910.[1] Until publication of their Plan de San Luis Potosí in November of 1910,

[1] Paragraph 3 of Article 3 of Plan de San Luis Potosí.

however, and indeed in that Plan, the Maderistas emphasized the establishment of formal democracy as their major goal.

It is the Madero revolution, later renewed and moved slightly Left by Carranza (1913–1917), that writers seem to have in mind when they call the Mexican Revolution a bourgeois revolution. For the PLM, however, and to a lesser extent for Zapata and his peasant army which adopted PLM's slogan of "Land and Liberty," the Mexican Revolution was one of urban and rural workers against the bourgeoisie.

Even for the Maderistas, the Revolution was not bourgeois in the usual sense of being an antifeudal revolution. How could the Maderistas create and forge a bourgeois revolution if they were already integrally part of a national bourgeoisie potentially on the defensive against a revolt of workers and peasants from below? In their criticisms of economic monopoly, especially of foreigners, the Maderistas could, of course, pursue to some extent revolutionary, nationalistic, bourgeois ends. However, in significant part, as Madero explained to his family and as his short-lived Presidency (1911–1913) suggested,[2] the Maderistas' revolution was a reform movement aimed at preserving and reinvigorating an already-existing "free enterprise" system. Díaz' top advisers themselves, as has been shown, recognized on the eve of the dictator's downfall the need for some modest economic reform, especially in the countryside. The Maderistas were not bourgeois revolutionaries in the historical sense of attempting to superimpose upon a feudal, outdated socio-economic system a capitalistic, modernized economy. Rather, the Maderistas sought to liberalize, stimulate, and increase the productive capacity of a capitalist system already established in Mexico, but blocked and slowed down by monopoly and recession under Porfirio Díaz, as well as threatened from classes below.

Madero and the PLM

Conflicts between Madero and the PLM established a pattern for division and civil war which came to prevail throughout the Mexican

2 Alfonso Taracena, *Madero. Vida del hombre y del político;* Charles C. Cumberland, *Mexican Revolution: Genesis under Madero;* Stanley R. Ross, *Francisco I. Madero, Apostle of Mexican Democracy.*

Revolution. Within the ranks of each contesting group, further divisions occurred along ideological lines of reform versus revolution. The history of the PLM between August, 1910, and March, 1911, reflected these patterns of conflict.

Released from an Arizona prison in August of 1910, Ricardo Flores Magón, Librado Rivera, and Antonio I. Villarreal went to Los Angeles, California, to renew publication of *Regeneración*. Throughout that autumn, *Regeneración* emphasized radical socio-economic goals sought by PLM revolutionaries and the need for the use of violence to achieve those goals. Disdainful of Madero's nonviolent electioneering, *Regeneración* boasted, in the September 3 issue: "Our electoral ballots will be bullets from our guns." Three weeks later, the newspaper proclaimed the Anarchists' motto of "Land and Liberty": " 'Land!' shouted Bakunin; 'Land!' shouted Ferrer; 'Land!' shouts the Mexican Revolution . . . 'Land and Liberty!' "[3] In the October 8 issue of *Regeneración,* the PLM asserted that Mexico was involved in a "class war," and that the political reform sought by Madero was not only inadequate but also "a crime, because the malady that afflicts the Mexican people cannot be cured by removing Díaz and putting in his place another man." On November 12, 1910, *Regeneración* excoriated "the imperialism of the United States." Villarreal contributed an article titled "Mexican, Your Best Friend Is a Gun" to the December 3 issue. A week later *Regeneración* stated: "Violence which frees is no crime; it is a virtue. Dynamite which destroys oppressors is the fruitful and glorious force of progress and emancipation."

The PLM Board of Ricardo and Enrique Flores Magón, Rivera, Práxedis G. Guerrero, and (nominally) Villarreal realized that many Mexicans, including some veterans of the Liberal Club movement of

---

[3] *Regeneración,* October 1, 1910. Francisco Ferrer Guardia (1859–1909) was a Spanish pedagogue whose Escuela Moderna (Barcelona, 1901–1906) and its publications emphasizing laical, "rational" education became world-famous. In 1907, he founded, with Malato and other Anarchists and left-wingers, the "International League for Rational Education of Children." On October 13, 1909, he was executed by the Spanish Government as an alleged chief of the revolutionary movement; European Anarchists made his case a *cause célèbre.*

1900–1903 and the PLM, had been won over to the Madero camp
during the many months of Madero's electioneering and their own imprisonment in Arizona. Hence, five days prior to the scheduled Madero revolt, the board issued a manifesto calling upon PLM members
and sympathizers to take advantage of any pro-Madero uprising by
adding the weight of their numbers and arms in fighting for "the economic revolution." The manifesto warned, however, that Madero represented "the conservative party," and it adjured PLM militants not to
make "common cause" with Madero's "personalist" movement. The
manifesto emphasized that no pact had been signed or could ever be
signed between the PLM and the Madero Anti-reelectionists. Later, on
January 3, 1911, "General Instructions" to PLM revolutionaries were
issued, repeating the 1906 and 1908 instructions and emphasizing the
struggle against "tyrants and the rapacity of capitalist exploiters, whatever their nationality." These new instructions permitted collaboration
with forces of Madero during actual combat, but reiterated the basic
differences between the two movements.[4]

Madero had delayed his call for a violent uprising until early November, 1910 (although he dated his Plan de San Luis Potosí October
5, in honor of the day he escaped San Luis Potosí to go into U.S. exile).
By setting November 20 as the date for revolt, Madero had left his
followers little time to prepare. Many Maderistas were surprised by
their leader's last-minute decision to cease months of nonviolent political campaigning and resort suddenly to armed rebellion, the tactic espoused by the PLM. The Maderistas needed time to collect arms and
co-ordinate military plans. Madero himself did not re-enter Mexico
from his U.S. exile until February 14, 1911. Even the followers of
Zapata in Morelos did not rebel until February and March of 1911.
Yet at the time of Madero's call for revolt, most of Mexico was already seething with discontent. In Morelos, for example, schoolteacher
and later Zapatista ideologist Otilio Montaño had delivered inflammatory speeches about the war "of the poor against the rich" as early as

[4] Text in Diego Abad de Santillán, *Ricardo Flores Magón, el apóstol de la Revolución Social Mexicana*, pp. 65–66; Florencio Barrera Fuentes, *Historia de la Revolución Mexicana: la etapa precursora*, pp. 300–301; Relaciones, L-E-953.

the 1909 gubernatorial campaign. Similar rhetoric, much of it inspired by PLM, was sweeping the country from Yucatán to Sonora.[5]

After February of 1911, revolutionary victories spread across Mexico with increasing rapidity—Zapatistas, Maderistas, "Magonistas" (as the press dubbed the radicals of the PLM), and innumerable smaller, localized groupings led by lawyers, schoolteachers, and peasant *caudillos*. Yet only the PLM had been agitating consistently for violent revolution over the previous five years. It should not be forgotten that when Madero suddenly switched from nonviolence to revolution, the only revolutionaries who had accumulated a supply of arms and who were seasoned with battlefield experience were veterans of the PLM. Many Maderistas had to move swiftly to procure sorely needed guns and ammunition. Many other Mexicans were already armed in a rudimentary manner—machetes being almost as common in rural Mexico as tortillas. But, in late 1910, few had PLM's experience in organizing and leading a rebellion.

The November, 1910—February, 1911, phase of the Mexican Revolution is perhaps the most obscure period, in terms of military history, which the historian of Mexico has to confront. Yet insofar as available data reveal, everything indicates that the Madero wing of the revolt did not succeed in its early phases. The PLM, on the other hand, produced manpower, arms, and military victories in the November, 1910 —February, 1911, period, all of which helped to sustain the momentum of revolution against Díaz. Only the followers of Pascual Orozco, Jr., in Chihuahua, could match the PLM's record of victories during this crucial period. Many of the Orozquistas were from the PLM; the two groups often acted in alliance.

Prior to February, 1911, significant if temporary PLM victories occurred in Veracruz (October, 1910), Baja California, and Chihuahua. On January 29, 1911, Mexicali, capital city of Baja California, fell into the hands of PLM insurgents. This represented the biggest single victory against Díaz on the battlefield until that time; soon, the PLM was sweeping over the rest of northern Baja California. Mexican Government officials learned of official U.S. interest in "sending Amer-

[5] Francisco Bulnes, *El verdadero Díaz y la Revolución*, pp. 404–407; Gral. Gildardo Magaña, *Emiliano Zapata y el agrarismo en México*, Vol. I.

ican troops into Mexican territory, solely in order to protect lives and interests." U.S. gunboats were dispatched to both coasts of Mexico. However, relations between Díaz and the U.S. Government were now strained. The aging dictator had refused an earlier request by the United States for a permanent lease of Magdalena Bay, Baja California, site of an American naval station. The United States feared that, under a later Mexican Government, Japanese interests might be ceded the site. Further aggravating Mexican–United States relations was the fact that Díaz, in the last years of his regime, had begun to favor British petroleum interests over those of Rockefeller and Doheny, in what apparently was an attempt to play off one set of interests against another. Díaz now rejected U.S. overtures for American military intervention and, shrewdly waving the nationalistic banner of his domestic opponents, accused the PLM in Baja California of being controlled by "Yankee" filibuster interests.[6]

Meanwhile, by February of 1911, the state of Chihuahua also had become engulfed in revolution. A journalist from the New York *Herald*, sent to Chihuahua to investigate, reported public sentiment to be heavily "Magonista" (PLM).[7] The main Maderista leader in Chihuahua was Pascual Orozco, Jr., whose troops had chalked up an estimated nine major victories against two major defeats.[8] Orozquistas and Magonistas often worked together in Chihuahua, which was only natural since Orozco had formed links with the PLM years earlier. As

6 This charge, unpersuasive at the time because of PLM's obvious anti-U.S. position, has since been refuted by a number of historians (e.g., works by Duffy Turner, Cué Cánovas, and Blaisdell in the Bibliography). Some U.S. citizens did fight for the PLM in Baja California, including "Wobblies" of the IWW and various adventurers, but not in a filibuster effort to annex more territory to the United States. The Baja California campaign is not discussed in detail here because it has been fully examined and documented elsewhere, e.g.: Lowell L. Blaisdell, *The Desert Revolution: Baja California, 1911*. Although Blaisdell did not have access to the Relaciones Archives, documents in L-E-933–934, 953 buttress his argument. On possible U.S. intervention in Mexico to oppose the PLM, consult Isidro Fabela (ed.), *Documentos históricos de la Revolución Mexicana*, I, 223, 266, and 290. On strained Mexican–United States relations at the end of the Porfiriato, consult Henry Bamford Parkes, *History of Mexico*, p. 314; Ross, pp. 136–137.

7 Text in Barrera Fuentes, p. 305.

8 Michael C. Meyer, *Mexican Rebel: Pascual Orozco and the Mexican Revolution, 1910–1915*, pp. 19–26.

early as October, 1906, Orozco had been observed reading "antigovernment literature" (probably *Regeneración*), according to state-govern-
ment correspondence. In May of 1909, José Inés Salazar, of PLM,
and Orozco had been accused by the *jefe político* of the Bravos District,
Chihuahua, of purchasing arms and ammunition in the United States
and bringing them into Mexico. Orozco's biographer is of the opinion
that Práxedis G. Guerrero was the main contact between the PLM
Board and the Orozco-Salazar group.[9]

In December, 1910, Orozco sent to the United States a request for
more of "Ricardo Flores Magón's combat forces."[10] Later that month,
PLM rebels led by Guerrero captured Casas Grandes, Chihuahua, site
of a humiliating defeat for Madero two months later (March 6,
1911).[11] Guerrero's troops moved on to take nearby towns. On December 30, 1910, Guerrero was killed in a battle at Janos, Chihuahua.

Guerrero's death did not cripple the PLM effort in Chihuahua. In
mid-January, 1911, the two major battlefield commanders of Chihuahua were Orozco, with seven hundred men, and PLM member Luis A.
García, with three hundred men, each of whom co-operated with the
other. In the North and West, hundreds of PLM troops under José de
la Luz Blanco were winning hit-and-run battles between Sonora and
Chihuahua, often in collaboration with Orozco's troops.[12]

Enrique and Jesús Flores Magón, the latter a Maderista in 1910–
1911, subsequently recalled heavy Maderista dependence on PLM soldiers and commanders. Some of the Flores Magóns' claims remain difficult to confirm—e.g., that the Pascual Orozcos (father and son) were
once PLM members. Pascual Orozco, Jr., a loyal Maderista, did co-
operate with PLM members during the anti-Díaz fighting; however,
there is no conclusive evidence that he himself was a PLM member.
On the other hand, Orozco did not always get along with Madero. By
pressing an attack on Ciudad Juárez, Chihuahua, May 8–10, 1911,

[9] *Ibid.*, pp. 11–12, 15, 17; correspondence between Michael C. Meyer and author
of the present work.

[10] Francisco R. Almada, *La revolución en el Estado de Chihuahua*, p. 187.

[11] *Ibid.*, pp. 200–201; Cumberland, pp. 131–133; Ross, pp. 144–149; Meyer, pp.
7–28.

[12] Almada, p. 189, and *passim;* Relaciones, L-E-934 and L-E-953.

Orozco disobeyed specific orders from Madero. On May 13, Orozco confronted Madero with a list of demands, of which the most controversial was that the defeated federal commander of Ciudad Juárez should be tried as a war criminal. These incidents caused much concern among revolutionaries, until Orozco and Madero repledged their loyalty to one another, a day later. A breach had opened between Orozco and Madero, however, and it never was to be completely closed.

Orozco's attack on Ciudad Juárez precipitated Díaz' surrender and flight from Mexico. Throughout the anti-Díaz campaign, Orozco's "army" had been Madero's most effective weapon. Orozco's battles were often fought with the aid of such PLM veterans as the following: Luis A. García, José de la Luz Blanco, José de la Luz Soto, Lázaro Alanís, Prisciliano G. and Benjamín Silva, Jesús M. Rangel, José Inés Salazar, Lázaro Gutiérrez de Lara, Elfego Lugo, Benjamín Aranda, and José C. Parra, to name only the best known.[13]

Enrique and Jesús Flores Magón later claimed PLM affiliation for a score of revolutionary heroes. Included in their list were the following men: in the North, Lucio Blanco (later famous for his distribution of land in Matamoros, Tamaulipas), Manuel Chao (Villista commander), José María Leyva (PLM victor in Mexicali), León Ibarra, Abraham González (initiator of Maderista revolt in Chihuahua and later, 1911–1913, governor of Chihuahua), and Antonio I. Villarreal; in the Durango-Zacatecas-La Laguna (Torreón) region of north-central Mexico, Emilio P. Campa, Luis Moya, Cheché Campos, Calixto Contreras, José Isabel Robles, César E. Canales, and Antonio Rojas; in the South and East, in the Veracruz-Oaxaca-Puebla region, Cándido Aguilar, Heriberto Jara, Gabriel Gavira (1915 governor of San Luis Potosí and responsible for the first official land distribution there), Rafael Tapia, Teodoro Hernández, Carlos Ramírez, Octavio Bertrand, Raúl Pérez, Camerino Mendoza, Hilario C. Salas, Ernesto E. Guerra, Gaspar Allende, Cándido D. Padua, and "Santanón" (Santana Rodríguez), among others.[14] Mention already has been made of the Sonoran PLM

13 The Flores Magóns' assertions about these men are confirmed by documents in Relaciones, L-E-934–953; on Ciudad Juárez incidents, see Ross, pp. 163–169, Cumberland, pp. 139–141, and Meyer, pp. 29–37.

14 Enrique Flores Magón, "Notas breves de un revolucionario en defensa del

nucleus, including Esteban Baca Calderón, later Nayarit governor and left-wing delegate to the Constitutional Convention of Querétaro, 1916–1917. When PLM influence on the labor movement and on the 1917 Constitution is considered, there remains little doubt that not only as a Precursor movement but also as an active force in the 1910–1917 Revolution, the PLM, like the Maderistas, played an extremely important role.

Madero was not unaware of the contributions PLM armed units were making during the early months of the 1910 Revolution. With or without Madero's approval, Maderistas sought PLM rank-and-file support by circulating the rumor that Madero would be President and Ricardo Flores Magón Vice President. Ricardo flatly denied this in the February 25, 1911, issue of *Regeneración,* reiterating his Anarchist view that "governments are protectors of the rich." However, by then, many PLM members had been deceived by the scheme and were marching side by side with Maderistas; moreover, circulation of *Regeneración* inside Mexico had declined because of war and confusion.

On February 11, 1911, three days prior to Madero's return to Mexican soil, Prisciliano G. Silva's PLM troops captured Guadalupe, Chihuahua, southeast of Ciudad Juárez, and raised the banner of "Tierra y Libertad." While, on the one hand, the PLM had won major victories at Casas Grandes, Guadalupe, and Mexicali—indeed, the Baja California campaign was going strong and spreading inland—Madero, on the other hand, was concerned because his forces were ineffective except in a small portion of the state of Chihuahua. As one of Madero's biographers, Charles C. Cumberland, has noted of this time, "Madero needed an important victory."[15]

Therefore Madero crossed the border to claim leadership of revolutionary forces operating in Chihuahua. In his first military action, he vainly sought to seize Zaragoza. According to Prisciliano G. Silva, Madero and his aides, including former PLM member José de la Luz Soto, ran into heavy federal resistance and asked Silva to send rein-

Partido Liberal Mexicano, iniciador de la Revolución Social Mexicana," *Gráfico,* January 23, 1931; Jesús Flores Magón, "Qué fue y cómo se desarrolló la Revolución que encabezó Flores Magón," *Gráfico,* November 22, 1930.

[15] Cumberland, p. 130; Blaisdell, pp. 41–162.

forcements and transportation to assist them in moving to the PLM stronghold of Guadalupe. There, by all accounts, Madero embraced Silva, while PLM member Lázaro Gutiérrez de Lara arrived from across the border with reinforcements. For the moment, in spite of Madero's late arrival on the scene and his failure to have won any battle yet, the Revolution seemed quite viable indeed.

Next day, Madero declared Silva his prisoner, an action made possible by Gutiérrez de Lara's agreement to ally his fresh PLM forces with those of Madero. Gutiérrez de Lara represented the Socialist wing of PLM, which felt resentment against the Anarchist majority of the PLM Board for having earlier agreed to keep revolt plans secret from Socialists like Antonio I. Villarreal and Manuel Sarabia. Gutiérrez de Lara's repudiation of the PLM was duplicated about two weeks later by that of Villarreal, and then by Eugene V. Debs and U.S. Socialists. The Socialists disparaged PLM's Anarchism and insistence on autonomy from Madero.[16]

Up until Silva's arrest by Madero in mid-February, 1911, Madero's revolution had been struggling for survival, while that of the PLM had been progressing, especially in Baja California and Chihuahua, even according to the evidence provided by Madero's biographers. Now, however, the PLM divided on the very issue that caused Silva and Gutiérrez de Lara to part company in Guadalupe: the question of the goals of the Revolution and the degree of co-operation with Maderista forces. A majority of the PLM "remained vitriolic critics of Madero and his work."[17]

It should be noted that Silva, not Madero, was arrested at the PLM stronghold of Guadalupe. Consequently, aside from ideological and social issues at stake, Ricardo Flores Magón's article "Francisco I. Madero Is a Traitor to the Cause of Freedom," which appeared in *Regeneración* on February 25, 1911, was an expected PLM response. Madero

[16] *Regeneración*, February 25, March 4, July 8, 1911; Ross, pp. 144–146; Almada, pp. 196–197. Ethel Duffy Turner (*Ricardo Flores Magón y el Partido Liberal Mexicano*, p. 239) provides an eye-witness account of Villarreal's final meeting with Ricardo Flores Magón and other PLM leaders on February 26, 1911; Villarreal then went to the Texas border to join Madero's forces, but he was arrested there by U.S. authorities.

[17] Ross, p. 145.

had, at worst, allowed himself to be rescued by the PLM and Silva and then had turned against them, or, at best, simply had declared war on PLM as well as on Díaz. In either case, what was involved was, at least on the ideological level, a civil war between conflicting coalitions within the anti-Díaz camp: the worker-peasant–lower-middle-class faction of the PLM and the (generally) upper and upper-middle-class grouping of Madero, now strengthened by the addition of PLM defectors and increasing numbers of peasant recruits.

Ricardo Flores Magón's article attacking Madero merely reiterated in stronger language what the newspaper had been proclaiming for months. Wrote Flores Magón:

The wolf has taken off his sheepskin and shown us his fangs and talons . . . Madero made Silva a prisoner because Silva refused to recognize Madero as "Provisional President of the Republic." . . . Salvation rests not only in the fall of Díaz but also . . . in the denial of the supposed right of Capital to expropriate for itself a portion of what workers produce. Mexicans: your "Provisional President," as he fancies himself, has begun to deliver blows against freedom. What will happen when the "Provisional" becomes actual?

Thus, the November, 1910—February, 1911, period of the Mexican Revolution was characterized by major PLM military successes, military failure in the Madero camp (even in March, when Madero lost his first major engagement, at Casas Grandes), and a scission between Maderistas and PLM moderates on the one hand, and PLM radicals on the other. There is abundant evidence to justify the hypothesis that the PLM played a critical role in maintaining revolutionary impetus during the November–February period, as well as during 1906–1910, without which impetus the Madero revolt might never have started or, ultimately, succeeded.

Ciudad Juárez Peace Treaties and Anti-Madero Revolts

From March to May of 1911, Díaz' forces suffered reverses throughout the nation. Maderistas and Zapatistas won new and important victories. The PLM advanced in Baja California. Madero, however, continued to insist that PLM troops follow his orders; when his strength permitted, he arrested those who held out for PLM autonomy. In April,

1911, he ordered the arrest and disarming of Luis A. García and five other PLM commanders in Chihuahua for having raised the PLM red flag of "Tierra y Libertad," and for having requested permission to act independently of, but not against, Madero's command. According to Madero, those leaders were acting "in rebellion against my Government."[18]

If a truce agreement had to be reached, Porfirio Díaz presumably preferred making peace with the moderate wing of the Revolution. The dictator had battled, off and on, for five years against the PLM. Confronted by PLM and Orozquista military successes during the period between November of 1910 and February of 1911, Díaz had reason to fear that the entire socio-economic system he had labored to develop and preserve might come tumbling down under a revolutionary leadership dominated by PLM elements. Madero's civil war against PLM radicals after February, 1911, presumably did not displease the dictator. The very radicalism of the PLM wing of the Revolution, combined with its military victories, may have helped incline Díaz to prefer peace with Madero and the moderates, to defeat at the hands of all branches of the Revolution, including PLM, Zapata, and the radicals.

However complicated the motives and forces at work, Díaz sought and achieved a peace arrangement with Madero in May, 1911. Within Madero's own camp, a Left-Right split became evident during the negotiations of the Ciudad Juárez peace treaties. Left-wing elements objected to Madero's reported willingness to permit Díaz to continue as President and Limantour as Finance Minister. Dr. Francisco Vázquez Gómez, who had been Madero's running mate in the fraudulent 1910 elections won by President Díaz, helped persuade Madero that Díaz must go. The Doctor was less successful in the case of Limantour, a long-time friend of the Madero family. Finally, Vázquez Gómez "maneuvered privately and without authorization to eliminate Limantour," leaving Madero faced with a *fait accompli*. This marked the start of a growing division between Vazquistas and Maderistas.[19] Luis

18 For letters by Madero and PLM leaders on this, consult Manuel González Ramírez (ed.), *Fuentes para la historia de la Revolución Mexicana,* IV, 376–377; Almada, pp. 219–222.

19 Ross, pp. 159–169; cf. Cumberland, pp. 146–151.

Cabrera and Carranza, both of whom formerly had been associated with the Reyes movement, viewed the Ciudad Juárez peace treaties as a compromise by Madero, bordering upon betrayal of the Revolution.[20]

In accordance with the Ciudad Juárez peace treaties, Foreign Minister Francisco León de la Barra became Interim President, and Porfirio Díaz left Mexico. Presidential elections were scheduled for October, 1911. All revolutionary armies were, in the meantime, to disarm.

During the period of the interim government, a number of events occurred which alienated not only PLM radicals but also many Maderistas. The left wing of the Madero movement, including intellectuals like Jesús Flores Magón, politicians like Vázquez Gómez, and military *caudillos* like Orozco, looked askance at Madero's tolerance for further compromise. Only three Maderistas were named to the interim Cabinet, and two of them were former Porfiristas—Dr. Vázquez Gómez and his brother, Emilio. On June 9, 1911, two days after his clamorous entrance into Mexico City, Madero made a pact with General Bernardo Reyes, who had just returned to Mexico from his exile on a military study mission in Europe. Madero promised Reyes the Ministry of War when he should become President. On June 12, Reyes announced his willingness to run for Vice President on a Madero ticket; seven weeks later Reyes declared his intention to run for President. Many Maderistas felt that the Revolution had not brought any change, since Porfiristas and Reyistas continued to wield so much influence.

Vazquistas were further antagonized by Madero's decision on July 9, 1911, to disband his Anti-reelectionist Party, in order to rebuild his crumbling political coalition around a new organization. In August–September, 1911, Madero's new party, the Partido Constitucional Progresista (PCP), held its first convention in Mexico City. In what many considered to be an "imposition" by Madero, the PCP convention replaced Dr. Vázquez Gómez with José María Pino Suárez as Madero's running mate for the October elections.

Finally, the violent disarming of revolutionary armies caused many

---

[20] Ross, p. 163; Luis Cabrera, "Carta abierta a Don Francisco I. Madero con motivo de los tratados de C. Juárez," April 27, 1911, in his *Obras políticas*, pp. 203–213. This famous letter, it should be noted, was conservative in tone, even if to the Left of Madero.

to doubt Madero's devotion to the Revolution. On July 12, 1911, federal troops under Colonel Aureliano Blanquet killed some eighty Maderista soldiers in Puebla, in a local dispute that shocked much of the nation. Maderistas were disarmed in other states as well. In the state of San Luis Potosí, the pro-Madero revolutionary leader and former schoolteacher Alberto Carrera Torres was arrested for alleged involvement in the unsuccessful agrarian-reform revolt of August, 1911, led by Andrés Molina Enríquez. Also in August, Madero assured Zapata that if Zapata disarmed his forces, lands would be distributed to the peasantry as soon as Madero became President. Zapata agreed to Madero's condition. A few days later, as Zapatistas were turning in their guns, General Victoriano Huerta launched a full-scale attack against them and put them to rout.

In the eyes of many, Madero could not be trusted if military forces of men like Blanquet and Huerta could so freely attack Maderistas and Zapatistas. It appeared as if the Porfirista *federales,* still Mexico's official Army, were moving to consolidate their power after the Ciudad Juárez peace treaties. Publicly, Madero never challenged the Army's position, perhaps because to do so might have caused an Army revolt against himself, or perhaps because he needed a well-trained, professional Army to defend the interim government and his own government, elected in the autumn of 1911, against the threat of continued worker-peasant revolution from below (PLM, Zapata, and others). Whatever the explanation, Madero's ostensible compromises with the military aided the *federales* in forcibly disarming revolutionaries and did not prevent Army generals from eventually plotting to overthrow Madero himself (Blanquet, Huerta, and Reyes were all top leaders of the *coup d'état* against Madero, in February, 1913).[21]

None of these developments came as a surprise for PLM radicals. The PLM had anticipated the Zapatista agrarian revolution in more than just its slogan of "Land and Liberty." It had served as well to adum-

---

21 On disarming of Maderistas, consult González Ramírez (ed.), *Fuentes,* IV, 311–312, *passim.* In Part Three of the present work, footnotes are not provided where the text is common knowledge and available in standard histories of diverse viewpoints.

brate the Zapata–Madero split[22]—by suffering earlier the same kind of military "betrayal" as that suffered by Zapata, and by insisting upon the fight for socio-economic goals in the countryside.

It should be pointed out, however, that PLM consistently was more aggressive in its politics and actions than was the Zapata movement. From the start, PLM applied pressure on other revolutionary groups to assume a position more to the Left, in the interest of workers and peasants. By means of its ideology and revolutionary behavior, it served as a constant force for radicalizing events, that is, moving the Revolution to the Left. In most other cases in the Revolution, events tended to radicalize revolutionary leaders rather than vice versa, suggesting the effect of the groundswell of revolt from below.

For example, although the Zapata movement did later serve to radicalize events and force other revolutionary groups toward the Left, it at first went no further in its ideology than did paragraph 3 of Article 3 of Madero's Plan de San Luis Potosí—judicial review of land exchanges and the eventual return of lands to original owners. Even the subsequent Zapatista Plan de Ayala, November, 1911, provided for restitution of land only to those peasants showing legal title, and expropriation of only one-third of the lands of *latifundios*, with prior indemnity. Rarely, and apparently never before 1913, did the Zapatistas sign their major manifestoes with the motto "Tierra y Libertad." Only in the post-1913 period did the Zapatistas radicalize their ideas more in accordance with the pattern established years earlier by the PLM and its revolutionary Program and slogans. It may be said, then, that prior to 1913, events served to radicalize many Mexican revolutionaries, including Zapata, but that only the PLM, even when faced with internal divisions and dwindling influence on post-Díaz governments, consistently served to radicalize events.

In October, 1911, Vazquistas declared themselves in revolt against Madero. According to the Vazquistas' Plan de Tacubaya, October 31, 1911, the aim of the revolt was to effect agrarian reform "at the very

---

[22] Technically, Madero did not betray Zapata—rather, General Huerta acted against Madero's wishes. Nevertheless, Madero never made up for such unfortunate incidents, never distributed land to the peasantry, and, in his caution, alienated even his own followers.

moment the revolution triumphs, without waiting any more, and without delaying for any reason the execution of solutions to the agrarian problem." This, of course, was a page out of PLM's revolutionary book, written in the revolts of 1906 and 1908. So too was the Plan's concluding argument, which emphasized that the Revolution was not intended merely to "remove one man from the Presidential chair in order to put in another, but rather to bring to fruition the ideals, or the only goal, of the Revolution: to resolve once and for all our agrarian problem, and to render Justice equally to all men."[23]

One of the principal authors of the Plan de Tacubaya was former schoolteacher Paulino Martínez, a veteran Precursor journalist. His exile (San Antonio, Texas) newspaper, *Monitor Democrático,* had been generally recognized as second to *Regeneración* in generating revolutionary potential in 1910.[24] Then a Maderista, Martínez was one of many of Madero's followers who grew impatient with the delay in effecting agrarian reform. When the Vázquez Gómez revolt lost momentum in 1912, Martínez joined the Zapatistas.

Complot de Tacubaya: Arriaga and Díaz Soto y Gama

Other Precursors had joined the Madero revolution in 1910 and early 1911, in the hope that it would bring about rapid socio-economic reform. The focal point of their activities had been Mexico City. There many former affiliates of the Liberal Clubs and PLM had begun to reassemble around the figure of Camilo Arriaga. Mainly urban intellectuals, these men were relatively unfamiliar with agrarian problems and uninformed about the PLM-Madero divisions taking place in the North. Under Arriaga's leadership, they planned the Complot de Tacubaya, of March, 1911. This pro-Madero scheme called for a rebellion at the San Diego Army barracks, just outside the nation's capital in the town of Tacubaya. The plot was betrayed, and many arrested on March 27, 1911.

However, the incident proved consistent with the Precursors' record of applying pressure from the Left. The movement's revolutionary "Political and Social Plan Proclaimed by the States of Guerrero, Mi-

---

23 Text in González Ramírez (ed.), *Fuentes*, I, 55–60.
24 Consul Ellsworth to Department of State, September 20, 1910, in Justice, 90755.

choacán, Tlaxcala, Campeche, Puebla, and the Federal District" (March 18, 1911) was, in fact, a forthright continuation of the principles set down in the PLM Program of 1906, with only slight modification.[25] This was not surprising, since the rebels, said to number more than ten thousand in six states, followed Arriaga as their leader and included many other Precursor figures, as well as left-wing elements who later joined the Zapata and Carranza revolts. José Vasconcelos represented the more moderate, Maderista elements in the Complot de Tacubaya. The movement's Political and Social Plan was written in main part by Arriaga's San Luis Potosí colleague poetess Dolores Jiménez y Muro, a veteran of the 1907 Mexican City group "Socialistas Mexicanos" (*Vésper's* Juana B. Gutiérrez de Mendoza, Elisa Acuña y Rosete, *et al.*).[26]

Upon the failure of the Complot de Tacubaya, Arriaga was jailed. He was released when Madero triumphed, in May, 1911. Sizing up the political situation as ominously compromising, especially after the return of General Reyes from exile, Arriaga joined his San Luis Potosí disciple Díaz Soto y Gama in drafting an anti-Reyes manifesto, dated June, 1911, and published in *Diario del Hogar*, June 12.[27]

Because of his responsibility for the support of his family, Díaz Soto y Gama had been relatively quiet between 1904 and 1910, limiting his political activity to occasional correspondence with the PLM. In 1910,

[25] See especially Points VI through XV (full text in González Ramírez [ed.], *Fuentes*, I, 68–70); Magaña (I, 103–110) is the best source for Complot de Tacubaya, because of the author's participation.

[26] Teodoro Hernández, "Precursores de la Revolución: José Edilberto Pinelo," *El Popular*, July 12, 1943. Important figures in the Complot de Tacubaya included the following: Dolores Jiménez y Muro, Juana B. Gutiérrez de Mendoza, José Neira, Santiago R. de la Vega, Alfredo B. Cuéllar, Cándido Navarro, Francisco J. Múgica, Carlos Múgica, Antonio Navarrete, Francisco Sánchez Correa, the Joaquín Mirandas (father and son), Alfonso Miranda, Gabriel Hernández, José Edilberto Pinelo, Francisco Fierro, Felipe Fierro, Francisco Maya, Miguel Frías, Felipe Sánchez, the brothers Melchor, Rodolfo, and Gildardo Magaña (the last-named, Zapata's biographer), José Rodríguez Cabo, Gustavo Durón González, Juan Jiménez Méndez, Domingo Ramírez Garrido, Porfirio Meneses Córdova, Flavio Solís, Juan Torices Mercado, Luis Cid, Santiago Orozco, José N. Valdés, José Carrillo, Fortino B. Serrano Ortiz, Samuel A. Ramírez, José Vasconcelos, and a militant group of medical students.

[27] The manifesto was signed by eighty-three persons in the name of the Centro Electoral Antirreyista.

he had been approached by Vasconcelos at the U.S. law firm of Warner, Johnson, and Galston, where the two young lawyers were employed. Vasconcelos had asked him to join the Madero revolution. According to Vasconcelos, "the very intelligent youth from the provinces" refused to co-operate because of a feeling of political disillusionment. However, Díaz Soto y Gama subsequently told this author that in those days he still identified with the PLM and its socio-economic revolution and therefore could not bring himself to collaborate with the political revolt of Madero, which he viewed as a "mere change of the guard."[28] Whatever the case, once the smoke of battle had settled in May, 1911, and Porfirio Díaz had left Mexico, Díaz Soto y Gama resumed active participation in politics.

Unlike most PLM members in the North, Díaz Soto y Gama had not been personally involved in armed combat. Revolutionary developments, so far as he was concerned, tended to moderate his "Jacobin" tendencies at this point, when elections and political propaganda were the main areas of action in San Luis Potosí and Mexico City. On June 7, 1911, he drafted a manifesto proposing Arriaga as gubernatorial candidate for San Luis Potosí; however, Arriaga refused the candidacy and asked Díaz Soto y Gama to run instead. On June 19, 1911, Arriaga became president of the Club Electoral Potosino Antonio Díaz Soto y Gama. This club claimed to represent the Partido Liberal and the old Club Liberal "Ponciano Arriaga."[29] Díaz Soto y Gama, by now aware of PLM's continued violent revolution in the North, decided to support instead the electoral path of reform offered him at home. He believed PLM radicals were fighting a noble battle, but one which had little chance of success.[30]

In San Luis Potosí, on the eve of Porfirio Díaz' overthrow, Governor Espinosa y Cuevas had founded, with unabashed cynicism, the Club Antirreeleccionista Potosino Aquiles Serdán—named by a Porfirista governor after the Maderista martyr of Puebla, who had died in a premature uprising of November 18, 1910. Resigning as governor, Es-

[28] José Vasconcelos, *Ulises criollo* in *Obras Completas*, I, 582–583; Díaz Soto y Gama, interviews.

[29] *Diario del Hogar*, June 8, 19, July 1, 1911.

[30] Díaz Soto y Gama, interviews.

pinosa y Cuevas then managed the 1911 political campaign of Pedro Barrenechea, gubernatorial candidate of the "elite families." Angered by these tactics of the "counter-revolution," Díaz Soto y Gama at first entered the gubernatorial campaign energetically, but subsequently withdrew and threw his support to Maderista candidate Dr. Rafael Cepeda, whom he considered more popular than himself and able to turn back the political machine of the Espinosa-Barrenechea group. Cepeda won, and Díaz Soto y Gama hailed his victory as a revolutionary one befitting a fellow "Liberal."[31]

At the start of his 1911 political campaign, Díaz Soto y Gama delivered a forty-one–point manifesto "To the People of San Luis Potosí" which, while glorifying the Reform Laws and democracy, introduced socio-economic issues into the political debate. He excoriated the state's elite families, blaming their corruption and greed for San Luis Potosí's failure to become "the Chicago of Mexico." This last reference was intended to appeal to local businessmen and industrialists, whose support Díaz Soto y Gama sought in an attempt to establish a broad coalition between upper, middle, and lower classes. To "save" the state, Díaz Soto y Gama appealed to the middle and lower classes. On behalf of workers, he called for freedom to organize, higher wages, reduced hours, accident indemnity, and other benefits. Concerning the agrarian problem, he promised "to dedicate special attention to the matter of dividing up lands . . ., giving preference to farm laborers and subsistence farmers." He also vowed "to return to Indians the lands and water rights which had been stolen from them."[32]

Díaz Soto y Gama was taking a position somewhere in the middle between Madero and the PLM. His main public complaint at this time was that the interim government had failed to carry out the Revolution's promises to rid the government of Reyistas, Porfiristas, and Científicos. He deliberately was reintroducing socio-economic issues into public debate gradually.[33] An article of his in *Diario del Hogar*, June 20, 1911, expressed concern with little more than "order," "decorum,"

[31] *Diario del Hogar*, July–September, 1911, especially September 25, 1911; *El Estandarte*, May 31, 1911, *passim*.
[32] Text in *Diario del Hogar*, July 1, 1911.
[33] Díaz Soto y Gama, interview, March 19, 1965.

"clean government," "the right of private property," and "patriotism." In the same article, Díaz Soto y Gama applauded defeats of PLM radicals in northern Baja California, an area the PLM had held for almost five months. PLM radicals reacted to Díaz Soto y Gama's moderation as critically as they had to Madero's "treasonous" arrest of Silva.

Juan Sarabia and a Divided PLM

The situations, aims, ambitions, and politics of the old Precursor colleagues now no longer ran on parallel courses. Precursor and PLM moderates were, by comparison with the ever Leftward-moving PLM radicals, now in a nonviolent position of gradual, slowed-down revolution, endorsing Madero while criticizing him from the Center-Left. When Juan Sarabia was released from San Juan de Ulúa Prison, in early June of 1911, he added his weight to the moderates' side. Juan's lawyer, who helped gain his freedom, was Jesús Flores Magón, the brother of Ricardo and Enrique who had sided with Madero. Viewing the PLM radicals' continued revolutionary warfare as impractical, reunited Precursor moderates decided to send a mission to Baja California and Los Angeles, California, to seek a *rapprochement*. As a symbol of their nascent alliance with certain political figures from the Madero movement's left wing, and in an effort to introduce an element of family loyalty, they chose Jesús Flores Magón to accompany Juan Sarabia north in the unenviable task of patching up the division with Ricardo Flores Magón.

In general, Mexico City's PLM moderates were in agreement about ultimate goals and immediate tactics. Their position was publicly stated by a letter from Juan Sarabia, Jesús Flores Magón, and Antonio I. Villarreal to Ricardo Flores Magón, printed in *Diario del Hogar* on June 22, 1911. An earlier letter to Ricardo from Sarabia, on the eve of his truce mission to Los Angeles, had expressed the position of the moderates in identical terms.

Sarabia appealed to Ricardo as a friend, rather than as a political rival. He emphasized the need for education in Mexico, in order to provide a peaceful evolution toward the egalitarian goals of Socialism and Anarchism. He acknowledged and praised Ricardo's Anarchism, but said that the PLM's revolutionary struggle in Baja California was impractical and premature, since the main goal of the Revolution had been achieved: the overthrow of Díaz. Ricardo, of course, viewed the main goal of the Revolution as more than Díaz' removal. Sarabia, however, urged Ricardo to lay down arms and join the nonviolent propaganda battle. "Your Anarchist revolutionary movement not only is unacceptable—it encounters downright hostility on the part of the vast majority of the Nation," Sarabia wrote. "On the other hand," he continued, "the political revolution that has triumphed has met with unanimous support, because it was desired and, above all, understood." Sarabia reminded Ricardo of "a natural law," one which could not be transcended: "the scientific principle of evolution." Finally, Sarabia affirmed his own "credo":

I believe in the irresistible force of universal progress and the constant, unlimited, but relatively slow advance of Humanity. . . . rather than a job of revolution, it is a long job of education. . . . we should accept the situation produced by the triumphant revolution, and, within the relative freedoms that we will enjoy under a democratic regime, we should constitute . . . an advanced and pure Party, which could be the Socialist Party.[34]

Perhaps Sarabia was correct in viewing Mexicans as unprepared for Anarchism or Socialism—the point is debatable—but facts throughout the 1910–1917 period indicate that PLM radicals were correct in claiming that peasants and workers were ready as early as 1910–1911 to seize properties, declare strikes, and pronounce themselves in socioeconomic revolution. Also, PLM radicals analyzed the conservative nature of Maderismo much more accurately than did PLM moderates—although eventually the moderates, after evolving to a realization of the inadequacies of the Madero government, arrived at radical positions on Maderismo.

Perhaps what is most noteworthy, however, is that, in their own divisions of 1911, the PLM Precursors were reflecting and anticipating—in general terms and tone—the innumerable divisions and conflicts within the Mexican Revolution of 1910–1917. For example, to look ahead briefly, well might Sarabia's peace mission to the PLM armed camp of the North in June of 1911 be compared to the one he made

[34] Sarabia's letter in archive of Eugenio Martínez Núñez.

from the North to the South in August of 1914. Then, as an unofficial spokesman for Carranza, Sarabia arranged for an attempted reconciliation between Zapata's radical forces and the more moderate ones of Carranza. Sarabia succeeded in getting Zapata to agree to a conference with Carranza's official representatives—Antonio I. Villarreal and Luis Cabrera—but the conference itself failed. In addition to the moderate-radical division involved, still largely along lines of political reform versus economic revolution, by 1914 there was the added complexity of divisions within divisions, since PLM moderates had by then divided among themselves. In 1914, Díaz Soto y Gama was serving as an important adviser to the radical, Zapata. His former PLM moderate ally Sarabia was beseeching him to confer with another of his former PLM moderate allies, Villarreal.[35]

To return to the June 13, 1911, interview between Sarabia and Jesús Flores Magón, on the one hand, and Jesús' brothers, Ricardo and Enrique Flores Magón, on the other, it was, by all accounts, as tense and unsuccessful as the 1914 Villarreal–Díaz Soto y Gama meeting arranged by Sarabia. Later on the same day of the interview, Sarabia and Jesús tried to persuade Librado Rivera and Anselmo L. Figueroa also to cease their revolutionary activities. According to Sarabia's report of his mission in his newspaper, *Diario del Hogar,* Ricardo Flores Magón and Rivera had insisted that the PLM would not lay down arms until land was distributed to the peasants and the instruments of production were in the hands of the workers. The next day, June 14, 1911, Ricardo and Enrique Flores Magón, Rivera, and Figueroa were surprised in their *Regeneración* offices and arrested; all PLM documents were confiscated.[36] Positive that Sarabia had been involved in arranging the arrest, Ricardo dipped his pen in the venom that was to become commonplace in the warring camps of the Mexican Revolution and wrote,

35 Robert E. Quirk, *The Mexican Revolution, 1914–1915: The Convention of Aguascalientes,* pp. 63–68; Eugenio Martínez Núñez, *Juan Sarabia, apóstol y mártir de la Revolución Mexicana,* I, 273–296; Díaz Soto y Gama, interviews, and *La revolución agraria del sur y Emiliano Zapata, su caudillo,* pp. 173–181.

36 *Diario del Hogar,* June 28, 1911. Sarabia's editorship of *Diario del Hogar* became official on July 1, 1911; the newspaper's founder, Filomeno Mata, had died the previous week.

in the July 2, 1911, issue of *Regeneración,* the first installment of PLM-radical-versus-moderate invective: "The Judas, Juan Sarabia."

Sarabia answered Ricardo's attack in *Diario del Hogar* on July 20, 1911. He asserted that he had had nothing to do with the arrests: "I am opposed to those persecutions." While admitting he "had sent an appeal to insurgents in Baja California, asking them to lay down their arms," Sarabia denied having told Rivera and Figueroa that "he would do all evil possible to members of the [PLM] Board." Furthermore, Sarabia said, he had not credited Madero with his release from San Juan de Ulúa, but rather "the popular endeavor." Finally, he said, "I am not a Maderista . . . but, because of that, I do not deny all merit or sympathy to Madero."

By September of 1911, PLM moderates and radicals were exchanging charges of "treason." However, only once did PLM moderates level the charge of "filibusterism" against the radicals in Baja California, a charge which the moderates ordinarily passed off as an invention of "the bourgeois press."[37]

Sarabia's *Diario del Hogar* led the moderates' attack, which reached a climax in the August 26 and September 27, 1911, issues, when Villarreal called Ricardo Flores Magón "a blackmailer, swindler, coward, drunken pervert, and scoundrel" who "shared his mistress with all men of bad taste." Villarreal accused Ricardo of obtaining economic assistance from the Científicos. He cited as evidence the testimony of Emilio P. Campa, a PLM military commander who had defected in August, 1911, and a letter from Ricardo to Campa which said: "If the Devil gives our movement money, then from the Devil we must take it, naturally without betraying our principles." Finally, Villarreal challenged Ricardo and the radicals to armed combat with himself and the moderates: "If I fall into his hands, then of course he should hang me; if I seize him, I will spit in his face and send him to a madhouse."[38]

This was pure bluster, of course. Moderates were quite committed to nonviolence at this stage. Their assuming of arms would not occur until much later (1913), and then not against the radicals but against

[37] *Ibid.,* August 1, September 27, 1911.
[38] González Ramírez (ed.), *Fuentes,* IV, 369–390.

the enemy whom radicals had claimed to be fighting from the start: the forces of counter-revolution.

Throughout 1911, the position of PLM radicals was one of thinly veiled Anarchism—in the sense that the word "Anarchism" was rarely used. The radicals never wavered from their revolutionary course, not even to make a land-for-arms bargain with Madero, which Zapata had vainly essayed in August, 1911. On May 24, 1911, Ricardo Flores Magón explained to PLM lawyer E. E. Kirk of San Diego, California:

> The Mexican Liberal Party has no compromise to make with either Díaz or Madero. The proposed peace treaty between Díaz and Madero will not stop the revolutionary activity of the Liberals, nor the activity of the other revolutionary forces independent of Madero. . . .
>
> Madero is not the revolution. Madero is simply a leader of the forces at present under his command.
>
> The Mexican Liberal Party has armed forces in all the states of the Mexican Republic, and has the northern portion of Lower California in complete control.
>
> . . . the lands will be given to the working classes with the machinery . . . The revolution of the Mexican Liberal Party is not a political but a true economic revolution.[39]

The July 8, 1911, issue of *Regeneración* claimed that the Revolution, far from being "triumphant," was still going on: "It cannot be denied that the hundreds of strikes taking place at this moment in almost every state of Mexico are revolutionary in character." On July 29, 1911, *Regeneración* asserted that "the capitalist press recognizes the purely economic movement of the PLM in almost all the states of the Republic . . . the seizing of lands by the inhabitants." The newspaper concluded: "See, then, Juan Sarabia, that we have not taken a stand diametrically opposed to the spirit that animated and goes on animating the Revolution." On September 2, 1911, *Regeneración* pointed to the land-grabs and anti-Madero war being conducted by Zapatistas as another indication of the Revolution in process. Mexicans, far from having to be "educated," as Sarabia claimed, were already prepared for radical actions and were acting accordingly, the newspaper said.

A PLM manifesto of September 23, 1911, signed by Ricardo Flores

[39] Ricardo Flores Magón to E. E. Kirk, May 24, 1911, in Relaciones, L-E-934.

Magón, Rivera, Figueroa, and Enrique Flores Magón, summed up earlier statements into a classically Mexican-Anarchist position:

The Mexican Liberal Party has unfurled the red flag in the field of action in Mexico, against Capital, Authority, and Church.

. . . .

All that is produced will be sent to the community general store, from which everyone will take according to his needs.

. . . .

The choice, then: either a new government, that is, a new yoke, or the redeeming expropriation of private property and the abolition of all imposition, be it religious, political, or any other kind.

LAND AND LIBERTY![40]

The Revolution was now breaking up and splintering into many distinct trajectories. On the Left, PLM radicals and Zapatistas were in open rebellion against Madero. At Center-Left, PLM moderates were gathering their forces to found a new party to oppose radicals of the Left and Porfiristas and Reyistas of the Right. Madero's followers had divided into Left and Right also, with Madero making more concessions to the Right than to the Left.

The Moderates' Liberal Party (PL)

PLM moderates founded a Mexico City version of *Regeneración*, known by the same name, in August, 1911. Directed by Sarabia and Villarreal, the newspaper became the official voice of the Junta Iniciadora de la Reorganización del Partido Liberal. This Junta was the main organizing body for the moderates' new Liberal Party, which eventually became known as the Partido Liberal (PL). Key participants in the PL included Sarabia, Villarreal, Arriaga, Díaz Soto y Gama, Jesús Flores Magón, Santiago R. de la Vega, and a number of older, distinguished Liberals, like Fernando Iglesias Calderón, Junta president. These traditional Liberals, though conservative on socio-economic matters, were outspoken anticlericals and helped lend the PL needed prestige among the upper classes. Sarabia had expressed the group's sentiments when

[40] González Ramírez (ed.), *Fuentes*, IV, pp. 369–375; Barrera Fuentes, pp. 311–319.

he earlier answered his Leftist critics by assuring them that "it now will not be possible for a counter-revolution to occur."[41]

Sarabia, Arriaga, Díaz Soto y Gama, Villarreal, and De la Vega, who earlier had formed the Centro Electoral Antirreyista to combat Reyistas in the Madero movement, brought the anti-Reyes group into the new PL. They renamed the Centro Electoral Antirreyista the Club Liberal "Ponciano Arriaga," thus retaining the anti-Reyes flavor of the 1901–1903 club of the same name. The historical parallel was not without significance. The San Luis Potosí leadership's old nemesis, Heriberto Barrón, leader of the goon-squad attack on San Luis Potosí Liberals in 1902, dashed off an urgent warning to Madero:

> *Camilo Arriaga, Sarabia, Díaz Soto y Gama, and all their supporters have separated from you and will be, you will see, your worst enemies.* They succeeded in their perfidious task of separating you from General Reyes, with whose alliance you were both very strong, and now they are separating from you.[42]

Barrón was very close to Madero. As Commercial Agent of the Government of Mexico in New York, he helped reassure American investors and bankers of Madero's reliability. He was, however, less successful in persuading General Reyes to go along with Madero. In December, 1911, the General launched an armed rebellion in Nuevo León. Article 4 of Reyes' revolutionary "Plan" called for agrarian reform, but peasants were wary of the General whose troops had oppressed them so often under Díaz. The Reyista revolt failed after twelve days, and the General was put in jail.

For about a year, most members of the PL stubbornly defended their policy of nonviolence and democratic debate against attacks from the Left, while at the same time suffering one disillusionment after another

[41] *Diario del Hogar,* June 28, 1911. Díaz Soto y Gama, in an interview of March 19, 1965, chuckled about the pragmatic politics involved in soliciting the support of traditional Liberals like Iglesias Calderón. First committeeman (*vocal*) of the Junta Iniciadora was Colonel Eduardo Hay, an engineer whom Madero and Zapata had secretly chosen as provisional governor of Morelos when they arranged their short-lived truce of August, 1911 (*Diario del Hogar,* July 26–29, 1911).

[42] Barrón to Madero, October 26, 1911, in Fabela, VI, 199–200 (emphasis Barrón's); *Diario del Hogar,* August 1, 1911.

with the cautious policies of Madero to their Right. Many were the ironies and embarrassments that occurred. Díaz Soto y Gama, considered to be one of the strongest voices at Center-Left, went out of his way to praise the Mexican Army (Porfirio Díaz' *federales*) and to condemn the liberties taken by a free press. Except for the PLM radicals, not one of the prominent revolutionaries of the time was guiltless of this fatal and ironic misjudgment of the military.[43] Moderates were disturbed by evidence of the spreading of the PLM rebellion in Chihuahua, Coahuila, Tabasco, Veracruz, "and other places in the Republic," as Sarabia's biographer, ordinarily unsympathetic to PLM radicals, has observed.[44] On August 13, 1911, Sarabia, Villarreal, and Jesús Flores Magón dispatched an "open letter" to PLM radicals, Zapatistas, and all other rebels in arms, urging them to lay down their weapons: "Other Liberals tell you that we are still ruled by a tyranny, when in fact the tyranny has died, and they tell you that you will be persecuted, even if you return to a peaceful life." Such Liberals were wrong, the letter asserted. Yet two weeks later, as has been seen, General Huerta launched his attack against disarmed Zapatistas.[45]

With gloomy foresight, Díaz Soto y Gama warned that the national government "carries within itself the germ of contradiction and incongruity, absurd and anomalous things which can produce only evil results."[46] As early as November 19, 1911, the PL's daily newspaper, *Diario del Hogar*, acknowledged the justice of the Zapatistas' cause: "There does not exist Zapatismo, but rather the agrarian problem." On December 15, *Diario del Hogar* became the first Mexico City newspaper to publish in full Zapata's Plan de Ayala. The newspaper always included sections exposing flagrant land injustices, especially those perpetrated by *latifundista* Iñigo Noriega in the state of Mexico. In addition, *Diario del Hogar* waged a steady campaign against the jailing of Liberals throughout Mexico, many of whom were arrested merely for

[43] Díaz Soto y Gama described the military as "the guardians of democracy" and the press, largely controlled by Porfiristas and Científicos, as "conspiratorial" (*Diario del Hogar*, August 3, 8, 1911). For praise of the military by other revolutionaries, consult González Ramírez (ed.), *Fuentes*, IV, 233–235.
[44] Martínez Núñez, *Juan Sarabia*, II, 82–85.
[45] *Ibid.*, and *Diario del Hogar*, August 22, 1911.
[46] *Diario del Hogar*, August 24, 1911.

having received the PLM radicals' *Regeneración* of Los Angeles, California (their names being on earlier mailing lists from 1906 and 1907).

Besides applying pressure on Madero from the Center-Left by means of *Diario del Hogar,* PL members acted individually to persuade Madero to take a more revolutionary position. One of PL's founders, Jesús Flores Magón, also belonged to the central committee of Madero's newly created PCP. Jesús represented an important link between the left wing of the Madero movement and the right wing (PL) of the PLM. One of Jesús' first appeals to Madero had been on behalf of the PLM radical Emilio P. Campa, who later defected to the PL. Jesús asked that Campa and his 280 PLM soldiers be granted their condition for disarmament in Coahuila's sierra: land to the area's peasants and political amnesty.[47]

Arriaga, for his part, joined a group of revolutionary "generals," including Juan Andreu Almazán (later a Zapatista and unsuccessful Presidential candidate in 1940), Cándido Navarro (Maderista, Zapatista), Gabriel Hernández, Heriberto Jara, J. Pesqueira, and Juan J. Múgica, to draft the "Agreement of the Principal Commanders of the Liberating Army in Support of the Plan of San Luis [Potosí]." Dated July 11, 1911, this agreement emphasized that all of Madero's program must be fulfilled, most importantly Article 3, paragraph 3 (modest agrarian reform) of the Plan de San Luis Potosí.[48] Arriaga also joined with the rest of the moderates' Junta Iniciadora de la Reorganización del Partido Liberal to declare the Ciudad Juárez peace treaties null and void, since neither Madero nor Díaz had signed them personally and since the Revolution had been "betrayed."[49]

On labor questions, PL members shifted between radical and conservative positions. Sarabia and Villarreal opposed the anti-Madero revolt of the Vázquez Gómez brothers (October, 1911) because of the Vazquistas' past record of Reyismo. Nevertheless, they joined with Paulino Martínez, main ideologist of the Vázquez Gómez movement, to head an organizational committee for the nascent Confederación

---

[47] *Ibid.,* July 22, 1911.
[48] González Ramírez (ed.), *Fuentes,* I, 54.
[49] *Diario del Hogar,* July 31, 1911.

Nacional de Trabajadores. Never successful, this labor organization defended "direct action," including "strike, boycott, sabotage."[50] Yet later, Sarabia wrote in Mexico City's *Regeneración* (December 2, 1911), an article which considered the strike as no more than "perhaps" a worthy goal.

In general, the moderates displayed great political caution throughout 1911. For example, they were unable to radicalize Madero's PCP by their attendance at its political convention in August and September. The best they could do was to incorporate the 1857 Constitution and Reform Laws into the PCP political platform—a step Madero resisted.[51] Moderates nominated their PL Junta president, Iglesias Calderón, for the Vice Presidential slot on the Madero electoral ticket. Iglesias Calderón polled 33 per cent and 25 per cent of the delegates' votes on the first and second ballots, before Pino Suárez won. The PCP convention elected Camilo Arriaga president of the Election Committee, a post equivalent to that of campaign manager for Madero.[52] This marked the beginning of a division within a division—Arriaga's separation from the Sarabia–Díaz Soto y Gama left-wing axis of PL, in order to back Madero wholeheartedly. Further divisions within divisions were evident in the breaking away of the Vázquez Gómez brothers from the Madero camp and the growing tensions between Orozco and Madero, as the Mexican Revolution became increasingly fractured.

The moderates maintained their cautious approach to social change

---

[50] *Ibid.*, August 10, 12, 1911.

[51] Cumberland, p. 164; González Ramírez (ed.), *Fuentes*, IV, 478–480; Mexico City's newspapers (*q.v.* in the Bibliography).

[52] Cumberland, pp. 164 ff.; González Ramírez (ed.), *Fuentes*, IV, 270–271, 484–497; Agustín Casasola (ed.), *Historia gráfica de la Revolución Mexicana*, I, 344–351; *Diario del Hogar*, August 30–31, September 3, 28, 1911. The PL also placed Arriaga as first vice-chairman of the Maderistas' PCP convention, Sarabia as fourth secretary, and Villarreal as one of four observers (*escrutadores*). The PL did not press the socio-economic issues underlying the Mexican Revolution. Díaz Soto y Gama engaged in a spectacular word duel with Félix Palavicini, later a leader of the conservatives at the 1916–1917 Constitutional Convention, on the need for a stronger anticlerical statement in the PCP program, climaxed by Díaz Soto y Gama's call for a PL walk-out from the convention. Sarabia rose to oppose this threatened break between the PL and PCP, asking his San Luis Potosí colleague to "calm down." Camilo Arriaga engaged in a similarly impassioned debate against Luis Cabrera in favor of including a fairer tax structure in the PCP program.

at their own political convention, in November, 1911, when they emphasized anticlerical and political issues instead of the socio-economic question. Delegates to the PL convention adopted a tentative program which was more moderate than that of the 1906 PLM, even though Sarabia and Díaz Soto y Gama played important roles in drafting both the 1906 and 1911 programs. Paradoxically, these two men, who earlier had been radicals, were acting as moderates now that the Revolution, in their eyes at least, had "triumphed." They retained much of the original PLM Program on labor, although the eight-hour day and minimum wage were now applied only to government jobs. On agrarian matters, the PL program paid lip service to the Zapatista cause of land redistribution, but emphasized the rights of private property. In order to fulfill Madero's Plan de San Luis Potosí, delegates promised to "study" agrarian reform.[53]

The PL itself threatened to split, even as the original PLM had done, along radical-moderate lines. As early as September 3, 1911, Díaz Soto y Gama, Villarreal, Sarabia, Luis Jasso, De la Vega, Gutiérrez de Lara, Rosalío Bustamante, and others, most of them former affiliates of PLM who had since joined PL, were calling for a "Gran Manifestación Popular" to denounce the brutality of "the Cossacks" of Minister of Government Alberto García Granados in putting down a transport strike in Mexico City. Their manifesto was radical and inflammatory. However, two days later, a new signature headed a more moderate manifesto calling off the demonstration: that of Madero's good friend and campaign manager, Camilo Arriaga. When the demonstration finally took place, October 8, Arriaga, Díaz Soto y Gama, and Sarabia did not participate, while relatively unknown newcomers like Socialist Rafael Pérez Taylor, later a leading left-wing labor organizer (1912–1915), did.[54] In Mexico City, the moderate PL was in danger of forfeiting its claims of nonviolent, Leftist opposition against Madero to representatives of the ascending labor movement.

On October 7, 1911, Sarabia penned an article for *Diario del Hogar* which, while limited to political issues, was titled: "The Present Gov-

[53] *Diario del Hogar*, July 29, October 2, November 22, December 11, 1911.
[54] *Ibid.*, September 4, 5, October 7, 9, 1911; José G. Escobedo and Rosendo Salazar, *Las pugnas de la gleba, 1907–1922.*

ernment Is Betraying the Revolution." On October 18, Villarreal's Partido Democrático, which included prestigious, but economically conservative, Liberals like Carlos Trejo y Lerdo de Tejada, merged with the PL. In the October 18 and 19 issues of *Diario del Hogar*, Sarabia denied that he or his newspaper were controlled, or had been "converted," by Iglesias Calderón, Trejo y Lerdo de Tejada, and Arriaga, implying thereby that he was not so conservative as they. The name of Luis Cabrera, a former Reyista, appeared on a list of PL members published by *Diario del Hogar* on October 29, 1911. To bridge this widening spectrum of political interests and ideologies being gathered under the banner of PL, delegates at the PL's November convention named "left-winger" Díaz Soto y Gama and "moderate or conservative" Arriaga to a special committee to defend striking workers before President Madero.[55]

In brief, the moderates' PL was expanding its political coalition beyond its capacity to maintain unity and good will among its own members. Iglesias Calderón, Trejo y Lerdo de Tejada, and less so Arriaga and Cabrera—all would play important political and ideological roles in causing the conservatives' break from the PL's "left wing," as in April, 1912, Sarabia and Díaz Soto y Gama would term their group. In 1911, however, all PL members agreed to the kind of compromising expansion that the new party had undertaken. Indeed, on December 27, 1911, *Diario del Hogar* sealed the party's fate with the publication of the PL's proposed program to be discussed at the disastrous convention of April, 1912. The tentative program, as published, made no significant reference to socio-economic problems.

In one of its last united actions and probably its most significant one, the PL addressed a strongly dissenting "Memorandum to President Madero," criticizing the compromises and oppression of the Madero regime. Dated December 23, 1911, this memorandum anticipated by more than one year a similar step taken by the more famed "Bloque Renovador" of the 26th Legislature (Luis Cabrera *et al.*), which, in late 1912, sensed that the counter-revolution was ascendant under Madero and might overthrow him, as it in fact did six weeks later. The

[55] *Ibid.,* October 19, November 27, 1911.

PL memorandum of 1911 warned Madero of the consequences of his compromising policies:

. . . as the new bureaucrats profit unduly from their posts in the manner of the old, as many of the old oppressive caciques continue enjoying power and influence, the friends of liberty and change, yesterday's revolutionaries, see themselves abandoned, persecuted, or humiliated, lose their patience, and, without considering the harm they cause the Fatherland or themselves, rise up once more in rebellion.

.   .   .   .

The policy of making deals with corrupt men and corrupt practices of the past can only occasion further disturbances and growing malaise, which will end by dragging us all down into the horrors of misery and anarchy.[56]

Through such criticisms, moderates of the PL now found themselves in the position of making life extremely difficult for Madero, a position for which they earlier had criticized PLM radicals.

Madero may have been disappointed to see the names of Camilo Arriaga and Juan Sarabia at the bottom of the PL memorandum. Only two days earlier he had received a letter from Arriaga beseeching him to provide a government job for Juan Lerdo de Tejada y Arriaga, Camilo's nephew. Two weeks prior to that, Madero had written a letter to Governor Rafael Cepeda of San Luis Potosí, asking that all possible assistance be given Arriaga in the sales of some of his properties. "We need Camilo Arriaga's services in the United States, and he only wants to know if he can complete this business transaction before departing," Madero wrote. Arriaga's signing of the PL memorandum was his last public criticism of Madero. Having agreed to provide services for Madero in the United States, Arriaga could no longer go along with the PL.[57]

Madero was less familiar with the name of Juan Sarabia. On December 4, 1911, he had received a letter from José Vasconcelos requesting a government pension for Sarabia. Vasconcelos explained that Sarabia, suffering from tuberculosis contracted while in San Juan de Ulúa Prison, needed funds to support his family. Sarabia did not know

---

56 Text in Fabela, VI, 450–456.
57 Arriaga to Madero, December 21, 1911, and Madero to Cepeda, December 6, 1911, in Fabela, VI, 387, 438.

of this letter, Vasconcelos said. It is not known how Madero responded to the request to lend assistance to one of his critics.[58]

It is known, however, that Madero replied with great indignation to the PL memorandum. Dating his reply December 27, 1911, Madero emphasized—as had the PL earlier to PLM radicals—that his regime was young. The President said that he needed time, and that the Revolution had to "evolve" gradually toward its proclaimed goals: ". . . during the short period of my Administration, I will only be able to lay the foundations for the future aggrandizement of Mexico." He denied all the PL's many charges and expressed "complete satisfaction" with his Cabinet, which was well known to include many former Porfiristas and Científicos. He protested that the new generation of revolutionaries could not possibly fill all the government's administrative posts and that to arbitrarily replace all public servants, most of whom had worked honestly and fairly under the Díaz regime, would be unfair to a large number of innocent, hard-working people.

Finally, Madero accused *Diario del Hogar* of supporting Zapata's revolt and of being part of a "sensationalist" press which had produced "uneasiness in people's consciences." He blamed the news media for frightening away "large amounts of foreign capital, which might otherwise have been invested in our Nation to fertilize our fields and make prosperous our industries, thereby augmenting the wages of workers." He explained the need for a new law, "indispensable" for controlling the "alarmist press . . . sowing panic and confusion among the people." With or without such a law, the President vowed that the press would, in "extreme cases," be controlled, in order to avoid its "bringing to the people anarchy and ruin."[59]

This reply by Madero, striking at the democratic principle of a free press that the President and the PL had championed for so long, galvanized the Sarabia–Díaz Soto y Gama left wing of the PL. After all, labor strikes were sweeping the country, as PLM radicals had pointed out and applauded. A general strike threatened to erupt at Orizaba, where textile manufacturers were demanding immediate troop rein-

[58] Vasconcelos to Madero, December 4, 1911, in Fabela, VI, 376–378.
[59] Texts in *Diario del Hogar,* December 25, 31, 1911, and Fabela, VI, 473–480. The PL denied supporting Zapata's revolt.

forcements and "mounted rural police."[60] Increasing numbers of disillusioned revolutionaries were taking up arms, partly in self-defense,
partly for revolutionary goals, even as the Zapatistas were doing. The
Vázquez Gómez brothers (August, 1911—February, 1912), Bernardo
Reyes (December, 1911), and Pascual Orozco (January–March,
1912) all were laying the ideological and material foundations for their
revolts against the Madero regime and, however demagogically, were
already taking a radical stand on agrarian reform and labor's rights.
Stubbornly refusing to approve of the use of violence, the PL continued to back Madero at least nominally. Nevertheless, events threatened
to overtake not only Madero but the PL as well. By criticizing Madero
from a Center-Left position, members of PL were pouring fuel on the
very flames which threatened to consume them—armed revolts running from Reyes on the Right to PLM radicals and Zapatistas on the
Left.

Ominously underlying PL's discomfort and the galvanization of its
left wing was the fundamental issue of the Mexican Revolution which
had divided leaders, parties, groups, and coalitions from the outset:
Was the Revolution a bourgeois one, or was it one of workers and
peasants against the bourgeoisie? Could it be both at the same time
without precipitating civil war? What would happen if the counter-
revolution did ascend under Madero and even overthrow him? Or if
the revolution of workers and peasants simply swept Madero aside?
As the year 1911 drew to a close, was the PL's goal of democratic reform viable, given such political realities as the following: an imperiled
bourgeoisie, a ruling but strained political coalition of upper and upper-
middle classes defended by some middle-class intellectuals, and a rising
swell of revolt from below led by low-status intellectuals and peasant
caudillos? In brief, what was the course of the Revolution?

Résumé

The polemics first between Madero and the PLM, and then within
the PLM and Madero camps themselves, may be said to have set the
pattern for the polemics within the Mexican Revolution overall. Ini-

[60] President of the Compañia Industrial de Orizaba, S.A., Manufacturas de Algodón
(Orizaba) to Madero (Mexico City), December 28, 1911, in Fabela, VI, 480–482.

tially along the line of political reform versus socio-economic revolution, these disputes bred a series of revolutionary and counter-revolutionary charges, divisions, and divisions within divisions, involving ideological, personalist, and economic issues. The year 1911, and specifically the divisive behavior of the PLM and Precursor veterans, may be said to have anticipated the complex and often chaotic nature of the Revolution and its civil war in the years immediately following.

CHAPTER NINE

Epilogue: Civil War, 1910-1917

M EXICO'S CIVIL WAR of 1910–1917 was an integral part of the Revolution. Conflicts in the minds of bourgeois reformers like Madero had become accentuated during the April–May, 1911, peace negotiations, which had aggravated the civil war by sowing tensions between Madero, on the one hand, and Vázquez Gómez and Orozco, on the other. In addition, a far deeper line of division had been drawn between political reformers, like Madero, and social revolutionaries, like Zapata and PLM leaders.

The pattern of division and debate on socio-economic issues had, in fact, long since been established by the Precursor Movement. During the period of renewed civil strife in 1911–1912 and, with greater violence, during 1913–1917, each contending faction inevitably included in its "armies" a number of peasants and workers. With varying degrees of legitimacy, each faction claimed to speak for the lower classes. Revolutionary groups moved toward the Left in the course of battle. Each faction had within it intellectual spokesmen who encouraged more progressive socio-economic measures. Each *caudillo*, sooner or later, paid lip service to agrarian reform. Radicals, best represented by Zapata, more clearly pursued the line of economic revolution; moderates, best represented by Carranza, who inherited Madero's mantle, defended the line of political reform.

From the ideological viewpoint of the PLM, even though its members and sympathizers had contributed to the divisions and divisions-within-divisions of the civil war, the greatest tragedy of the heightened warfare was that, at a crucial point in early 1915, urban workers pitted themselves against the peasantry. How this happened, and how veterans of the Precursor Movement contributed to its occurrence, relates to the pattern of divisions analyzed already and summarized in what follows. (Diagram 2 presents a graphic view of the divisions and civil war of 1910–1917.)

Madero's Loss of Support and Huerta's Coup d'Etat

In 1911 and 1912, a clear pattern of social and political division set in, as group after group broke with Madero and declared itself in rebellion against his government. Even right-wing rebels like Reyes proclaimed agrarian reform as an important cause to be defended. In this way, the groundswell of revolt from below, and not bourgeois reformism, came at least tacitly to be recognized as the driving force of the Mexican Revolution.

Pascual Orozco, Jr., officially declared his anti-Madero revolt in March of 1912, when, with the approval of the state legislature, thousands of armed rebels took over all of Chihuahua and pushed into Coahuila and Durango. Orozco's top military leaders and ideological guides were PLM veterans like César E. Canales, Emilio P. Campa, José de la Luz Soto, José Inés Salazar, "Cheché" Campos, Lázaro L. Alanís, and Benjamín Argumedo.[1]

Orozco's revolutionary "Plan," dated March 25, 1912, so resembled the PLM Program of 1906 as to make these men's collaboration obvious. As Orozco's biographer, Michael C. Meyer, has pointed out, the

---

[1] Jesús Silva Herzog, *Breve historia de la Revolución Mexicana*, I, 247, 259; Eugenio Martínez Núñez, *Juan Sarabia, apóstol y mártir de la Revolución Mexicana*, II, 169 ff.; *El País*, April 13, 1912; *Diario del Hogar*, March 17, 28, 1912, *passim*.

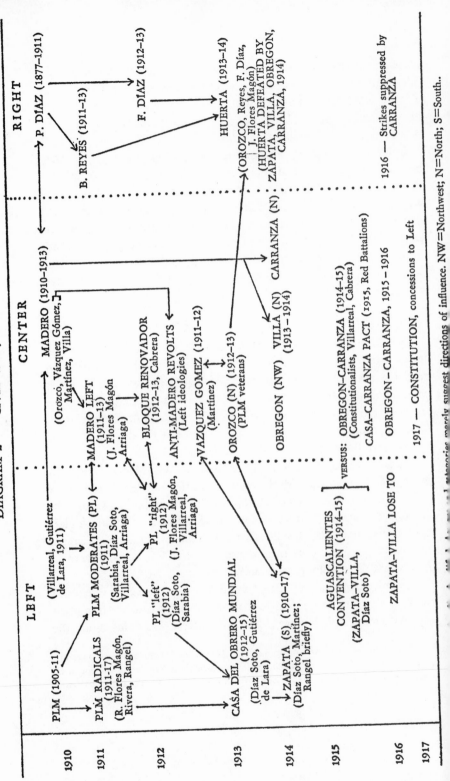

DIAGRAM 2 — CIVIL WAR, 1910–1917

RIGHT

P. DÍAZ (1877–1911)

B. REYES (1911–13)

F. DÍAZ (1912–13)

HUERTA (1913–14)
(OROZCO, Reyes, F. Díaz, J. Flores Magón)
(HUERTA DEFEATED BY ZAPATA, VILLA, OBREGON, CARRANZA, 1914)

1916 — Strikes suppressed by CARRANZA

CENTER

MADERO (1910–1913)
(Orozco, Vázquez Gómez, Martínez, Villa)

CARRANZA (N)

VILLA (N) (1913–1914)

OBREGON (NW)

OBREGON-CARRANZA (1914–15)
(Constitutionalists, Villarreal, Cabrera)

CASA-CARRANZA PACT (1915, Red Battalions)

OBREGON–CARRANZA, 1915–1916

1917 — CONSTITUTION, concessions to Left

LEFT

(Villarreal, Gutiérrez de Lara, 1911)

PLM (1905-11)

PLM RADICALS (1911-17) (R. Flores Magón, Rivera, Rangel)

PLM MODERATES (PL) (1911) (Sarabia, Díaz Soto, Villarreal, Arriaga)

MADERO LEFT (1911–13) (J. Flores Magón, Arriaga)

BLOQUE RENOVADOR (1912–13, Cabrera)

PL "right" (1912) (J. Flores Magón, Villarreal, Arriaga)

ANTI-MADERO REVOLTS (1911–12) (Left ideologies)

VAZQUEZ GOMEZ (1911–12) (Martínez)

PL "left" (1912) (Díaz Soto, Sarabia)

OROZCO (N) (1912–13) PLM veterans

CASA DEL OBRERO MUNDIAL (1912–15) (Díaz Soto, Gutiérrez de Lara)

ZAPATA (S) (1910–17) (Díaz Soto, Martínez; Rangel briefly)

AGUASCALIENTES CONVENTION (1914–15) (ZAPATA-VILLA, Díaz Soto)

} versus: {

ZAPATA-VILLA LOSE TO

1910
1911
1912
1913
1914
1915
1916
1917

Black dots and categories merely suggest directions of influence. NW=Northwest; N=North; S=South.

Plan Orozquista "was inspired by the [1906] manifesto of the Mexican Liberal Party." It even employed the old PLM slogan of "Reform, Liberty, and Justice"—although not specifically mentioning "Land and Liberty." (However, many Orozquistas, no doubt influenced by PLM veterans, used the slogan "Land and Liberty" as an official one prior to Orozco's public declaration of his Plan—these Orozquistas having launched their rebellion before their leader's final decision to rebel.) Expressing support for the earlier revolts of the Vazquistas and Zapatistas, the Plan Orozquista provided for basic PLM-style labor reforms and a land-distribution program intended to give the agrarian problem "a violent solution that hits the mark."[2]

Zapata's Plan de Ayala, which antedated Orozco's revolt by four months, had named Orozco as President of Mexico. This implied a burgeoning consensus between revolutionary leaders of North and South on the question of agrarian reform. By the spring of 1912, Madero was contributing to the hysteria of the yellow press and the fears of the bourgeoisie by describing Zapatistas as "Vandalic hordes."[3]

Orozco's revolt, however, drew criticism from many quarters for its acceptance of financial support from Chihuahua's "elite families," known popularly as the Terrazas-Creel clique. According to Meyer, Terrazas-Creel interests agreed to radical ideas in the Plan Orozquista "to entice mass support and—more importantly—to attract the leadership that would give the movement the name they desired." Whether Orozco was conscious of the machinations of these men or not, most leaders of his movement in 1912 remained revolutionary in their ideology and intent, in spite of being "financed, at least in part, by reactionary elements in Chihauhua."[4]

After the military *coup d'état* against Madero in February, 1913, Orozco and his followers recognized the Huerta regime. Rather than "proof" that Orozco and his PLM allies had always been "reactionaries," this was a case of complicated political maneuvering which involved many anomalies. Having been badly beaten by Madero's troops in

[2] Text in Silva Herzog, *Breve historia,* I, 246–259; Michael C. Meyer, *Mexican Rebel: Pascual Orozco and the Mexican Revolution,* p. 65.

[3] Silva Herzog, *Breve historia,* p. 223.

[4] Meyer, pp. 65–66.

1912, Orozquistas had reason to welcome the overthrow of Madero. On the other hand, even some PL moderates and friends of Madero, including Jesús Flores Magón and Trejo y Lerdo de Tejada, recognized the Huerta regime. Jesús, in fact, became Huerta's ranking Cabinet member: Secretary of Government. By 1913, the process of division within the Revolution had become so severe that more than a few "revolutionaries" found themselves amenable to joining the Huerta camp.

Mexicans in general, and many foreigners as well, including U.S. President-elect Woodrow Wilson, reacted with horror and indignation at the crude manner in which Madero was removed from power. On February 9, the military revolt against Madero began when military forces of Porfirio Díaz' still intact Army released Generals Bernardo Reyes and Félix Díaz (Porfirio's nephew) from prison (Reyes had been arrested in December, 1911, and Díaz in October, 1912, both for earlier abortive revolts against Madero). Bernardo Reyes was killed in battle that same day, but his son, Rodolfo, continued as the Reyistas' leader. American Ambassador Henry Lane Wilson helped Madero's opponents plot his downfall. On February 8, he offered the American Embassy as a meeting place for Rodolfo Reyes, Generals Huerta and Díaz, and other commanders of the Mexican Army. These men drew up and signed the Pact of the Ciudadela at the Embassy, on the basis that it was "neutral ground." Ambassador Wilson then confided to his aides that "everything was arranged."[5] President Madero and Vice President Pino Suárez were arrested, as Huerta became provisional President in accordance with the Pact of the Ciudadela. On the night of February 21, 1913, outside the gates of the federal prison in Mexico City, Madero and Pino Suárez were shot and killed by military officers. This deed was a classical political assassination in the tradition of Mexico's *ley fuga*—murder of prisoners on the pretext that they were "attempting to escape."

There followed almost instant response from the Mexican people. Workers and peasants rushed to join already-established revolutionary

5 Stanley R. Ross, *Francisco I. Madero, Apostle of Mexican Democracy*, p. 310; Charles C. Cumberland, *Mexican Revolution: Genesis under Madero*, p. 238.

contingents, like those of Zapata in the South. They also flocked in large numbers to new units being organized by Pancho Villa and Carranza in the North and Alvaro Obregón in the Northwest. The Carranza-Obregón forces became known as the "Constitutionalist" army, in symbolic representation of their leaders' defense of constitutional norms and repulsion at the brutal manner in which Madero had been replaced by Huerta. For a brief moment, Mexico's revolutionary forces, led mainly by Zapata, Villa, Carranza, and Obregón, united against the common enemy: Huerta. While occasional moderates from the PL went over to Huerta's side, many moved to the Left, recognizing that the course of revolution had to be pressed onward if social revolution was to be achieved (as PLM radicals had long been arguing).

That events were again radicalizing the Revolution's main leaders in this 1913–1914 period was illustrated in less than six months' time by Carranza's ideological recognition of the need to accept the "class war" and to effect at least some of its socio-economic goals. Landowner Carranza was years behind the Mexican Revolution when he first proclaimed the "Constitutionalist" revolution in his socially and economically innocuous Plan de Guadalupe, March 27, 1913. However, fighting the same enemy (Huerta) and co-operating with the Constitutionalist army were some social reformers, including Obregón, who would form the "left wing" of the 1916–1917 Constitutional Convention. Many of them were in the audience on September 23, 1913, when Carranza addressed a rally in Obregón's bailiwick, Hermosillo, capital of Sonora, the same state where the PLM had been agitating workers since 1905 (Cananea strike, 1906; PLM revolts, 1906 and 1908). In one of his few and rare statements capturing the flavor of the times, Carranza acknowledged the central problem that PLM radicals had proclaimed in their manifesto of exactly two years earlier:

Once the armed conflict called for by the Plan de Guadalupe is over, the formidable and majestic social struggle will have to begin, the class war, whether we ourselves want it or not, and whatever the forces that oppose it—the new social ideas will have to take root among our masses; and it is not merely to divide up lands and natural resources, it is not "Effective Suffrage," it is not opening up more schools, it is not dividing up equally the nation's wealth; it is something greater and more sacred; it is the establishment of justice, it is the quest for equality, it is the disappearance of the powerful, in order to establish balance in the national economy.[6]

Revolutionary Factionalism: Zapata, Villa, and Carranza

Except for the peasant grouping under Zapata, Mexico's classes were not rigidly aligned in a "class war," even though peasants and workers under rival *caudillos* vaguely believed that they were fighting for class ends. Divisions and geography were driving wedges not only into the Revolution but also into the classes involved in it. No sooner was Huerta driven from power in July, 1914, than Mexico's civil war intensified. Revolutionary armies under Zapata and Villa, who briefly if ineffectually united at the 1914 Aguascalientes Convention, waged relentless war, ultimately a defensive one, against the combined forces of Carranza and Obregón (the Constitutionalist army), during the 1914–1917 civil-war phase of the Revolution. Ideological issues were involved again, as the Zapatistas claimed to represent the agrarian cause —or economic cause, in their eyes—and the Constitutionalists initially emphasized the political cause of rule of law, constitutionalism, democracy, and Maderismo. Adding to the complexity of the divisions plaguing the Mexican Revolution were personalist and geographical factors. This pattern too had been established by the Precursor Movement— one has only to recall the abrasive personalities of Ricardo Flores Magón and Villarreal, or the distance separating PLM radicals in Los Angeles and Baja California from PLM moderates in Mexico City (PL).

Of the three major contending factions—Zapatistas, Villistas, Carrancistas—the Zapatistas most clearly defended the agrarian goals of the 1906 PLM Program. Indeed, the Zapatistas were so preoccupied with peasant and land-tenure problems that they rarely appreciated the corresponding problems for urban industrial labor. PLM radicals, dispersed as they were by 1913, predictably supported Zapatistas against Carrancistas. Jesús M. Rangel and other PLM radicals carried out missions to Zapata's headquarters in Morelos in 1913. Various PLM radicals joined Zapata's peasant army. Others, like Rangel, regrouped in

6 Silva Herzog, *Breve historia,* I, 34–35.

Texas and attempted an assault against Huerta's troops in September of 1913. However, they were intercepted by U.S. authorities and jailed, leading to a left-wing campaign in the United States in defense of "the martyrs of Texas," reminiscent of the events of the period 1906–1911.[7]

Villistas, in general, were not considered as progressive as Zapatistas. Nor were they as localized or as specifically peasant-oriented. Various cowboy, migrant-laborer, miner, and unemployed elements merged in Villa's giant, well-armed, wide-ranging army. Because of its social diversity, because of its dependence on the United States for armaments, and because of its domination by cowboy *caudillos* (*rancheros*) rather than communal peasant farmers (*ejidatarios*), the Villista movement was not as radical on the land question as the Zapatista movement or even, necessarily, the Carrancista movement. As foremen of large estates or as independent ranchers, cowboy *caudillos* had often commanded peasants, but rarely had they experienced the peasants' land hunger firsthand. Their expectations and ambitions were more commercial than those of the landless peasantry. U.S. properties in Mexico's North, like the sprawling Hearst estates and the large mines, went untouched by Villa's troops, who depended heavily on cattle-for-guns trade arrangements with merchants in the United States. In sending its battalions to distant points across the immense expanses of Mexico's North, the Villa movement needed a rather large bureaucracy to manage and administer military and government affairs. For this purpose, much of the old Madero bureaucracy was absorbed by the Villistas.

Villa had maintained a fanatical worship of Madero ever since the martyred President had helped save his life in 1912, when General Huerta, under whom Villa had then served to fight the Orozquistas, had almost executed Villa for insubordination. Whatever his motley troops may have been thinking, Villa saw his cause as identical with that of Madero. Nevertheless, forces of geography and circumstances contributed some radicals to Villa's cause—e.g., northern *caudillos* like Alberto Carrera Torres, and a score of PLM veterans unable to fight

[7] Ethel Duffy Turner, *Ricardo Flores Magón y el Partido Liberal Mexican*, pp. 288–299.

effectively elsewhere. Similarly, Villa's nominal alliance with Zapata helped radicalize Villistas.[8]

Carrancistas faced two politically united but geographically separated enemies: the Zapatistas and the Villistas. In the ranks of the Constitutionalist army too were represented many different social types. The Constitutionalists were able to claim some of the Revolution's radical banners as their own, including, on the level of diplomacy, the one of "anti-imperialism," anticipated by the PLM. Depending for their armaments on Europe (especially Germany), rather than on the United States, the Veracruz-based Constitutionalists were much more vehement than their rivals in protesting the U.S. occupation of Veracruz in 1914. Zapata, characteristically preoccupied with his *patria chica* of Morelos, rarely meddled in the mundane and complex matters of foreign affairs. Carrancistas also, by their defense of the 1857 Constitution, laid claim to the anticlericalism banner of Liberalism. However, to win the civil war, Carranza and his chief advisers—middle-class intellectuals like Luis Cabrera—realized that it was imperative to command some legitimacy in matters of socio-economic reform. Carranza's 1914–1915 labor and agrarian-reform decrees contributed some to such legitimacy —yet the civil war dragged on.

Something more than ideological appeals and promises of socioeconomic reform was needed if the Mexican bourgeoisie, as represented by its more progressive elements in the Carranza camp, was to survive the threat of worker and peasant forces already armed throughout Mexico and at least partially united in the Villa-Zapata camp. In the tense days of the 1914–1915 civil war, bourgeois revolutionaries in Carranza's camp were not concerned with toppling a mythological aristocracy. Rather, they were concerned with winning over important revolutionary groups from the lower classes which threatened to turn the course of the Revolution completely against them. At stake was not the survival of a nonexistent feudal order, but rather the stability and endurance, if not the strengthening, of a bourgeois order, however divided the bourgeoisie and workers and peasants were. The largest radical contribution to the Carrancista cause occurred when the indus-

---

[8] Especially insightful on Villismo is Friedrich Katz, *Deutschland, Díaz und die mexikanische Revolution. Die deutsche Politik im Mexiko 1870–1920.*

trial workers' Casa del Obrero Mundial, through a deal negotiated with Obregón, swung its support to Carranza. The Casa contributed its subsequent famous "red battalions" to the military effort, which helped tip the balance to Carranza and defeat Villa in early 1915; Zapatista troops fought a guerrilla holding action in Morelos until their eventual attrition and Zapata's assassination in 1919. Thus, each of the contending factions laid some claim to legitimacy in defending the socioeconomic goals of the Mexican Revolution—in agrarian matters the Zapatistas, in labor the Carrancistas, and, at least through their alliance with Zapata, in agrarian matters, on a modest scale, the Villistas.

Divided Precursors

Following the usual pattern of division within the Revolution, Arriaga, Díaz Soto y Gama, Ricardo Flores Magón, Rivera, and Sarabia themselves went different ways during the 1912–1917 period. Of the five, Ricardo Flores Magón and Rivera remained closest together. The two PLM radicals maintained their determined but vain Anarchism until their deaths in 1922 and 1932, respectively, spending much of the 1911–1916 period in U.S. jails. Díaz Soto y Gama and Sarabia also retained certain personal and ideological affinities, although the former moved further Left. Arriaga withdrew from the furor of left-wing politics as early as 1912. He did not attend the April, 1912, political convention of the PL and, after the Huerta *coup d'état,* went into exile. What remained in common among the five intellectuals was their Precursor heritage and their varying degrees of opposition to Carranza. Not one of them could bring himself to believe that Carranza adequately represented the socio-economic aims of the Revolution. Indeed, in the eyes of Flores Magón, Rivera, and Díaz Soto y Gama, Carranza became the "counter-revolutionary" enemy, to be fought until the end.

Up until the eve of the April, 1912, PL convention, Sarabia and Díaz Soto y Gama maintained their firm opposition against all anti-Madero revolutions, including that of Zapata. However, they increasingly criticized the compromises of the Madero government and its "purges" of such revolutionaries as the Zapatistas. Their aims were to effect Cabinet changes in the government—that is, political aims, not socio-economic ones. Even when addressing some of his former PLM colleagues at public meetings in the Orozco-dominated state of Chihuahua in March, 1912, when there on another of his "peace" missions, Sarabia scarcely mentioned socio-economic matters, instead emphasizing the Reform Laws, the 1857 Constitution, and traditional anticlerical Liberalism.[9] Only at the April, 1912, PL convention itself did Sarabia and Díaz Soto y Gama begin organizing the "extreme left wing of the Liberal Party" (*extrema izquierda del Partido Liberal*), and not until June was the PL division officially completed.

The move to the Left by Sarabia and Díaz Soto y Gama was precipitated by revolutionary events, especially the increasing urgency of the agrarian problem, as Díaz Soto y Gama explained in July, 1912.[10] Political causes involved *Diario del Hogar*'s replies to Madero's rejection of the PL's "Memorandum" to him of December, 1911, and the question of the legitimacy or illegitimacy of the Zapata movement. *Diario del Hogar* denied Madero's charge that it was promoting "uneasiness in people's consciences," claiming instead that "that uneasiness is not a result of our work, but, on the contrary, our work is the reflection of that uneasiness."[11] The newspaper's issues of January 3 and 27, 1912, defended the rank-and-file peasant soldiers of Zapata's army, without defending the Morelos *caudillo* himself; the President was blamed for pressing the military campaign against Zapata at such a high cost of life and low level of comprehension of social forces (e.g., the land hunger of the peasantry).

Díaz Soto y Gama was then offered the position of "Secretary of Government" of the new Morelos state government established under Francisco Naranjo, a veteran of the Precursor Movement since his days in the Liberal Club of Lampazos, Nuevo León (1901). While applauding Madero's choice of Naranjo as a step in the right direction, Díaz Soto y Gama rejected the offer to join the government on the grounds that he could not become a part of Madero's policy of "war to the death" against Zapatistas. In an interview published by *Diario del Hogar*, January 25, 1912, Díaz Soto y Gama explained in language

9 Martínez Núñez, *Juan Sarabia*, II, 153 ff.
10 Díaz Soto y Gama, letter to *El País*, July 22, 1912.
11 *Diario del Hogar*, January 7, 1912.

reminiscent of his 1899 and 1901 speeches and briefly borrowing from the PLM radicals' emphasis on "class war":

Everywhere, even in Russia, the social question is accepted . . . as something that derives from conditions of tyranny in which there develops the war between Capital and Labor. Everywhere . . . it is recognized that the tendency of capitalists is to abuse, while that of the worker is to defend himself against those who have more powerful weapons than he. . . . All this does not mean that we advanced Liberals aspire for agrarian communism or an impossible utopia of absolute equality, but one does not have to go so far to desire that the government, instead of buying haciendas in Coahuila, should acquire them and divide them up in Morelos.

Díaz Soto y Gama returned to this theme in the February 7, 1912, issue of *Diaro del Hogar*. There, he reiterated three points he had made publicly at a free-press rally on January 7, at which Sarabia also had appeared:[12] Madero's PCP was a self-seeking "anti-Constitutional Maderista party"; Madero's introduction of obligatory military service was a grave mistake; and the people would not be deceived by Madero's "thinly cloaked autocratic tendencies." More importantly, Díaz Soto y Gama warned that the nation was being swept by an agrarian tide, and that unless reform measures were enacted quickly, "communism" would be hailed as the remedy, Zapata as "the Savior," and "the oppressed people" would explode as "an avalanche . . . and then, good-bye, nationhood, and good-bye, Fatherland!" If these words were somewhat incongruous with his 1903 self-proclaimed "communism" and later role as chief adviser to Zapata, Díaz Soto y Gama's recommended remedies were not: "If it is necessary to restore to the people the *ejidos*, woodlands, and watering places that have been snatched from them, then that restoration should be brought about by every means possible."

It was this kind of agrarian radicalism, becoming ever more manifest as events pushed Díaz Soto y Gama to the Left, that underlay the PL division in April, 1912. Yet, besides this and the political sniping at Madero, the most publicly discussed cause of the PL split was a trip made by Sarabia to Chihuahua, in March of 1912. There Sarabia was

[12] Agustín Casasola (ed.), *Historia gráfica de la Revolución Mexicana*, I, 410–411.

feted by the Orozquistas, then on the threshold of their revolt against Madero.

Sarabia had resigned as editor of *Diario del Hogar* on February 16, 1912, ostensibly so that he and other PL leaders might make a political fund-raising tour for the April convention. At first, Sarabia's trip to Chihuahua was reported as an official peace mission approved by the top-ranking Madero Cabinet member—recently appointed Secretary of Government Jesús Flores Magón.[13] Sarabia's peace mission with Jesús to the PLM radicals in Los Angeles, California, in June, 1911, also had been reported as an official one, although Sarabia had denied it. This time, Sarabia conceded at least the semiofficial nature of his mission, claiming that the PL wanted to "support the work of Jesús Flores Magón and take advantage of my old personal friendship with chief leaders of the North to see if I could use my influence in arranging an equitable pacification agreement."[14] Unlike that of 1911, the dispute concerning this Sarabia peace mission in 1912 did not involve the question of his collaborating with the government to have the rebels lay down their arms or be jailed, but rather the question of his collaborating with the rebels to overthrow the government, so much had revolutionary events radicalized Sarabia.

In Chihuahua, Sarabia went on a whirlwind speaking tour. Although later denying that he had solicited funds, Sarabia collected much money for PL coffers. Everywhere he was acclaimed by the aroused populace. Sarabia himself signed a receipt for money handed him by Orozco. In self-defense, Sarabia, the man who earlier had published the PLM moderates' attacks on PLM radicals for accepting money from "the Devil," as Ricardo Flores Magón had expressed it, now adopted Ricardo's argument of being unable to refuse money offered for a progressive cause so long as no compromise of principles was involved.[15]

Sarabia's apparent embrace of the Orozco cause, no matter how much he cloaked it in terms of a peace mission, alienated many traditional Liberals of the PL who feared that he was supporting a violent revolution against Madero. Especially galling to PL moderates and admirers

13 *Diario del Hogar,* March 17, 1912.   14 *Ibid.,* March 28, 1912.
15 *Ibid.,* March 22, 28, June 17, 1912.

of Madero were Sarabia's apologies for Orozco. According to Sarabia, "The revolutionaries claim to be Liberals and seek, fundamentally, a solution to the agrarian question, with ample distribution of lands to the people." Sarabia quoted Orozco as follows: "We have nourished our spirit on the teachings of the PLM . . . the only group to have fought the tyrant openly and energetically during the Porfirian dictatorship, and the one movement that, by means of its propaganda, revolts, and sacrifices, prepared and touched off the revolution that Madero sought to take advantage of without knowing how to direct or sustain it."[16] If Ricardo Flores Magón and PLM radicals could find little to quarrel with in that kind of speech attributed to Orozco by their former adversary Juan Sarabia, a number of pro-Madero moderates in the PL could—and did.

The PL convention of March 31, 1912—April 7, 1912, ended in disaster for the "left wing." Sarabia delivered the keynote address, which finally acknowledged the agrarian problem as the principal one in Mexico but remained steadfastly pacifist and anticlerical in tone. The PL's "right wing" engineered an ingenious voting scheme whereby it maneuvered to capture the only four important posts in the powerful Directorate (*Centro Director*—Iglesias Calderón, Trejo y Lerdo de Tejada, Jesús Flores Magón, and Francisco Escudero). Radical measures on agrarian reform, parliamentarianism, nonrecognition of the Ciudad Juárez peace treaties, and fulfillment of the Plan de San Luis Potosí, proposed and defended by Díaz Soto y Gama and Sarabia, were diluted into half-hearted generalities. Villarreal sided with PL's right wing. The "Leftists" were, in effect, read out of the party for their alleged collaboration with Orozco against Madero. Díaz Soto y Gama performed as if rehearsing for his more famous speeches and actions at the 1914 Aguascalientes Convention, where he was to be the major Zapatista orator. Walking out at one point with various of his colleagues in a defiant gesture that cost his side key votes on the agrarian question, Díaz Soto y Gama shouted that the convention had ended up by representing "the bourgeois minority," that "the people" were out-

16 *Ibid.*, March 22, 1912.

side the convention's halls, and that tragic days loomed ahead if the agrarian problem was left unsolved.[17]

In spite of the defeat of the PL's "left wing" at the April, 1912, convention, Díaz Soto y Gama and Sarabia still defended PL candidates in the Congressional elections of June. They remained opposed to the PLM radicals' claim that elections could not resolve the problems confronting Mexico.[18] Díaz Soto y Gama, Sarabia, and Arriaga all ran for Congress in San Luis Potosí districts—Sarabia alone winning. PCP candidate Pedro Antonio de los Santos defeated Díaz Soto y Gama. De los Santos would later die in the fighting against Huerta in 1913, a martyr to Madero's cause.[19]

The final scission between PL's right and left wings occurred in mid-June, 1912. According to Sarabia, the right wing's anger at his accepting donations from Orozquistas caused the minority left wing to withdraw its token representation from the PL Directorate and act independently as the "extreme left wing of the Liberal Party."[20] Following the Precursor pattern of divisions within divisions, the PL's right wing divided three ways in December of 1912, by which time the PL's "extreme left wing" had ceased co-operating with the PL majority on most issues.[21]

In May of 1912, Díaz Soto y Gama, Sarabia, and Arriaga engaged in their last significant collaboration before going separate ways for the remainder of the civil-war days of the Revolution. The three San Luis Potosí Precursors founded an "Escuela Socialista," which sought to propagandize for easier, more healthful working conditions, higher wages, and fringe benefits. However, their program was less advanced than the old PLM Program of 1906. For example, it made no mention of the eight-hour work day except for "office workers." Nor was their movement Socialist, in spite of the school's name, but rather "advanced

17 *Ibid.,* April 7, 1912; *El Imparcial, El País,* and *La Prensa,* April 7, 1912, *passim.*
18 *Diario del Hogar,* April 11, 1912, *passim; La Prensa,* April 11, 1912.
19 *Diario del Hogar,* June 13, 15, 1912; *El País,* June 14, July 18, 1912.
20 Sarabia, letter in both of *ibid.,* June 15, 1912.
21 PL's "right wing" divided into (1) Maderistas, led by Escudero and favoring a pact with the PCP; (2) oppositionists, led by Trejo y Lerdo de Tejada; and (3) independents, led by Iglesias Calderón (*El País,* December 19, 20, 1912).

Liberal," as Sarabia's biographer has expressed it.[22] When the "Escuela Socialista" failed, Díaz Soto y Gama moved Left to help found the industrial workers' Casa del Obrero Mundial. Sarabia, on the other hand, entered Congress, refusing an invitation from the Casa del Obrero Mundial to join either the Casa or the Socialist Party. Sarabia said that he preferred to defend the workers' cause from a position of "advanced Liberalism, not Socialism."[23]

Casa del Obrero Mundial and Díaz Soto y Gama

The Casa del Obrero Mundial, founded in July of 1912, was initially dominated by Anarchists, although PLM radicals had little to do directly with its founding. The Casa's two principal founders were primary schoolteacher Francisco Moncaleano, a Spanish Anarchist who headed the stonecutters' union in Mexico City, and tailor Luis Méndez, a friend of Díaz Soto y Gama and a self-proclaimed Anarchist with Socialist leanings. The Casa's members initially held their meetings at Méndez' tailor shop, where they read from Kropotkin's *La conquista del pan* and Max Simon Nordau's *Las mentiras convencionales de la civilización*. On July 15, 1912, they began publishing their official newspaper, *Luz*. At the same time, they established an "Escuela Racional," a school for workers based on the pedagogic principles of Spain's martyred professor, Francisco Ferrer Guardia (1859–1909). Moncaleano's Anarchist incantation "Grito Rojo" (Red Yell) was recited regularly at the Casa's meetings. Thus, even in the hour of their decline, the PLM radicals' major ideology, that of Anarchism, came to have a profound effect on the founding of Mexico's modern labor movement.[24]

[22] Martínez Núñez, *Juan Sarabia*, II, 172–180.

[23] Sarabia, speech to Congress, March 27, 1913, in *ibid.*, p. 228.

[24] José G. Escobedo and Rosendo Salazar, *Las pugnas de la gleba, 1907–1922*, I, 41. In addition, works by Luis F. Bustamante and Salazar, listed in the Bibliography, provide firsthand knowledge of the history of the Casa. As Salazar was not an Anarchist, his account need not be suspected of a bias in that direction. He was a left-wing participant in Casa affairs and approved the Casa–Carranza pact of 1915. Max Simon Nordau was an Austrian Zionist and philosopher, who lived in Paris after 1890. His works, which tend toward individualistic Anarchism and the gospel of self-realization, include *Les mensonges conventionnels de notre civilisation* (1888) and *Dégénérescence* (1894).

In addition to the Anarchists and their sympathizers—including Díaz Soto y Gama, who retained his long-standing preference for such Anarchist principles as communitarian democracy—various Socialists, Anarcho-Syndicalists, and independent intellectuals began frequenting the Casa's meetings. A score of primary schoolteachers, led by the Casa's main leader, Moncaleano, became involved in the movement. The Madero government responded to this new threat from the Left by expelling Moncaleano, a Spaniard, from the country, closing down the Casa's Escuela Racional, and jailing the "Anarchist group of *Luz*."[25]

However, the Casa del Obrero Mundial gained the co-operation of the Mexican Socialist Party, then dominated by PLM and Precursor veterans like Gutiérrez de Lara, Manuel Sarabia, and De la Vega, as well as by new Socialist leaders like Rafael Pérez Taylor. The Casa's campaign for an eight-hour day, Sunday rest, and other labor goals originally outlined in the PLM Program of 1906 gained momentum during the next year and a half.

On June 2, 1913, Díaz Soto y Gama joined Méndez, De la Vega, and Jacinto Huitrón in signing a manifesto which added to the Casa's Anarchism a Syndicalist orientation. According to the manifesto, "The Casa del Obrero Mundial once more ratifies its profession of syndicalist faith, declaring its job specifically to be the organization of workers into trade unions." The Casa's major weapon would be "direct action of worker against capitalist, that is, a struggle supported by syndicalist organizations directing strikes." The manifesto retained the Anarchists' disdain for participation in political affairs: "Direct action, thus understood, excludes political work, for we syndicalists do not want the worker to be distracted from his great objective, the class war."[26]

In effect, Díaz Soto y Gama now accepted the PLM radicals' critique of political activity, for he dropped politics to emerge in 1913 and 1914 as one of the most charismatic spokesmen for the Revolution's Left, denouncing parliamentary delays and urging upon workers the course of "direct action." In spite of severe repression of labor-organizing and strikes by police and soldiers of the Huerta regime, Díaz Soto y Gama harangued massive crowds of protesting workers on May 1

25 *Ibid.*, I, 20, 40–45, 53; Silva Herzog, *Breve historia*, I, 225–226.
26 Escobedo and Salazar, I, 69–70.

and May 25, 1913. Once again, on March 18, 1914, only two months prior to the closing down of the offices of the Casa del Obrero Mundial by Huerta's police, Díaz Soto y Gama orated before a throng of disgruntled laborers in Mexico City.[27]

Now a leading public figure of the Left, Díaz Soto y Gama provided Zapatista General Rodolfo Magaña with quinine for Zapata's troops. He formed his links with the Zapata movement through his friend, Luis Méndez, who regularly corresponded with Zapata and made financial contributions to the cause of the Morelos peasantry. Méndez later left the Casa to attend the 1914 Aguascalientes Convention with the Zapatistas. Díaz Soto y Gama vaguely sensed that the Casa might not survive in urban Mexico, where it was being suppressed by Huerta, unless the rural fight was won. The Casa clearly was being driven underground in 1914. Díaz Soto y Gama was impressed by the action of Cuban Anarchist Prudencio R. Casals, who left the Casa to join Zapata's forces. Also, he feared that the Anarcho-Syndicalist direction of the Casa was giving way to one of political compromise, perhaps a deal with the Carranza camp. As a result of these considerations, Díaz Soto y Gama left Mexico City, in late March of 1914, to join the Zapata forces, for whom he soon became a leading adviser, speaker, and planner.[28]

Juan Sarabia, Futile Peace-maker

Juan Sarabia, in contrast to Díaz Soto y Gama, continued the line of political activity, debate, and compromise through his performance in Congress. Like Díaz Soto y Gama, however, he moved Left and, on October 5, 1912, told Congress: "The time has come to say it, gentlemen. The Revolution has turned in the wrong direction—I'm in agreement with that—the promises have not been fulfilled." In language remarkably similar to that of PLM radicals whom he had previously denounced, Sarabia went on to assert that "true revolutionaries" concerned themselves with "the agrarian question, the labor question . . . [for] we do not believe that [the goals of] the Revolution has been

---

[27] *Ibid.*, I, 53–84; Rafael Pérez Taylor, *El socialismo en México*, pp. 79–81.
[28] Díaz Soto y Gama, interview, March 19, 1965.

fulfilled merely because Francisco I. Madero occupies the place of Porfirio Díaz."[29]

On October 14, 1912, Sarabia introduced before Congress an agrarian-reform proposal drafted by lawyers Díaz Soto y Gama and Eduardo Fuentes for the "extreme left wing of the Liberal Party." Except for the original PLM Program's Points 36 and 37, which guaranteed poor peasants land and credits, Sarabia's proposed agrarian law was equivalent in substance to the PLM Program of 1906. It was more detailed on many points of procedure and, unlike the PLM Program, proposed that specific limits be established on the size of estates. This agrarian-reform proposal by Sarabia, radical in its Congressional implications, never passed into law because of the Huerta *coup d'état*, but it preceded by three weeks the more famous speech of Luis Cabrera, who eloquently called for the return of *ejidos* to the peasantry—one of the points in Sarabia's proposal.[30]

Also in Congress, Sarabia introduced a proposal that Madero's Cabinet resign. However, he withdrew it in order to throw his support behind the Madero regime when Félix Díaz rebelled in Veracruz (October 16, 1912). On December 7, 1912, Sarabia spoke in favor of a free press and greater amnesty for political dissidents.[31] Unlike Díaz Soto y Gama, who had given up on political action as fruitless, Sarabia stayed on in Congress under Huerta in order to oppose the new dictatorship. When Huerta closed down Congress, in October, 1913, Sarabia was jailed.

Upon his release from prison in April, 1914, Sarabia had to go into hiding. Huerta had threatened to kill him because of his past record and his association with Díaz Soto y Gama, then a leading Zapatista. Sarabia escaped to Monterrey, Nuevo León, where, in July, 1914, he was threatened with arrest by Carrancistas, who accused him of having collaborated in the 1912 Orozco revolt against Madero. In August, 1914, he went to Zapata's headquarters in Cuernavaca and arranged

29 Diego Arenas Guzmán (ed.), *Historia de la Cámara de Diputados de la XXVI Legislatura Federal*, I, 430.

30 Texts in *ibid.*, III, 273–288, 363–386, and Jesús Silva Herzog (ed.), *Colección de folletos para la historia de la Revolución Mexicana: la cuestión de la tierra*, II, 219–237, 277–310.

31 Arenas Guzmán, III, 283–288, and IV, 33–47, 151–153.

for the unsuccessful conference of the Constitutionalists' Villarreal and Cabrera with Zapata and Díaz Soto y Gama. When the talks failed, he returned to Mexico City with Antonio I. Villarreal and Luis Cabrera. By December of 1914, Sarabia found all his peace-making efforts futile.

Refusing to accept the adamant anti-Villa and anti-Zapata attitude of Carranza, Sarabia traveled to El Paso, Texas, to try to found an independent revolutionary newspaper. In early 1915, he returned to Mexico City to work in the National Library and direct the "Industrial School of Orphans." On a nonpolitical trip to Veracruz, headquarters of Carranza, Sarabia was jailed for fifteen days by the Carrancistas. Constitutionalist General Pablo González, a former PLM member, helped effect his release. Sarabia then worked for General González as a speech-writer. In 1916, he vainly tried to re-establish the moderates' version of the PLM. In June of 1917, he ran for governor in San Luis Potosí as an independent. Peasant leaders Magdaleno Cedillo and Saturnino Cedillo, brothers, the two most important pro-Zapata *caudillos* in San Luis Potosí, promised Sarabia they would lay down their arms if he was elected. Sarabia lost, however, to Carrancista candidate Juan Barragán, whose *latifundista* background has already been described.[32]

Juan Sarabia's political career was cut short in 1920 by death from heart disease and tuberculosis contracted a decade earlier in San Juan de Ulúa Prison. At the time, Sarabia was a newly elected member of Congress, under Obregón. Thus, the Precursor Movement's youngest leader was one of the first to die, only thirty-eight years of age.

Carranza-Casa Pact and Dispersion of the Precursors

Sarabia's name has often been linked with the Carranza forces of moderation affecting the behavior of the Casa del Obrero Mundial after Díaz Soto y Gama, Méndez, and other Anarchist-oriented elements left it in 1914.[33] Sarabia's contribution to the Carranza-Casa deal of Feb-

---

[32] Luis F. Bustamante, *Perfiles y bocetos revolucionarios*, p. 71; Víctor A. Monjaras, "Los precursores de la Revolución: Juan Sarabia," *Todo*, October 31, 1933; Aquiles Elorduy, "Juan Sarabia," *Excélsior*, October 13, 1932; Martínez Núñez, *Juan Sarabia*, II, 273–338; Antonio Díaz Soto y Gama, *La revolución agraria del sur y Emiliano Zapata, su caudillo*, pp. 173–181, and interviews.

[33] Roberto de la Cerda Silva, *El movimiento obrero en México*, pp. 115–117, and Rosendo Salazar, *La carta del trabajo de la Revolución Mexicana: fundamentos de una evolución*, pp. 48, 52–53.

ruary, 1915, can best be viewed as an indirect one, in the sense that the forces of moderation on the Left finally triumphed over the radicals within the Casa. Sarabia did not belong to the Casa. Moreover, the Carranza-Casa pact was not merely a triumph of moderates over extreme Leftists. Carranza too made concessions. After all, the Revolution's Leftist-moderate current of thought succeeded in persuading the moderate-to-conservative strain represented by Carranza to accept the Leftist implication of Casa collaboration.

Another indirect contribution by Precursor veterans to the Carranza-Casa alliance may have been the failure of Anarchists among them to achieve labor's goals in the course of their years of agitation. The PLM had always retained, even in the cases of its moderates, an active sympathy for Anarchism. PLM propaganda had helped make possible the high degree of Anarchist influence in the founding of the Casa. Yet the very failure of Anarchists ever to attain meaningful power at either the level of government or the level of communal democratic control (except in Baja California, 1911) may have contributed to the discouragement of Casa elements in the face of the Revolution's intensified civil war. When Obregón, acting for Carranza although without the "First Chief's" approval, offered the Casa much-needed food, money, equipment, meeting halls, and printing presses, as well as guaranteed freedom to act, the temptation to the heretofore suppressed and defeated labor organizers, as well as to hungry workers in poorly supplied Mexico City, must have been great. According to Casa apologist Rosendo Salazar, the essence of the Carranza-Casa pact, which Salazar approved, was that, in difficult conditions, the Casa allowed itself to be "bought out" by Obregón in February, 1915.[34]

PLM and Casa veterans like Díaz Soto y Gama, Ricardo Flores Magón, and Rivera, the last two scarcely a year out of jail in the United States, could only protest from their Zapatista and Anarchist viewpoints, respectively, that the labor movement in Mexico had "sold out." In fact, from that time forward, organized labor remained closely associated with the Mexican Government. At times, labor prospered from this association; at other times, the government came close to crushing

---

[34] Consult Salazar's works in Section II-F of the Bibliography. I am indebted to Enrique Semo Caler, editor of the Mexico City journal *Sociedad e Historia*, for his suggestions about the effects of Anarchism's failure in Mexico's labor movement.

labor as a political force. Even the Casa's best apologists—those who, like Salazar, signed the pact with Carranza and helped lead the formation of workers' "red battalions" in February, 1915—later would admit that they had signed the Casa's death warrant.[35]

No sooner had the Carrancistas triumphed militarily over the Zapatistas and Villistas, in battles which the Casa's "red battalions" had helped fight, than Carranza's provisional government began to suppress labor unions throughout the Republic. During its short-lived honeymoon with Carranza, labor had begun to organize with great success throughout Mexico, and mainly along Socialist lines (Anarchists could not accept the Carranza-Casa pact, of course). When a general strike in the summer of 1916 was declared, and Carranza realized how strong labor had become, the "First Chief" issued his famous decree of August 1, 1916, invoking the old war measure of January 25, 1862, which provided the death penalty for anyone "disturbing the public order." The strike was suppressed, its leaders jailed. "Death warrant" in this case took on a literal meaning.[36]

Thus, in one of the Mexican Revolution's more complicated incidents, the forces unleashed by the Precursors continued to determine events. In the context of the radical-moderate line of dispute established earlier when the PLM divided, the Casa may be said to have gone over to the moderates in February of 1915. Again the radicals, this time represented by Díaz Soto y Gama, could say later: "We told you so!" From the viewpoint of most of the PLM Precursors, the larger tragedy of the Carranza-Casa pact was that it pitted workers against peasants and thus facilitated the triumph of bourgeois reformers like Carranza over radical revolutionaries like Zapata.

In 1915, Díaz Soto y Gama denounced all Carrancistas as "traitors" and "counter-revolutionaries." He even sought to purge from his own camp—that of Zapata and, via the Aguascalientes Convention, that of Villa—all moderates who might be suspected of "counter-revolutionary tendencies." On April 28, 1915, he called for the formation, within the Aguascalientes Convention, of a Committee of Public Safety.[37]

[35] *Ibid.*, and Escobedo and Salazar, I, 159.

[36] *Ibid.*

[37] Robert E. Quirk, *The Mexican Revolution, 1914–1915: The Convention of Aguascalientes*, pp. 242–243; Díaz Soto y Gama, interviews.

True to his Anarchist spirit, Díaz Soto y Gama refused to serve in various government posts offered him by the Convention. In the mountains of Morelos, the Revolution's Danton was reduced to atypical silence— and in the course of the Zapatistas' twilight years (1916–1919), Díaz Soto y Gama underwent a conversion to mystical Catholicism.[38]

This, however, did not prevent Díaz Soto y Gama from pursuing agrarian goals, as indicated by his founding of the peasant-based Partido Nacional Agrarista in 1920 and his serving as congressman under Obregón. In Congress in 1929, he defended religious teaching in the schools "so that children might learn Christian morals."[39]

Díaz Soto y Gama had thus come full circle since his anticlerical days of 1899–1919. A sometime-defender of Obregón, as in the 1927– 1928 Presidential campaign, Díaz Soto y Gama opposed what he viewed as the "personalist" movement of Calles and became a prominent member of the Confederación Revolucionaria de Partidos Independientes. In 1934, this movement unsuccessfully ran Díaz Soto y Gama's 1911 ally and 1914 adversary Antonio I. Villarreal for President. Calles and the national party supported winning candidate Lázaro Cárdenas. Díaz Soto y Gama and former San Luis Potosí Governor (1923–1925) Aurelio Manrique, Jr., were Villarreal's main companions during the campaign.[40]

Although he defended President Cárdenas in 1935 against what he feared was an attempt by Calles to return to power, Díaz Soto y Gama continued to move Right during the 1930's, while the Cárdenas regime was carrying Mexico toward the Left. In spite of his opposition to most of Cárdenas' policies, Díaz Soto y Gama approved of Cárdenas' land distribution wherever it was successfully and fairly carried out. In his last bedside interviews with this author, Díaz Soto y Gama reiterated his loyalty to the cause of the peasantry in clear and articulate terms. On March 14, 1967, Díaz Soto y Gama died in Mexico City, age eighty-seven.

The Precursor Movement's oldest leader, Camilo Arriaga, went into exile when Madero was overthrown. He chose as his haven New Orleans, Louisiana, perhaps because that was where his idol, the great

---

[38] Díaz Soto y Gama, interview, January 23, 1965.
[39] John W. F. Dulles, *Yesterday in Mexico*, p. 562.
[40] *Ibid.*, pp. 582–585; Manrique, Jr., and Díaz Soto y Gama, interviews.

Liberal Benito Juárez, had gone into exile in the nineteenth century. From there, according to one biographer, Arriaga supplied arms for the Constitutionalists. However, according to Vasconcelos, Arriaga did not get along with Carranza. Arriaga did not reappear as a public political figure until 1920, when he became head of the Department of Forestry, Hunting, and Fishing, under Obregón. By then he was more than sixty years old, however, and, until his death in 1945, he generally abstained from an active role in politics. That Arriaga did not move to the Right in his old age is suggested by his support for the Spanish Republic and the U.S.S.R. and his opposition to the Nazis and to Mexico's fascist Sinarquistas.[41]

Rivera and Ricardo Flores Magón spent the period 1911–1914 in jail, during which time Rivera's wife died. During 1914–1918, Rivera and Flores Magón published *Regeneración*—rather sporadically, because of its frequent suppression. Together, they issued the PLM radicals' last manifesto, in March, 1918: a final and defiant call for the world Anarchist revolution.[42] U.S. authorities then sentenced the two Anarchists to prison: twenty years for Flores Magón and fifteen years for Rivera. They began serving their terms in August of 1918. Díaz Soto y Gama, in Congress, worked to effect their release and return to Mexico, as well as for government pensions on their behalf. True to their Anarchist principles, Rivera and Flores Magón refused all such support. When President Obregón finally gained U.S. approval of their return to Mexico, in November, 1922, Ricardo Flores Magón mysteriously died in his jail cell (November 21, 1922)—"murdered," according to Rivera.

Rivera returned to San Luis Potosí (1923–1925), where he refused the offer of the Partido Reformista "Juan Sarabia," composed of old Precursor elements in the state, to run for Congress, protesting anew his Anarchism. After 1926, he directed a prolabor newspaper, *Avante*, in Ciudad Cecilia, Tamaulipas. Government authorities suppressed

---

41 On Arriaga's supplying arms to the Constitutionalists, see Pedro María Anaya Ibarra, *Precursores de la Revolución Mexicana*, p. 77; Vasconcelos, "Camilo Arriaga," *Novedades,* July 6, 1945; José Mancisidor, "Dos precursores," *El Nacional*, July 2, 1945; and the press of the 1930's and 1940's.

42 Text in Florencio Barrera Fuentes, *Historia de la Revolución Mexicana: la etapa precursora*, pp. 326–328.

Avante, taking Rivera to prison in Mexico City. Later released, he renewed his Anarchist fight by editing another prolabor newspaper, *Paso.*

During 1930–1932, Rivera shared living quarters in Mexico City with Nicolás T. Bernal, an old Anarchist friend of Ricardo Flores Magón. As the result of an automobile accident in February of 1932, in which he was run over, Rivera contracted a fatal case of tetanus. He refused to press charges against the driver, who "might be a worker and head of a family." In his final days of semiconsciousness, March of 1932, Rivera weakly waved his hand against a sheet being lifted to cover his face from the flies in his hospital room. The girl attending him exclaimed: "Still so rebellious, comrade!" Rivera whispered: "Always I have fought, and still I fight, against the injustices of the strong." A short while later, he died. Members of Mexico City's labor organization Federación de Trabajadores bore his corpse to a municipal graveyard, where not even a nameplate was left to mark his grave.[43]

CONCLUSIONS

In sum, Mexico's intellectuals, except for the Precursor Movement prior to Madero's triumph and PLM radicals after it, generally were radicalized by revolutionary events, rather than serving to radicalize events. Some, like PLM moderates in 1911, were moderated by events before being radicalized. Then, in cases like that of Díaz Soto y Gama, intellectuals helped to push the Revolution to the Left, at least for a while. Some intellectuals, like Arriaga, became more or less alienated by the Revolution's complications. Others, like Jesús Flores Magón, moved to the Right. All intellectuals active in the Mexican Revolution

---

[43] Librada Rivera, "Prólogo," *in* Diego Abad de Santillán, *Ricardo Flores Magón: el apóstol de la Revolución Social Mexicana,* pp. vii–xiii, and Librado Rivera, "Persecución y asesinato de Ricardo Magón," in *Ricardo Flores Magón: vida y obra,* V, 70–90; Víctor A. Monjaras, "Librado Rivera," *El Nacional,* March 11, 1932; Ramos Pedrueza, "Librado Rivera," *El Popular,* May 4, 1942; Bernal, interview. To the best of this author's knowledge, the accusations and mystery surrounding Flores Magón's death have not been resolved in the courts of justice or scholarship.

tended to fight among themselves rather than to unite behind a single revolutionary group or leader. In part, this pattern of division among its intellectuals caused the Mexican Revolution's worker and peasant followers to end up fighting one another, instead of uniting behind antibourgeois goals as initially outlined by the PLM.

After mid-1911, PLM radicals failed to play a pivotal role in the Mexican Revolution—except indirectly, through their influence on organized labor, ideological controversy, and occasional fighting units among Zapatistas and Villistas. Most historians have argued that, during 1910–1911, PLM radicals, by their Anarchism, became international revolutionaries and therefore ceased being "Mexican." But no scholar has taken note of a fundamental connection between the position of PLM radicals during 1910–1911 and that of the Revolution's somehow more "Mexican" radicals of subsequent years—the Zapatistas, certain Obregonistas and Villistas, and, ironically, some PLM moderates (PL) after 1912. That connection was the contention that a revolution, to be more than a political change of the guard, cannot be cut short, or considered "triumphant," with its socio-economic promises unfulfilled. PLM radicals did advocate international revolution, but this did not make them any less "Mexican." Events between 1910 and 1917, including the grabbing of lands by peasants and the militant organizing of labor along Anarcho-Syndicalist lines, suggest just how Mexican the PLM radicals in fact were.

After Madero's tragic death, Arriaga, Díaz Soto y Gama, Ricardo Flores Magón, Rivera, and Juan Sarabia all followed more or less divergent paths. None of them achieved political victory. All five rejected Carranza. Yet all five, as well as other intellectuals like them, were critically important figures in the Mexican Revolution—not only in the Precursor Movement, which laid the military and ideological groundwork of the Revolution, but also in the Revolution's pattern of complex divisions and civil war.

Except for a handful of intellectuals in the Constitutionalist movement, Mexico's Precursors could claim little concrete political victory, as distinguished from an ideological victory, when, on February 5, 1917, Venustiano Carranza promulgated the 1917 Constitution. Militarily and politically, Carranza had triumphed—not the PLM, not the

Zapata and Villa forces which most of the Precursors had preferred to Carranza.

Carranza has rightfully been credited with signing the new Constitution, even though it went far beyond what he had proposed when convoking the Querétaro Constitutional Convention. On the other hand, he systematically violated the Constitution as President, as in the cases of his suppression of labor unions during 1916–1920, and his failure to carry out its mandates for agrarian reform. Carranza's approval of the 1917 Constitution, however, appears to have been an act of political pragmatism he could well afford. Not to have signed the Constitution might have again unleashed the very forces that had produced the Revolution in the first place. Those forces had been generated by the Precursor Movement, the Madero movement, Madero's assassination, and the increasingly violent civil war of 1910–1917. Carranza's triumph did not eliminate those forces, but his signing of the 1917 Constitution at least recognized, in theory, the justice of the workers' and peasants' causes during the Revolution and thereby satisfied, if only on paper, some of the Left's expectations.

Carranza himself was assassinated in 1920, and the forces of revolution and counter-revolution continued to struggle, often violently, during the next decades. Although the Porfiristas were generally beaten as of 1917, in diverse ways their conservative policies were still championed in Mexico. Military rebellions in subsequent years had some Porfirista characteristics, as did the bloody "Cristero revolt" of 1926–1929, when militant Catholics fought to the death against the governments of Obregón and Calles. Supporters of left-wing revolution also remained active. They re-emerged as especially influential figures in the 1930's under Lázaro Cárdenas, and they are still by no means eliminated or satisfied in Mexico today.

The 1917 Constitution represented the Mexican Revolution's only clear-cut, unanimously recognized, and lasting victory: the ideological one. Significantly, more than just the Precursor pattern of radical-moderate division took place at the Querétaro Constitutional Convention of 1916–1917. For the first time, the radicals, or "Jacobins," as the Convention delegates in favor of substantial socio-economic change were called, won a major battle: Articles 27 and 123, agrarian reform and labor's "Bill of Rights." Thus, while not going so far as some Precursors would have liked, the 1917 Constitution did, to the distress of moderates, go a long way toward laying the ideological basis for radical social and economic change in Mexico. The PLM and Precursor intellectuals who had agitated for so long for such a program could point to at least that much success after their many political divisions and setbacks.

From the innumerable conflicts between Mexico's revolutionary intellectuals, political leaders, social groups, and political coalitions between classes; from the many years of struggle for the basic rights of workers and peasants; from the Precursor Movement's formulation of radical socio-economic goals for the Revolution; from all the disputes and divisions that derived from and followed the Precursor pattern; from the bloodied battlefields and explosive convention halls of civil war—there finally emerged, in 1917, the first clearly recognizable results of the Mexican Revolution. Those results were: a defeated peasantry, a crippled and dependent labor movement, a wounded but victorious bourgeoisie, and, for a divided Mexican people, a paper triumph—the 1917 Constitution.

APPENDIXES

APPENDIX A

PROGRAM[1] OF THE LIBERAL PARTY (PLM), 1906

Constitutional Reforms

1. Reduction of the Presidential term to four years.*

2. No re-election for President and state governors.* These public officials can be newly elected only after the elapse of two terms following the ones in which they have served.

3. The Vice President shall not carry out legislative functions or any other duty resulting from popular election, but he shall be allowed to perform duties assigned by the Executive.

4. Elimination of obligatory military service and the establishment of a National Guard. Those who serve in the standing Army will do so freely and voluntarily. Military ordinance will be reviewed in order to remove from it anything considered oppressive or humiliating to the dignity of man, and the incomes of those who serve in the national militia will be increased.**

5. Reform and regulation of Articles 6 and 7 of the Constitution, removing restrictions that private life and public safety impose upon the freedom of speech and press, but declaring that falsehoods involving fraud, blackmail, and lawless immorality will be punished.*[2]

6. Abolition of the death penalty except for those who are traitors to their country.**[3]

---

[1] A single asterisk indicates that the provision called for in the PLM Program was later adopted in the 1917 Constitution; double asterisks indicate that the provision called for in the Program went further in its demands than those incorporated into the 1917 Constitution.

[2] The PLM Program left out freedom of travel (Article 11 of the 1917 Constitution. Also, although implicit in Point 5, the Program did not mention freedom of assembly (Article 9 of the Constitution).

[3] Article 22 of the Constitution allowed the death penalty for other crimes: "The death penalty for political crimes is likewise prohibited; and for other types of of-

7. Increase in the responsibility of public officials, imposing severe prison sentences on offenders.*

8. Restoration of the territory of Quintana Roo to Yucatán.**

9. Elimination of military tribunals in time of peace.*

Improvement and Development of Education

10. Multiplication of elementary schools,** on such a scale that educational institutions closed down because they belong to the Clergy can be advantageously replaced.*

11. Obligation to provide completely secular education in all schools of the Republic, be they public or private; those directors who do not comply shall be held responsible.*

12. Compulsory education to the age of fourteen; the government shall be responsible for providing protection in whatever form possible to poor children who, because of their poverty, might lose out on the benefits of an education.*

13. Good salaries for elementary schoolteachers.**

14. Obligatory instruction in the rudiments of arts and crafts and military instruction for all schools of the Republic, with special attention to civic instruction, which today receives so little notice.*

Foreigners

15. Prescribe that foreigners, by the sole act of acquiring real estate, lose their former nationality and become Mexican citizens.**

16. Prohibit Chinese immigration.**4

---

fenses, it may be imposed only upon traitors to the Fatherland in a foreign war, parricides, homicides by treachery, premeditation, or gain, incendiaries, kidnapers, highway robbers, pirates, and offenders who have committed grave crimes of a military character."

4 The Constitution permitted foreigners to hold properties if they were granted concessions by the State "provided they agree before the Ministry of Foreign Relations to consider themselves as nationals with respect to said properties and not to invoke the protection of their governments in reference to same; should they fail to respect the agreement, they will be penalized by having to return to the Nation the properties they may have acquired. Under no consideration may foreigners acquire direct ownership over lands and waters within a zone one hundred kilometers wide along the Nation's borders, or fifty kilometers along the coast" (Article 27). Subsoil rights were reserved to the nation (Article 27). Foreigners could be sent out of Mexico on a simple order from the President and were forbidden to participate in

Restrictions on Abuses by the Catholic Clergy

17. Churches are considered to be business concerns, and must, therefore, keep accounts and pay corresponding taxes.*

18. Nationalization, according to law, of real estate held in trusteeship for the Clergy.*

19. Increase in the punishment that the Reform Laws decree for violators of the same.*

20. Elimination of schools run by the Clergy.*

Capital and Labor

21. Establishment of a maximum of eight hours of work a day and a minimum salary* on the following scale: a peso for each part of the country in which the average salary is less than a peso, and more than a peso for those regions in which the cost of living is higher and one peso would not suffice to save the workers from poverty.[5]

22. Regulation of domestic service and servants in residences.**

23. Adoption of measures preventing employers from evading application of maximum time and minimum salary to piecework.**

24. Prohibition of employment of children under fourteen years of age.**[6]

---

the nation's politics (Article 33). PLM Point 15, though briefer, is more restrictive of foreigners in economic matters. The prejudice against Chinese in Point 16 reflected the sentiment of a large number of Mexico's Northerners, who viewed Chinese immigrant laborers as unfair competition, or "dirty," or convenient scapegoats for their angers. In the "Exposition" of its Program, the PLM explained the ban on Chinese immigration as a step toward eliminating wage competition of Chinese workers, who "accept the lowest wages."

[5] The Constitution did not fix the amount of the minimum wage, leaving that to the discretion of municipal and state commissions (Article 123, Part IX). However, the Constitution went beyond the PLM Program by providing for overtime pay (Article 123, Part XI) and for profit-sharing, amounts to be determined in the same fashion as the minimum wage (Article 123, Parts VI and IX).

[6] The Constitution was much weaker (Article 123, Parts II and III): "Unhealthful or dangerous work is forbidden for women in general and for youth less than sixteen years of age. Industrial night work is also forbidden for these two classes; and they may not work in commercial establishments beyond ten o'clock at night. Young persons more than twelve and less than sixteen years of age shall have six hours as a maximum day's work. The labor of children under twelve years of age is not subject to contract." On the other hand, the Constitution made generous provisions for pregnant women (Article 23, Part V).

25. All owners of mines, factories, shops, etc., must maintain the best hygienic conditions on their properties and must service danger areas in a manner guaranteeing the safety of the lives of workers.*

26. All employers or rural property owners must provide hygienic lodgings for employees when the nature of their work necessitates their receiving shelter from said employers or proprietors.*

27. All employers must pay indemnity for accidents occurring on the job.*7

28. All debts of rural day laborers to their employers are hereby declared null and void.**8

29. Adoption of measures to prevent landowners from abusing sharecroppers.*

30. All landowners and overseers of fields and houses must compensate tenants for necessary improvements which tenants make on their property.**

31. All employers, under pain of severe penalty, must pay employees in cash; fining of workers, deducting from their day wages, delaying payment of set wages for more than one week, and refusing to pay immediately a worker leaving a job his accumulated earnings, are all prohibited and subject to punishment; company stores [*tiendas de raya*] are outlawed.*

32. All enterprises or businesses must hire only a minimum of foreigners. At no time may a Mexican be paid less than a foreigner doing equivalent work in the same establishment, and Mexicans must never be paid in a manner different from the way in which a foreigner is paid.**9

33. Sunday is an obligatory day of rest.*

Lands10

34. Landowners must make all the land they possess productive; any ex-

---

7 The Constitution extended these points slightly, to include provision for housing, medical care, markets, recreation, and municipal services, under certain conditions (Article 123, Parts XII and XIII). Also, social security was encouraged, although not instituted (Article 123, Part XXIX), and employment agencies were provided for (Article 123, Part XXV).

8 The PLM Program omitted strictures against monopolies (Article 28 of the Constitution) and said nothing about abolishing slavery and titles of nobility (Articles 2 and 12 of the Constitution), although PLM's Points 28 and 29 served, in part, the latter purpose.

9 The Constitution's Article 32 was much less stringent. Curious omissions from the PLM Program were the right to form labor unions and co-operatives and the right to strike (Article 123, Parts XVI, XVII, and XXX of the Constitution).

10 The brevity of this section is misleading. The PLM's Point 50 provided for the

tension of land that the owner leaves unproductive will be confiscated by the State, and the State will employ it in accordance with the following articles.*

35. For those Mexicans residing abroad who so solicit, the Government will provide repatriation, paying the transportation cost of the trip and allotting them lands that they can cultivate.**

36. The Government will grant land to anyone who solicits it, without any conditions other than that the land be used for agricultural production and not be sold. The maximum amount of land that the Government may allot to one person will be fixed.*

37. In order that the benefits in this section should extend not only to a few who have resources for cultivating land but also to the poor who lack resources, the State will either create or develop an agricultural bank which will lend money to poor farmers at low interest rates, payable in installments.**

Taxes

38. Abolition of the present tax on corporations and on individuals, leaving the Government the task of studying the best means of lowering the stamp tax until it becomes possible to abolish it.**

39. Elimination of tax on capital of under a hundred pesos, exempting from this privilege churches and other businesses considered harmful or unworthy of guarantees granted to useful enterprises.**

40. Increase in the tax rate on usury, luxury items, and vices [e.g., alcohol and tobacco—JDC], and decrease in taxes on basic staples. The rich shall not be permitted to make arrangements with the Government to pay less taxes than those imposed by the law.**

General Points

41. To make practicable the writ of *amparo*, simplifying the procedures.*11

---

restitution of *ejidos*, as did the "Exposition" preceding the Program: "The restitution of *ejidos* to those communities that have been dispossessed of them is a matter of clear justice." By not raising the question of indemnity for expropriated lands, the PLM went further than the 1917 Constitution, which provided for indemnity (Article 27). In other agrarian respects, the PLM Program was equal to the later Constitution, or went beyond it, as indicated by double asterisks.

11 There is no exact translation of *juicio de amparo*, which in Mexico is roughly equivalent to a writ of appeal. Consult: David S. Stern (ed.), *Mexico: A Symposium*

42. Restitution of the free-trade zone.**

43. Establishment of civil equality for all children of the same father, eliminating the differences between legitimate and illegitimate children which the present law now establishes.**

44. Establishment, whenever possible, of reform colonies, instead of the jails and penitentiaries in which offenders suffer punishment today.**

45. Elimination of political bosses [*jefes políticos*].**

46. Reorganization of municipalities [*municipios*] which have been suppressed or weakened, and strengthening of municipal power.*

47. Measures to eliminate or restrict usury, pauperism, and scarcity of basic staples.**

48. Protection of the Indian race.**

49. Establishment of ties of union with Latin American countries.**

50. Upon the triumph of the Liberal Party, properties of public officials who make themselves rich under the present dictatorship will be confiscated, and these properties will be applied toward the fulfillment of the section on Lands—especially to restore to Yaquis, Mayas, and other tribes, communities, or individuals the land of which they have been dispossessed*— and toward amortization of the National Debt.

51. The first National Congress to function after the fall of the dictatorship will annul all reforms of our Constitution made by the Government of Porfirio Díaz; it will reform our Magna Carta, wherever necessary to put into effect this Program; it will create laws necessary for the same end; it will regulate articles of the Constitution and of other laws that so require, and it will study all those things considered of interest to the Fatherland, whether or not they are enunciated in the present Program, and it will reinforce the points listed herein, especially in the matter of Labor and Land.

Special Clause

52. It remains the duty of the Recruitment Board of the Liberal Party to address itself as quickly as possible to all foreign governments, informing them, in the name of the party, that the Mexican people do not want any more debts burdening the Fatherland and that, therefore, it will not recognize any debts that the dictatorship, under any form or pretext, thrusts upon

---

on Law and Government, and Richard D. Baker, "The Judicial Control of Constitutionality in Mexico: A Study of the Juicio de Amparo" (Ph.D. dissertation).

the Nation, whether by contracting loans, or by recognizing, too late, previous obligations which no longer have legal value.**

Reform, Liberty, and Justice

St. Louis, Missouri, July 1, 1906

President, RICARDO FLORES MAGON
Vice-President, JUAN SARABIA
Secretary, ANTONIO I. VILLARREAL
Treasurer, ENRIQUE FLORES MAGON
First Committeeman, PROFESSOR LIBRADO RIVERA
Second Committeeman, MANUEL SARABIA
Third Committeeman, ROSALIO BUSTAMANTE

APPENDIX B

GLOSSARY

alcabala. State and municipal import and marketing taxes, officially eliminated in 1896.

amparo (juicio de). Mexican version of a writ of appeal.

Antirreeleccionista (Anti-reelectionist). Supporter of the Madero movement, 1909–1910—"Effective Suffrage, No Re-election."

baldío laws. "Vacant-land" laws of 1883 and 1894 facilitating land giveaways.

Belén. Mexico City prison.

bracero. Mexican migrant farm laborer employed in the United States at harvest time.

caballada. "Herd of tame horses," Díaz' way of referring to his Congress.

Carrancista (Carranza). Supporter of "First Chief" Venustiano Carranza in 1913–1917 civil war and as President, 1917–1920.

Casa (Casa del Obrero Mundial). Labor movement, 1912–1916.

caudillo. Military leader of guerrilla forces; also, any "strong-man" ruler who maintains his supremacy by some combination of charisma and military might.

Científicos. Díaz' braintrust of Positivists and Social Darwinists.

Ciudad Juárez peace treaties. Madero-Díaz truce agreements of May 17–21, 1911, paving the way for Díaz' exile and the interim government of Francisco León de la Barra.

Conservative (-ism). Nineteenth-century movement for political centralism, clericalism, inviolability of private property.

Constitutionalist (-a). The name of Carranza's movement against Huerta (1913–1914) and later against other revolutionary factions (1914–1917), which sought to restore the 1857 Constitution and civilian rule by law.

Corralista (Corral). Supporter of Vice President Ramón Corral during 1909–1910 politicking.

Creelman interview. James Creelman published his interview with Díaz in *Pearson's Magazine* in 1908, under the subtitle "Thrilling Story of President Díaz, the Greatest Man on the Continent," in which Díaz said he would retire in 1910 and make way for democratic elections.

ejidatario. Peasant farming communal lands.

ejido. Traditional communal land farmed by Indians.

empleomanía. Government-job mania, infecting many middle-class intellectuals and adding to the growth of bureaucracy under Díaz.

Federal District. Greater Mexico City.

gente decente. Aristocracy or upper class.

guayule. A shrub from which rubber is extracted, common to north-central Mexico.

hacendado. Large landowner.

Huasteca. Thinly populated, well-watered, jagged eastern slopes and tropical lowlands of the extreme eastern part of San Luis Potosí; part of the larger geographical and cultural section of Mexico called "Huasteca" after the Huaxteco Indians, incorporating parts of Tamaulipas, Querétaro, Hidalgo, Tlaxcala, and Veracruz.

Independence. Climax of the 1810–1821 Mexican revolution against Spain, resulting in Mexico's independence.

ixtle. A fiber extracted from a cactus-like plant grown in arid parts of the north-central Mexico tableland and used to make blankets, nets, handbags, sacks, and coarse rope.

jefe político. District political official, often a local tyrant during the Porfiriato.

Juarista (Juárez). Devotee of Liberal President (1860–1872) Juárez.

Laguna. A basin area two hundred miles west of Monterrey on the border of Coahuila and Durango, which in modern times became the source of half of Mexico's cotton crop and much of its wheat.

latifundio. Large landholding.

latifundista. Owner of one or more *latifundios.*

lechuguilla. A fiber extracted from a cactus-like plant grown in arid parts of the north-central Mexican tableland and used to make handbags, sacks, and coarse rope.

leva. Forced conscription into the Army, used throughout Mexico during the Porfiriato. The *leva* system was sometimes employed in the transfer of Yaqui Indians from Sonora to henequen plantations in Yucatán and to tobacco fields of the Valle Nacional.

ley fuga. "Law of flight," commonly used to justify shooting prisoners "while attempting to escape" during Porfiriato.

Liberal (-ism). Nineteenth-century movement for political federalism (decentralization), anticlericalism, political freedoms, free trade, free enterprise, and the rights of private property. The 1810–1812 Spanish Cortes (parliament) of Cádiz introduced the concept "Liberal" into the Spanish-speaking world. Juárez and the Reform Laws emphasized its anticlerical implications in Mexico, 1855–1872. After 1905, the PLM gave Liberalism a socio-economic interpretation, calling for agrarian reform and the defense of workingmen's rights. Liberalism's anticlericalism never diminished, as evidenced in the 1917 Constitution and post-1917 Mexican politics.

Liberal Clubs. Political groups formed in the 1900–1903 period to oppose resurgent clericalism and loss of political freedoms under Díaz, initiated in response to Camilo Arriaga's 1900 Liberal manifesto.

Maderista. Supporter of Francisco I. Madero, 1909–1913.

Magonista. PLM radical; follower of Ricardo Flores Magón, 1910–1918.

Obregonista (Obregón). Supporter of Alvaro Obregón during 1913–1917 civil war and as President, 1920–1924.

Orozquista (Orozco). Supporter of Pascual Orozco, Jr., main Maderista field commander in campaign against Díaz, 1911; Orozco rebelled against Madero, 1912–1913.

Partido Democrático. A Reyista political party of 1909–1910, initially backed by Madero.

Partido Nacional Antirreeleccionista. Madero's political party, 1910–1911.

patria chica. "Little fatherland," commanding loyalty of a given population to its specific region.

PCP. The Partido Constitucional Progresista, founded by Madero in August, 1911, to replace his earlier Partido Nacional Antirreeleccionista.

PL. Partido Liberal, the PLM moderates' version of the PLM; a left-wing minority of the PL, including Antonio Díaz Soto y Gama and Juan Sarabia, broke off to form the "extreme left wing of the Liberal Party" in 1912.

PLM. Partido Liberal Mexicano, 1905–1911, political core of the Precursor Movement. In 1911, the PLM divided between moderates (Juan Sarabia, Antonio Díaz Soto y Gama, *et al.*) and radicals (Anarchists Ricardo Flores Magón, Librado Rivera, *et al.*). The PLM moderates renamed their group the PL. The PLM radicals' last manifesto was issued in 1918.

Porfiriato. The reign of Porfirio Díaz, 1877–1911.

Porfirista. Supporter of Díaz or his government, 1877–1911.

Potosino. Native of San Luis Potosí.

Precursor Movement. All political precedents (manifestoes, strikes, armed uprisings, etc.) of the Mexican Revolution of 1910–1917, dating from the 1900 founding of the Club Liberal "Ponciano Arriaga" in San Luis Potosí to the 1911 overthrow of Díaz.

ranchero. Cowboy.

Reform, Reform Laws. 1855–1862 period of Liberal agitation for, and passing of, anticlerical laws, as exemplified in the 1857 Constitution.

Reyista (Reyes). Supporter of General Bernardo Reyes, 1900–1913, the Porfiriato's leading military figure.

Rurales. Díaz' crack rural police force of "rehabilitated" bandits and outlaws.

San Juan de Ulúa Prison. Military fortress prison off the coast of Veracruz, to which more than a thousand Precursors were sent, half of whom died in its damp dungeons.

tienda de raya. Company store.

Valle Nacional. Area in northern Oaxaca, near Veracruz border, where Yaqui Indians and political dissidents were forcibly sent during the Porfiriato to harvest tobacco and other crops in a kind of "slave labor" system.

Vazquista (Vázquez Gómez). Supporter of Francisco Vázquez Gómez, Madero's running mate in 1910 elections. He rebelled against Madero in 1911–1912.

Villista (Villa). Supporter of Pancho Villa, 1911–1916; Villa opposed Carranza.

Zapatista (Zapata). Supporter of Emiliano Zapata, 1910–1919; supporter of the peasants' revolution led by Zapata, who opposed Carranza.

APPENDIX C

CHRONOLOGY FOR THE MEXICAN PRECURSOR
MOVEMENT AND REVOLUTION OF 1910

1857 New Constitution proclaimed by Liberals; period of anticlerical Reform Laws.
1861 Benito Juárez, President, after three years of Liberal-Conservative civil war.
1862 Camilo Arriaga born.
1862 To 1867——French military intervention; Emperor Maximilian.
1864 Librado Rivera born.
1867 To 1872——Benito Juárez, President.
1872 To 1876—Sebastián Lerdo de Tejada, President.
1873 Francisco I. Madero born.
1874 Ricardo Flores Magón born.
1876 General Porfirio Díaz revolts against Lerdo de Tejada under banner of "Effective Suffrage" and "No Re-election," expressed in Plan de Tuxtepec.
1877 General Díaz becomes President; thirty-four-year Porfiriato begins.
1879 To 1883——peasant revolt in Huasteca of SLP[1]
1880 Antonio Díaz Soto y Gama born.
      —To 1884——Manuel González, President; Díaz is main power.
1882 Juan Sarabia born.
1883 And 1894, *baldío* laws facilitating land giveaways.
1884 To 1911—Díaz, President.
1888 Arriaga becomes deputy to SLP legislature; opening of Laredo–Mexico City railroad in SLP.
1890 Arriaga takes father's seat in Congress.
1892 Student protests in Mexico City (R. Flores Magón *et al.*).
      —To 1895——Economic crisis, especially in silver, hits Arriagas and nation in general.
1896 SLP elite families ask Díaz to change state governor.

---

[1] SLP = San Luis Potosí.

1898 Arriaga's anticlerical protest causes his dismissal from Congress.
—To 1904——Blas Escontría SLP governor.

1899 Arriaga's economic assistance to Juan Sarabia, who publishes *El Demócrata*; Díaz Soto y Gama sparks student protests in SLP.

1900 *El Demócrata* closed down; Sarabia publishes *El Porvenir*.
—June 6——SLP. Bishop Ignacio Montes de Oca y Obregón's Paris speech boasting of Church's resurgence under Díaz.
—August 7——First issue of *Regeneración*, Mexico City.
—August 30——Arriaga's "Invitación al Partido Liberal."
—September 13——organization of Club Liberal "Ponciano Arriaga," SLP.

1901—January——Díaz Soto y Gama jailed one week, SLP.
—February 5——First Liberal Congress, SLP.
—March——Manifesto "to the nation" by Club Liberal "Ponciano Arriaga."
—April——Smashing of Liberal Club in Lampazos, Nuevo León.
—May——Ricardo and Jesús Flores Magón jailed.
—June–September——Publication of *Diario del Hogar* in SLP; Arriaga jailed.

July 18——Díaz Soto y Gama jailed after Pinos (Zacatecas) speech.
—October 7——*Regeneración* closed down.
—November 4——Manifesto by Club Liberal "Ponciano Arriaga" calls for social and agrarian reform.
—December——Díaz Soto y Gama released from jail.

1902—January 24——Goon-squad attack on Club Liberal "Ponciano Arriaga"; Arriaga, Sarabia, Rivera jailed.
—April——Díaz Soto y Gama jailed.
—April 6——Jailed Potosinos found *El Demófilo*.
—April 30——R. and J. Flores Magón released from Belén.
—July 16——R. Flores Magón edits *El Hijo del Ahuizote*; J. Flores Magón becomes inactive in movement.
—July 30——*El Demófilo* press confiscated.
—August 10——Last edition of *El Demófilo*.
—September 12——*El Hijo del Ahuizote* staff, including R. and Enrique Flores Magón, jailed.
—September——Sarabia, Díaz Soto y Gama, Rivera released from jail.
—November 23——*El Hijo del Ahuizote* reissued by Juan Sarabia; Manuel Sarabia joins movement.

1903—January 10——Arriaga released from Belén.

—January 23——R. and E. Flores Magón released from jail.

—February 23——Manifesto by Club Liberal "Ponciano Arriaga."

—February 27——Manifesto by Club Liberal "Ponciano Arriaga" emphasizing socio-economic injustices, implying call for revolution.

—March——Founding of Anti-reelectionist Club Redención, with its newspaper *Excélsior*.

—April 2——Demonstrators against General Bernardo Reyes shot upon in Monterrey; Arriaga and Díaz Soto y Gama flee to United States.

—April 11——Club Redención manifesto calling for support of Liberal candidate against Díaz, raising possibility of revolution.

—April 16——Police raid on *El Hijo del Ahuizote;* J. Sarabia, Rivera, R. and E. Flores Magón, *et al.* jailed. Rest of opposition press closed down soon thereafter.

—June 9——Decree against publication of any article written by journalists of *El Hijo del Ahuizote* jailed earlier.

—July——Rivera released from prison.

—October——J. Sarabia, R. and E. Flores Magón, *et al.* released from Belén.

1904   Funds exhausted from work with exile press, Díaz Soto y Gama returns to Mexico to get job, help support family.

—January 3——R. and E. Flores Magón, J. Sarabia, *et al.* arrive in Laredo, Texas.

—March——*El Colmillo Público* founded, Mexico City; after quarrel with R. Flores Magón, Arriaga, accompanied by Santiago R. de la Vega, goes to San Antonio, Texas.

—March 22——Santiago de la Hoz drowns.

—November 5——*Regeneración* reissued, San Antonio, Texas.

1905   To 1911——José María Espinosa y Cuevas SLP governor.

—February——Arriaga, J. Sarabia, R. and E. Flores Magón flee Texas harassment for St. Louis, Missouri.

—February 27——*Regeneración* reissued from St. Louis, Missouri.

—May 27——Centro Agrícola e Industrial founded, SLP.

—September 28——PLM statutes issued.

—October 12——*Regeneración* office raided by Pinkerton detectives; J. Sarabia, R. and E. Flores Magón jailed.

—October——In *El Colmillo Público*, R. Flores Magón calls Arriaga a traitor.

—December——J. Sarabia, R. and E. Flores Magón released from jail.

1906—February 1——*Regeneración* renews publication, St. Louis, Missouri.

—March 20——R. and E. Flores Magón, J. Sarabia flee to Canada.

—June 1–4——Cananea strike.

—July 1——PLM Program issued.

—July 1–7——Editors of *El Colmillo Público* jailed.

—August 3——Rafael de Zayas Enríquez submits report to Díaz about imminence of "socialist" revolution with popular support.

—September 2——J. Sarabia and R. Flores Magón arrive in El Paso, Texas, meet Antonio I. Villarreal, Prisciliano G. Silva, and other PLM revolutionaries.

—September 4——Arizona PLM headquarters raided; *El Demócrata* and arms confiscated.

—September 12——Rivera arrested in St. Louis, Missouri.

—September 15 to October 1——*Regeneración* operation smashed by U.S. authorities and Pinkerton detectives, St. Louis.

—September 24——Madero refuses arms and aid to PLM's Silva.

—September 26——PLM revolt in Jiménez, Coahuila.

—September 30 to October 3——PLM revolt in Acayucán, Veracruz.

—October——PLM revolt in Camargo, Tamaulipas.

—October 19——J. Sarabia, Canales, and De la Torre arrested in Cd. Juárez; PLM conspirators arrested in Texas; El Paso, Texas, headquarters of PLM, raided; R. Flores Magón flees to California.

—November 30——Rivera declared innocent by U.S. Commissioner in St. Louis, Missouri.

—December 4——Nationwide textile strike begins.

1907 To 1911——Economic crisis throughout Mexico.

—January 7——J. Sarabia's "trial" in Chihuahua—sentenced to seven years in San Juan de Ulúa Prison.

—January 8——Río Blanco massacre; textile strike ends.

—February——"Balance Sheet of Events in 1906" issued by R. Flores Magón and Villarreal for PLM.

—June 1——First issue of PLM's *Revolución*, Los Angeles, California.

—June 16——Rivera arrives in Los Angeles after six months of harassment and flight through Texas and Colorado.

—July 1——Manuel Sarabia "kidnaped" in Douglas, Arizona.

—August 23——R. Flores Magón, Rivera, Villarreal, and Modesto Díaz arrested in Los Angeles, California.

—October 7——E. Flores Magón arrives in Los Angeles.

1908   Crisis in credit; new banking laws; protests against new restrictions led by Toribio Esquivel Obregón, who in 1909 joins with Madero.

—February 17——In "Creelman interview," Díaz promises to retire at end of term (1910), welcomes "opposition" party.

—May 30—Díaz announces he will run for another term.

—June——R. and E. Flores Magón, Rivera, and Práxedis G. Guerrero agree to cut Manuel Sarabia and Villarreal out of PLM Board and to fight for Anarchism.

—June 22——Silva's El Paso, Texas, home raided.

—June 24–25——PLM revolt in Viesca, Coahuila.

—June 26——PLM revolt in Las Vacas, Coahuila.

—June 30 to July 1——PLM revolt in Palomas, Chihuahua.

—Summer——Arriaga returns to SLP to attend to financial matters; rejects political overtures from Díaz and Madero, renews political contacts in Mexico City.

—August 9——PLM guerrillas ambush federal troops in Sierra del Burro, Coahuila.

—September 5——Acayucán guerrillas repledge allegiance to PLM.

1909   Unrest spreading throughout Mexico; economic crisis continues.

—January——Hesitant opposition movements emerge; Reyistas strong; Madero's *La sucesión presidencial en 1910* appears.

—August——PLM's Jesús M. Rangel, Tomás Sarabia arrested.

—November——General Reyes exiled; Madero seeks Reyistas' support; Ateneo de la Juventud founded, Mexico City.

1910   Madero's Anti-reelectionist campaign repressed; Madero jailed in SLP.

—June——Revolts in Valladolid, Yucatán, and Cabrera de Inzunza, Sinaloa.

—July 22——Release of Madero from SLP jail on bond.

—August——R. Flores Magón, Rivera, and Villarreal released from Arizona prison.

—September 3——*Regeneración* reissued in Los Angeles, California.

—October——Santanón-PLM revolt in Veracruz.

—October 1——*Regeneración* for revolution, "Tierra y Libertad."

—October 5——Madero flees SLP to go into U.S. exile; date of Madero's Plan de SLP, although Plan was not completed until early November, from U.S. exile.

—November 20——Date set for nationwide uprising, according to Madero's Plan de SLP.

December——Casas Grandes, Chihuahua, captured by PLM and P. Guerrero.

—December 30——P. Guerrero killed in battle of Janos, Chihuahua.

1911—January 29——Mexicali, B.C., captured by PLM.

—February 11——P. Silva's PLM troops take Guadalupe, Chihuahua.

—February 14——Madero re-enters Mexico from U.S. exile, is welcomed at Guadalupe; PLM's Silva taken prisoner by Madero.

—February 25——*Regeneración* calls Madero a traitor.

—February 26——Villarreal leaves PLM to join Maderistas.

—March 6——Madero defeated at Casas Grandes, Chihuahua.

—March 18——PLM-style program of the "Complot de Tacubaya," led by Arriaga *et al.* (pro-Madero).

—March 27——Arrest of plotters of "Complot de Tacubaya"; Arriaga jailed.

—April 17——Various PLM commanders disarmed by Madero's troops.

—May 10——Pascual Orozco's troops take Cd. Juárez, Chihuahua, precipitating Díaz' downfall.

—May 17 to 21——Madero-Díaz Cd. Juárez peace treaties.

—May 25——Díaz resigns.

—May (?)——Arriaga released from prison.

—May 31——Díaz leaves Mexico for exile.

—June——J. Sarabia released from jail; joins Díaz Soto y Gama and other PLM moderates in Mexico City.

—June 7——Madero enters Mexico City triumphant.

—June 9——Madero promises War Ministry to General Reyes.

—June 11——Arriaga, Díaz Soto y Gama, *et al.* print anti-Reyes manifesto.

—June 13——J. Sarabia, J. Flores Magón peace mission to R. Flores Magón and PLM radicals fails.

—June 14——R. and E. Flores Magón, Rivera, and Figueroa jailed, Los Angeles, California.

—June 19——Díaz Soto y Gama named gubernatorial candidate for SLP, instead of Arriaga.

—July 11——"Agreement of the Principal Commanders of the Liberating Army in Support of the Plan of San Luis," signed by Arriaga.

—July 12——Colonel Blanquet's troops kill eighty Maderista soldiers in Puebla.

—July 28——Junta Iniciadora de la Reorganización del Partido Liberal formed by Sarabia, Díaz Soto y Gama, Arriaga, *et al.* (PL).

—July 31——PL's *Diario del Hogar* declares Cd. Juárez treaties nonexistent, Revolution "betrayed."

—August——PL's *Regeneración* appears, Mexico City. Andrés Molina Enríquez' agrarian revolt (Plan de Texcoco).

—August 2——Emilio Vázquez Gómez resigns from Cabinet.

—August 4——General Reyes announces candidacy for President.

—August 27——Madero-Zapata truce; General Huerta routs disarmed Zapata forces; Zapata then plans revolt against Madero.

—August–September——PCP convention; Arriaga as Madero's campaign manager.

—September 23——PLM radicals' Mexican-Anarchist manifesto.

—October——Elections: Madero elected President; Rafael Cepeda, SLP governor.

—October 31——Plan de Tacubaya (Vazquistas).

—November——PL's convention.

—November 6——Madero takes office as President.

—November 25 or 28——Plan de Ayala (Zapata).

—December——General Reyes declares revolt.

—December 23——PL's "Memorandum to President Madero," criticizing his regime.

1912—February——Juan Sarabia peace mission to Orozco forces, Chihuahua.

—March 25——Orozco revolt with PLM-style program.

—March–April——PL convention.

—June—PL split; J. Sarabia and Díaz Soto y Gama lead "extreme left wing of the Liberal Party."

—July——Casa del Obrero Mundial founded by Díaz Soto y Gama *et al.*

—October 16——Félix Díaz rebellion, Veracruz.

—December——Three-way division of PL "right wing."

1913—February——Huerta *coup d'état*; Madero assassinated.

—March 27——Plan de Guadalupe (Carranza).

—October ——Congress dissolved; Sarabia jailed.

1914—March——Díaz Soto y Gama joins Zapata forces.

—April——Sarabia released from jail.

—May——Casa del Obrero Mundial closed down by Huerta police.

—July——Huerta driven from power.

—August 21–22——Sarabia arranges Villarreal-Cabrera mission to Zapata.

—August 29——Villarreal-Cabrera Constitutionalist mission to Zapata, Díaz Soto y Gama, *et al.* in Cuernavaca, fails.

—October–December—Aguascalientes Convention (Villistas and Zapatistas); Díaz Soto y Gama orates for Left; Carranza government moves to Veracruz.

—December 12——Carranza's labor and agrarian-reform decree.

—1914 to 1918——R. Flores Magón and Rivera released from jail; sporadically publish *Regeneración*.

1915 Sarabia jailed by Carrancistas, Veracruz.

—January 6——Carranza's agrarian-reform decree.

—February——Carranza–Casa del Obrero Mundial alliance; Carrancistas defeat Villistas and Zapatistas soon thereafter.

1916 To 1917——Querétaro Constitutional Convention.

—August 1——Carranza invokes death penalty against strikers.

1917—February 5——Constitution promulgated (cf. PLM Program).

—June——Sarabia runs as independent for governor, SLP; loses.

1918—March——Rivera, R. Flores Magón issue last PLM manifesto (Anarchist).

—August——Rivera and R. Flores Magón sentenced to fifteen and twenty years, respectively, in U.S. prison.

1919 Zapata assassinated.

1920 Carranza assassinated; Obregón ascends to power. Díaz Soto y Gama forms Partido Nacional Agrarista; serves in Congress; turns to Catholic mysticism. Arriaga heads Department of Forestry, Hunting, and Fishing.

—July——Sarabia elected to Senate; dies (age thirty-eight) while serving his term.

1922—November——R. Flores Magón dies in U.S. jail cell.

1923 To 1930—Rivera in SLP and Tamaulipas, continuing Anarchist struggle.

1932 Rivera hit in car accident, dies.

1945 Arriaga dies.

1967 Díaz Soto y Gama dies.

ABBREVIATIONS

Bib.—The publisher Biblioteca del Instituto Nacional de Estudios Históricos de la Revolución Mexicana.

FCE—The publisher Fondo de Cultura Económica.

SLP—Place of publication, San Luis Potosí.

Justice—U.S. Department of Justice Archives (file number follows entry).

Relaciones—Archivo de la Secretaría de Relaciones Exteriores (colocación number follows entry).

State—U.S. Department of State Archives, Numerical File, 1906–1910 (file number follows entry).

UNAM—Universidad Nacional Autónoma de México.

Unless stated otherwise, all Mexican works were published in Mexico City. In some instances it has been impossible to ascertain the publisher. No assertions from secondary sources and no material from published collections of primary sources have been accepted without first cross-checking the relevant primary sources, normally to be found in the various public and private archival and library collections listed in Section II-A of the Bibliography (Archival Materials). The title "Dr." refers only to a doctor of medicine.

BIBLIOGRAPHY

Primary sources include material by major participants in the Precursor Movement or their close friends; material on post-1876 San Luis Potosí events; biographical material on Arriaga, Díaz Soto y Gama, Ricardo Flores Magón, Madero, Rivera, and Sarabia; books, articles, and published interviews containing large amounts of primary documents or memoirs (letters, etc.). Works of various European left-wing political figures, mostly Anarchists, mentioned in the text and footnotes, are not listed in the Bibliography because it is impossible to know what particular editions Mexican Precursors were reading during the Porfiriato (cf. comments on Editorial Maucci in Chapter Three).

The Bibliography is organized as follows (cf. "Abbreviations"):

I. BIBLIOGRAPHIES

Alcorta Guerrero, Ramón, and José Francisco Pedraza.
Bibliografía histórica y geográfica del Estado de San Luis Potosí. Instituto Panamericano de Geografía e Historia, 1941.

————. *Primeras adiciones a la bibliografía histórica y geográfica del Estado de San Luis Potosí.* Sociedad Mexicana de Geografía y Estadística, 1947.

Basave del Castillo Negrete, Carlos. *Exploraciones y anotaciones en libros y folletos que tratan de la Revolución Mexicana.* Talleres Linotipográficos H. Barrales Sucre, 1931.

Bibliografía de la Secretaría de Hacienda y Crédito Público, 1821–1942. Imprenta del Gobierno Federal, 1943.

Bullejos, José. *La bibliografía económica y sus fuentes en México.* Instituto de Investigaciones Económicas, UNAM, 1954.

Castillo, Ignacio B. del. *Bibliografía de la Revolución Mexicana de 1910 a 1916.* Talleres Gráficos de la Secretaría de Comunicaciones y Obras Públicas, 1918.

García Cuvas, Antonio. *Diccionario geográfico histórico de México.* 1888–1891.

Gómez, Marte R., et al. *Bibliografía agrícola y agraria de México.* 2 vols. Talleres Gráficos de la Nación, 1946.

González, Luis, et al. *Fuentes de la historia contemporánea de México. Libros y folletos.* 3 vols. Colegio de México, 1961–1963.

Jones, C. K. "Recent acquisitions in the Library of Congress treating of Mexico in Revolution," *Hispanic American Historical Review*, I, No. 4 (November, 1918), 480–481.

Lombardo Toledano, Vicente. *Bibliografía del trabajo y de la previsión social en México.* Imprenta de la Secretaría de Relaciones Exteriores, 1928.

Priestley, H. I. "Mexican Literature of the Recent Revolution," *Hispanic American Historical Review*, II, No. 2 (May, 1919), 286–311.

Ramos, Roberto. *Bibliografía de la Revolución Mexicana.* 3 vols. Bib., 1959–1960.

Ross, Stanley R. (compiler), et al. *Fuentes de la historia contemporánea de México: periódicos y revistas.* 2 vols. Colegio de México, 1965–1967.

Velázquez, Primo Feliciano. "Bibliografía científica potosina," in his *Obras.* Imp. de Victoriano Agueros, Editor, 1901.

II.   PRIMARY SOURCES
    A.   Archival Materials
      1.   Public

Archivo Económico de la Biblioteca de la Hacienda.
Archivo Espinosa de los Monteros, Museo Nacional de Historia.
Archivo General del Estado de San Luis Potosí.
Archivo General de la Nación.

Archivo de la Presidencia de la República.
Archivo de la Secretaría de Relaciones Exteriores. *Asunto: Flores Magón, Enrique y Ricardo—Juan Sarabia—Antonio I. Villarreal, etc., y disturbios en la frontera del norte.* Colocación L-E-918–954. 36 vols.
Bancroft Library, University of California, Berkeley.
Biblioteca del Colegio de México.
Biblioteca de México.
Biblioteca National de México.
Biblioteca de la Secretaría de Hacienda.
Biblioteca de la Sociedad Mexicana de Geografía y Estadística.
Biblioteca de la Universidad Autónoma de San Luis Potosí.
Biblioteca de la UNAM.
Colección de Carlos Basave del Castillo Negrete, Biblioteca de México.
Hemeroteca Nacional de México.
Instituto de Historia, UNAM.
Library of Congress, Washington, D.C.
U.S. Department of Justice, Archives. Files 90755 and 43718.
U.S. Department of State, Archives. Decimal File, 1910–1929; Numerical File, 1906–1910 (Nos. 100, 283, 1730–1750, 2787, 3916, 5028, 7418, 7722, 8183, 21057); *Despatches from United States Ministers to Mexico, 1823–1906.*
U.S. National Archives, Washington, D.C.

2. Private

Alcorta Guerrero, Ramón. San Luis Potosí.
Chávez Orozco, Luis. Cuernavaca.
Díaz Soto y Gama, Antonio. Mexico City.
Duffy Turner, Ethel. Cuernavaca.
Martínez Núñez, Eugenio. Mexico City.

B. Manuscripts

Carrera Torres, Alberto. Unpublished letters.
————. *A mis siempre estimados y finos hermanos los Tamaulipecos del Distrito de Tula y demás pueblos del Estado.* Tula, Tamaulipas: June, 1912.
Díaz Soto y Gama, Antonio. *Breves consideraciones sobre la importancia del municipio.* Tesis que presenta al Jurado Calificador. SLP: Imprenta del Comercio, 1901.
Martínez Núñez, Eugenio. "Antonio Díaz Soto y Gama."

————. "Camilo Arriaga."

————. "Humberto Macías Valadés."

————. *Juan Sarabia, apóstol y mártir de la Revolución Mexicana.* 2 vols. To be published by Bib.

————. "Librado Rivera."

————. "Manuel Sarabia."

Meade, Joaquín. *Diccionario biográfico, histórico, geográfico y estadístico del Estado de San Luis Potosí.* N.d.

C. Public Documents

Arenas Guzmán, Diego (ed.). *Historia de la Cámara de Diputados de la XXVI Legislatura Federal.* 4 vols. Comisión Nacional para la Celebración del Sesquicentenario de la Independencia Nacional y del Cincuentenario de la Revolución Mexicana, 1961–1963.

Barrera Fuentes, Florencio (ed.). *Crónicas y debates de las sesiones de la soberana Convención Revolucionaria.* Bib., 1964.

Cepeda, Rafael. *Informe.* SLP: Tipografía de la Escuela Industrial Militar, 1912.

Constitución Política de los Estados Unidos Mexicanos. Imprenta de la Secretaría de Gobernación, 1917.

Diario de los debates del Congreso Constituyente, 1916–1917. 2 vols. Comisión Nacional para la Celebración del Sesquicentenario de la Independencia Nacional y del Cincuentenario de la Revolución Mexicana, 1960.

Dirección General de Estadística. *Censo, 1900.* Oficina Tipográfica de la Secretaría de Fomento, 1904.

————. *División territorial de los Estados Unidos Mexicanos correspondiente al censo de 1910. Estado de San Luis Potosí.* Oficina Impresora de la Secretaría de Hacienda, 1918.

————. *Censo general de habitantes, 30 de noviembre de 1921. Estado de San Luis Potosí.* Talleres Gráficos de la Nación, 1927.

Ley reglamentaria del decreto 17 de mayo del presente año que reforma la constitución del Estado suprimiendo las jefaturas políticas y estableciendo las presidencias municipales. SLP: Tip. de la Escuela Industrial Militar, 1912.

Suprema circular del Ministerio de Fomento sobre deslinde de terrenos baldíos, sancionada y promulgada en México el 15 de mayo de 1886. SLP: Imprenta y Litografía de Esquivel y Salas, 1886.

U.S. Department of State. *Papers Relating to the Foreign Relations of the*

United States. Washington: U.S. Government Printing Office, various publication dates.

U.S. House of Representatives. *Hearings on House Joint Resolution 201 Providing for a Joint Committee to Investigate Alleged Persecutions of Mexican Citizens by the Government of Mexico*. Hearings held before the Committee on Rules, U.S. House of Representatives, June 8–14, 1910. Washington: Government Printing Office, 1910.

U.S. Senate. *Investigation of Mexican Affairs. Report and Hearing pursuant to Senate Resolution 106*. Hearings held before Subcommittee on Foreign Relations, U.S. Senate, 66th Congress, 1st Session. Senate Document No. 285, 2 vols. (Serial Nos. 7665 and 7666). Washington: Government Printing Office, 1920.

U.S. Supreme Court. *In the Matter of the Application of R. Flores Magón, Antonio I. Villarreal and Librado Rivera, for a Writ of Habeas Corpus*. Transcript of Record on Appeal from the Circuit Court of the United States of America, of the Ninth Judicial Circuit, in and for the Southern District of California, Southern Division. 1908.

D. Articles

Alessio Robles, Vito. "Gajos de historia," *Excélsior*, May 17, 1951 ff.

Anonymous. "Datos biográficos de Juan Sarabia," *El Nacional*, November 27, 1932.

Anonymous. "Don Camilo Arriaga, ilustre precursor de la Revolución," *El Popular*, June 27, 1945.

Anonymous. "Procesos por rebelión en 1906, instruídos en los juzgados de distrito de Oaxaca y San Luis Potosí, contra el periodista Plutarco Gallegos y otros," *El Legionairo*, March 31, 1955.

Arriaga, Camilo, and Antonio Díaz Soto y Gama. "El proceso del General Bernardo Reyes [June, 1903]," *Diario del Hogar*, August 21–23, 1911.

Brayer, Herbert O. "The Cananea Incident," *New Mexico Historical Review*, XIII, No. 4 (October, 1938), 387–415.

Brown, Lyle C. "Los liberales mexicanos y su lucha en contra de la dictadura de Porfirio Díaz, 1900–1906," *Antología MCC, 1956* (Mexico City College Press, 1956), 89–136.

———. "The Mexican Liberals and Their Struggle Against the Díaz Dictatorship," *Antología MCC, 1956* (Mexico City College Press, 1956), 318–362.

Cockcroft, James D. "El maestro de primaria en la Revolución Mexicana," *Historia Mexicana,* XVI, No. 4 (April–June, 1967), 565–587.

Cravioto, Alfonso. "Algunos recuerdos de Belén," *El Nacional,* March 22, 1933.

Creelman, James. "Interview with Porfirio Díaz," *Pearson's Magazine,* XIX, No. 3 (March, 1908), 241–277.

Cué Cánovas, Agustín. "Ricardo Flores Magón," *El Nacional,* February 3 and 10, 1957.

Debs, Eugene V. "This Plot Must Be Foiled. Conspiracy to Murder Mexican Comrades Now Imprisoned in This Country by Order of Díaz," *Appeal to Reason,* October 10, 1908, published as a separate pamphlet.

El Demócrata, August 29 through September 30, 1924 (series of articles containing government correspondence, interviews, etc.).

Díaz Soto y Gama, Antonio. "Ricardo y Enrique Flores Magón," *El Universal,* November 10, 1954.

Elorduy, Aquiles. "Juan Sarabia," *Excélsior,* October 31, 1932.

Escobedo Acevedo, Antonio. "Periódicos Socialistas de México, 1871–1880," *El Libro y el Pueblo,* XIII, No. 1 (January–February, 1935), 3–14.

Esquivel Obregón, Toribio. "Las consecuencias de nuestra política ferrocarrilera," *El Estandarte,* June 16, 1908.

———. " 'El Imparcial' y política bancaria y ferrocarrilera del gobierno," *El Estandarte,* July 14–17, 1908.

———. "El verdadero objeto de la circular de la Secretaría de Hacienda a las instituciones de crédito," *El Estandarte,* May 12, 1908.

Ferrer, Gabriel. "Camilo Arriaga, el revolucionario," *El Nacional,* July 3, 1945.

Flores Magón, Enrique. "Añoranzas," *El Nacional,* April 30, 1945, through February 3, 1947.

———. "Apuntes históricos para mis memorias," *Todo,* April 2, May 28, June 18, July 16, August 13, 20, and November 26, 1953.

———. "Los genuinos precursores," *Todo,* November 22, 1945.

———. "Notas breves de un viejo revolucionario en defensa del Partido Liberal Mexicano, iniciador de la Revolución Social Mexicana," *Gráfico,* January 11–24, 1931.

———. "El Partido Liberal (acción e ideología)," *El Nacional,* January 13–18, 1954.

———. Untitled series of articles, *El Universal,* February 23, 1951, through October 29, 1954.

————. "La vida de los Flores Magón," *Todo*, January 2 through June 19, 1934.

————. "Vida y hechos de los hermanos Flores Magón," *El Nacional*, January 7 through April 22, 1945.

Flores Magón, Jesús. "El amparo de Juan Sarabia," *El Tiempo*, May 27, 1911.

————. "Qué fue y cómo se desarrolló la Revolución que encabezó Flores Magón," *Gráfico*, November 22, 1930.

González Ramírez, Manuel. "Ricardo Flores Magón," *Novedades*, November 23–December 7, 1956.

Hernández, Teodoro. "Las tinajas de Ulúa: Juan Sarabia y su odisea," *El Universal Gráfico*, August 18–20, 1943.

————. Various articles. *La Prensa*: November 20, 1935; November 20, 1940; January 1, 1941; May 3, 10, and 17, 1942; February 5 and November 21, 1951; November 21, 1952; November 23–27, 1953; all 1955; June 30, 1956; July 1 and November 5, 1957. *El Popular*: July 12, 1943; February 5, 1944; April 28 and November 22, 1945; December 15, 1947; October 17 and November 19, 1948; July 2, 1949; all 1950. *Todo*: November 17, 1955. *El Nacional*: all 1958.

Ledesma Zavala, Juan Antonio. "Juan Sarabia," *El Nacional*, January 8, 1954.

Magaña Cerda, Octavio. "Historia documental de la Revolución," *El Universal*, May 19, 1950.

Mancisidor, José. "Dos precursores," *El Nacional*, July 2, 1945.

Martínez Núñez, Eugenio. "Antonio Díaz Soto y Gama, caballero del ideal," *El Universal*, October 14, 1958.

————. "Precursores de la Revolución: Antonio Díaz Soto y Gama," *Boletín Bibliográfico de la Secretaría de Hacienda y Crédito Público*, November 20, 1964.

————. "Los precursores de la Revolución, Juan Sarabia," *Boletín Bibliográfico de la Secretaría de Hacienda y Crédito Público*, June 1, 1961.

Meade, Joaquín. "Semblanza de Don Benigno Arriaga," *El Sol de San Luis*, February 19, 1956.

Monjaras, Víctor A. "Librado Rivera," *El Nacional*, March 11, 1932.

————. "Los precursores de la Revolución: Juan Sarabia," *Todo*, October 31, 1933.

Morales Jiménez, Alberto. "Camilo Arriaga, una vida ejemplar," *El Nacional*, June 28, 1945.

Murray, John. "Cases of Mexicans Persecuted by the United States Officials," *Congressional Record*, 61st Congress, 2nd Session, House, 1910, XLV, p. 5137.

———. "The Men Díaz Dreads—Mexico's Revolutionists and Their Third Uprising," *The Border*, January, 1909.

———. "San Juan de Ulua, the Private Prison of Díaz," *The Border*, February, 1909.

Olvera, Isidro. "Proyecto de ley," *Derecho público mexicano* (Imprenta del Gobierno en Palacio, 1871), IV, 417–424.

Pérez, Abel R. "El brote revolucionario de septiembre de 1906 en Minatitlán y Acayucán," *Excélsior*, June 9 through July 8, 1935.

Ramírez Arriaga, Manuel. "Camilo Arriaga," *Repertorio de la Revolución*, No. 4 (May 1, 1960), 7–28.

Ramos Pedrueza, Rafael. "Librado Rivera," *El Popular*, May 4, 1942.

———. "Semblanzas revolucionarias: Juan Sarabia," *El Popular*, December 22, 1942.

Rangel Gaspar, Eliseo. "Precursores de la Revolución: Juan Sarabia, defensor de la causa del pueblo," *Boletín Bibliográfico de la Secretaría de Hacienda y Crédito Público*, June 15, 1963.

Ríos, Plácido Cruz. Interview, *Excélsior*, October 2, 1965.

Rivera, Librado. "La mano férrea de la dictadura y el Congreso Liberal de San Luis," *Gráfico*, December 12–14, 1930.

———. "Persecución y asesinato de Ricardo Flores Magón," *Ricardo Flores Magón: vida y obra*, Vol. V, *Rayos de luz* (Mexico City: Ediciones del Grupo Cultural "Ricardo Flores Magón," 1924), 70–90.

———. "Prólogo," *in* Diego Abad de Santillán's *Ricardo Flores Magón: el apóstol de la Revolución Social Mexicana*, vii–xiii.

Salazar, Rosendo. "Camilo Arriaga trajo de Francia el socialismo," *El Nacional*, November 25, 1959.

Sarabia, Manuel. "How I was Kidnaped," *The Border*, December, 1908.

Sodi de Pallares, María Elena. "Charlando con el Lic. Antonio Díaz Soto y Gama," *El Universal*, November 20, 1941.

Valadés, José C. "El archivo de Madero," *La Opinión*, November 19, 1933.

———. "El hombre que derrumbó un régimen: Ricardo Flores Magón," *Todo*, March 5 through August 6, 1942.

———. "Los precursores de D. Francisco I. Madero," *La Opinión*, December 13, 1929, through January 24, 1930.

Vasconcelos, José. "Camilo Arriaga," *Novedades*, July 6, 1945.

Vázquez, Francisco. "Asuntos graves de justicia," *El Contemporáneo*, September 30, 1900.

Vega, Santiago R. de la. "Los precursores de la Revolución," *El Universal*, November 20, 1932.

E. Pamphlets

Ahualulco, Ayuntamiento de. *Representaciones que el Ayuntamiento y vecinos de la Villa de Ahualulco, han elevado al Sr. Prefecto Superior Político, en las cuestiones que tienen con la Hacienda Estancia de Bocas.* SLP: Tipografía del Gobierno, 1865.

Alcerreca, Félix M. *Viaje a San Luis Potosí, con motivo de la inauguración del Ferrocarril Nacional.* Tipografía de Alfonso E. López, 1888.

Alegre, Manuel M. *¡Aun es tiempo!* Tip. y Lit. "La Europea" de J. Aguilar Vera y Compañía, 1907.

Alonso, Antonio F. *El Germanofilismo Carrancista y la guerra de las naciones.* 1920.

Amaya, Arturo A. *Ignacio Montes de Oca y Obregón versus Elpidio Rodríguez. Juicio Sumario.* SLP: "El Precio Fijo," Tip., August, 1912.

Arriaga, Camilo, et al. *Invitación al Partido Liberal.* SLP: August 30, 1900. Photocopy in *Letras Potosinas*, VII, No. 83–84 (November–December, 1949), 13.

Arriaga, Camilo, and José María Facha. *Petición de amparo.* SLP: Imprenta de Rafael B. Vélez, 1902.

Arriaga, Ponciano. *Voto particular del C. Ponciano Arriaga sobre el derecho de propiedad.* SLP: Impreso "Al Libro de Caja," 1959.

Banco de San Luis Potosí, S.A. *Banco de San Luis Potosí, S.A. Concesiones, estatutos y extractos de la ley general de 19 de marzo de 1897 de Instituciones de Crédito.* SLP: Imprenta Municipal, 1898.

Barragán, Juan B. *Discurso pronunciado el 15 de septiembre de 1879 por el C. Lic. Juan B. Barragán, en la inauguración del primer tramo de Ferrocarril construido en el Estado.* SLP: Imprenta de Bruno E. García, 1879.

Berlanga, David G. *Soluciones del socialismo, conferencia del teniente coronel David G. Berlanga en el Teatro "Morelos" 9 de agosto de 1914.* Aguascalientes: Imp. Pedroza e Hijos, 1914.

Bolio, Edmundo. *Pluma obrera, cuestiones sociales.* 1918.

Casino Obrero Potosino. *Estatutos.* SLP: Imprenta y Encuadernación de J. Kaiser y Hno., 1910.

Centro Agrícola e Industrial Potosino. *Primer Concurso de Ganadería, septiembre de 1906.* SLP: Tip. de la E. Industrial Militar, 1906.

————. *Reglamento para la admisión de artículos que han de exhibirse, espacio que deben ocupar los exhibidores, instalación y cuidado de las exhibiciones y concursos de ganadería.* SLP: Tip. de la E. Industrial Militar, 1906.

Centro Liberal Independiente. *La candidatura Liberal Calero-Flores Magón.* Imprenta Eusebio Sánchez, 1913.

Cepeda, Rafael. *De mis memorias—Apuntes anecdóticos de la revolución.* 1916.

Chávez, Eduardo. *Estación Agrícola Experimental de Río Verde, San Luis Potosí.* Imprenta y Fototipia de la Secretaría de Fomento, 1909.

Ciudad del Maíz, Ayuntamiento de y Junta Local del Centenario. *Corona patriótica a la memoria de los héroes de la Independencia Nacional en el Primer Centenario de su gloriosa iniciación.* SLP: 1910.

Clubs Electorales del Estado. *Homenaje al Sr. Ing. Don José M. Espinosa y Cuevas al tomar posesión por segunda vez del Gobierno de San Luis Potosí.* SLP: Imprenta de Elpidio Ramírez, 1910.

Comité Conmemorativo "Juan Sarabia." *1920–1932 Homenaje a Juan Sarabia.* SLP: Talleres Tipográficos de la Escuela Industrial Militar, 1932.

Compañía Anónima de Santa María de La Paz y Anexas. *Estatutos de la Negociación Minera Santa María de La Paz y Anexas, en Matehuala, S.A., aprobados en Asamblea General de Accionistas el 17 de febrero de 1903, y elevados a escritura pública el día 20 del mismo mes y año.* SLP: Imprenta de J. Kaiser, 1903.

————. *Informes que a la Asamblea General Ordinaria de 31 de enero de 1901, rindieron los señores Presidente, Comisario y Director, acuerdos tomados y cuenta de producción y gastos del año de 1900.* SLP: Talleres de Imprenta, Litografía y Encuadernación de M. Esquivel y Cía., 1901.

Compañía Anónima Restauradora del Mineral de Ramos. *Estatutos de la Compañía Anónima Restauradora del Mineral de Ramos de San Luis Potosí, aprobados en junta celebrada el 7 de diciembre de 1887.* SLP: Imprenta y Litografía de M. Esquivel y Compañía, 1887.

Compañía de la Mina del Refugio y Socabón de la Luz. *Reglamento de la Negociación de la Luz en Catorce.* SLP: Imp. del Colegio Polimático, 1870.

Compañía Industrial "Cervecería de San Luis," S.A. *Estatutos de la Compañía Industrial "Cervecería de San Luis" Sociedad Anónima.* SLP: Imprento, Linografía y Encuadernación de M. Esquivel y Cía., 1897.

Compañía Mexicana de Petróleo "La Nacional," S.A. *Estatutos.* SLP: Tip. M. Esquivel e Hijos, 1913.

Compañía Minera Anónima de Esmeralda y Anexas. *Estatutos*. SLP: Imp., Litografía y Encuadernación de M. Esquivel y Compañía, 1899.

Compañía Minera de la Concepción. *Contrato celebrado entre la Junta Directiva de la Compañía propietaria y explotadora de la Mina de la Concepción y Anexas, sitas en el Mineral de Catorce, Estado de San Luis Potosí, por una parte, y el Sr. Benigno Arriaga por sí o por la Compañía o Compañías que se organicen, para la compraventa de los metales de dichas minas*. SLP: Imprenta de Dávalos, 1883.

————. *Estatutos aprobados para el trabajo y laborío de la Mina de la concepción ubicada en el Mineral de Catorce*. SLP: Tip. de Bruno E. García, 1880.

————. *Reseña de los trabajos ejecutados durante el primer semestre del año de 1889*. SLP. Imprenta de M. Esquivel y Cía., 1889.

Compañía Minera de "La Victoria." *Reglamento de la Compañía Minera de "La Victoria" explotadora del Socayón aventurero del mismo nombre en el Mineral de San Pedro*. SLP: Imprenta de Dávalos, 1880.

Compañía Minera "Hidalgo." *Reglamento*. SLP: Imprenta de Dávalos, 1881.

Compañía Minera Potosina Restauradora de Charcas. *Reglamento*. SLP: Imprenta del Gobierno a cargo del C. José María Infante, 1836.

Compañía Minera "San Pedro el Alto y Anexas." *Escritura de avío y estatutos de la Compañía*. SLP: Imprenta de Dávalos, 1879.

Compañía Minera Unión Santa Ritense. *Informe que la Junta Directiva de la Compañía Minera "Unión Santa Ritense" presenta a los Sres. accionistas en la Junta General Ordinaria del día 15 de enero de 1882*. SLP: Imprenta de Dávalos, 1882.

————. *Memoria de la Junta Directiva presentada a la Compañía Minera Unión Ritense*. SLP: Imprenta de Dávalos, 1885.

————. *Memoria de la Negociación Minera Unión Ritense, Correspondiente al año de 1885*. SLP: Imprenta de Dávalos, 1886.

Compañía Petrolífera "La Carolina," S.A. *Compañía Petrolífera Mexicana "La Carolina," S.A.* SLP: Linotipografía de la Escuela Industrial Militar, 1914.

Compañía Potosina Explotadora de Sales. *Estatutos*. SLP: Imprenta del Comercio, 1883.

Compañía Restauradora de la Mina de Purísima. *Reglamento*. SLP: Imprenta de Dávalos, 1878.

Compañía Telefónica Potosina. *Estatutos*. SLP: Tip. de la E. Industrial Militar, 1901.

Díaz Soto y Gama, Antonio, *et al. Discursos pronunciados por Juan Ramón Solís, José R. Saucedo, Antonio Díaz Soto y Gama, Diego Arenas Guzmán y Antonio I. Villarreal en el mitin con que el Partido Nacional Antirreeleccionista, la Confederación Revolucionaria de Partidos Independientes y otras agrupaciones políticas celebraron el XXIII Aniversario de la Revolución Mexicana.* Eds. de "El Hombre Libre," 1933.

Doheny, E. L. *A Brief Statement of the results accomplished by the Mexican Petroleum Company at Ebano, San Luis Potosí, México.* Imprenta y Fototipia de la Secretaría de Fomento, 1906.

Espinosa y Cuevas, Hermanos. *Las aguas de "El Nacimiento" en "Oaxcamá."* SLP: Talleres de Imprenta y Encuadernación de J. Kaiser y Hno., 1908.

Fremont, A. *Obras de irrigación en las Haciendas Anexas y abastecimiento de la Presa de Guadalupe, San Luis Potosí.* 1907.

Fundición de Fierro de San Luis Potosi. *Estatutos de la Fundición de Fierro de San Luis Potosí, Sociedad Anónima incorporada bajo las leyes de la República Mexicana.* SLP: "Al Libro Mayor," Imprenta Litografía y Encuadernación, 1905.

Guardiola, Bartolo, and Juan Rentería. *Informe presentado ante el IV Congreso Nacional de Educación por los Delegados Oficiales del Gobierno.* SLP: Linotipografía de la Escuela Industrial Militar, 1913.

Mendoza, Paulino de la Luz. *Los burgueses potosinos y su censor.* SLP: 1912.

———. *Queja.* SLP: Imprenta de Mendoza e hijo, 1909.

Murillo, Gerardo (Dr. Atl, pseudonym). *Confederación revolucionaria, conferencias públicas.* Teatro Arbeu: February 5, 1915.

Nieto, José G. *En defensa propia.* SLP: July 28, 1913.

Nieto, Rafael. *Exposición de los motivos que el Ejecutivo del Edo. tuvo para pedir al H. Congreso, la expedición de la Ley Agraria.* SLP: Talls. Gráficos de la E. I. "Benito Juárez," 1921.

O. L. A. *Origen y progreso de la Revolución de Sierra Gorda.* SLP: Imprenta del Pueblo, 1849.

Orozco, Wistano L. *Amparo promovido por el Lic. Wistano L. Orozco contra su detención y prisión, ordenadas por el Juez de Primera Instancia de Alaquines, San Luis Potosí.* Tip. de la Vda. de Francisco Díaz de León, 1906.

———. *De los elementos esenciales de toda acción civil y de los términos clásicos de su fórmula.* Talleres Tipográficos de "El Tiempo," 1905.

———. *El fusilamiento de Pedro López.* SLP: Tip. de la Escuela Industrial Militar, 1897.

———. *Interdicto de recuperar la posesión*. SLP: Imprenta, Litografía y Encuadernación de M. Esquivel y Cía., 1906.

———. *Las aguas subterráneas*. SLP: Imprenta, Litografía y Encuadernación de M. Esquivel y Cía., 1897.

———. *Las tierras de los Moctezuma*. Talleres Tipográficos de "El Tiempo," 1905.

———. *Las víctimas de Río Abajo o sea la propiedad inmueble y las acciones penales*. Talleres Linotipográficos de "El Tiempo," 1905.

Othón, Juan. *Observaciones*. SLP: Tip. de Abraham Exiga, 1865.

Othón, Manuel José. *Apuntes que, para alegar de buena prueba ante el Señor Juez 3° de Letras del Partido de Mapimí, produce Don Jesús Revilla, patrocinado por el Lic. Manuel J. Othón, y representante jurídico de la Compañía Minera "Siderita" y Anexas, S.A. de S. Luis Potosí en el interdicto de despojo promovido contra la Compañía Minera y Fundidora "Descubridora."* Torreón: Tipografía Dramática de Alberto N. Swain, 1900.

Partido Nacionalista Democrático. *La candidatura del C. profesor y general insurgente Cándido Navarro, para el gobierno del estado de Guanajuato, y su biografía*. 1911.

Pérez, Romualdo. *Cuestión de ejidos y linderos. Documentos oficiales. Informes del Archivo General y Público de la Nación y de la Dirección Agraria, rendidos a la Secretaría de Fomento, sobre los linderos de la Hacienda de Gogorrón y los ejidos de Villa de Reyes*. SLP: Talleres Tipográficos de "El Estandarte," 1912.

Pérez Salazar, Alicia. *Discurso a Ricardo Flores Magón*. Tribuna de Mexico, November 22, 1963.

Perogordo, Moisés. *Informe y cuentas a la Cía. Minera del Gran Socavón "García Salinas" en Zacatecas*. SLP: Imprenta de Dávalos, 1884.

Potreritos, dueños y vecinos de. *Manifestación que los dueños y vecinos de Potreritos, sito en Guadalcázar, San Luis Potosí, hacen a sus amigos y a las personas amantes de la justicia*. Guadalcázar, San Luis Potosí: 1906.

Quintana, Pedro. *Representación que los vecinos de San Juan Salinillas y algunos de otros puntos elevan al Hon. Congreso del Edo., para que se sirva declarar a aquel lugar el Título de Villa, y refutación de la esposición hecha a la misma Legislatura, por el apoderado de la Sra. Doña Francisca de P. Pérez Gálvez, oponiéndose a aquella pretensión*. SLP: Imprenta del Estado a cargo de V. Carrillo, 1850.

Quiroz, Eleuterio. *Plan Político y Eminentemente Social*. Río Verde, San

Luis Potosí, March 13, 1849, in *Colección de Planes*, Editor Vargas Rea, 1962.

Ramírez Martínez, Julián. *Discurso por el Profesor Normalista D. Julián Ramírez Martínez, en la velada con que la Sociedad Mutua de Artesanos celebró el IX Aniversario de su instalación, la noche del 20 de julio de 1906, en el Teatro de la Paz.* SLP: Imprenta Popular, 1906.

Rebelión y plan de los indios huaxtecos de Tantoyuca, 1856. Editor Vargas Rea, 1956.

Reyes, Bernardo. *La declaratoria de absolución en favor del Sr. Gral. Reyes, ante la opinión pública nacional.* N.d.

Rito Escocès Antiguo y Aceptado. *Código penal masónico.* 1910.

Rodríguez, Elpidio. *El crimen y su expiación Monseñor Pirene Obispo de Peregrina, Drama moral y religioso en prosa y tre actos.* SLP: Imprenta y Fotografía de Mendoza é hijo, 1906.

Santa María del Río, San Luis Potosí. *Títulos de propiedad particular que amparan los terrenos que disfrutan los indígenas de Santa María del Río.* SLP: Imp. del Eco de la Moda, 1882.

Santa María del Río, Vecinos de. *Ocurso dirigido al C. Gefe Superior de Hacienda del Estado, por varios vecinos de Santa María del Río, solicitando la declaración de que ni las aguas de riego de esa ciudad, ni los baños de Ojo Caliente, están comprendidos en la Ley de 25 de Junio de 1856.* SLP: Tip. de Dávalos y Ca., 1868.

Santibañez, Felipe. *Estudios para el programa del Partido Liberal: Derechos del hombre y los bienes naturales, y la solución del problema agrario.* Apartado 28, 1912.

Sarabia, Antonio. *Problema agrario y emancipación del peón y proletario mexicanos.* Tipografía y Litografía de Muller Hnos., 1914.

Sarabia, Juan. *Defensa del C. Juan Sarabia.* San Antonio, Texas: Imprenta de J. C. Mendoza, 1907.

———. *Proyecto de ley sobre adiciones a la Constitución General respecto a la materia agraria, presentado por el C. Diputado Juan Sarabia.* Imp. de la Cámara de Diputados, 1912.

Sociedad Mutua de Artesanos. *Estatutos.* SLP. Imprenta del Comercio, 1902.

Sociedad Mutualista de Profesores. *Reglamento.* SLP: Imprenta Municipal, 1901.

Sociedad Progresista de Artesanos. *Reglamento y Estatutos.* SLP: Imprenta Económica, 1894.

Tinoco, Manuel. *Informe sobre los minerales de Guadalcázar, Sta. María del*

Tecomite y Rincón de Petros, del Estado de San Luis Potosí. The Electric Engraving Company, 1901.

Trowbridge, Elizabeth D. *Political Prisoners Held in the United States.* Tucson, Arizona: The Border Publishing Company, 1909.

F. Books

Alessio Robles, Miguel. *Mi generación y mi época.* Editorial Stylo, 1949.

Alvarez, Alfredo (ed.). *Madero y su obra.* Talleres Gráficos de la Nación, 1935.

———. *El limantourismo de Francisco Madero.* Talleres Tipográficos de la Casa de Orientación para Varones, 1934.

Amezcua, Genaro. *¿Quién es Flores Magón y cuál su obra?* Editorial Avance, 1943.

Anaya Ibarra, Pedro María. *Precursores de la Revolución Mexicana.* Secretaría de Educación Pública, 1955.

Arnáiz y Freg, Arturo. *Madero y Pino Suárez.* Secretaría de Educación Pública, 1963.

Ateneo de la Juventud. *Conferencias del Ateneo de la Juventud.* Imprenta Lacaud, 1910.

Baca Calderón, Esteban. *Juicio sobre la guerra del Yaqui y génesis de la huelga de Cananea.* Ediciones del Sindicato Mexicano de Electricistas, 1956.

Barragán Rodríguez, Juan. *Historia del Ejército de la Revolución Constitucionalista.* 2 vols. Antigua Librería Robredo, 1946.

Barrera Fuentes, Florencio. *Historia de la Revolución Mexicana: la etapa precursora.* Bib., 1955.

Barrera Lavalle, Francisco. *Estudios sobre el origen desenvolvimiento y legislación de las instituciones de crédito en México.* Tip. D. García y Cia, 1909.

Batalla, Diódoro, *et al. Una campaña política.* Imprenta Estampa, 1902.

Blaisdell, Lowell L. *The Desert Revolution: Baja California, 1911.* Madison: University of Wisconsin Press, 1962.

Breceda, Alfredo. *México revolucionario, 1913-1917.* Madrid: Tip. Artística Cervantes, 1920.

Bustamante, Luis F. *El anarquismo científico.* 1916.

———. *Bajo el terror Huertista.* 1916.

———. *Perfiles y bocetos revolucionarios.* Talleres de "El Constitucional," 1917.

———. *Savia roja (socialismo mexicano).* SLP: Imp. Económica, 1914.

Cabrera, Luis (Lic. Blas Urrea). *Obras políticas.* Imprenta Nacional, S.A., 1921.

———. *El pensamiento de Luis Cabrera.* Bib., 1960.

Calero, Manuel. *Cuestiones electorales.* Imprenta de Ignacio Escalante, 1908.

———. *El problema actual: la vice-presidencia de la República.* Tipografía Económica, 1903.

Carrasco Puente, Rafael. *La caricatura en México.* UNAM, 1953.

Carrillo, Rafael. *Ricardo Flores Magón, esbozo biográfico.* 1945.

Casasola, Agustín (ed.). *Historia gráfica de la Revolución Mexicana.* Vols. I and II. Archivo Casasola, n.d.

Casasús, Joaquín D. *Las reformas a la ley de instituciones de crédito y las instituciones de crédito en México en 1908.* Tip. de la Oficina Impresora de Estampillas Palacio Nacional, 1908.

Castillo, José T. del. *Historia de la Revolución Social de México.* 1915.

Chávez Orozco, Luis. *La agonia del artesanado mexicano.* Editorial "Aloma," 1958.

———. *La crisis agrícola de México en 1908, en su aspecto crediticio.* Publicaciones del Banco Nacional de Crédito Agrícola y Ganadero, S.A., 1954.

———. *Documentos para la historia económica de México.* 11 vols. Publicaciones de la Secretaría de la Economía Nacional, 1933–1936.

Chism, Richard E. *Una contribución a la historia masónica de México.* Imprenta de el Minero Mexicano, 1899.

Cué Cánovas, Agustín. *Ricardo Flores Magón, la Baja California y los Estados Unidos.* Libro Mex Editores, 1957.

Cumberland, Charles C. *Mexican Revolution: Genesis under Madero.* Austin: University of Texas Press, 1952.

Díaz de León, Rafael. *Nuestros Prohombres.* SLP: Imprenta de la Escuela Industrial Militar, 1926.

Díaz Soto y Gama, Antonio. *La revolución agraria del sur y Emiliano Zapata, su caudillo.* Imprenta Policromia, 1960.

Duffy Turner, Ethel. *Ricardo Flores Magón y el Partido Liberal Mexicano.* Morelia, Michoacán: Editorial "Erandi," 1960.

Escobedo, José G., and Rosendo Salazar. *Las pugnas de la gleba, 1907–1922.* 2 vols. 1922.

Esquivel Obregón, Toribio. *La crisis agrícola de México en 1908, en su aspecto crediticio* (Recopilación de Luis Chávez Orozco). Publicaciones del Banco Nacional de Crédito Agrícola y Ganadero, S.A., 1954.

————. *Democracia y personalismo—relatos y comentarios sobre política actual.* Imp. de A. Carranza e hijos, 1911.

————. *Mi labor en servicio de México.* Imprenta Linomex, 1934.

Estrada, Roque. *La revolución y Francisco I. Madero.* Guadalajara: Tall. de la Imp. Americana, 1912.

Fabela, Isidro (ed.). *Documentos históricos de la Revolución Mexicana.* 10 vols. Vols. I–V, FCE, 1960–1964; Vols. VI–X, Editorial Jus, S.A., 1965–1966.

Fabila, Manuel. *Cinco siglos de legislación agraria en México (1493–1940).* Talleres de Industrial Gráfica, 1941.

Ferrer Mendiolea, Gabriel. *Vida de Francisco Madero.* Secretaría de Educación Pública, 1945.

Flores Magón, Ricardo. *Epistolario revolucionario e íntimo.* 3 vols. Grupo Cultural "Ricardo Flores Magón," 1925.

————. *Ricardo Flores Magón, vida y obra.* 6 vols. Grupo Cultural "Ricardo Flores Magón," 1923–1925.

Gavira, Gabriel. *Su actuación político–militar revolucionaria.* Talleres Tip. de A. del Bosque, 1933.

González, A. B. *Album Rioverdense, colección de escritos, datos históricos y estadísticos recogidos.* SLP: Tip. E. Católica, 1902.

González, Antonio P., and J. Figueroa Domenech. *La Revolución y sus héroes.* Herrero Hnos. Sucesores, 1912.

González Garza, Federico. *La Revolución Mexicana. Mi contribución político–literaria.* A. del Bosque, 1936.

————. *El testamento político de Madero.* Imprenta Victoria, 1921.

González Monroy, Jesús. *Ricardo Flores Magón y su actitud en la Baja California.* Editorial Academia Literaria, 1962.

González Ramírez, Manuel (ed.). *Epistolario y textos de Ricardo Flores Magón.* FCE, 1964.

————. *Fuentes para la historia de la Revolución Mexicana.* 4 vols. FCE, 1954–1957.

González Roa, Fernando. *El aspecto agrario de la revolución.* Poder Ejecutivo Federal, Departamento de Aprovisionamientos Generales, Dirección de Talleres Gráficos, 1919.

Goytortúa Santos, Jesús. *Pensativa.* Editorial Porrúa, 1945.

Guerrero, Práxedis G. *Práxedis G. Guerrero: artículos literarios y de combate; pensamientos; crónicas revolucionarias, etc.* Grupo Cultural "Ricardo Flores Magón," 1924.

Gutiérrez de Lara, Lázaro. *The Mexican People—Their Struggle for Freedom.* New York: Doubleday, Page & Co., 1914.

——. *El pueblo mexicano y sus luchas por la libertad.* Los Angeles, California: Citizen Print Shop, n.d.

Hernández, Teodoro. *La historia de la Revolución debe hacerse.* 1950.

——. *Las tinajas de Ulúa.* Editorial "Hermida," 1943.

Kaplan, Samuel. *Combatimos la tiranía (conversaciones con Enrique Flores Magón).* Bib., 1958.

Lara Pardo, Luis. *De Porfirio Díaz a Francisco Madero.* New York: Polyglot Publish. & Commercial Co., 1912.

Lepino, K. *Sangre y humo, o "El tigre de la Huasteca."* 1918.

Leyva, José María. *Aportaciones a la historia de la Revolución.* N.d.

Limantour, José Yves. *Apuntes sobre mi vida pública.* Editorial Porrúa, 1965.

López–Portillo y Rojas, José. *Elevación y caída de Porfirio Díaz.* Librería Española, 1912.

——. *Fuertes y débiles.* Librería Española, 1919.

Madero, Francisco I. *Archivo de Francisco I. Madero: Epistolario (1900–1909).* Ediciones de la Secretaría de Hacienda, 1963.

——. *El Partido Antirreeleccionista y la próxima lucha electoral. Su programa, sus trabajos, tendencias y aspiraciones.* San Pedro, Coahuila: ed. de "El Demócrata," 1910.

——. *La sucesión presidencial en 1910.* 3rd ed. (1st ed., San Pedro, Coahuila, 1908; 2nd ed., Mexico City, 1909). Libr. de Viuda de Ch. Bouret, 1911.

Magaña, Gral. Gildardo. *Emiliano Zapata y el agrarismo en México.* 5 vols. Editorial Ruta, 1951.

Maqueo Castellanos, Esteban. *Algunos problemas nacionales.* Edit. Eusebio Gómez de la Puente, 1909.

María y Campos, Armando de (ed.). *Las memorias y las mejores cartas de Francisco I. Madero.* Libro–Mex Editores, S. De R. L., 1956.

Márquez Sterling, Manuel. *Los últimos días del Presidente Madero.* Havana: Ed. Siglo XX, 1917.

Martínez, Pablo L. *El magonismo en Baja California.* Editorial "Baja California," 1958.

Martínez, Paulino. *Causas de la Revolución de México y cómo efectuar la paz.* Havana: Imprenta Hourcade, Crews & Co., 1914.

——. *Rayos de luz.* Imprenta Fiat Lux, 1910.

Martínez, Rafael, and E. Guerra. *Madero, su vida y su obra.* Monterrey: 1914.

Martínez Núñez, Eugenio. *La revolución en el estado de San Luis Potosí (1900–1917).* Bib., 1963.

————. *La vida heroica de Práxedis G. Guerrero (apuntes históricos del movimiento social mexicano desde 1900 hasta 1910).* Bib., 1960.

Meade, Joaquín. *Semblanza de D. José Encarnación Ipiña.* SLP: Impresos del Centro, S.A., 1956.

Meléndez, Jose F., Juan Sánchez Azcona, and Octavio Paz (eds.). *Historia de la Revolución Mexicana.* Talleres Gráficos de la Nación, 1936.

Menéndez, Carlos R. *La primera chispa de la Revolución Mexicana.* Mérida: 1919.

Moheno, Querido. *¿Hacia dónde vamos?* Talleres de I. Lara, 1908.

Molina Enríquez, Andrés. *Los grandes problemas nacionales.* Imprenta de A. Carranza e Hijos, 1909.

————. *La revolución agraria de México de 1910 a 1920.* 5 vols. Talleres Gráficos del Museo Nacional de Arqueología, Historia, y Etnografía, 1933–1937.

Mota, Gonzalo, and Ignacio Morales. *El General Esteban Baca Calderón.* 1917.

Muñoz Cota, José. *Ricardo Flores Magón, un sol clavado en la sombra.* Editores Mexicanos Unidos, S.A., 1963.

Muro, Manuel. *Historia de San Luis Potosí.* 3 vols. SLP: Imprenta, Litografía y Encuadernación de M. Esquivel y Cía. (Vols. 1 and 2), Imprenta Moderna de Fernando H. González (Vol. 3), 1910.

Naranjo, Francisco. *Diccionario Biográfico Revolucionario.* Imprenta Editorial "Cosmos," 1935.

Niemeyer, E. Victor. *El General Bernardo Reyes.* Trans. Juan Antonio Ayala. Monterrey: Centro de Estudios Humanísticos de la Universidad de Nuevo León. 1966.

Nieto, Rafael, *Más allá de la patria. Ensayos económicos y políticos.* Imprenta Politécnica, 1922.

Obregón, Alvaro. *Ocho mil kilómetros en campaña.* FCE, [1917], 1960.

Orozco, Wistano Luis. *La cuestión agraria.* Guadalajara: 1911.

————. *Legislación y jurisprudencia sobre terrenos baldíos.* Imp. El Tiempo, 1895.

————. *Los negocios sobre terrenos baldíos resoluciones judiciales y estudios del Lic. Wistano Luis Orozco, en el caso especial de Agustín R. de Ortiz contra los Moctezumas.* SLP: Tip. de M. Esquivel y Cía., 1902.

Ortiz Rubio, Pascual. *La Revolución de 1910. Apuntes históricos.* Ediciones Botas, 1937.

Otero, Mariano. *Ensayo sobre el verdadero estado de la cuestión social y política que agita en la República Mexicana.* Instituto Nacional de la Juventud Mexicana, [1842], 1964.

Padua, Cándido Donato. *Movimiento revolucionario 1906 en Veracruz.* Tlalpan, D.F.: 1941.

Palavicini, Félix F. *Historia de la Constitución de 1917.* 2 vols. 1938.

————. *Mi vida revolucionaria.* Ediciones Botas, 1937.

Pani, Alberto J. *Apuntes autobiográficos.* 2 vols. Librería de Manuel Porrúa, 1950

Pérez Gálvez, Francisca de Paula. *Representación que eleva a la Cámara de Diputados, Doña Francisca de Paula Pérez Gálvez, con motivo de los denuncios de vertientes y pozos de agua salada, hechos en haciendas de su pertenencia y de la testamentaría de su hermano, Don Juan de Dios Pérez Gálvez.* Imprenta de Ignacio Cumplido, 1851.

Pérez Salazar, Alicia. *Librado Rivera: un soñador en llamas.* Edición de los Amigos, 1964.

Pérez Taylor, Rafael. *El socialismo en México.* 1914.

Portes Gil, Emilio. *La lucha entre el poder civil y el clero.* 1934.

Pruneda, Salvador. *La caricatura como arma política.* Bib., 1958.

Puente, Ramón. *Pascual Orozco y la revuelta de Chihuahua.* Eusebio Gómez de la Puente, 1912.

Reyes, Bernardo. *Defensa: que por sí mismo produce el General de División Bernardo Reyes acusado del delito de rebelión.* Impr. Lacaud, 1912.

Reyes, Rodolfo. *De mi vida. Memorias políticas (1899–1913).* 2 vols. Madrid: Biblioteca Nueva, 1929.

Rodarte, Fernando. *7 de enero de 1907. Puebla–Orizaba.* A. del Bosque, Impresor, 1940.

Rodríguez, Blas. *Informe acusatorio presentado por el estudiante de jurisprudencia Blas E. Rodríguez, ante el juez de la 1° instancia de Tancanhuitz, en la vista de los procesos acumulados contra Salomón Morales y Socios por el homicidio del Sr. Don Francisco Morales.* Talleres de Imprenta y Encuadernación de F. Bustillos, 1906.

Rodríguez Barragán, Nereo. *El canónigo Mauricio Zavala, apóstol del agrarismo en el Valle del Maíz.* SLP: Universidad Autónoma de San Luis Potosí, 1958.

Ross, Stanley R. *Francisco I. Madero, Apostle of Mexican Democracy.* New York: Columbia University Press, 1955.

Salazar, Rosendo. *La carta del trabajo de la Revolución Mexicana: fundamentos de una evolución.* Libro Mex, Editores, 1960.

――――. *La Casa del Obrero Mundial.* Costa–Amic, Editor, 1962.

――――. *Hacia el porvenir.* Editores Avante, 1916.

――――. *México en pensamiento y en acción.* Editorial Avante, 1926.

――――. *Los primeros de mayo en México.* Costa–Amic, Editor, 1965.

――――. *Al rojo libertario.* Orizaba, Veracruz: Talleres Gráficos de la "Casa del Obrero Mundial," 1915.

Santillán, Diego Abad de. *Ricardo Flores Magón, el apóstol de la Revolución Social Mexicana.* Grupo Cultural "Ricardo Flores Magón," 1925.

Secretaría de Economía, Dirección General de Estadística. *Estadísticas sociales del Porfiriato, 1877–1910.* Talleres Gráficos de la Nación, 1956.

Sentíes, Francisco de P. *La organización política de México.* Imp. y Lib. de Inocencio Arriola, 1908.

Sierra, Justo (ed.). *México, su evolución social.* 3 vols. 1900–1902.

Silva Herzog, Jesús (ed.). *Colección de folletos para la historia de la Revolución Mexicana: la cuestión de la tierra.* 4 vols. Instituto Mexicano de Investigaciones Económicas, 1960–1962.

Taracena, Alfonso. *Madero. Vida del hombre y del político.* Ediciones Botas, 1937.

Trejo y Lerdo de Tejada, Carlos. *Nuestra verdadera situación política y el Partido Democrático.* Talleres Tipográficos de "El Tiempo," 1910.

Trowbridge, Elizabeth D. *Mexico Today and Tomorrow.* New York: Macmillan, 1919.

Turner, John Kenneth. *Barbarous Mexico.* Chicago: Charles H. Kerr & Company, 1910.

Valdés, Manuel. *Memorias de la Guerra de Reforma. Diario del Cornl. Manuel Valdés.* Sociedad Mexicana de Geografía y Estadística, 1912.

Vasconcelos, José. *Don Evaristo Madero; biografía de un Patricio.* Impresiones Modernas, 1958.

――――. *Obras completas.* 4 vols. Libreros Mexicanos Unidos, S.A., 1961.

Vázquez Gómez, Francisco. *Memorias políticas (1909–1913).* Imprenta Mundial, 1933.

Velázquez, Primo Feliciano. *Colección de documentos para la historia de San Luis Potosí.* SLP: Imprenta del Editor, 1897.

――――. *Historia de San Luis Potosí.* 4 vols. Sociedad Mexicana de Geografía y Estadística, 1946.

Vera, Agustín. *En la profunda sombra.* SLP: M. Sancho, 1916.

――――. *La revancha.* SLP: Talleres Linotipográficos Acción, n.d.

————. *Tradiciones potosinas.* SLP: A. Macías, 1941.

Vera Estañol, Jorge. *La Revolución Mexicana, orígenes y resultados.* Editorial Porrúa, 1957.

————. *Partido Popular Evolucionista. Programa y bases de organización.* 1911.

Zayas Enríquez, Rafael de. *The Case of Mexico and the Policy of President Wilson.* New York: A. and C. Boni, 1914.

————. *Porfirio Díaz, la evolución de su vida.* New York: D. Appleton & Co., 1908.

Zepeda, Manuel. *Opiniones de la prensa sobre las fiestas de inauguración del Ferrocarril Nacional Mexicano verificadas en la ciudad de San Luis Potosí los días 1°, 2, 3, y 4 de noviembre de 1888.* SLP: Tip. de la Escuela Industrial Militar, 1888.

G.   Interviews[1]

Bernal, Nicolás T.; in Mexico City.

Díaz Soto y Gama, Antonio; in Mexico City.

Duffy Turner, Ethel; in Cuernavaca.

Guzmán, Martín Luis; in Mexico City.

Manrique, Jr., Aurelio; in Mexico City.

Martínez Núñez, Eugenio; in Mexico City.

Silva Herzog, Jesús; in Mexico City.

III.   NEWSPAPERS

Acción Mundial, 1916.

El Antirreeleccionista, 1909–1910.

Appeal to Reason (Girard, Kansas), 1908–1910.

Arizona Daily Star (Tucson), 1906–1910.

The Border (Tucson, Arizona), 1908–1909.

El Colmillo Público, 1905–1906.

El Constitucional, 1910.

El Contemporáneo (SLP), 1899–1905.

Daily Express (San Antonio, Texas), 1906–1910.

El Debate, 1909–1911.

El Defensor del Pueblo (Tucson, Arizona), 1908.

El Demócrata, 1924.

[1] For additional Mexican scholars interviewed, consult Acknowledgments.

El Demófilo (SLP), 1902.
El Diario, 1911–1913.
Diario del Hogar, 1908–1913.
Diario Oficial, 1906–1910.
El Estandarte (SLP), 1892–1912.
La Estrella (San Antonio, Texas), 1909.
Excélsior, 1903.
Globe Democrat (St. Louis, Missouri), 1906–1909.
Gráfico, 1930–1932.
El Hijo del Ahuizote, 1902–1903.
El Imparcial, 1900–1913.
El Liberal (Del Rio, Texas), 1908.
Mexican Herald, 1906–1913.
México Nuevo, 1911, 1913.
Monitor Democrático (San Antonio, Texas), 1910.
El Nacional, 1932–1958.
Nueva Era, 1912–1913.
La Ofrenda Escolar (SLP), 1907–1909.
La Opinión (Los Angeles, California), 1929–1938.
El País, 1900–1913.
El Partido Democrático, 1909.
Periódico Oficial del Gobierno del Estado Libre y Soberano de San Luis Potosí, 1900–1913.
El Popular, 1943–1958.
Post-Dispatch (St. Louis, Missouri), 1906–1909.
La Prensa, 1911–1913.
El Progreso (San Antonio, Texas), 1907–1908.
Punto Rojo (Del Rio, Texas), 1909.
Reforma, Libertad y Justicia (Austin, Texas), 1908.
Regeneración, 1900–1901; (San Antonio, Texas), 1904; (St. Louis, Missouri), 1905–1906; (Los Angeles, California), 1910–1911.
Regeneración (of the PLM moderates), 1911.
Revolución (Los Angeles, California), 1907–1908.
Star Chronicle (St. Louis, Missouri), 1906–1909.
El Tiempo, 1900–1913.
Todo, 1934–1954.
La Unión Industrial (Phoenix, Arizona), 1911.
El Universal, 1913–1964.
Vésper, 1901.

La Voz de Juárez (San Antonio, Texas), 1910.

La Voz de la Mujer (El Paso, Texas), 1907.

IV.   SECONDARY SOURCES

    A.   Articles

Anderson, Bo, and Morris Zelditch, Jr. "Rank Equilibration and Political Behavior," *European Journal of Sociology*, V (1964), 112–125.

Bazant, Jan. "La desamortización de los bienes corporativos en 1856," *Historia Mexicana*, XVI, No. 2 (October–December, 1966), 193–212.

Bernstein, Marvin D. "Colonel William C. Greene and the Cananea Copper Bubble," *Bulletin of the Business Historical Society* (December, 1952), 179–198.

Blanquel, Eduardo. "El anarco-magonismo," *Historia Mexicana*, XIII, No. 3 (January–March, 1964), 394–427.

Bloch, Marc. "European Feudalism," *Encyclopedia of the Social Sciences* (New York: The Macmillan Company, 1957), VI, 203–210.

Bustamante, Luis F. "Cándido Navarro," *El Estandarte*, May 27, 1911.

Carrillo, Alejandro. "Una historia de amistad yanqui-mexicana," *Mañana*, April 10, 1954.

Clark, John Maurice. "Monopoly," *Encyclopedia of the Social Sciences* (New York: The Macmillan Company, 1957), X, 623–630.

Cumberland, Charles C. "Precursors of the Mexican Revolution of 1910," *Hispanic American Historical Review*, XXII (May, 1942), 344.

Díaz Soto y Gama, Antonio. "Los hermanos Cedillo, destacados agraristas," *El Universal*, July 1, 1953.

————. "Hombres de la Revolución: las proezas de Cándido Navarro," *El Universal*, June 20, 1951.

Ferrer Mendiolea, Gabriel. "Precursores de la Revolución: la rebeldía liberal," *El Nacional*, January 1, 10, 16, and 25, 1951.

————. "Sucedió en México," *El Nacional*, January 3, 1956.

Frank, Andre G. "¿Con qué modo de producción convierte la gallina maíz en huevos de oro?," *El Día*, October 31, 1965.

————. "Not Feudalism: Capitalism," *Monthly Review*, XV, No. 8 (December, 1963), 468–478.

Friedrich, Paul. "A Mexican Cacicazgo," *Ethnology*, IV, No. 2 (April, 1965), 190–209.

Gama, Valentín. "La propiedad en México. La reforma agraria," *Revista Mexicana de Ingeniería y Arquitectura*, Nos. 6, 8, 9, and 10 (1931).

García Briseño, Filiberto. "50 aniversaria del manifiesto del Partido Liberal Mexicano," *El Popular*, July 3, 1956.

Gill, Mario. "Turner, Flores Magón y los filibusteros," *Historia Mexicana*, V, No. 4 (April–June, 1956), 642–663.

González Navarro, Moisés. "La huelga de Río Blanco," *El Colegio de México*, VI, No. 4 (April–June, 1957), 510–533.

———. "Las huelgas textiles en el Porfiriato," *El Colegio de México*, II, No. 2 (October–December, 1956), 201–216.

———. "La ideología de la Revolución Mexicana," *Historia Mexicana*, X, No. 4 (April–June, 1961), 628–636.

González Ramírez, Manuel. "El nacionalismo mexicano de la Revolución," *Excélsior*, November 24, 1957.

Guillén, Francisco R. "Hombres de la Revolución," *Nosotros*, May 19, 1956–March 22, 1958.

Hale, Charles A. "José María Luis Mora and the Structure of Mexican Liberalism," *Hispanic American Historical Review*, XLV, No. 2 (May, 1965), 196–227.

Jiménez Rueda, Julio. "La defensa de los intelectuales," *Excélsior*, November 10, 1929.

Magaña San Juan, Rodolfo. "Precursores de la Revolución," *Nosotros*, November 17, 1951.

Mancisidor, José. "El programa del Partido Liberal," *El Nacional*, July 5, 1948.

Michels, Roberto. "Intellectuals," *Encyclopedia of the Social Sciences* (New York: The Macmillan Company, 1957), VII, 118–124.

Mignone, A. Frederick. "A Fief for Mexico: Colonel Greene's Empire Ends," *Southwest Review*, XLIV (Autumn, 1959), 332–339.

Montejano y Aguiñaga, Rafael. "Dos periodistas potosinos recientemente fallecidos," *Fichas de Bibliografía Potosina*, I, No. 5 (March–April, 1950), 2–3.

Morales Jiménez, Alberto. "Hombres de México: Jesús M. Rangel," *El Nacional*, November 24, 1941.

Muñoz y Pérez, Daniel. "Lic. Enrique Flores Magón, precursor de la Revolución," *El Universal*, July 31, 1955.

Núñez y Domínguez, Roberto. "Los precursores de la Revolución," *Revista de Revistas*, November 20, 1932.

Ochoa Campos, Moisés. "Reseña histórica del periodismo mexicano," *El Nacional*, May 8, 1942.

Romero Flores, Jesús. "Esteban B. Calderón: precursor de la Revolución, maestro de escuela y constituyente," *El Nacional*, October 11, 1955.

Rosenzweig, Fernando. "El desarrollo económico de México de 1877 a 1911," *El Trimestre Económico*, XXXII, No. 127 (July–September, 1965), 405–454.

Schmitt, Karl M. "Catholic Adjustment to the Secular State: the Case of Mexico, 1867–1911," *The Catholic Historical Review*, XLVIII, No. 2 (July, 1962), 182–204.

—————. "The Díaz Conciliation Policy on State and Local Levels, 1876–1911," *Hispanic American Historical Review*, XL, No. 4 (November, 1960), 513–532.

Tovar y Bueno, W. "Los precursores de la Revolución," *La Prensa*, September 19–October 21, 1932.

Valadés, José C. "Doña Juana B. Gutiérrez de Mendoza," *Todo*, July 23, 1942.

B. Books

Agetro, Leafar. *Las luchas proletarias de Veracruz: historia y autocrítica*. Jalapa, Veracruz: Editorial "Barricada," 1942.

Aguirre, Manuel J. *Cananea: garras del imperialismo en las entrañas de México*. Libro Mex, Editores, 1958.

Alba, Víctor. *Las ideas sociales contemporáneas en México*. FCE, 1960.

Aldrete, Enrique. *Baja California heroica*. Frumentum, 1958.

Alessio Robles, Miguel. *Historia política de la Revolución*. Ediciones Botas, 1946.

—————. *Ideales de la Revolución*. Editorial "Cultura," 1935.

Almada, Francisco R. *La revolución en el Estado de Chihuahua*. Bib., 1964.

Anonymous. *Pedro Antonio de los Santos: soldado y mártir de la Revolución de México*. SLP: 1944.

Araquistáin, Luis. *La Revolución Mexicana, sus orígenes, sus hombres, su obra*. Madrid: Renacimiento, 1929.

Arenas Guzmán, Diego. *Del maderismo a los tratados de Teoloyucán*. Bib., 1955.

Baerlein, Henry. *Mexico, the Land of Unrest: Being Chiefly an Account of What Produced the Outbreak of 1910*. London: Herbert and Daniel, 1913.

Balbás, Manuel. *Recuerdos del Yaqui: principales episodios durante la campaña de 1899 a 1901*. Sociedad de Edición y Librería Franco Americana, S.A., 1927.

Barreiro Tablada, E. *Práxedis Guerrero*. Departamento de Bibliotecas, 1935.

Beals, Carleton. *Porfirio Díaz: Dictator of Mexico*. Philadelphia: Lippincott, 1932.

Beltrán, Enrique, *et al. México: cinquenta años de revolución*. 4 vols. FCE, 1960–1964.

Bernstein, Marvin D. *The Mexican Mining Industry*. Albany: The State University of New York, 1966.

Blasco Ibáñez, Vicente. *Mexico in Revolution*. New York: E. P. Dutton & Company, 1920.

Bonilla Jr., Manuel. *Diez años de guerra: sinopsis de la historia verdadera de la Revolución Mexicana*. Mazatlán, Sinaloa: Impr. Avendano, 1922.

Bórquez, Djed (pseud. of Juan de Dios Bojórquez). *Crónica del constituyente*. Ediciones Botas, 1938.

————. *Forjadores de la Revolución Mexicana*. Bib., 1960.

————. *Monzón: semblanza de un revolucionario*. Talleres de A. Artís, 1942.

Borregán, María Teresa. *Figuras de actualidad*. SLP: Taller Gráfico Escuela Industrial Militar, 1930.

Brandenburg, Frank R. *The Making of Modern Mexico*. Englewood Cliffs, New Jersey: Prentice-Hall, Inc., 1964.

Bremauntz, Alberto. *La batalla ideológica en México*. Ediciones Jurídico Sociales, 1962.

————. *Panorama social de las revoluciones de México*. Ediciones Jurídicas Sociales, 1960.

Brenner, Anita, and George R. Leighton. *The Wind that Swept Mexico*. New York: Harper, 1943.

Brinton, Crane. *The Anatomy of Revolution*. New York: Vintage Books, 1959.

Bulnes, Francisco. *El verdadero Díaz y la Revolución*. Editora Nacional, 1960.

————. *The Whole Truth about Mexico—President Wilson's Responsibility*. New York: M. Bulnes Book Company, 1916.

Bustamante, Luis F. *La Defensa de "El Ebano." Los libertarios*. Tampico, Tamaulipas: Imprenta "El Constitucional," 1915.

————. *De El Ebano a Torreón*. Monterrey: Tip. El Constitucional, 1915.

————. *Quién es el Crol. Juan B. Barragán*. SLP: Talleres de "El Constitucionalista," 1917.

Cabrera, Antonio. *El Estado de San Luis Potosí*. 2 vols. SLP: Imprenta y Encuadernación de Antonio Cabrera, 1902.

Cabrera Ipiña de Corci, Matilde. *Cuatro grandes dinastías mexicanas en los descendientes de los hermanos Fernández de Lima y Barragán.* SLP: Talleres Gráficos de la Editorial Universitaria Potosina, 1956.

Callcott, Wilfred Hardy. *Liberalism in Mexico, 1857–1929.* Palo Alto, California: Stanford University Press, 1931.

Cerda Silva, Roberto de la. *El movimiento obrero en México.* Instituto de Investigaciones Sociales, UNAM, 1961.

Chávez Orozco, Luis. *Historia económica y social de México.* Ediciones Botas, 1938.

———. *La prehistoria de socialismo en México.* Secretaría de Educación Pública, 1936.

———. *La revolución industrial, la revolución política.* Ed. D. A. P. P., 1937.

Clark, Marjorie Ruth. *Organized Labor in Mexico.* Chapel Hill: University of North Carolina Press, 1934.

Clendenen, Clarence C. *The United States and Pancho Villa.* Ithaca, New York: Cornell University Press, 1961.

Cole, G. D. H. *Socialist Thought: Marxism and Anarchism, 1850–1890.* London: Macmillan & Co., Ltd., 1957.

Cosío Villegas, Daniel (ed.). *Historia moderna de México.* 8 vols. Editorial Hermes, 1948–1965. See also, Moisés González Navarro and Fernando Rosenzweig.

———. *The United States versus Porfirio Díaz.* Lincoln: University of Nebraska Press, 1963.

Creelman, James. *Díaz, Master of Mexico.* New York: Appleton, 1911.

Dabdoub, Claudio. *Historia del Valle del Yaqui.* Librería de Manuel Porrúa, 1964.

de Tocqueville, Alexis. *The Old Régime and the French Revolution.* New York: Doubleday Anchor Books, 1955.

Díaz Cárdenas, León. *Cananea, primer brote del sindicalismo en México.* Departamento de Bibliotecas de la Secretaría de Educación Pública, 1936.

Díaz Dufoo, Carlos. *La evolución industrial en México y su evolución social.* 2 vols. J. Ballescá, 1901.

Díaz Ramírez, Manuel. *Apuntes históricos del movimiento obrero y campesino de México, 1844–1880.* FCE, 1954.

Dromundo, Baltasar. *Emiliano Zapata.* Imprenta Mundial, 1934.

Dulles, John W. F. *Yesterday in Mexico.* Austin: University of Texas Press, 1961.

Escobedo, José G. *Notas biográficas. Los valores morales e intelectuales y fallas de quienes promovieron la agremiación obrera y campesina de México—ya extintos—y actuaron en los últimos 50 años.* 1951.

Espinosa de los Reyes, Jorge. *Relaciones económicas entre México y Estados Unidos, 1870–1910.* Nacional Financiera, 1951.

Ferrer Mendiolea, Gabriel. *Historia del Congreso Constituyente de 1916–1917.* Bib., 1957.

Figueroa Uriza, Arturo. *Ciudadanos en armas. Antecedencia y datos para la historia de la Revolución Mexicana.* 2 vols. B. Costa–Amic, Editor, 1960.

Frank, Andre G. *Capitalism and Underdevelopment in Latin America.* New York: Monthly Review Press, 1967.

Fuentes Díaz, Vicente. *Los partidos políticos en México.* Talleres Impresiones Perfectas, 1954.

García Cruz, Miguel. *Evolución mexicana del ideario del seguridad social.* Instituto de Investigaciones Sociales, UNAM, 1962.

García Granados, Ricardo. *Historia de México desde la Restauración de la República en 1867 hasta la caída de Porfirio Díaz.* 4 vols. Ediciones Botas, 1923–1928.

Gerth, H. H., and C. Wright Mills (eds.). *From Max Weber.* New York: Oxford University Press, 1958.

Gill, Mario. *Episodios mexicanos. México en la hoguera.* Editorial Azteca, S.A., 1960.

Ginger, Ray. *Eugene V. Debs: A Biography.* New York: Collier Books, 1962.

Gómez, Marte R. *Las comisiones agrarias del sur.* Librería de M. Porrúa, 1961.

González de Cossío, Francisco. *Historia de la tenencia y explotación del campo desde la época precortesiana hasta las leyes del 6 de enero de 1915.* 2 vols. Bib., 1957.

González Navarro, Moisés. *Historia moderna de México. El Porfiriato: la vida social.* Editorial Hermes, 1957.

González Ramírez, Manuel. *La revolución social de México: las ideas—la violencia.* FCE, 1960.

Grimaldo, Isaac. *Gobernantes potosinos, 1590–1939.* SLP: Tip. Esc. Hijos del Ejército No. 10, 1939.

———. *Rasgos biográficos del Dr. Rafael Cepeda.* SLP: Tipografía de El Heraldo, 1912.

———. *Vida del C. Divisionario Saturnino Cedillo.* SLP: Imprenta Fénix, 1935.

Gruening, Ernest. *Mexico and Its Heritage*. New York: Appleton-Century-Crofts, 1928.

Guzmán, Martín Luis. *El águila y la serpiente*. Compañía General de Ediciones, S.A., 1961.

————. *Memorias de Pancho Villa*. Compañía General de Ediciones, S.A., 1963.

Hofstadter, Richard. *The Age of Reform: From Bryan to F. D. R.* New York: Alfred A. Knopf, 1955.

————. *Social Darwinism in American Thought*. Boston: The Beacon Press, 1955.

Huszar, George B. de (ed.). *The Intellectuals*. Glencoe, Illinois: The Free Press, 1960.

Joll, James. *The Anarchists*. Boston: Little, Brown and Company, 1965.

Jordan, David Starr. *The Days of a Man, Being Memories of a Naturalist, Teacher and Minor Prophet of Democracy*. 2 vols. New York: World Book Company, 1922.

Katz, Friedrich. *Deutschland, Díaz und die mexikanische Revolution. Die deutsche Politik im Mexiko 1870–1920*. Berlin: VEB Deutscher Verlag der Wissenschaften, 1964.

Lefebvre, Georges. *The Coming of the French Revolution*. New York: Random House, 1947.

Lewis, Oscar. *Life in a Mexican Village: Tepoztlán Restudied*. Urbana: University of Illinois Press, 1963.

List Arzubide, Armando. *Apuntes sobre la prehistoria de la Revolución*. 1958.

————. *La huelga de Río Blanco*. Publicaciones del Departamento de Bibliotecas de la Secretaría de Educación Pública, 1935.

López y Fuentes, Gregorio. *Huasteca*. Ediciones Botas, 1939.

Lozano, Fortunato. *Antonio I. Villarreal: vida de un gran Mexicano*. Monterrey, N.L.: Impresora Monterrey, S.A., 1959.

McBride, George McCutchen. *The Land Systems of Mexico*. New York: American Geographical Society, 1923.

Mancisidor, José. *La Revolución Mexicana*. Ediciones El Gusano de Luz, 1958.

Mannheim, Karl. *Ideology and Utopia*. New York: Harcourt, Brace & World, Inc., 1964.

María y Campos, Armando de. *Múgica, crónica biográfica*. Compañía de Ediciones Populares, S.A., 1939.

Martínez, Pablo L. *¿Como anda la cultura en Baja California?* Editorial Baja California, 1961.

————. *Historia de Baja California.* Libros Mexicanos, 1956.

————. *Sobre el libro "Baja California heroica" (contra la defensa de una falsedad histórica).* 1960.

Mata, Luis I. *Filomeno Mata: su vida y su labor.* Secretaría de Educación Pública, 1945.

Meade, Joaquín. *Hemerografía potosina, historia del periodismo en San Luis Potosí, 1828–1956.* SLP: Letras Potosinas, 1956.

————. *La huasteca veracruzana.* 2 vols. Editorial Citlaltepetl, 1962.

Mendieta y Núñez, Lucio. *El problema agrario de México.* Editorial Porrúa, S.A., 1964.

————. *Teoría de la revolución.* UNAM, 1958.

Menéndez, Gabriel Antonio. *Doheny el cruel.* Imprenta Didot, 1958.

Meyer, Michael C. *Mexican Rebel: Pascual Orozco and the Mexican Revolution, 1910–1915.* Lincoln: University of Nebraska Press, 1967.

Morales, Julian. *El socialismo en México, o sea la explotación del obrero mexicano. Episodios de la vida social obrera de 1910–1923.* Tacuba (Mexico City): Libertad y Trabajo, n.d.

Morales Jiménez, Alberto. *Hombres de la Revolución Mexicana.* Bib., 1960.

Navarrete, Félix. *La masonería en la historia y en las leyes de México.* Editorial Jus, 1957.

Noyola Barragán, Luis. *Como murieron los generales Magdaleno y Saturnino Cedillo.* SLP: Ediciones "Peritos," 1964.

O'Connor, Harvey. *The Guggenheims.* New York: Covici Friede, 1937.

Othón de Mendizábal, Miguel, *et al. Las clases sociales en México.* Sociedad Mexicana de Difusión Cultural, n.d.

Packard, Sidney R. *The Process of Historical Revision: New Viewpoints in Medieval European History.* Northampton, Massachusetts: Smith College, 1962.

Parkes, Henry Bamford. *A History of Mexico.* 3rd ed. Boston: Houghton Mifflin Company, 1960.

Peña, Moisés T. de la. *El pueblo y su tierra: mito y realidad de la reforma agraria en México.* Cuadernos Americanos, 1964.

Penilla López, Salvador. *Apuntes de San Luis Potosí.* SLP: Talleres Gráficos El Aguila, 1942.

Pérez Gallardo, Reynaldo. *Apuntes para la historia. ¿Dónde surgió la primera chispa de la Revolución?* SLP: Camarades de Haro, Quintanilla y Dávila, 1938.

Pletcher, David M. *Rails, Mines, and Progress: Seven American Promoters in Mexico, 1867–1911.* Ithaca, New York: Cornell University Press, 1958.

Quirk, Robert E. *The Mexican Revolution, 1914–1915: the Convention of Aguascalientes.* New York: The Citadel Press, 1963.

Ramos, Samuel. *Historia de la filosofía en México.* Imprenta Universitaria, 1943.

Ramos Pedrueza, Rafael. *La lucha de clases a través de la historia de México, revolución democraticoburguesa.* 2 vols. Talleres Gráficos de la Nación, 1941.

Rangel Gaspar, Eliseo. *Hacia una teoria de la Revolución Mexicana.* Talleres Gráficos de la Nación, 1964.

Reed, John. *Insurgent Mexico.* New York: D. Appleton & Co., 1914.

Reed, Nelson. *The Caste War of Yucatan.* Stanford, California: Stanford University Press, 1964.

Reyes, Alfonso. *Pasado inmediato y otros ensayos.* El Colegio de México, 1941.

Reyes Heroles, Jesús. *El liberalismo mexicano.* 3 vols. Facultad de Derecho, UNAM, 1957–1961.

Rodea, Marcelo N. *Historia del movimiento obrero ferrocarrilero en México (1890–1943).* 1944.

Roeder, Ralph. *Juárez and His Mexico.* 2 vols. New York: The Viking Press, 1947.

Romero Flores, Jesús. *Anales históricas de la Revolución Mexicana.* 3 vols. Libro Mex Editores, 1960.

———. *Historia de los Estados de la República Mexicana.* Ediciones Botas, 1964.

———. *La Revolución como nosotros la vimos.* Bib., 1963.

Rosenzweig, Fernando, *et al. Historia moderna de México. El Porfiriato: la vida económica.* 2 vols. Editorial Hermes, 1965.

Rouaix, Pastor. *Génesis de los artículos 27 y 123 de la Constitución política de 1917.* Bib., 1959.

Ruiz, Ramón Eduardo. *Mexico: the Challenge of Poverty and Illiteracy.* San Marino, California: The Huntington Library, 1963.

Ruiz, Rodolfo D. *Del lírico verjel potosino. Semblanzas y pergenios.* SLP: 1919.

Salvemini, Gaetano. *The French Revolution, 1788–1792.* New York: W. W. Norton & Company, Inc., 1962.

Sánchez Lamego, Miguel A. *Historia militar de la Revolución Mexicana.* Bib., 1956–1957.

Sánchez Valle, Manuel. *El profesor y general Cándido Navarro.* Guanajuato: Publicaciones de la Unión de Estudiantes Socialistas Guanajuatenses, 1937.

Silva Herzog, Jesús. *El agrarismo mexicano y la reforma agraria.* FCE, 1959.

———. *Breve historia de la Revolución Mexicana.* 2 vols. FCE, 1960.

———. *El pensamiento económico de México.* FCE, 1947.

———. *Trayectoria ideológica de la Revolución Mexicana, 1910–1917.* Cuadernos Americanos, 1963.

Simpson, Eyler N. *The Ejido: Mexico's Way Out.* Chapel Hill: University of North Carolina Press, 1937.

Simpson, Lesley Byrd. *Many Mexicos.* Berkeley and Los Angeles: University of California Press, 1960.

Sotelo Inclán, Jesús. *Raíz y razón de Zapata.* Ed. Etnos, 1943.

Stern, David S. (ed.). *Mexico: A Symposium on Law and Government.* Coral Gables, Florida: University of Miami Press, 1958.

Tannenbaum, Frank. *The Mexican Agrarian Revolution.* Washington, D.C.: The Brookings Institute, 1929.

———. *Mexico, the Struggle for Peace and Bread.* New York: Alfred A. Knopf, 1950.

———. *Peace by Revolution—an Interpretation of Mexico.* New York: Columbia University Press, 1933.

Taracena, Alfonso. *Mi vida en el vértigo de la Revolución Mexicana (anales sintéticos, 1900–1930).* Ediciones Botas, 1936.

———. *La verdadera Revolución Mexicana.* 6 vols. Editorial Jus, 1960–1961.

Tischendorf, Alfred. *Great Britain and Mexico in the Era of Porfirio Díaz.* Durham, North Carolina: Duke University Press, 1961.

Tweedie, Ethel B. *Mexico as I Saw It.* New York: 1901.

Urquizo, Francisco L. *Origen del Ejército Constitucionalista.* Bib., 1964.

Valadés, José C. *Historia general de la Revolución Mexicana.* 3 vols. Manuel Quesada Brandi, Editor, 1963–1965.

———. *Imaginación y realidad de Francisco I. Madero.* Antigua Librería Robredo, 1960.

———. *El porfirismo, historia de un régimen.* 3 vols. Editorial Patria, 1948.

Velasco Ceballos, R. *¿Se apoderará Estados Unidos de América de Baja California? (la invasión filibustera de 1911).* Imprenta Nacional, 1920.

Velasco Valdés, Miguel. *La prerrevolución y el hombre de la calle*. Editorial B. Costa-Amic, 1964.

Vernon, Raymond. *The Dilemma of Mexico's Development: the Roles of the Private and Public Sectors*. Cambridge, Massachusetts: Harvard University Press, 1963.

Whetten, Nathan L. *Rural Mexico*. Chicago: University of Chicago Press, 1948.

Woodcock, George. *Anarchism: A History of Libertarian Ideas and Movements*. Cleveland and New York: The World Publishing Co. (Meridian Books), 1962.

Yáñez, Agustín. *Don Justo Sierra: su vida, sus ideas y su obra*. UNAM, 1962.

Zalco y Rodríguez, Luis J. *Apuntes para la historia de la masonería en México*. 2 vols. Talleres Tipográficos de la Penetencearía del Distrito Federal, 1950.

Zea, Leopoldo. *Apogeo y decadencia del positivismo en México*. El Colegio de México, 1944.

――――. *Del liberalismo a la Revolución en la educación mexicana*. Bib., 1956.

――――. *El positivismo en México*. Ediciones Studium, 1953.

C. Unpublished Material

Anderson, Bo. "On Systems of Stratification in Maya Communities." Stanford University, n.d. (Mimeographed.)

Baker, Richard D. "The Judicial Control of Constitutionality in Mexico: A Study of the Juicio de Amparo" (Ph.D. dissertation, University of North Carolina, 1963).

Blanquel, Eduardo. "El pensamiento político de Ricardo Flores Magón, precursor de la Revolución Mexicana" (Master's thesis, Facultad de Filosofía y Letras, UNAM, 1963).

Brown, Lyle C. "A 'Magonista' Bibliography." Baylor University, n.d. (Mimeographed.)

――――." 'Magonista' Chronology." Baylor University, n.d. (Mimeographed.)

De Vore, Blanche B. "The Influence of Antonio Díaz Soto y Gama on the Agrarian Movement in Mexico" (Ph.D. dissertation, University of Southern California, 1963).

Levenstein, Harvey A. "The U. S. Labor Movement and Mexico, 1910–1951" (Ph.D. dissertation, University of Wisconsin, 1966).

Mascona Davidoff, Linda. "Orígenes del socialismo en México, 1867–1876" (thesis, Facultad de Ciencias Sociales, UNAM, 1963).

Muñoz Rosas, Jerónimo. "La ideología de Ricardo Flores Magón" (thesis, Facultad de Filosofía y Letras, UNAM, 1965).

Niemeyer, Jr., E. Victor. "The Public Career of General Bernardo Reyes" (Ph.D. dissertation, University of Texas, 1958). Published in Mexico under the title *El Géneral Bernardo Reyes* (see Section II–F, "Books," of the Bibliography).

Phillips, Richard B. "José Vasconcelos and the Mexican Revolution of 1910" (Ph.D. dissertation, Stanford University, 1953).

INDEX

Acayucán: PLM charge on, 147; guerrilla struggle by revolutionaries of, 154

Acuña y Rosete, Elisa: founds newspaper, 102; sides with Arriaga, 118; in "Socialistas Mexicanas," 189

"Agrarian Proclamation of Social Order": issued, 52–53

"Agreement of the Principal Commanders of the Liberating Army in Support of the Plan of San Luis": drafted, 200

agriculture: effect of Mexican Revolution on, 6; economic interests in, 13; investment outside of, 18; elite families in, 26; acquisition of land for, 28; capitalist nature of Mexican, 29, 30–33, 49; effect of weather on, 43–44; Madero studies, 62; San Luis Potosí centers for, 82; first manifesto dealing with, 99; Madero family interests in, 158; Díaz Soto y Gama on, 191, 219, 230; *Diario del Hogar* on, 199; PL program on, 202, 221; radical stand on program for, 206; Zapatista concern with, 217; Sarabia on, 225, 226; 1917 Constitution on, 234. *See also* plants (agricultural)

—, revolutionary programs for: types of, 50–51; influence revolts, 52–53; influence Díaz, 54; Carrancista, 59, 216; engineers' contributions to, 69; lawyers' contributions to, 75–76; incorporated into 1917 Constitution, 77; of PLM, 132, 144, 154, 161; of Reyes, 198, 209; of Orozquistas, 211; of Zapatistas, 214.

Agua Prieta: customs house at, 146

Aguascalientes: railroad to, 14; PLM movements in, 55; rail strike in, 141

Aguascalientes Convention (1914): 75, 86, 214, 225, 229

Aguilar, Cándido: 180

Aguirre, Lauro: in co-ordination of revolt plans, 147; U.S. authorities arrest, 149

Ahualulco: rebel victories at, 52

Alacrán, El: journalists from, jailed, 102

Alanís, Lázaro L.: aids Orozco, 180, 209

Alcázar, Ramón: banking interests of, 25

Allende, Gaspar: 180

Alonso, Dr. Antonio F.: withdraws from Precursor Movement, 69

Alvarado, Salvadro: receives *Regeneración*, 124

American Federation of Labor: R. Flores Magón on, 151

American Magazine, The: *Barbarous Mexico* published in, 127

American Smelting and Refining Company: 18

Amsterdam Congress: Malatesta's role in, 121

Anaconda (mining firm): 135

Anarchism: political influence of, under Díaz, 7; Arriaga's readings in, 66; Guerrero's commitment to, 68; as intellectual ideology, 70; influence of, on Díaz Soto y Gama, 72, 98; Sarabia moves toward, 80; Bustamante propagandizes for, 80–81; European betrayal of Mexican, 84–85; revolutionaries agree to con-